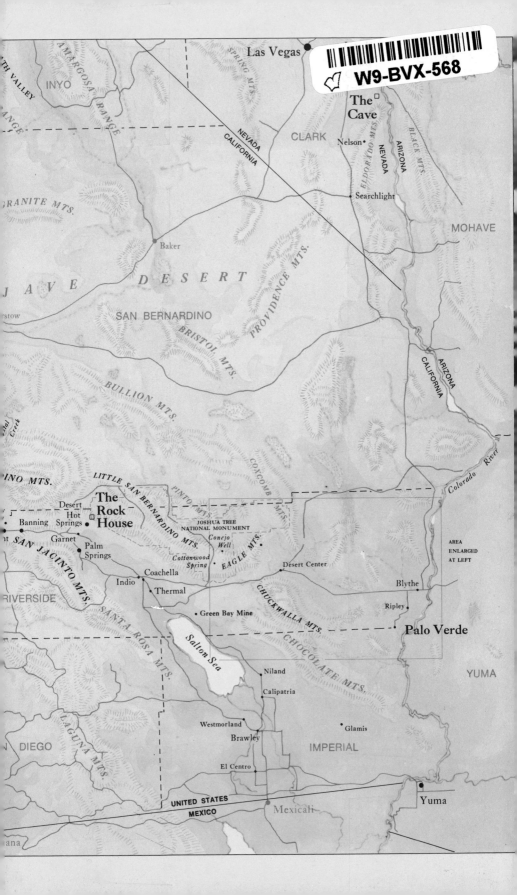

DEATH VALLEY

INYO

AMARGOSA RANGE

GRANITE MTS.

Las Vegas

SPRING MTS.

NEVADA
CALIFORNIA

The
Cave

CLARK

Nelson

ELDORADO MTS.

NEVADA
ARIZONA

BLACK MTS.

MOHAVE

Searchlight

Baker

MOJAVE

DESERT

SAN BERNARDINO

BRISTOL MTS.

PROVIDENCE MTS.

BULLION MTS.

CALIFORNIA
ARIZONA

Colorado River

COXCOMB MTS.

INO MTS.

LITTLE SAN BERNARDINO MTS.

PINTO MTS.

Whitewater Creek

Desert
Hot
Springs

The
Rock
House

Banning

Garnet

Palm
Springs

SAN JACINTO MTS.

JOSHUA TREE
NATIONAL MONUMENT

Conejo
Well

Cottonwood
Spring

EAGLE MTS.

Desert Center

AREA
ENLARGED
AT LEFT

Blythe

Ripley

Coachella

Indio

Thermal

SANTA ROSA MTS.

RIVERSIDE

Green Bay Mine

CHUCKWALLA MTS.

CHOCOLATE MTS.

Palo Verde

Salton Sea

YUMA

Niland

Calipatria

LAGUNA MTS.

DIEGO

Westmorland

Brawley

Glamis

IMPERIAL

El Centro

Yuma

UNITED STATES
MEXICO

Mexicali

ana

Also by Colin Fletcher

*The New Complete Walker*
(1974)

*The Winds of Mara*
(1973)

*The Man Who Walked Through Time*
(1968)

*The Thousand-Mile Summer*
(1964)

THE MAN FROM THE CAVE

# COLIN FLETCHER

# The Man From
# The Cave

ALFRED A. KNOPF   NEW YORK   1981

THIS IS A BORZOI BOOK
PUBLISHED BY ALFRED A. KNOPF, INC.

Library of Congress Cataloging in Publication Data
Fletcher, Colin.   (date)
The man from the cave.
1. Simon, William Anthony, 1875–1950.
2. United States—Biography.   3. Fletcher, Colin.
I. Title.
CT275.S5214F55   1981   978'.031'0924 [B]   80–22548
ISBN 0–394–40695–8

Manufactured in the United States of America
First Edition

TO CARL D. BRANDT

literary agent, book doctor, friend

# Contents

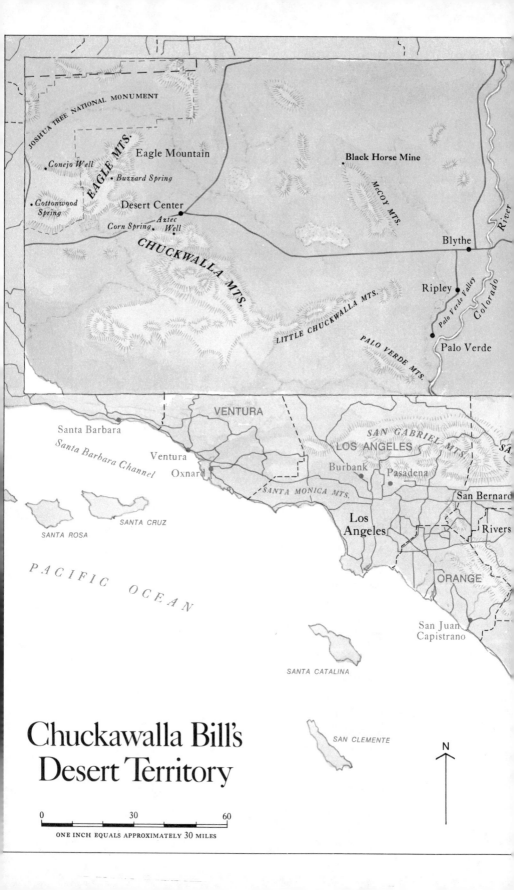

JOSHUA TREE NATIONAL MONUMENT

EAGLE MTS.

*Conejo Well*

Eagle Mountain

*Buzzard Spring*

Black Horse Mine

*McCOY MTS.*

*Cottonwood Spring*

Desert Center

*Corn Spring*  *Aztec Well*

CHUCKWALLA MTS.

Blythe

*River*

Ripley

*Palo Verde Valley*

*Colorado*

LITTLE CHUCKWALLA MTS.

PALO VERDE MTS.

Palo Verde

VENTURA

Santa Barbara

*Santa Barbara Channel*

Ventura

Oxnard

SAN GABRIEL MTS.

LOS ANGELES

Burbank   Pasadena

SA

SANTA MONICA MTS.

San Bernard

SANTA CRUZ

SANTA ROSA

Los
Angeles

Rivers

ORANGE

P A C I F I C   O C E A N

San Juan
Capistrano

SANTA CATALINA

# Chuckawalla Bill's
# Desert Territory

SAN CLEMENTE

N

0        30        60

ONE INCH EQUALS APPROXIMATELY 30 MILES

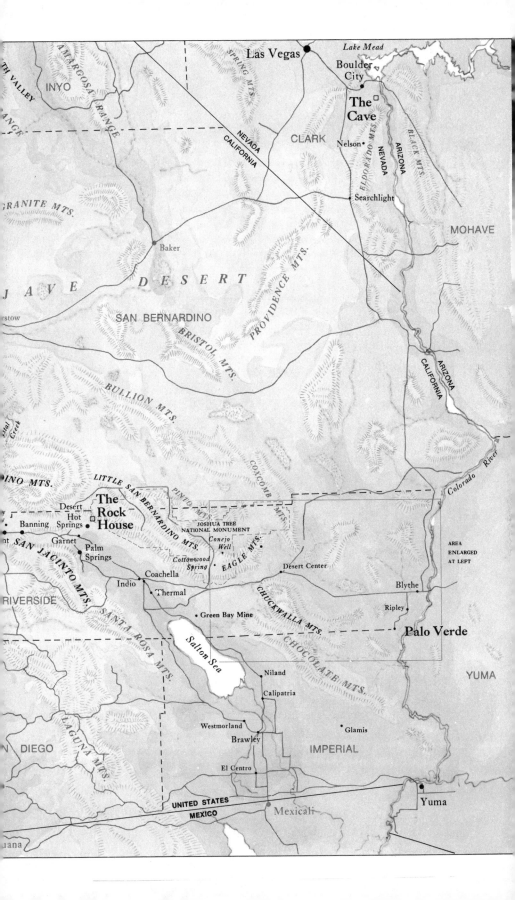

THE MAN FROM THE CAVE

# PART I

# I   The Cave

IT WAS FOUR O'CLOCK in the afternoon, Nevada time, November. I was walking up a narrow desert canyon, twenty miles east of Vegas but light-years from neon. Hours had passed since the last sign of man. Cliffs and silence enveloped me. Then I came around a rock buttress and saw, thirty paces ahead, standing in the middle of a gravel patch as if on display, a trunk.

I stopped in my tracks.

Now I want you to see, clearly, the place in which this trunk stood; and to understand certain other things, too.

Somebody once ruled that "landscape is cows, scenery is when you think it's going to fall down on you." Even by such stern standards, this trunk stood in scenery. And I am not talking only about the canyon I was following.

Just before noon that day—the second day of a week-long walk—I had been moving along the edge of an almost level plain when there opened up in front of me a gigantic rock basin—a deep, two-mile-wide rubble hole. Ridges and canyons ribbed and furrowed it. At its sump they converged into chaos. "Thou shalt not pass!" the place seemed to say.

I think I said, aloud, "Oh, my God!" I know the weight of the pack on my back had suddenly doubled.

Now the rock basin was really a bay—an arm of a chasm that the Colorado River has cut through this country in an echo of its Grand Canyon, not far upstream—and I knew that if I wanted to I could avoid it by detouring, out on the plain. But when you are walking the way I was walking that week, your eye is fixed not merely on getting someplace but on the going.

3

I was walking for the good of my soul or something. In part, the week was a contribution to an ongoing project: sometime in the next hundred and fifty years I plan to complete a piecemeal walk along the entire Colorado River. Straying too far from the river would therefore have come close to cheating (only an impassable stretch of chasm had forced me up onto the plain for a mile or so). But I was also walking to smooth out certain creases that furrowed my life, and I had already achieved some success. So I was in a holiday mood: unchained, carefree and curious. And when I came to the edge of that huge rock basin I did not hesitate for long.

I took off my pack, sat down, lifted binoculars.

What I saw was hardly people country. But before long I thought I detected a way through. I heaved the pack onto my back again and went over the rim.

Now, I picked my way downward through a stark, staccato rockscape. Crumbling brown ridges. Gray rubble slopes. Black lava. Yet the place less barren than it had looked. A sparse but stalwart community of shrubs. Here and there, a tree hanging grimly on. Soon, coyote tracks. Then bighorn sheep droppings. Once, a tortoise's empty shell. But nothing moved. The rock ruled.

I went on down, deeper.

It was very, very quiet now. Rock walls closed in. I stopped for lunch, dozed, moved on. Several routes offered themselves. I chose one. Soon, cliffs were rising sheer, pressing tight. The silence solidified. Then, as I began to climb out of the basin's sump, up a narrow canyon, I came around the rock buttress.

Beyond it, the canyon ran almost straight for thirty or forty paces. To the left rose a hundred-foot cliff, part overhung. And at the foot of this cliff stood the trunk. It looked perfectly preserved—the kind of period piece you might find in a hushed-voice downtown antique shop where everything, owner included, looks lacquered. And in that first moment I felt as if I had walked in on one of those fey TV ads that feature a car perched on a butte or an immaculate jet-setter sipping wine in mid-howling wilderness.

I hope you see, now, why I stopped in my tracks; and will understand certain things that followed.

When the surprise had ebbed, I walked forward.

Close up, the trunk looked less lacquered but more intriguing. Its wood was gray and stained. But the metal sheathing, embossed with a faint flower pattern, had rusted to a warm, almost glowing, chestnut brown. So the trunk, though obviously very old, did not look at all decrepit. It had

[Scale: Shadowed part of cave (lower left in picture) is about 15 feet at apexes; visible part of cliff rises about 70 feet sheer, before slope starts; and peak at top left stands half a mile from cave and 600 feet higher.

Lava stone (see plan, page 8) shows at center of lower edge of cave shadow.]

simply weathered to a rich and evocative maturity.

Scattered haphazardly beyond it, I now saw, was an assortment of camp gear: an ancient canteen, a washbasin, a rusty stove chimney, a shovel, a bucket, two empty five-gallon cans and a bleached yellow measuring tape that snaked erratically across the gravel.

I lifted the trunk's lid.

Empty. Empty, that is, except for two ordinary brown paper bags—the kind you would pick up in a grocery store to hold half-a-dozen apples. But the paper-lined lid bore a print. The print was cracked, yet unfaded. From it, a damsel in a broad-brimmed hat smiled out. Fussy flowers and pastoral scenes surrounded her. Clearly, they all belonged to the past; belonged, I guessed, to the turn of the century.

I closed the trunk, walked a few paces through the scattered camp gear, then glanced to my left. A little above me, cut into the cliff, was a cave. A natural ramp led up into its main chamber. I slipped off my pack and walked up the ramp.

A long time ago, a man had lived in the cave. But his primitive furniture and belongings now lay jumbled, random, their relationships gone. They were mere junk, mute of immediate meanings; and even in the thin, late light I could see dust coating everything, thick. So the scene at first looked forlorn and pitiful, like a bombed and looted house. Then I began to discern detail—to move behind the dust and disarray, striving to reconstruct relationships, messages.

Near the head of the ramp stood a metate—one of those massive granite stones on whose smooth, concave upper surface Indians used to grind their grain. Among nearby articles my eye noted a stool and a small table—both made from wooden boxes, both tipped on their sides; also four smooth pebbles. Off to the right, at the end of the cave, a rectangle of cut grass had clearly been a bed. Beside it nestled the upper halves of three tortoise shells.

But the densest body of relics lay off to the left in a small, low-roofed annex: an assortment of wooden boxes and metal cans, a frying pan, a coffeepot, a heavy iron "Dutch oven," a wooden folding chair, a pair of very small and tattered green shoes lacking soles, a rusty "sheepherder's" stove and a chimney that clearly belonged to it and was also brother to the one lying outside near the trunk.

I stepped into the annex.

The relics lay on and among a jumble of cut firewood. I knelt down. The firewood half hid many smaller items. There was a lot more stuff than I had thought—enough to tell me something about the man who had once lived in the cave. If I spent an hour or two sifting through his effects . . .

I straightened my back. Outside, the rock world had grown gray. Within an hour it would be too dark for safe walking. I glanced at my pack, propped up against the walking staff: barely a gallon of water left in my canteens; and even if I left at once I could not be sure of reaching either the river or a spring before next afternoon.

There was only one thing to do. I went back down into the wash, marked the cave's location on my map, swung the pack onto my back and walked on up the canyon.

A year later I returned.

Now I do not want you to think of me as having spent that year dreaming about the old-timer's cave. It was not like that at all. I had a busy year and rarely thought of the cave. But when I did it still intrigued me, and I soon decided that the next time I needed to smooth out creases—alone, away from the man-world—I would go back. I would photograph everything (I had carried no camera the first time) and make a list of the dusty relics. Mostly, though, I would just live quietly in the cave. And by putting myself in the old-timer's place, among the things he had left behind, I would try to learn something of the way he had lived. With luck I might even discover his name. Anyway, it ought to be fun—a pleasant lubricant for deeper needs.

In the beginning, it was as simple and casual as that.

At least, I think it was. But perhaps I harbored, even then, more than a vague curiosity about the cave and its long-gone occupant.

It was November again—November of 1969—before I developed my next unshruggable need for a spell of solitude. By that time I had arranged with the superintendent of Lake Mead National Recreational Area, within which the cave lay, that after living for ten days in the cave I would show the Park Service where it was and then help pack out the "artifacts." For I had decided that with desert vandalism rampant and spreading it would be criminal to leave the old-timer's belongings where they were.

At the cave, I found everything as it had been a year earlier—untouched, as if in a museum.

The first night, I camped a little way up the wash, well clear of the scattered gear, so that nothing would be disturbed before I photographed it next day. After dinner I lay looking up at towering black rock walls and a wedge of less than black, star-spangled sky. It felt good to be back. The desert was always clean and bitingly real, yet soothing. And this time I had ten clear days stretching ahead. As I slid down into sleep I looked forward to my first insights into how it had been the last time any human—a man or men, or even a woman (I must not jump to conclusions)—had lived and moved around this now silent place.

As things turned out, it was not until the third day that I really began, in an unexpected flash of enlightenment, to piece the story together. But in the course of the first two days I formulated some fundamental questions and even glimpsed a few tentative answers.

The first morning, waiting for afternoon sun to floodlight wash and cave for photography, I just sniffed around, taking care to disturb nothing.

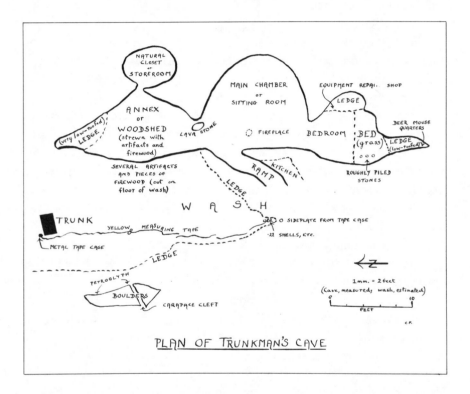

PLAN OF TRUNKMAN'S CAVE

On the natural ramp leading up to the cave lay a thin, whippy stick, five feet long, gently curving, with its thicker end bent in a natural handle. A year earlier I had assumed "walking stick." But when I squatted beside it that first morning, with time to let my mind run, I saw that, sadomasochism aside, it had to be a weapon for prodding and if necessary whacking into obedience certain notoriously obstinate beasts of burden. But that raised new questions. Was there a feasible route down to the cave for laden burros? Why had the old-timer left the stick behind, along with everything else? Had he died nearby? Or had his burros died—or bolted?

I examined the stick more carefully. It even told me something about the kind of man its owner had been. For he had selected a piece of wood with just the right curves and then had carefully peeled and cut and smoothed it. Tip and handle, in particular, were neat beyond the demands of everyday use.

When I moved up into the cave, stepping only on rock so as to leave no footprints, I found confirmation that its occupant had been a neat, meticulous man, even something of an artist. Various cut sticks lying around—some apparently made for such jobs as stirring food, some for purposes still hidden from me—were all beautifully fashioned. He was also, I saw, a practical handyman. At the foot of the grass bed, along the inner wall, a curving ledge tapered into a small natural pocket, and in it lay a miniature "equipment repair shop": a collection of washers and nails and carpet tacks, a piece of wire, half a dozen unused grommets and two small buckles.

The repair shop told me something else, too.

It was possible to imagine a man passing through this basin with his loaded burros, pausing at the cave overnight or for a day or two, but then for some reason being forced to jettison his belongings—because his burros bolted, for example. But the repair shop, laid out on the ledge rather than kept in a portable can or box, proved beyond reasonable doubt that their owner had at least intended to stay longer than a day or two.

No matter how long he stayed, though, he needed water, and I spent most of that first morning looking for a water source. I found only one tiny seep, a hundred yards down the canyon. It was a mere dampness on steep rock. But desert springs are fickle. Fifty years earlier, that seep could have been a gusher. Or it might have been dry. If it had been dry, my old-timer could have relied on the Colorado, by packing big loads up on burros.

I soon tested that theory. By now I knew that I would certainly have to rely on the river; and early on the second morning I set off down-canyon with an empty pack. Seven hours later, after making several scabrous detours around sheer drop-offs, and after finding no trace whatever of a man-made trail, I arrived back in camp with three precious gallons of river water and the knowledge that no burro could have used such a route.

That night I slept in the cave.

As a precaution against damaging things that might not at first seem significant, I lit no fire. And after dinner I sat looking at the cave's contents in the faint and flickering glow of my candle lantern. From the first, I had been puzzled by the way the gear lay. Why some inside the cave, some scattered around outside? Perhaps, I thought, the old-timer carried only lighter articles up into the cave when he left—probably in a hurry, after his burros bolted. (I was beginning to like the "lost burro" theory.) But if so, why the tape measure and other small items near the trunk? And why was the trunk empty, except for the two paper bags?

Then there was the odd distribution of gear inside the cave.

The main chamber, with its high roof, was the place you would live. And sure enough, the fireplace was there, with smoke stains on the roof. Yet most of the gear, including the stove, lay in the annex—where the roof lacked smoke stains and was so low that I could not stand upright. It did not make sense. And it made even less sense that the jumble of gear was concentrated toward the back of the annex, near the rather small opening to a surprisingly big but almost empty natural closet. Back there, the roof came very low indeed. You could hardly sit, let alone stand. The sticks of firewood intermixed with the gear suggested that the annex had been a woodshed. That, at least, made sense: you could toss firewood up into it from the wash, and the low roof would hardly matter when you reached in from the main chamber for a few sticks. But nothing else fitted.

When I blew out the candle at last and slid down into my sleeping bag, I felt glad that I had eight full days left for finding the answers to my puzzle.

Next morning I began to list the "artifacts." Under this rather pretentious title I included everything in or near the cave that could have been made or habitually used by humans, and the job turned out to be far bigger than I had expected. It filled most of the next six days.

From the start, it was hard, dirty work. At times it grew tedious. Yet as the hours and days passed I became more and more engrossed. For I soon began to jigsaw answers together.

The most dramatic moment came near the end of the first morning's listing. Its catalyst was the bleached yellow measuring tape that snaked down the gravel patch.

It is important that you have a clear picture of this tape and its metal case.

The case, which lay near the trunk, measured three-and-a-half inches in diameter. One side plate was missing. The other, though corroded and encrusted, bore on its brass or alloy bushing what seemed to be the beginning of the maker's name: "E. O. SIM . . ." The exposed spindle still held a few turns of the yellow linen tape.

The rest of the tape meandered up the gravel patch to the foot of a rock ledge, thirty feet away. It was extensively but erratically twisted. There were three breaks in it, and at each break a few inches of tape had vanished. The free ends seemed to have been gnawed through by rodents, then frayed as they flapped in the wind. In one place, the wind had figure-of-eighted the tape loosely around two big stones.

All this was straightforward enough. But the tape also passed directly beneath several items that, given their sheltered positions in the lee of the rock ledge, seemed too solid to have been moved by wind: a good-sized stone; a five-gallon can; a rusty tin box; the lid that had obviously once been hinged to the box. And how that had happened was something I could not immediately explain.

When I had listed the tape and its case and everything else on the gravel patch, I moved up onto the lip of the rock ledge.

The first item I found was a disk of rusty metal about three inches across. Beside it lay a brass or alloy washer and bushing that obviously fitted a hole in its center. I picked up the three pieces of metal and laid them on the palm of one hand. At once, I saw that the rusty disk was the missing side plate from the metal tape case down by the trunk. And almost in the same instant I knew—in a flash of enlightenment—exactly what had happened in that place, years before.

I turned and looked down across the gravel patch, toward the trunk. A long time ago, somebody had stood on that ledge and pried the side plate loose from its case and dropped it at his feet; then he had grasped the end of the tape in one hand and with the other had thrown the case high and hard. The case had arched out over the gravel patch; the tape, twisting off the exposed spindle, had traced a parabola behind it. Standing there on the lip of the ledge, I could see that parabola arching out over the gravel patch, yellow against black rock; could see it almost as vividly as if the throwing had happened in front of my eyes, with the tape twisting, twisting, twisting off its spindle.

The case had landed near the place the trunk now stood—and perhaps stood then. The tape, suddenly slack, had fluttered down onto the gravel, already snaking in the wind—if there was a wind that day, that hour. Soon afterward, the thrower or an accomplice had by chance dropped on top of the tape several things too heavy to be moved by wind—including a tin box from which he had just ripped the lid.

In that first catalytic moment I knew that this was how it had been.

And as I stood there on the rock ledge with the parabola scene still vivid across my mind, I saw that a vital sector of my jigsaw puzzle had snapped into place. For the scene drew together all manner of hints that I had not understood: boards and stones lying at the mouth of the natural closet in the annex; that concentration of gear just below them, intermixed with the firewood; directly beneath the annex, down on the gravel, more firewood mixed in with more artifacts; three empty .22-caliber shells lying beside the tape in the lee of the rock ledge; even the empty trunk—empty, that is, except for two ordinary brown paper bags.

Suddenly, these clues had clicked home.

For as I should have seen from the start, it was ridiculous to suppose that my neat, meticulous trunk man had strewn his own belongings about the place. What he had done, of course, was to cache them neatly away in the natural closet, then block its mouth with boards and stones. He had cached almost everything, including the trunk. He had left in their original places only such things as the heavy metate, his grass bed and the fiddling little repair items on their ledge. And then—because his burros had bolted or for some other reason—he had left.

Later—though I had no idea how much later—two or more vandals had stumbled on his cave, just as I had done. (There had been more than one vandal, I felt sure: a man on his own does not vandalize, unprovoked; does not throw things, anyway, in unconscious exhibitionism. Besides, why did the trunk hold two ordinary brown paper bags of the kind that two men would pack lunches in if they were making a day trip out into the desert?)

The vandals had seen the boards and stones blocking the entrance to the natural closet, had found the trunk man's gear inside and had dragged everything out onto the firewood he had left in his woodshed. They had let some of the gear lie there, among the firewood. They had tossed a few items into the main chamber. They had thrown or kicked others, including the trunk, down into the wash, along with several sticks of firewood. Then they had gone to work—these symbols of the chaos that is always lurking, ready to tear order apart, when the bonds of decency loosen or are left safely behind. They had torn apart the carefully cached private belongings of the neat and meticulous man who had once lived in that quiet place. At least once, they had thrown what they had torn apart. They had also fired three or more rounds from a .22 rifle or pistol. More than likely, they had stuffed into pockets or rucksacks the most valuable items from the looted trunk.

And then they had gone.

Silence had flowed back into the canyon. Peace had settled over the trunk man's belongings—over the sheepherder's stove now lying tilted on its side in his woodshed and over his empty trunk left standing on the gravel patch with his yellow measuring tape snaking away from it toward the rock ledge. In the cave, dust had begun to settle. Outside in the wash, sunlight had begun to bleach the tape, rodents to gnaw it, the wind to flap and fray it. And that was how it had been ever since: dust and sun and wind, year after year after year, in silence.

All this I saw in that first catalytic moment when I stood on the rock ledge with the rusty side plate lying in the palm of my hand. At least, I think so. It is possible, I suppose, that I have come to attribute too much to that first moment. But I doubt it. And even if I have slipped in a few jig-saw pieces that actually remained unfitted for a little longer, it does not matter much. In that first flash of enlightenment I certainly grasped the broad outline of what had happened at my cave in the half-century before I came.

And no doubts ever rose to cloud that picture.

When I checked the footage markings on the measuring tape, and the way the slack lay, both supported my yellow parabola scenario. And the tape's metal case turned out to be dented much as you would expect it to be if its side plate had been pried off and then it had landed not too heavily on gravel with the tape half holding it back. (I had left the side plate up on the ledge and did not bother to mate it with the case until five days later, when I began to reconstruct my trunk man's camp. Then, sure enough, it fitted, snap. Note that I already thought of the old-timer as "my" man—silly as that may sound if you have never tackled a project of this kind.)

When I checked the trunk for signs that it had been thrown or dropped from annex to gravel patch, I found the metal sheathing torn at one corner. The underlying wood looked sounder than I had expected; but the vandals, I decided, could have carried the trunk out of the cave, looted it up on the ledge and then, when it was empty, slung it down onto the gravel patch. Or strong winds might have blown it down, later. I felt sure, anyway, that if the trunk had been damaged while it belonged to my trunk man he would at least have nailed the metal back in place.

Next I rechecked the annex. Most if not all the jumbled gear had indeed been pulled down on top of the firewood. And up in the natural closet three large stones had been carefully piled, then wedged firm with smaller ones: they could hardly have been put there, I now saw, for any reason but to level off some large object, such as a trunk. And all this double-har-monized—with both the new scenario and my picture of a neat, meticu-lous Trunkman. (About this time, the "old-timer" who had become the "trunk man" first appeared in my notes as "trunkman," then "Trunk-man." It seemed an apt name for the central character in what looked like becoming a sort of amateur archaeological project. By association, the "vandals" soon became the "Vandals.")

With the new scenario pretty well blocked out, I resumed my listing of artifacts outside the cave—and soon confirmed that the Vandals had indeed been Throwers.

Above the rock ledge, beyond a big boulder, I found a steel-jaw animal trap, similar to two others lying on the gravel patch below the cave. This one lay on its side. The jaws were closed and the securing chain was piled in an untidy heap, not attached to something, the way it would have been had someone deliberately set the trap among the bushes in which it lay. The straight-line distance from cave to trap was less than fifty feet—an easy lob over the big boulder, especially using the chain for a good swing.

As soon as I began listing in the cave I got my first real line on when Trunkman had lived there.

Something half hidden under the metate's sloping flank caught my eye. I bent down. Lodged between metate and one supporting chockstone was a fragment of weathered paper. I kneeled, cricked my head sideways. A page heading proclaimed: POPULAR MECHANICS.

Gently, I took the brittle fragment between forefinger and thumb. It came free without resistance. I laid it on top of the metate. Small mouths, no doubt attached to small rodents, had nibbled at the paper's edges—had notched it so continuously that it looked like a piece from a jigsaw puzzle. Beneath a bold-type heading, INTENSE HEAT DEVELOPED BY NEW GAS BURNER, ran a few unnibbled lines of text: "Very high temperatures have been attained with a gas burner lately designed by a St. Louis inventor in which combustion takes place, as it does in the cylinders of gasoline engines, within an airtight chamber. The flame is not subjected to the cooling effect of a surrounding atmos . . ."

I sat back on my heels. The words refined my original "turn of the century" guesstimate to "twentieth century—first decade or two." Tenderly, I turned the paper over: a few more snatches of text, all with the same time ring.

I leaned forward again, peered under the overhanging, chockstoned metate and found another small fragment, very rodent-notched. It jigsawed neatly into a top corner of the larger one. And each side bore a number: 667; 668. I smiled. Together, these fragments would fit my larger jigsaw puzzle. Would fit it accurately—if I chose to carry the problem home with me. For now that I knew the page numbers I should be able to establish, in any good library, which issue of *Popular Mechanics* Trunkman had brought down to his cave. And that would pretty well pin down the date of his occupancy.

Of course, I had no hard, logical evidence that the magazine ever belonged to Trunkman. But I felt in my bones that he had once read that issue of *Popular Mechanics.* And bones and feelings, though just as fallible as brains and logic, are much warmer and much nicer and, at their moments, incomparably more convincing.

For the rest of that day—and most of the next week—I pressed ahead with my listing. Item after item after item. Sitting room. Bedroom. Woodshed. It was back- and leg-wearying work, and from time to time I would put down the clipboard on which I made my lists and walk away for five minutes, or half an hour, to sample the desert's delights.

Do not overlook these delights.

My account to date may have suggested a grim, nose-to-the-grindstone business carried out in a grim, godforsaken place, and so may have led you to imagine that any man who chose to live there must have been a grim, blindly-down-to-earth kind of person.

Not at all.

To begin with, the canyon was no hellhole. As often happens in desert, the place had looked hostile only from a distance. Close up, it was, in its way, beautiful. But remember that desert beauty is an acquired taste. Anyone untuned to rocky desert landscape would likely call that canyon "godforsaken." But when men say "godforsaken" they mostly mean "manforsaken." And that the canyon certainly was. For me, in fact, solitude was its prime appeal. For Trunkman, too, I suspected.

But its attractions by no means ended there.

In desert, the starkness you see from a distance tends to focus, close up, into intricate detail: flowing rock and talus patterns; curving cactus needles, staunch against desiccation; a polka-dotted leopard lizard, sunbathing for his digestion, that flicks into a fleeing blur. Yet behind these filigrees, even when your eye has begun to enjoy them, the desert retains a clean, stark simplicity. If you must, call it barrenness. But this underlying simplicity means that the desert acts, more than most landscapes, as a tabula rasa for light.

One morning I felt the need for a longer than usual break from listing and scrambled up the canyon's easy west slope. I went mostly for exercise but also to look for a possible burro route and for water in a half-hidden gully. I found neither. But near the rim I discovered a bighorn sheep resting place that commanded a panoramic view of the basin's jagged peaks. And as I stood beside the little hollowed-out patch of bare earth I saw these peaks spring to life.

The day had dawned gray and lowering. Its early clouds had even drooled a few spittles of rain. But by nine o'clock the clouds had lost their steely grip. Then, as I stood beside the bighorn resting place, sunlight

broke through. And it transformed the peaks from dark, glowering sentinels into pink and smiling guardians.

I do not mean that they glowed with the startling incandescence that
sunset can strike into black desert hills. But they shone, now, with a clean,
new-day purity. They were forward-looking and full of hope—yet in no
way Panglossian, saccharine, Disnoid. For as the sunlight moved forward,
embracing ridge after angled ridge and spur after echeloned spur, touching them into life, it built behind each a somber black shadow. And such
shadows keep you honest. They remind you that in the end, everywhere, a
night must fall.

For long moments the vivid light held. Then, very slowly, its intensity
faded.

I glanced down at the cave. From up there where the bighorns sat, it
looked very small. Had the bighorns, I wondered, watched me moving
around down below? Had they, earlier, watched another indistinguishable
speck that had been Trunkman?

I looked back at the still-sunlit peaks. Had Trunkman been the kind of
man who appreciated the magic that light can paint on desert canvas?
Would he stand, entranced, and watch the colors go on? Watch them hold
briefly, then fade? I decided, tentatively or a bit firmer, that he would.
Such sun paintings are very much a part of what draws people to the desert. Draws them back again and again.

I began to walk down steep talus toward the cave.

The paintings were a part of what drew me back, certainly. My intro-
duction to the desert had come during a summer spent walking the length
of California. That walk had expanded my awareness of what light can do
with landscape—and had plunged me in love with the desert. I had not
moved there to live, but I had kept coming back. Trunkman had chosen to
live there—though for how long, I could not guess. As I walked down toward the cave I wondered at what stage of life he had discovered it. I had
been thirty-six when I walked up California. On a hunch, monumentally
unsupported by logic, I decided that Trunkman, too, had probably discovered the desert, and fallen in love with it, in his middle years.

Back at the cave, refreshed, I buckled down again to my artifacts list.
By now I knew that Indians, as well as Trunkman, had lived there.

The metate was only the first piece of evidence. The cave yielded many
more: two chert arrowheads; a fragment of what I felt fervently sure was
black Indian pottery; five stones, some equipped with notches for forefin-
gers, that fitted neatly into my hand and collectively drew from my deep
well of archaeological ignorance the designation "instruments" (one stone

had clearly been used for pounding things, and another was a strong candidate for metate-matching pestle); also seven smooth pebbles, mostly lying near the metate—undoubted imports, probably from the river. If an Indian had gone to the trouble of carrying the pebbles up, I decided, then they must have held hidden meanings.

All these artifacts could conceivably have been brought to the cave by white men. But scattered on and just below the dirt floor I found a vast cemetery of small mammal bones, densest around the fireplace. My tentative but barely avoidable conclusion: the debris of many long-past suppers.

The clinchers for Indian occupation came from just outside the cave. Directly opposite the annex stood two boulders with a deep, narrow cleavage between them. I named it "carapace cleft": it held a bighorn sheep skull and the smashed remains of at least six tortoise shells. These shells looked much older than the three carapaces lying beside the grass bed and were, I felt sure, debris from long-dead Indians' meals. My neat Trunkman would not have smashed them. He would certainly not have discarded such smelly garbage on his doorstep.

Finally, there was the petroglyph: a strong, fishbone-like pattern on one of the dark boulders that formed "carapace cleft." It was barely three feet long, and its lines had been scraped, not deeply cut. But once seen, it stood out like a billboard. To my Western eye it suggested a signpost, perhaps pointing toward water. To an Indian eye it no doubt signaled something entirely different. Like the seven smooth pebbles, and many other things in and around the cave, it probably held hidden meanings—though I knew I might not even recognize as "things" what earlier eyes had seen as specific entities.

But although the petroglyph, billboarding it out in the cave's front yard, seemed to clinch my case for Indian occupation, it did not necessarily signal their permanent residence. The cave was hardly what you would call a Stone Age mansion. It was not much more than a large and deeply cut ledge, really. And I would have hated to defend it. Besides, if it had been an Indian home or even storeroom, its owners—from what I had seen of similar caves up in Grand Canyon—would have built a stone wall along the lip. Here, somebody, probably white, had rough-piled a few stones at the head of the grass bed. Nothing more. Most likely solution: an occasional Indian night stop, a convenience on local journeys—perhaps clear up to Trunkman's time.

All along, I had been trying to pin down that time—trying to refine even further the whisper from *Popular Mechanics*: "Early twentieth century—first decade or two." And slowly, haphazardly, as I compiled my artifacts list, clues surfaced. Two suspender fittings inscribed "PAT DEC 1900." Raised letters on the rusty door of the sheepherder's stove: "GOLDBERG BROS. DENVER. PAT. Jan. 21 – 13." Another shard of *Popular Mechanics:* "On a cruise to the Mediterranean in 1913 hundreds of [U.S. Navy] bluejackets spent nine days touring Italy, France, Austria, and Switzerland." Yet another shard, with figures for shipping use of the Panama Canal, and including the date "August 1915."

But the newspaper fragments were what finally did it.

I found them everywhere: on the gravel patch; up under the rock ledge; in the cave's main chamber. They lay thickest in the woodshed, but there were some, too, in the natural closet I was beginning to call "the store-room." The fragments were yellow or bleached, depending on whether the articles holding them in place through years of desert wind had allowed light to fall on the paper; but all were brittle. Many were dime-size, some big as a silver dollar. A few measured six inches across. Almost all their edges had been nibbled or brittled away.

Most of the fragments were want ads. When I had read them I filed them tenderly in plastic bags, then stored the bags between sheets of cardboard. In my notebook I scribbled, "So here I am handling fifty-year-old want ads as if they were the Dead Sea Scrolls."

The first few I read offered little information. But as the collection grew, and as I sat or squatted, peering at the faded type, I kept catching glimpses of a long-gone world—and also finding new clues: "BUSINESS MAN LEAVING for Mexico City will undertake any commissi . . ." "LEAV-ING FOR SAN FRANCISCO 16th. High class car. Want 4 passenge . . ." "WANTED: WHAT HAVE YOU TO OFFER IN A silver prospect or developed mine located in Southern California . . ." "Address AB, Box 40, TIMES OFFICE." "PIANO LESSONS, 50 CENTS . . ." "MOVING—$1.00 a room . . ." "WANTED—YOUNG MEN WITH BICYCLES, GOOD pay, steady positions. Apply WESTERN UNION TELEGRAPH CO. 610 S. SPRING ST." "STUTZ BULLDOG, PERFECT IN EVERY respect. Packard, as classy a car as shown. Hupmobile, a classy little car." "FOR SALE—1915 Moon . . ." ". . . 1916 FORD TOURING CAR . . ."

Then, pregnant with suggestion: ". . . CAR, STOLEN Sept. 7, 1916 . . ."

And finally I got the break I had been waiting for.

It was late afternoon, the light al, ost gone. Among the last half dozen unlisted items—on a tapering, low-roofed ledge beyond the woodshed—I found two big newspaper fragments. Crouching under the low roof, half lying in the dust, I laid them carefully on my clipboard and angled it to catch the light.

They were obviously neighbors, from the top of a page. Close neighbors. For across them, in the big, ornate *Times*-style type used by newspapers all over the world, there ran: "LO .... ANGELES."

I turned over one fragment: in similar but smaller type, "SUNDAY TIMES."

"Ah!" I said to the dusty floor.

Then, handling the second fragment with Qumran care, I turned it over, too.

The heading leaped out at me: "SEPTEMBER 10, 1916."

"Got him!" I shouted to cave and canyon.

Then, cradling the clipboard as if it were a newborn babe, I backed slowly into the woodshed, sat on its lip, legs dangling, and smiled happily at the trunk, down on the gravel patch.

So that was that. Trunkman had brought down to his cave at least the want-ads section of a Sunday edition of the Los Angeles *Times*. It made little difference whether he had brought it to read or for packing things; either way, it would almost certainly be an issue from the last few days before he left civilization. And for the moment I would assume that he had arrived at the cave in mid-September 1916.

Deciding when the Vandals came proved much harder.

It had obviously been many years before I arrived. Thick dust coated everything in the cave. And much sunlight had beaten down on the gear scattered around the gravel patch. Up near the rock ledge I found two ordinary wooden mousetraps. One lay wrong side up, and the black words stamped on its long-protected face still stood out crisp as charcoal: "KLINCHER MOUSETRAP—SIMMONS HARDWARE CO. INC.—ST. LOUIS, MO. USA." The other trap lay face up—with not a letter left on its bleached woodwork.

When I had finished my listing, nothing pinned the Vandals to a year or even a decade; but I did find three windows that looked as if they might eventually open.

Among artifacts lying in the lee of the rock ledge were the end of the yellow measuring tape, the three empty .22 shells and a fragment of newspaper. I found them all directly under the cut-back center of the ledge, where it formed a spout and where even the slightest water runoff would have left them covered with a fine coating of silt. But they lay clean and clear, on the very surface of the fine gravel. And the newsprint was undamaged and entirely readable. So it seemed safe to say that no heavy rain had fallen in that canyon since the Vandals left. Back home I would be able to check weather records and—in theory—fix an "earliest possible date."

But desert rainfall often falls like a crazy quilt—a cloudburst can turn one wash into a torrent yet leave its neighbor a dust bowl—and I did not feel confident about converting my rainfall theory into practice.

The .22 shells, presumably the Vandals', looked a better bet. With luck I could get a gunsmith to date them, closely.

With still more luck I might cash in the two brown-paper bags in the trunk. Each had a black six-figure number stamped on its base. At a guess, these were quality-control codes, so if I could identify the maker I stood a chance of getting an accurate dating. And I now felt sure the bags were the Vandals': the woodshed had yielded a similar bag, half eaten by rodents, with red figures on its base, and it looked much older.

There could, of course, have been a second wave of Vandals—Visigoths, perhaps—but I decided to ignore that unlikely and inconvenient possibility.

By the end of my eighth day at the cave I had almost finished the artifacts list. For most of the six days of listing—broken only by a second, half-day water trip to the river—I had been swamped by the sheer volume of piece-by-piece information and had failed to see beyond the details. But at last, often as spin-offs from still-unassembled jigsaw pieces, I began to catch glimpses of my Trunkman as a flesh-and-blood individual.

My first insights touched only superficial, routine matters. But some were the kind that would have colored his life, the way daily routines, chosen or imposed, color all our lives.

From the dust of the sitting-room floor I lifted a small black fragment that went into my list as "unidentified piece of something that broke in my hand—very probably part of a pipe stem." Close by lay a can lid inscribed: "STEEL CUT." Deep in the woodshed clutter, screened from sunlight, I found an unfaded green pocket-size can of "PATTERSON'S TUXEDO TOBACCO—Specially prepared for pipe and cigarettes—Does not bite the tongue nor make the mouth sore." In the storeroom entrance, also safe from sunlight, stood a large, red, gold-lettered can that would have held two pounds of "UNION LEADER CUT PLUG—Smoke and chew." So I knew my man had smoked a lot; had smoked a pipe or rolled his own cigarettes, or both.

I got a line on his food, too.

He drank coffee, copiously. In woodshed and main chamber I found five cans labeled FOLGERS, MJB, RED HUSSAR. Total: six pounds of the stuff—and Lord knows how much more in the forty-six unlabeled cans scattered around cave and gravel patch. He used unsweetened evaporated milk: one can of LILY BRAND ("Cut the Bunch of Lilies from twelve labels, mail them to our office . . . and receive by return mail a Pretty Pincushion"). He liked highly seasoned foods: no less than three cans of pepper (SCHILLING, BEN HUR, TILLMAN). And out in the wash, tinted by sunlight to the purple hue that delights desert aficionados, lay a small stoppered bottle almost full of pale brown powder and inscribed: CHILI POWDER—GEBHART EAGLE. Trunkman also used REX CORNED BEEF, QUAIL BRAND SUGAR CORN, TEA GARDEN BRAND SYRUP and THE ORIGINAL SNOW FLAKE SODAS.

There was one hint that he had been a card player: the torn-off corner of a playing card tucked under a stone at the head of the bed. Yet I hesitated to draw a conclusion that seemed curiously out of character with the Trunkman I was beginning to bring into focus. A buried fragment of blue denim suggested the safer theory that he wore jeans.

By now I had confirmed that he was a highly competent handyman. Two hand-carved wooden lids for five-gallon cans had been beveled so accurately that they fitted the cans as if machined. And a fragile-looking wooden folding chair, legs braced with twisted wire, presumably by Trunkman, not only slid open as if greased when I picked it up but also accepted my 195 pounds without a whimper.

Then there was the garbage pit.

In the wash, fifty paces above the cave, tucked inconspicuously under an overhanging boulder, I found a small stone-walled basin. It was only a couple of feet across but neatly built. It held forty-two rusty tin cans. Some lay on the surface, some were half buried. Often, two or three cans had been telescoped together. All but three of them had apparently been opened with the same kind of old-style lift-and-press opener, operated with the same kind of rhythm and so probably by the same man. The three exceptions had partly attached lids with holes in the center and edges cut clean, as with a knife. But one of this kind was telescoped inside a standard type. Conclusion: all cans opened by Trunkman.

Forty-two cans implied a surprisingly short stay. In my notebook I wrote, "Two weeks?—though care in building basin suggests he meant to stay longer."

The garbage pit, I felt, fitted my portrait of Trunkman. Even today, such neat trash disposal is regrettably rare in the desert. I guessed that in 1916 it must have been remarkable. And although you could, if you wanted to, see the pit as the work of a merely tidy man—a bit of a fuddyduddy, even—you could also read it as the signature of a man with a decent sense of humility, a respect for the nonhuman world.

Soon, I found myself venturing onto even more slippery, speculative ground.

The canyon was not one of your teeming desert places—not a living zoo of beautifully adapted birds and beasts. But it supported many animals other than man. Small, stealthy creatures, no doubt insectile, lived in or near the grass bed and emerged at night for bloody sustenance, leaving on pale human skin raised welts about the size of a quarter—welts that itched only mildly but took four days to begin to subside. For several evenings, a finch and a phoebe kept fluttering around the cave entrance, as if they had established prior roosting rights. Day after day, a pair of ravens patrolled the canyon, swinging high past dark pinnacles, quothing. I saw only one bighorn sheep, far up the canyon; but the grass of the bed held hard, round evidence that a bighorn or two had discovered its comforts. In Trunkman's time there had been pack rats, too: countless generations of them had left their history writ in pack rat fashion—layer upon hard, almost geological layer of droppings—in a mini-echo of the main cave, twenty paces south of it; and several pieces of nail-studded shoe leather and one wooden thread bobbin showed that the inhabitants had patrolled up to the main cave and "exchanged" these items for the small, spiny cactus bases I had found there. The pack rats had died out or moved. But three deer mice still lived in the cave. They lived on a ledge near the grass bed, among stones, and they soon learned to come to dinner. To my dinner, that is: their breakfast. By the end of a week, the mice and I were on very neighborly terms. When the bravest of them came scurrying close under my wrist, then stopped to sample some stew I had put out for him (while the other two lurked timorous and distant, outside the flashlight beam), I began to finger-stroke his back. He did not turn a whisker. Soon I was running two fingertips along his back and pressing so hard that his little legs were bending and I could feel every detail of his backbone and tiny, whipcord muscles. The mouse went on with his meal.

Fingertips still massaging his back, I began to wonder if his ancestors had known Trunkman. If so, how had Trunkman treated them?

He had trapped them, I knew that. The pack rats, too. At least, he had tried to: in addition to the two mousetraps I had found a big homemade rattrap. But defensive trapping of animals need not imply callousness. I would have trapped them, though reluctantly, if I had meant to stay for long and if they had become a nuisance, as they almost certainly would have. But had Trunkman understood that mice, like us, have a part to play? Did he have fun with them, too? Did he feed them his leftovers, let them scurry close under his wrist? When he fell asleep to their soft scurry-ings, did he sometimes feel a warm sense of affinity with all his other neighbors—pack rats and bighorns, finch and phoebe and raven? Was he that sort of man—able to see beyond the arrogant self-centeredness of the human world?

Suddenly, still massaging the mouse's tiny whipcord muscles, I knew the answer was yes. And it made no difference that I recognized this con-viction as totally unbackupable by anything except wishful thinking.

It seemed safe to say, though, that Trunkman had been something of a reader. I found tantalizing hints of what he liked to read, beyond *Popular Mechanics* and the Los Angeles *Times:* several fragments from magazine-type advertisements—with one featuring Pennsylvania private schools on both sides—and a mouse-gnawed page heading from *Young's Magazine Advertiser;* also six small pieces and one almost complete page from what were clearly fiction stories. The complete page apparently came from a magazine: it had been neatly folded twice, lengthwise, as if someone had pushed it into a pocket.

But the other fiction could have come from a book—from between a matching pair of stiff, gray-green, cloth-and-cardboard book covers. These covers had been cleanly cut along the outer edge of the spine. They bore no lettering; the black lining papers, no writing. But scattered about the linings were short, straight, tapering pencil marks—as if someone had with a ruler drawn many straight lines, such as columns, on sheets of paper that had rested on the covers.

These covers remained a puzzle. And so did other things.

I found empty shells of no less than six different calibers of spent ammu-nition—from rifles (.44, .41, and .25-20 as well as the .22s), a pistol (.38) and a shotgun (12 gauge). Some of the empty shells remained intact. In others, primer caps had been removed. And several shells—from pistols, rifles and shotguns—had been cut to various lengths. The cuts, in both metal and cardboard, looked neat and Trunkmanlike. But I could not even guess at why they had been made.

Then there were what I came to call, collectively, the "thin-and-toggle sticks." The thin sticks were pliable, pointed at one end; the toggle sticks, stubby and rigid with, in their completed form, small wooden toggles at-tached by lengths of braided string. Colonies of both kinds of sticks lay scattered, in equal numbers, around the cave. All were beautifully made. In my notes I jotted down that the toggle sticks looked "like some kind of animal trap" and that the thin sticks probably had something to do with them. But I could go no further.

Finally, there were the pale green shoes from the woodshed. Somehow,  ›
they did not go with the cave. They looked like very light town shoes, and
their outer soles had been ripped off and the top parts of both uppers cut
away; and while this cutting could have been done to convert them into
comfortable slip-on camp shoes, their toes were not scuffed, the way they
would have been with even limited desert use. Yet they had seen so much
use, somewhere, that the leather had worn through at both outer-toe
bulges. The worn-through holes had been neatly stitched around the
edges. What puzzled me most, though, was the shoes' size. They were just
9½ inches long and 3½ inches at their widest. Even allowing for shrink-
age—and where they lay, no rain could have fallen on them, and only
weak, late-afternoon winter sun—they looked more like women's shoes
than men's. On my list I jotted down: "Foot fetishist? Memorabilia?
What?"

Among the last items on my list was a fragment of paper that cast unexpected light. It clearly came from a timetable. And in addition to departure times it bore snippets of text: "Rates over the Salt . . .," "Between
California and . . .," and ". . . Los Angeles/Chicago." Trunkman, it
seemed likely, had arrived in Las Vegas by rail. That was at least mildly
interesting. But it gave me no help with the two basic puzzles: "Did he live
alone?" "Just what was he doing down here?"

The variety of ammunition suggested "more than one man." So did
four heavy steel chisels and a massive chain, almost five feet long, that
were startling exceptions to the general run of gear—all lightweight stuff,
suitable for back- or burro-packing. And one end of the chain had been
wired into a loop in a rough and un-Trunkmanlike way. Again, the tiny
green shoes hinted at a woman. But these unsupported clues failed to convince me. In the end, I decided that although several white men could have
used the cave at different times, a lone old-timer as longish-term occupant
made the most sense.

The traditional answer to "what was he doing?" would be "trapping or
prospecting." But the thin-and-toggle sticks, even if parts of traps, suggested small, flimsy affairs; and three steel-jaw traps would be nowhere
near enough for a professional. Besides, the canyon hardly seemed a place
any trapper would choose. And neither was it prospecting country. No
man who knew gold from glitter would waste time on the basin's volcanic
rock. But most significant was the lack of a certain telltale sign. When you
go prospecting you carry pocketfuls or even satchelfuls of samples back to
camp each day, and at your leisure you break them with your hammer. I

found no trace of the fragments such hammering always leaves. And to me that was conclusive.

So when I at last finished my artifacts list, the question "Just what was he doing down here?" still hung unanswered.

I finished the list—which ran to about four hundred items—early on my ninth day at the cave. And after a third and final water trip to the river I spent twenty-four hours reconstructing Trunkman's cave camp.

From the start, it was fun. Setting up the dusty pieces of junk in logical places—and seeing them turn into furniture. Wondering why, having the collapsible wooden chair, Trunkman had bothered to make a stool from a box—and deciding he maybe kept the stool by his bed. Wedding a wooden tripod to a length of hooked wire, then hanging the Dutch oven from the wire and finding that the three might have been made for each other—and assuming they had. Siting the tripodded Dutch oven over the fireplace. Mating the sheepherders' stove with its chimney lengths and fitting the unit neatly into the "kitchen" (a mildly ash-strewn alcove, halfway down the ramp but protected from rain by the overhanging cliff). Putting the trunk at the foot of the bed and leveling it off with stones, the way Trunkman had cached it in his storeroom. Lining up all the five-gallon cans—the painted along with the rusted—and finding they made a colorful parade. Leaning a large but broken piece of mirror against a big lava stone at the narrows between sitting room and woodshed—and discovering that a rock ledge below it cradled the washbasin as if cast for the job. Setting the "ta-bletop" of the "desk" with matching, gray-flecked cup, bowl and coffee-pot, along with cutlery, some colorful, still-labeled cans and other bric-a-brac—and feeling the cave begin to take on a welcoming, lived-in warmth. Hanging the water canteen and a wire-handled can and a couple of smaller utensils from stick-jammed-in-crevice roof fixtures—and deciding they did as much for the feel of the place as lampshades do for a still half-empty house. Moving a few things around to satisfy my sense of order. Moving a few more. And then standing back to admire my handiwork—and discovering that the rich red-brown rust on most of the metal articles harmonized with the paler but still rich brown of weathered wood, and that with this warm undercoat gaily set off by splashes of color from labeled and painted cans and by the unexpected complexity of the bric-a-brac, all laid out as Trunkman might have laid them out, what I now had was a home.

And suddenly Trunkman was no mere abstract of such laboriously de-duced characteristics as tidiness and handymanness. He was a flesh-and-blood person who had also cooked and eaten in this place, had also carried

water and sweated and slept and snored and been bitten by insects that raised red welts the size of quarters on his skin—welts that took four days to begin to subside.

Now I do not mean that once I had reconstructed his camp I had learned any more facts about Trunkman. I had not. But something changed. I began at last to move into his place. And this is not just penetrating hindsight: in my notebook I jotted down, "LO, THE TRUNKMAN LIVETH!"

By this time I was therefore ready to shuck all stereotyped notions of what an "old-timer" might have been doing. I could see now that the very word imprisoned you. You tended to think of "old-timers" as old. But now I saw Trunkman as . . . well, not a young man, necessarily, but a man still full of vigor and fire, physically and mentally. And I saw that he had probably not been a traditional old-timer at all. There was more to him than that, whatever he had been doing. I would have been hard put to explain this conviction but it was there all right—deep and solid, bones and feeling.

He could, I saw, have been a recent college or even high school graduate: a biologist, perhaps, determined to experience the desert, pure—to live utterly on his own for a spell before he took his first job. (Had he brought the L.A. *Times* for the "Help Wanted" section? And what about those ads for Pennsylvania private schools?)

Or he could have been escaping from something. I did not, somehow, see him as an ordinary criminal on the lam. But he could have been a deserter who, because it was the fall of 1916 and he felt sure the U.S. would soon be sucked into "The Great War," needed time to think things over without harassment. After all, young men still did the same sort of thing. Or he could have retreated to the cave to convalesce from woman trouble. At such times, I well knew, the desert can exert a powerful pull.

I also knew, though, that my guesses were only guesses.

When I photographed the results of my camp reconstruction, I doubled for Trunkman. This playacting—just sitting in his chair as I imagined he might have sat, whittling away with his knife at a thin stick or toggle stick—carried things a stage further. And when dusk fell and I lit my first fire in the cave, that helped even more. For the fire added the final touch. Its smoke curled gently up, away from the sitting room and out into the night. Its light warmed the furnishings and built deep, dancing shadows. The walls glowed red. Bumps and bubukles pulsated. Now, leavened by hint and mystery, the cave lived. For the first time, I was seeing it as

Trunkman had seen it, every night of his stay. For a long time I just sat and watched.

Finally, I took some night shots.

For several of them I moved quickly away from the camera on its tripod and sat in the chair, as motionless as I could, waiting out long, stopped-down self-portraits—hoping the partial exposure and inevitable slight movement would make me look like a wraith appearing faintly through the mists of half a century. This final playacting, this oddly eerie little performance, seemed for brief moments to carry me back, as nothing had so far done, into that earlier occupation of the cave. And afterward I felt that it had somehow been a fitting curtain.

For the first time since opening night I camped out in the wash. After dinner I lay looking up at a familiar pattern of black rock walls and less than black, star-spangled sky. Once again, it felt good and clean out there—bitingly real, honed to essentials. And if it no longer soothed me in the way it had nine days earlier that was only because I no longer needed soothing.

I lay back, zippered up my sleeping bag.

So the ten days had worked out well. They had met my deeper needs: I felt rested, calmed, ready. But the Trunkman part had been something of a surprise. The plan was that park personnel and I would pack out the artifacts, and then I would go home. But as I slid down into sleep I knew that I might not be able to let go quite as easily as that.

Early next morning I went back up into the cave. I was wearing heavy, lugged walking boots, not my smooth-soled camp shoes, and they left sharp, patterned tracks. It looked all wrong, not 1916 at all, and I resmoothed the dust. Then I went back down the ramp and stood on the opposite side of the wash, beyond the petroglyph, and let my eyes run over everything. It was the last time I would have it like that, all to myself, with Trunkman's belongings set up the way they had once been, the way they were meant to be. And I saw that now I had lived with them for ten days it was going to be a real tearing away.

But I turned at last, went down onto the gravel patch and heaved the pack onto my back. Then I faced the cave again.

"Goodbye, Trunkman," I said, not too loudly. You do such things, I find, when you have been a long time on your own, miles from anywhere, and I guess it does very little harm, provided no one ever finds out.

After that, everything was just a matter of winding the trip down.

By noon I was at park HQ in Boulder City, and next morning a ranger and the park naturalist-archaeologist and I drove to the rim of the basin.

We stuffed our packs with newspapers to pad the artifacts and tarpaulins to cover them, then walked down to the cave.

The archaeologist tended to agree with my tentative conclusions. "And the Vandals must have been here at least ten years ago," he said. "Probably more. Today's vandals really tear things apart."

While we were dismantling the camp and packing everything into five one-man loads, the ranger suddenly said, "It still worries me that you don't have a good explanation of why he came down here in the first place."

"I know," I said. "It's getting to me, too. I guess I'll just have to ferret out some more information."

Next morning I brought up the two remaining loads.

Before leaving the cave for the last time, I stood and took a farewell look. Bare now except for metate and grass bed and a few sticks of firewood, it looked even sadder and more forlorn than when I had walked up into it a year earlier and seen dust lying thick on the jumbled junk. Not for the first time, I felt a shaft of guilt at having stripped the place of Trunkman's belongings and carried them ignominiously away.

"I hope you don't mind, Trunkman," I said aloud. Then, after a pause, I added, quietly and mostly to myself, "I don't think you would." After all, if I had not taken his belongings some more destructive vandals would surely have come down before long and found the cave and "really torn things apart." Now, with luck, his trunk and other belongings would someday form an exhibit at park HQ or a museum. And I had a hunch that Trunkman would have approved of such a resurrection.

At five o'clock that evening the 707 lifted off from Vegas' McCarran Field. We angled up, leveled off, arrowed toward the setting sun. Far below, the desert glowed.

I leaned back in my seat. The ten days were finally over and I was duly rested and calmed—ready to hurl myself back at the outside world. But it seemed clear now that my "old-timer's cave" was not yet ready to melt obediently into memory.

A few feet below me, in the cold belly of the jet, Dead-Sea-Scrolled away in plastic bags inside my pack, were sundry brittle fragments of *Popular Mechanics* and the Los Angeles *Times;* also a pair of dilapidated green shoes, a number of neatly carved little sticks, a collection of spent shells and three old grocery bags. And these selected items were no longer mere artifacts. Nor just mementos. They were exhibits; clues. They had become evidence in what was beginning to look like a sort of do-it-yourself detective mystery.

I knew that for a while I would not be able to devote much time to the mystery: back in the outside world, other things would loom too large. But I also knew, now, that I would somehow carve out wedges of free time. Come to think of it, the next day—November 16—would be the anniversary of my stumbling on the cave, and that seemed an apt date on which to launch a little preparatory sleuthing.

The jet sliced on westward. I peered out of my window. Spinning time had quenched the evening fireball. Below us, the earth had subsided to blue and gray and lingering brown.

I leaned back again. I might as well admit it, I decided: my little fun project at the cave had in ten days evolved almost beyond recognition, into a full-fledged mystery. At first I had told myself that I just wanted to get the feel of how the old-timer had lived. Then I began wondering what kind of person Trunkman had been—and liked what I saw, or imagined I saw. But now it looked as if I intended to track him down. Almost behind my own back, I seemed to have halfway committed myself to trying to ferret out his name and at least an outline of his history.

Sitting there in the jet, westering homeward, I did not understand how much difference that would make. I did not dream that the project's evolution had only just begun. I certainly did not grasp the impact these changes would bring to bear on the years of my own life.

# 2  First Sleuthings

Back home I devoted a week, full time, to my Trunkman mystery; and for several months after that, every time I saw a chance to snatch a few hours for research, I snatched.

The first week, I started a whole hutch of hares. One after another, they vanished into the undergrowth, apparently forever. But I found myself keeping at it, very happily. And in the end perseverance paid off. It even turned out that some of the early hares were not lost, only in hiding.

That first week, I began by gnawing at "Just what was he doing down there?"

Someone suggested "animal-specimen collector." At the U.C. Museum of Vertebrate Zoology, ten blocks from my Berkeley apartment, a consensus of helpful inmates saw the thin-and-toggle sticks as parts for some kind of deadfall trap—in which a heavy weight such as a stone slab is, when tripped, dropped onto the prey. That certainly fitted "specimen collector," as did the three steel-jaw traps—and the hodgepodge of empty shells, particularly the shotgun and .38 shells. For I learned that collectors, needing a wide range of shot but wanting to limit the weaponry, often carried .38 rifle barrels for insertion in shotguns. Trunkman's doctored shells made sense, too: collectors need a mix of loads and charges.

Some of my evidence even fitted that particular museum, snugly. The staff used paper the same size as the gray-green cloth-and-cardboard book covers, and for field trips some of the collectors still made stiff cardboard protectors very like them. So the pencil marks on the book covers' black lining papers could have come from preparing tabulated lists. Again, the museum often stored specimens in trunks. And the outfit list of a 1917 specimen-collecting expedition included, among other cave echoes, Graniteware crockery—the gray-flecked kind I had assembled on Trunkman's tabletop—and a Dutch oven. Down in the museum basement we even found a Dutch oven that collectors had used on field trips for fifty years, and still did. It was soulmate to Trunkman's.

By the end of that first week I was halfway convinced, seven-eighths excited.

Then the museum put me in touch with a man who had collected specimens all over California for a dozen years around 1916. He studied my finds and photographs, nodded a good deal and shook his head a lot more. Then, in the kindest but firmest way, he let the air out of my balloon. A collector would have had many more traps, he said—probably hundreds of them. The ammunition calibers were wrong, too. And the way the shells had been cut did not make sense for a collector. Nor did a fifty-foot measuring tape. Again, collectors of that period did not use burros: horses or mules perhaps, but by 1916, mostly cars. Above all, though, the feel of it was wrong. "A collector has a scientific mind, and that's not the way he operates. Too leisurely. You want to get as much information as you can in the most efficient way. No, I'd say it's much more likely this guy was a bum. A good bum, mind you. But a bum. A man who just liked living there."

And for the moment I had to live with this verdict.

Meanwhile, I had begun to decipher some of the written-word clues.

At the library, pages 668 and 669 quickly pinned the issue of *Popular Mechanics:* November 1915. Trunkman had apparently taken the whole magazine down to his cave, for other fragments I had found came from pages scattered throughout that issue. And the magazine's contents suggested several reasons he might have bought it. The lead article dangled an obvious bait for a man wondering how to get a trunk down into a rough canyon: "Piano Transported up Mountain by Burros" (by lashing the piano amidships on a pair of long timbers and securing the timbers' ends to the packsaddles of two burros). Other articles could have intrigued Trunkman, too: "Recovering Gold from River Beds," "The Shotgun and How to Use It," and—if he were indeed a deserter or simply a veteran—several stories on the war raging in Europe. Among many handyman items (for details, consult your friendly neighborhood library), one suggested an explanation for the doctored shells: "A brass cartridge makes a good bearing to fit in a wood driving rod used to run a small piece of foot-power machinery. . . . Cut the cartridge to the proper length, and ream out the cap hole even with the diameter of the bore of the shell."

When a gunsmith said he felt sure the cap-removing and the cutting of

Trunkman's shells had nothing to do with shooting, I settled for the "reamed-out bearing" solution—even though I could not guess what he might have wanted the bearings for.

Deciphering the other written-word clues took longer.

A hurried scanning of the Los Angeles *Times* for Sunday, September 10, 1916, confirmed that most of the newspaper fragments from the cave indeed appeared in it. But a few did not. By this time I had discovered that one small fragment bore as part of a page heading, ". . . DAY, DECEMB . . ." I failed to trace the paper from which this fragment came—the type was different from the *Times*'s—but the dates in certain "Automobiles for Sale" ads convinced me that the maverick December fragment came from a 1916 paper—and that Trunkman either had gone down to the cave for the first time during that month or, more likely, had done so in September and made one or more supply trips to Vegas and returned with current newspapers.

The remaining written-word clues, although they generated nothing that seemed likely to help identify him, tended to support the "amiable bum" hypothesis.

A search that ended in correspondence with the National Archives revealed that *Young's Magazine,* a monthly published in New York that folded in 1933, had been a miscellany of short stories and novelettes—mostly romantic affairs, often with emphasis on stage life. All but one of the fiction fragments from the cave appeared in its issue of September 1912. And that, I felt, fitted my scenario: a man might well take down to a remote cave a four-year-old magazine of short stories that appealed to him.

The same issue of *Young's* also featured all the magazine ads I had found except those for Pennsylvania private schools. These ads did not come from *Popular Mechanics* either, or from the *National Geographic* (a prime suspect) or from any Pennsylvania magazine that an experienced researcher could find in the Carnegie or public libraries in Pittsburgh.

During snatched hours of Trunkman sleuthing, spread over many months, I test-launched a battery of other leads brought home in pack bag and mind.

Some never took off. I failed, for example, to find any archaeologist who could throw light on the petroglyph's meaning. Other leads ran head on into brick walls. Even those that flew would often peter out in beguiling but apparently impenetrable thickets.

The thin-and-toggle sticks did just that. Months after he had helped me pack out Trunkman's gear, the park archaeologist solved the basic puzzle. In a book on Indians of that region he found virtual proof that the sticks had indeed been parts for deadfall traps; and a white man, he said, could easily have learned this technique from an Indian, then made the sticks himself. All along, I had felt sure the sticks would tell me something important about Trunkman. Yet once nailed down they seemed to lead nowhere—except, perhaps, back to the now discredited "specimen collector."

The ammunition leads looked at first as if they would also peter out.

Every shell had been made by Remington or Winchester, and I wrote to both manufacturers. It was "highly probable" that the Remington shells had all been made "prior to 1917." The Winchester shells could be dated accurately but broadly: between the mid-1880's and 1940. So I at least knew that all the older ammunition could have belonged to Trunkman.

That left only the three .22 shells I had found lying on the gravel patch, close to the measuring tape. If my scenario was correct they had belonged to the Vandals; and it had by now occurred to me that the Vandals might hold the key to my mystery.

When Trunkman cached everything in the storeroom he would have put his most intimate belongings in the trunk: letters, for example, and other personal papers. And when the Vandals looted the trunk they no doubt scattered such papers to the wind or stuffed them into pockets or rucksacks. Either way, they would have read them—or at least, from sheer curiosity, skimmed through them. So they would likely have learned his name. And if they were still alive and I could find them I might take a vital first jump toward discovering who Trunkman had been: once I had his name I should be able to track down some record of him, somewhere.

But first I had to find the Vandals. And before I could even begin that long-shot journey I needed to know when they had vandalized the cave.

So when I wrote to Winchester about the older ammunition I also asked about the three .22 shells.

Winchester replied that cartridges of that type and marking had been introduced in 1932 and were still being made. In other words, they had not belonged to Trunkman—and the Vandals could not have come to the cave before 1932.

Before long I had a firm, though less precise, "latest possible date."

The two grocery bags from the trunk had been made by Union Camp. (The third bag, from the woodshed, had not, and I never did trace its maker.) The black quality-control numbers on the two bags showed that both had been made on machines in Union Camp's Chicago plant, built in 1915 and closed in 1942. The numbers also indicated the week, month and year of manufacture. "But," wrote Union Camp, "since only one digit was used for the year, it does not tell us which decade." The year figure was definitely "9" on one bag and probably on the other. So the bags had been made in 1919, 1929 or 1939. But the normal time lag betwen manufacture and use of bags varied widely—from two or three months to as long as four or five years. I therefore assumed that because the Vandals could not have been at the cave before 1932 the bags were almost certainly not made in 1919, and probably in 1939 rather than 1929.

Final deductions: The Vandals' bracket—1932–44. Prime time—about 1940–41.

Now Boulder Dam was built between 1931 and 1936, and I had all along thought that the Vandals might have come from survey parties connected with it. Not far from the cave had lain a wooden peg with an alloy tag, and on the tag was scratched "BM ELEV—1804." The U.S. Geological Service office in San Francisco assured me that no surveyors of theirs ever used such tags. That left the Bureau of Reclamation, the Bureau of Land Management, and several power-line companies. All their relevant offices, I found, were in Boulder City. And that discovery triggered a decision.

By this time, nearly a year had passed since my second visit to the cave. Mostly I had been grappling with other matters and the Trunkman mystery would for months lie as forgotten as I could forget it; but whenever I dusted it off to chase a lead, it glittered—and for a while I was hooked again.

The Boulder City block in my surveyor line of inquiry loomed up at a time when I had taken a much-needed rest from other matters and become rehooked by Trunkman. And one September morning I flew to Vegas.

First, I rented a car and drove to Nelson, fifteen miles south of the cave, to see Murl Emery.

Emery, who had lived thereabouts since 1918, was now the oldest local resident as well as a minor celebrity. Erle Stanley Gardner, a longtime friend, had written about him in a book, *Hunting the Desert Whale.*

He was about sixty, Hemingway-faced and -bearded—but solid. He seemed rooted in the desert, yet in no way rootbound.

"Sure they could have been surveyors," he said. "In the thirties, when the dam was building, that country was full of 'em. They built the jeep roads in to the breakover. But if you want to find those guys you've got a hell of a job on your hands." He reeled off a list of organizations they could have worked for.

Meanwhile, he was examining my photographs and artifacts.

No, he had never heard of anyone living in a cave in that basin. But he did not come into the country until 1918, and by then the guy would have vanished without trace. "I wonder what he was up to. No prospector would waste an hour down there. Hot rock, all of it."

"Hot rock?"

"Volcanic. Maybe some Precambrian down by the river, but once he was out of that he'd turn back because of the float he'd see. No sign of samples? Then you're right—that proves it. Hardly a trapper, either. Not back in there. So I wonder why he went down. Barren, inhospitable place. No water. . . . Oh, wait a minute, wait a minute. . . . Fifty years ago that was a different world. We had twice the rainfall then, and all those valleys had grass this deep. The place was green—springs all over. . . ."

"Grass?" I said. "Of course! I should have thought of that. He'd made a bed out of grass. Long grass, too. But now I think about it, I'm almost sure I didn't see any grass growing within miles. And springs all over, you say? I did find a little seep close by. Just damp rock, really. . . ."

"Probably ran fifty feet on the surface in his time. Why, he likely had running water right there at the cave."

"Ah," I said. "Now it makes more sense."

Trunkman could easily have been packed in by burro, Emery thought. There were outfits in Vegas—and probably in Searchlight, which in those days was the big town thereabouts, especially for mining, and was also about twenty miles away. But a man could have had a car and backpacked down from the breakover: it wouldn't be too many loads. "Still, that's a lot of gear for one man. You know, I'll bet he'd been there at least once before and liked it and decided to come back with all the heavy stuff."

That would account for the stool, I said, as well as September and December papers. He could have made the stool on his first visit, then brought the folding chair later. But the forty-two cans in the garbage pit seemed to suggest that he hadn't stayed more than a couple of weeks altogether.

Emery disagreed. "He'd have all the usual things along with the canned stuff, don't forget. Flour and crackers and so on. And back then, with all that grass, he'd have a whole lot of game. Jackrabbits, bighorn, deer. And coyotes and foxes . . ."

"Desert kit foxes?"

"And the little red ones, too. Your man seems to have done some trapping and maybe some shooting, so he had plenty going for him. Could probably have lived on jackrabbits alone. Oh yes, forty-two cans could mean a month, easy. And maybe a whole lot longer."

Emery picked up my photo of the reconstructed camp. "Quail Brand, eh? Very popular corn, that was. And here's a five-gallon can with 'Pearl Oil' on it. That was a trade name for kerosene. But it doesn't mean he used kerosene. Five-gallon cans made the West, you know. They were everywhere."

I nodded. "Yes, it was the same in East Africa when I lived there, twenty years ago."

"He could have used these for water or food or just keeping pack rats and mice out of things. Could be that's why he made those wooden tops for some of 'em. Hm, he sure was neat with his hands. . . . The trunk could have been to keep pack rats out, too. Or burros."

Emery agreed that in 1916 only an unusual man would have built the garbage pit. "But then, I think he *was* an unusual man. Like you, I don't see him as a misfit—one of those men who just wanted to get away from it all. This was an interesting man. An educated man, I'd say, not like me—I only went to fourth grade. Probably young, too. Or anyway not too old."

"I'm glad you said that before I did. I'd come to the same conclusion, though I'm not sure why."

Emery smiled. "Guess I'm not sure either. But what the hell?"

He leaned back in his chair. "On the run from the law? No, I agree, probably not. But a man can be on the run from many things, including himself. If I had to guess, I'd say he was a remittance man. In those days the West was thick with 'em. Spent their time waiting around for checks, just the same as our old men sit around now waiting for welfare checks, except that these checks came from wealthy families in England or back East. Yes, I'd bet he was a remittance man."

We talked for two hours or more. When I left, Emery came out to the car. "Yes," he said as we shook hands, "that's an interesting man you've got there. A man who thought for himself. I'd like to have met him."

Next day, I went back down to the cave.

The moment I walked around the rock buttress and saw the gravel patch where the trunk had stood, I knew something was different. But it was several minutes before I understood. There had been rain. Heavy rain. And its runoff had deposited a new layer of gravel. This layer was about four inches thick. When I examined the wash carefully I saw that a minia-ture waterfall must have poured over the spout of the ledge: below it, a sizable mound now covered the place where the empty .22 shells had lain, beside the end of the measuring tape and the rusty tobacco can that the Vandals had broken open.

I stood looking down at this mound.

Twelve months earlier it had been clear that since the Vandals left there had never been heavy enough rain in the canyon to create a surface flow. Otherwise I would not have been able to read the whole story inscribed on the gravel's surface by tape and shells and rusty tobacco can. (Rainfall records, though inconclusive, as I had feared, tended to support my scenario.) But now I could see that if I had arrived just a few months later I would probably not have found even the tape. I would certainly not have found its wrenched-off side plate in the place it had fallen, at the spout of the ledge, or the three .22 shells down below, beside the tobacco can. Everything would have been swept far down the canyon or buried under that silent mound of gravel.

In the cave itself, nothing had changed. But as I climbed back up out of the canyon I ruminated on how lucky I had been with the rainfall—and it occurred to me that, the way things were going with my little mystery, I would need every last percentage point of luck I could lay hands on.

I spent the next four days scouring first Boulder City, then Las Vegas—fruitlessly. Finally, I went on a Vegas TV program, told the cave story and offered a $100 reward for information leading to Trunkman. I also contracted to write an article, offering the same reward, for the Las Vegas *Sun*.

The article appeared in November. Total viable harvest: nil.

Then, in February, just when my Trunkman energies were flagging because I frankly did not know where to look next, the San Francisco *Chronicle* decided, almost by chance, to reprint the article. And this time it generated—in addition to a bizarre crank letter and another from a man who said he owned a trunk that "came from somewhere in the Midwest" and was almost identical to that shown in my cave pictures—a note that bore the address of a hotel in Santa Cruz, California:

> *Dear Sir:*
>
> *I believe I have knowledge of "the Trunkman" you wrote of in This World Magazine of S.F. Chronicle. I have tried to be very sure before contacting you. If you wish to phone or write me for the investigation of my knowledge please do so, I'll be glad to have you do so. I'm elderly but of good memory.*
>
> *Late afternoon or evenings I am at home for appointments.*
>
> *Sincerely, (Mrs.) Grace Mazeris*

I phoned Mrs. Mazeris that evening.

Her voice was vital, her mind sharp, her memory indeed good—going on amazing. At first, she seemed loath to reveal anything on the phone; but soon, thawing, she began to furnish vivid detail. And her story had a ring to it. At moments, it almost sounded too plausible: I kept remembering the $100 reward. But in the end she at least blunted my skepticism, and I arranged to go and talk to her at her hotel.

Next morning I woke at five o'clock, my mind gnawing. A peripheral detail of Mrs. Mazeris' story had the man she said was Trunkman visiting "the World's Fair in San Francisco at the end of 1915" and having an old interest in minerals renewed by it. I got up and checked an encyclopedia. From February 20 through December 4, 1915, there had been a "Panama-Pacific Exhibition" in San Francisco, timed to celebrate the opening of the Panama Canal. The encyclopedia mentioned only exhibits of "architecture and the arts"; but it did not rule out others. I went back to my warm bed, convinced that Mrs. Mazeris either was telling the truth or was an accomplished and artistic liar.

A few days later I drove down to Santa Cruz.

# 3　Grace

THE HOTEL was downtown, square, passed by. I walked through finger-marked doors into a big, echoing lobby. In one corner stood a piano, closed. Stage center, a TV set flickered black and white. The dozen souls in its grip switched channels to watch me cross the lobby. They went on watching while I inquired for Room 212 from the surly desk clerk, then climbed a broad, still halfway-elegant staircase.

Alone again in a long corridor, I walked slowly, marshaling my thoughts for the interview ahead.

The nub of the story Mrs. Mazeris had told me on the phone was that for two or three years in the early 1930's she had lived in "a rock house" in a desert canyon near Palm Springs with a certain Bill Simmons, also known as "Chuckawalla Bill." And Simmons had repeatedly asked her to drive him up to "some place in Nevada" where he had cached a trunk many years before.

Mrs. Mazeris had fleshed out this frail linkage to Trunkman with convincing details of her life with Bill Simmons. She had sketched in his background and character, too. And everything she had said meshed with what I knew of Trunkman. But Simmons had conveniently died in the late 1930's, and I knew I would have to check Mrs. Mazeris' story closely. After all, she had a hundred-dollar reason for lying.

Although her answers to my leading questions had all fitted Trunkman, I realized afterward that they could have been tailored to my newspaper article. And in my pocket there now nestled a list of questions about matters not mentioned in the article. The answers to them would have to fit, too. And later I should be able to check facts with other people. But for the moment much would depend on the kind of person Mrs. Mazeris turned out to be. She had said she was nearly eighty. The rest was guess-work.

The door of Room 212 stood ajar. I knocked. A voice said, "Oh, hello." Footsteps advanced. The door opened.

My first impression: an avocado. She was barely five feet tall and, if you measured low enough, about the same around. She had red hair and wore sunglasses. Outside the sunglasses, her face was smiling. And somehow, even in that first moment, just standing in the doorway, she bounced.

"I'm so glad you chose today. It's St. Patrick's Day and I'm half Irish. Do come in."

She wore a green dress, too.

After the lobby, the room was a surprise: large and bright and high-ceilinged; solid, but with irregularities to keep it alive. Late-afternoon sun-shine, streaming through white curtains, painted everything cheerful. And the furnishings, ordinary but apt, made the place a home.

"Well, thank you. Of course, the proportions are all wrong. Just look at the height of it. Still, I could certainly do worse. It's nice and private—and I've been here through two earthquakes and the place hardly moved."

We prattled on, skirting business, feeling each other out. A lot hung in the balance. My story. Her hundred dollars. So there was caution in the room as well as hope.

Suddenly, the smile surrounding the sunglasses broadened. "Well, you really do exist! I'd begun to wonder. It cost me eight dollars to track you down." Her voice was strong—not at all the voice of an eighty-year-old. And she scattered huge, unexpected emphases, so that everything came out in theatrical italics.

"Yes, eight *dollars!* Phone calls to the *newspaper* and so on. I wasn't going to let them read my letter *first.* But do sit down. This one's *very comfortable.*"

I leaned back. On a shelf in front of me sat a Wollensak tape recorder. It was twin to the one I had left down in the car for fear of alarming an old lady of eighty.

"Why, of course I wouldn't mind," said Mrs. Mazeris. "I'm perfectly used to being recorded. I was in show business, you know. Eleven years singing and then in motion pictures. In motion pictures I did stunt riding for Billie Burke and many, many other stars. They kept me on hand to ride for these gals that had never straddled a horse. You'd never guess it now, Mr. Fletcher, but I can say, proudly, that I was a good horsewoman. I wasn't afraid of any kind of horse. I loved horses. I was born and raised in Kentucky and horses were my father's life and vocation. . . . No, I don't mind at all. Go right ahead and bring up your recorder."

On the way down to the car I decided, tentatively, "a warring mixture of Irish charm and Los Angeles grab."

When I came back, the sun was off the window and the room no longer so bright and Mrs. Mazeris had taken off her sunglasses and put on a pair of clear-lens bifocals. Her eyes were leprechaun green, and they smiled, too.

She was all set for business.

"Is it running now? Good." And she began to read, rather stiltedly, from an account she had written on a sheet of yellow paper. "Bill was born in 1866, in Pennsylvania, of French-Canadian origin. He was married there and had one son. He was in the Spanish-American War in 1898, aged thirty-one. He left the Army as top sergeant in the Philippines in 1908. When he got out of uniform he went to Pennsylvania to see his family, and he signed with the Harriman railroads as prospector and mineralogist for survey of roads. In 1914 he won a restaurant in a poker game in Seattle, Washington. He improved it and married the head waitress. He cooked and she managed. After one year he discovered he had been had, and she was having an affair with a policeman that posed as Bill's friend. He made a bill of sale to the woman, whose name was Marge, and drew all the money he could out of the bank and took a train to San Francisco—with a new trunk."

Mrs. Mazeris laid heavy emphasis on "trunk"—too much emphasis, even by her standards. But that, I told myself, need not make her a liar; only someone very conscious of the hundred-dollar reward.

"In San Francisco he spent days in the mineral exhibit rooms of the World's Fair and the urge to go back to prospecting came back to him. That was in 1915. He went direct to Las Vegas and after some days there—no, it was some months there instead of days, I think—he outfitted for the desert and hills. Some fate took him to the cave, but he realized the difficulties of getting to town for mail and checks. . . ."

"Checks?"

"Yes, he was a pensioner. A Spanish-American War pensioner."

"Are you sure he was getting a pension when he lived in the cave?"

"Well, no. But when we were together his whole life revolved around the monthly check, just like mine does now. But I lived four years around that man and I never knew how much he got. 'None of your damned business,' he'd say. . . . I draw a social security check now. A hundred and eight dollars a month my government gives me."

Mrs. Mazeris sniffed eloquently before returning to her yellow paper:

". . . for mail and checks. So he started out again and went to the mountains, where he found old claims, some lost diggings and the Lost Dutchman Mine. He's on record for finding that. For several years Bill made lots of money and he decided to go back to Pennsylvania in style. He bought a Cadillac, filled it with food and liquor, hired a driver and started out. He got as far as New Mexico, probably got sober, and ended the trip. He sold the car and dismissed the driver. He visited some mineral spring baths for a few days, then outfitted for the hills of California and the desert. He came to the Chocolate Mountains and this is where he again found a mine, in 1931. I met him in 1932, at the Salton Sea, at Eilers' Place."

Mrs. Mazeris put down her yellow paper. "Eilers was the last of a *multi*millionaire family of piano makers," she said.

I glanced at the careful, tight-packed handwriting on the yellow sheet. If you discounted some probable romanticizing by both parties, it all sounded very much as if it could be my Trunkman's history. But then, so would many men's histories. And I had to remember that the whole account was attenuated hearsay: what a man of unknown reliability might or might not have said, filtered through the forty-year-old memories of an eighty-year-old woman. All the same . . .

"You will understand, Mr. Fletcher, that everything I say about Bill is from my knowledge of living with him and listening to him, and I would swear to it, notarize it. But you say you're a writer, and if you should ever write anything about all this you will please use a name that I have published a little something under. I went to Alaska once, for a newspaper, under the name Grace Mazeris. At another time I can show you my clippings."

I checked the spelling of "Mazeris." "Was that your maiden name, or a purely fictional one?"

"No, that's a fictiona . . . it was a . . . a name, that's all. It's not my son's or my daughter's name, or my grandchildren's name, and that's the only thing that bothers me." Then, with a sudden, sad anger: "In some ways I don't give a damn. I gave them so much when I was young. I worked so hard for them, I . . . But no, you must promise never to use their names."

I promised. And quickly, to cover the rift in her composure, I asked the first of the questions on the list that nestled in my pocket. "What kind of things did Bill like to read?"

"Oh, almost everything. He was a great reader. He liked detective stories, magazines about minerals . . . yes, especially those, because he could have arguments about them in front of me and make out the writer didn't know what he was talking about. He was a smart fellow, Bill was, really smart. Not very formally educated, though he'd had some schooling. At a parochial school, I think. A Catholic school. No college, though. Yes, that's right, he used to call himself a . . . now what was it? . . . a . . ."

Deciding that it did not matter much when we got back to my questions, I let things roll.

". . . a fallen Catholic, that was it. A fallen Catholic. And he'd tell me how he didn't have any use for Catholics any more and if it hadn't been for the damned Catholics what he could have done and so forth. He wasn't a religious man, except that he loved God's world and God's properties. He loved 'em like no man ever loved 'em. The sky . . . 'Come and look at the sky,' he'd say. . . ."

I smiled at the memory of my unsupported speculations about Trunkman and the animal world and the magic that sunlight can paint on desert canvas.

"Yes, Bill loved skies. He was the one that taught me '*Abend ist rot, Morgen ist gut.*' That's German for 'If the evening is red, the morning is good.' He had picked up phrases in German and Spanish, and he spoke French well. I remember we went to Los Angeles once—Bill hated the place—and we had dinner in a French family-style restaurant and Bill talked to the people there. But it was a kind of peasant French from Canada, I think, nothing like my boarding school French and the little bit I got abroad."

"Did he speak English with a French accent?"

"Oh no . . . Though come to think of it he did have maybe just a little bit of a southern accent. I don't know where he got it. Maybe in the Army."

The room had darkened and Mrs. Mazeris got up to switch on a lamp. As she came back I touched an ashtray on a small table beside me. "Could I possibly bum a cigarette? I pay a nickel, always."

Mrs. Mazeris stopped dead. "I'll be happy to roll you one," she said. "Just the way Uncle Bill taught me. . . . That's what I always called him—Uncle Bill. And he always introduced me as his niece. It made things easier with other people, you know. Because Bill was sixty-seven then and I was only forty."

"He rolled his own cigarettes?"

"Always. And smoked a pipe, too."

I nodded. There had been no mention of smoking in my newspaper article. "Do you remember what kind of tobacco he liked?"

"Oh, clear-cut or king-cut or something. Maybe it was steel-cut. . . ."

"Ah!"

"You found a can of steel-cut in the cave?"

"The lid of a can."

"Hm. Anyway, he'd buy *cans* of tobacco—for his pipe and for rolling cigarettes. And ever since then I've liked to roll my own. But I hid the tobacco away before you came. I was afraid you wouldn't have any of my vices." She half turned toward a door, hesitated, then swung back, her smile full leprechaun. "Would you like a drink?"

"I'd love one."

"Good. I've got a half-bottle of Liebfraumilch in the icebox. It's 1969, which was a very good year, so if we mix it with Seven-Up it'll taste just like a Piper Heidsieck cocktail."

And after that we never looked back.

Mrs. Mazeris produced a copy of my San Francisco *Chronicle* article with comments scrawled in its margins. "When I read this," she said, "I was still in bed. And I'd only gotten down to here when I said, 'Why, for God's sake . . . you fool, that was Uncle Bill!' (I talk to myself a whole lot when there's nobody around.) And I went back and started again. I don't know why I did, but I put that down in writing, so that I'd remember it. And then I went through to the finish of it and saw about the reward. But until then I thought you were someone that knew Bill. It sounded like you'd copped something from my brain—something I'd put away there for years. This I take on an oath, Mr. Fletcher. I cross myself and tell you. . . . And one thing you described . . . why, I almost cried. Because Bill *always* had a pedsal—made out of stone, like the Indians use, and the Mexicans—and he pounded meats and vegetables on it. Nearly everything he cooked went through this pedsal. . . ."

"Ah, a metate?"

"Yes, a metate. I don't know where he got it but he had it when I met him, and he carried it around in the car. I'd say, 'That dirty old rock?' and he'd say, 'That rock is clean, kid'—that's what he often called me, 'kid'— and he'd wash it. . . . That's the thing that broke me down in this—that pedsal and the tape measure. Because those are two absolutely true things of Bill." He had owned several tape measures, she said, including linen ones in metal containers, and certainly knew how to use them.

"Then . . . well, some funny little things touch you sometimes. Really touch you. There was this can of corn in the picture here. Bill was the greatest corn eater that ever came from Cornville. When I went to get supplies it was always 'Did you get the corn?' The big-sized cans. He always bought things in big cans. Yes, when I saw that corn I laughed because . . . oh, Bill and his corn! He used to make corn fritters. Make a whole meal of them with fried bacon and a can of tomatoes. Yes, he was really a cook, Bill was. You'd think he was on Fifth Avenue."

I asked about foods not mentioned in my article.

Yes, Bill had liked corned beef. The men had grumbled about it in the Army but he said it was damned good stuff. Especially if it came from South America. Certainly he had used crackers. And condensed and evaporated milk—in coffee but not tea. His favorite coffee brands were M.J.B., Hills Brothers and Folgers—and also Arbuckles, from back East. Chili? Oh yes, especially in chili beans. Yes, he was very fond of chili.

Encouraged, I went on down my question list. Some of Mrs. Mazeris' answers were negative, some neutral, many decidedly positive. But I noticed that she could have avoided several negative answers, or at least softened them, by heeding hints or statements in my article. And by now there was no hint of any holding back. I began to feel more and more strongly, in spite of a natural and necessary skepticism, that she was telling the truth.

I asked if Bill had used the kind of utensils shown in one unpublished photograph of Trunkman's camp. "They're a special sort of mottled enamelware. I've forgotten the name now. . . ."

"Graniteware," prompted Mrs. Mazeris. "Yes, he had Graniteware, sure. A coffeepot and . . . oh, this looks like a layout of Bill's like I can't tell you. He could get up a kitchen in nothing flat."

I nodded. There had been no mention of Graniteware in my article.

Yes, Mrs. Mazeris remembered lots of square five-gallon cans around camp. They were the kind kerosene came in, but Bill used the sort restaurants got syrup in. He used to ask for them. He'd cut the tops out with a can opener and put wooden carrying handles across the opening. No, no recollection of neatly fitting lids. He used the cans to soak his clothes in, overnight, before he took them up to the spring. Mostly, he wore Levi's.

I ran on down my question list, making parenthetical mental notes and in some cases awarding grades.

Yes, Bill had a rifle and a six-shooter. But no shotgun. (My article had been unclear on this subject.)

A "repair shop"? Well, it was astonishing what Bill carried around. He was such a gatherer-upper that by the time they moved into the rock house she didn't know what all he'd got. But she certainly remembered lots of grommets and similar repair items. (No mention in the article.)

Bill always buried garbage. Otherwise, he said, you attracted animals. He would "make a place quite a ways off" and was "apt to do it down in a draw." (I gave this answer three grades. Superficially, negative. But neutral if you accepted that the cave was Bill's first desert camp and he would have refined his practices later. Highly positive as a truth indicator, because Mrs. Mazeris had not tailored her answer to the clear description of the garbage pit in my article.)

Bill often brought pocketfuls of prospecting samples back to camp and crushed them with his hammer and examined them under his prospecting glass. (Negative, neutral and positive, as above.)

Among Bill's several kinds of camp slippers had been a pair made from ordinary town shoes, with the backs cut completely away and just a strap left in front. He wore size 8's: his feet were his pride and joy. (Apparently rather positive—until we measured the tattered green shoes against Mrs. Mazeris' tiny, size-5 feet and found them too small.)

Bill had carried one or two steel-jaw traps in case they were troubled by big animals like coyotes. "And he used to make wooden traps at night, as he sat there in camp. They were for small animals like gophers and rats that bothered us or that he was afraid would fall into our spring. Yes, the traps had a trip mechanism. Little things up, like this, and they fell and captured animals alive. Bill said so, anyway. But I never actually saw one in operation."

I brought out some thin-and-toggle sticks.

"Is *that* the kind you found in the cave? Oh gosh, those aren't original. Many, many people made them. No, not only Indians. I saw them time and time again in the camps." (So offhandedly positive, when she could easily have made a big deal of it, that after my difficulties in identifying the sticks I wondered if some mistake had not crept in.)

Mrs. Mazeris sipped her "champagne cocktail." "You know, there's nothing about this that is *not* Uncle Bill. I can see it all. And I believe that I discovered him in your article, here, at least ten minutes before I finished it. Before I got to the bit about the reward. 'Goddamnit!' I said to myself, '*that's* why he wanted to go back for that trunk!' And I scribbled all these notes in the margins. At first, I had no intention of doing anything—the hundred dollars didn't upset me—and it was five days before I had the courage to call the *Chronicle.* But some of the things you wrote were so right. Neat and meticulous. . . . Was Bill ever neat and meticulous! He never went into town with me without a bath, clean shirt and shiny shoes. And he shaved. He used to shave up in the hills all the time. Finally he started to grow a Kentucky colonel's goatee beard."

"Hm. There was a mirror in the cave."

Behind her glasses, Mrs. Mazeris' eyes grew round and big. "No!" she breathed. The eyes were moist now, the face puckered. "When we were together he had a washbasin and a mirror and a shaving . . ." Her voice trailed off.

"Of course," I said, "if you're going to shave you've pretty well got to have a mirror." I said it firmly, cynically—hearing the plain common sense behind the words. Yet I could not forget the look on Mrs. Mazeris' face. True, she had been in show business. Yet at that moment I had lost all but the most residual disbelief in her story.

She took a deep breath, regained her composure. "He was meticulous in other ways, too. He hated any kind of mess."

"Meticulous almost to the point of being overmeticulous?"

"You have him down! That was Bill—getting on your nerves. 'Did you leave this damn pot here? You know why you shouldn't leave it there? You pick it up and get a scorpion in your finger and you'll know.' Oh boy! Always had some reason."

I laughed. "On occasions, an annoying sonofabitch. I know. I'm like that."

"Are you? Yes, you're a bit like him in some ways. . . . Then there was this business about hiding his things. That's Bill all over again. When we left the Chocolate Mountains he hid things there that, honest to God . . . they were there when he went back, just as good as new. He had a good way of hiding things. I always thought he learned that in the Army."

"How did he hide things?"

"Oh, he'd dig out a place and rock it in and put stuff over it and . . . now what did he call doing that? He had a name for it."

"Cache?"

"That's it! Cache! His cache. 'This cache'll be here when I come back,' he'd say."

I nodded. So the storeroom fitted, too. I took from their envelope some photographs that had not appeared with the article and handed one to Mrs. Mazeris.

"Why, there's the stove! That's the kind we bought to take to the Chocolate Mountains. But what's he got that long chimney on it for? We only had a short chimney, because he'd put it up high. Not when we were on the road, though. But even on the road he'd just as leave bake a pie or a cake or anything. . . ."

"What did he bake in?"

"A big pot. An oven. What do you call them? Dutch ovens. He used to hang it on . . . on hangers, you know . . ."

My hand was already lifting another photograph that had not appeared with my article. But at the word "hangers" I froze. For the photograph showed the Dutch oven as I had set it up in Trunkman's reconstructed camp, hanging from a tripod—hanging in a way that everybody I had talked to said they had never seen a Dutch oven hang. And although my article mentioned the Dutch oven, it said nothing about a tripod.

"How did he hang the pot?" I asked. I did my best to make the question sound casual.

"Well, he made a three-stick thing to hang it up sometimes. To hang over a fire, over ashes. . . ."

"A three-stick thing? You mean a tripod?"

"Yes, a tripod. I remember he made one the first time he showed off he could make bread, up in the Chocolate Mountains."

I handed over the photograph. "Like this?"

"That's it! He makes a tripod and he puts a wire around it here and it comes down through the middle like this with a hook here and then . . ." Mrs. Mazeris broke off. Tears flooded her eyes. And suddenly her face crumpled; just fell apart. "Oh, you're going to make me cry in a minute."

This time I felt sure that no one, in or out of show business, could have faked such a flood of fond memory. Then I was telling myself sternly that although Bill Simmons had clearly existed, that did not make him Trunkman. Not yet—even if Mrs. Mazeris thought so.

When she had recovered her composure Mrs. Mazeris said, very quietly, "This is the first time this has come in between you and I, isn't it? . . . You're different than I thought you were going to be, you know."

"Why?"

"Well . . . I'm probably different than what you expected."

"Yeah."

"I like it better the way it is. I figured you were coming in for just cold hard facts and figures and . . ."

"Oh no. For one thing, I've got to find out if your Bill Simmons 'feels' like my Trunkman. But . . . but there's more to it than that, somehow."

"Yes," said Mrs. Mazeris. "There is."

Now fully at ease, she launched into the story of her life with Bill. This time she did it without her yellow-paper prop, and again I let things roll. The story did not unfold tidily, but in the end it was all clear enough. Although some chapters emerged as bare outline, others rolled rich and revealing, and I began to glimpse this Bill Simmons who I already half-believed—well, quarter-believed—was indeed my Trunkman. Began to glimpse, I mean, more than a shadowy, one-dimensional figure.

Mrs. Mazeris had met Bill at "Eilers' Place" on the Salton Sea in early 1932, or perhaps December 1931. Soon, they had gone "on safari" together into the Chocolate and then the Eagle Mountains, east of the Sea. Mrs. Mazeris drove. "It was a funny thing, Bill had no feel for cars. He liked to drive his Model T truck—the old pedal-style, you know—but he couldn't tackle anything else. So we went in my big Buick. A beautiful car that was. Curtains and all that.

"The whole thing was fascinating to me. To be out there in the hills. Always I'd been a curious person and I thought, 'Well, I'll learn something'—and there was nothing I could do back in Los Angeles, back at my own work. In the theatrical life you get to be a bohemian and here I was a desert rat, and I didn't have to think about the Depression and the banks failing . . . and my own nephew at the lunch table and when he went back to work at the bank it was closed and I had lost seventeen thousand dollars that day and he knew nothing about it. And although I thought, 'Oh well, I'll go back and be on top again,' it was something I liked to slide off of my back. And this was the way I did it—going with Bill. I was in my forties then, you know, when every woman has a little struggle to know what she's on earth for. I was disgusted and worried and trying to find a new me, and I thought I was pretty smart—going on a Palm Springs vacation in the mountains that would cost me nothing and maybe even make me some money. And frankly I've never regretted it."

Mrs. Mazeris let her face smile. Tentatively. With trial bravado.

"Out in the hills it was all a new world to me and Bill knew that world and explained it. One time, on the way out to the Eagle Mountains, he said, 'We don't have to find gold or silver to be rich, Grace. We have to find what the government wants. There's isinglass out here but they don't want that any more.' And he told me all about isinglass—I'd never *dreamed* what isinglass was—and he showed me the papers where he sold it to the government in 1918.

"And we went up there and made camp. I tell you, Bill knew how to order things. He made my little 'twa-ley' down here and his 'twa-ley' over there, about three hundred yards away. And he put a branch across . . . two for the female to sit on—he was a very thoughtful man, I never saw that done before or since—and around mine he put this little brush stuff, you know. One time I happened to go over to his, just out of curiosity, and saw Bill's. . . . You see, he would go out every day to look for this old mine. He had a map of it but he didn't know for sure just where it was. And every day for the two weeks we were there I stayed in that camp, *alone.*

"And then he came in one night all feathered up: 'I've found it, honey, I've found it! Now we've got it!' *'What* have we got?' 'Whatever . . . what d'you want?' And Bill gave it to me. Gave me the mine. 'This is my first present to you,' he said. 'For you and your kids.' So I said, 'First, I want to see it.'

"Oh, that was an awful place to be! My legs were scratched with all this stuff. And here's this outcropping and he'd worked on it and, boy, it was galena, really galena. Silver and gold all over the place. And Bill said, 'Do you know how much this is worth?' 'No.' And he said, 'Neither do I. But we'll get all we can.' Well, he made the map and worked on the road to get there better, and we rested and worked together and then went back to Banning.

"We went to Banning because there was nowhere else to stay in those days except Palm Springs, and we couldn't afford that because the movie people were just starting to take it up. And we put an ad for the claim in the Banning paper and in the end I sold that damned thing to a big German who owned an undertaking parlor in town. I got a thousand dollars and a brand-new car. A Dodge it was. A beautiful roadster car. Just what I wanted for my son. He got the car. . . ." Mrs. Mazeris suddenly looked up at me, uncertain, pleading. I could almost see the trust and confidence draining out of her features. "You think I'm an awful person, don't you?"

"No. No. On the contrary."

She smiled, took a deep breath, relaunched. "So we got a thousand dollars for the mine. Or was it fifteen hundred? And after we'd sold another mine we went to Garnet."

That was when they moved into the "rock house," up a canyon in the mountains. "Bill made me so comfortable! He got two old redwood railroad ties and shaved them down until he'd made me a four-poster redwood bed with a crossbar of pine. The prettiest bed you ever saw. . . ."

Mrs. Mazeris sighed.

"Most days he'd go off on foot to set traps or something like that and I'd stay at the rock house, occupied or resting. And then in the evening we'd sit outside in the twilight with our dogs and Bill would tell me what he was going to do next day, like when that picture was taken. . . . Oh, I meant to tell you. I found two photographs of Bill in among my papers. . . ." She got up, went to a cupboard and brought back two small, faded snapshots.

One showed a man and woman and a dog outside a primitive, flat-roofed stone cabin set in rough desert. Details were fuzzy but the woman sitting in the chair could clearly be Mrs. Mazeris, forty years younger. Bright sunlight, slanting low, made the man standing beside her a shadowy figure. He seemed rather small. But he stood very upright. And very posed. He was wearing a dark sweater and nondescript slacks. Even through a magnifying glass I could not really make out his features, but his hair, receding sharply from a high forehead, was long and unruly behind the ears. He had a little goatee beard and seemed to be wearing glasses.

I turned the snapshot over. On the back was written: "Rex the dog . . . Reina."

"That's right," said Mrs. Mazeris. "Reina was Bill's dog."

I turned the snap back over and peered at the man's face.

"This one's clearer," said Mrs. Mazeris. "It was taken down in Garnet. That's a waitress at the restaurant there. Name of Rose. You see how neat and tidy Bill was when he went to town? And he always wore a ten-gallon hat like that."

The hat's shadow obscured the man's eyes but the exposed part of his face had character. And above the little goatee it creased in an amused smile. The woman was Eleanor Roosevelt-plain.

"Bill didn't like her too well," said Mrs. Mazeris over my shoulder. "She was so masculine, you know. I don't think he could ever have fallen in love with her. She came from New Jersey. . . . Oh, look! In that one of the rock house you can see Bill's Model T truck. My Buick's there too, I think. And you can see how well Bill built the doorways. And those crossbeams. . . . Why, yes, *that's* when he told me about his trunk!"

Mrs. Mazeris leaned back and shut her eyes.

"Wait, I'll tell you what it was. . . . The roof. . . . The beams. . . . That's it, the beams! He said that if he had his trunk there he could have his instruments and that would make the beams . . . Oh God, what word did he use? Abutted? Butts? Make the butts better? The crossbeams would butt better? Something like that. I remember this word because I said to him, 'It isn't only the butt in the ceiling that's getting on my nerves, it's your butt. Stop this thing about . . .' "

Her voice tailed off.

"Was this the first time he mentioned the cave?"

"Oh, he never told me he lived in a cave. I've never said he called it a cave. Just his camp. Where he had his things hidden. What did you call it? Cached. Cached away. His 'camp' he called it. I don't remember the word 'cave.' If he used it, I wasn't paying attention. But right at the beginning, when we'd sold the mine to the German in Banning and I had this money and the new car, he asked me to drive him to this camp up in Nevada. And after that he kept worrying at me to drive him there, to pick up these things. When I talked to him sensibly he would agree that somebody probably went in there after he left and got everything. But he would keep

coming back to it. He didn't say 'cave,' though. Just his 'camp.' Or later on, his 'trunk.' Bill wouldn't like to say he lived in a cave because that would leave him open to ridicule—and he was very sensitive to ridicule."

We began to discuss why he had gone to live in the cave.

"The way I see it," said Mrs. Mazeris, "he was healing. He was trying to get himself together. Because he'd just had this breakup with his second wife, remember, in Seattle."

"Yes, that makes sense. I know."

"Bill never liked to speak of sorrow, but he did tell me the story of his wife." It seemed that Bill had caught her more or less *in flagrante delicto* with the policeman. "He told me one time, 'Grace, the only reason I didn't do anything was because I walked and I talked to myself. Otherwise I'd have been a murderer.' He was that kind of person, Uncle Bill was. He could analyze and talk himself in and out of things. So although his first impulse was to shoot the policeman and beat the hell out of her, he did neither one. He outsmarted them by taking all the money. So he had money when he went to Las Vegas.

"But when he went down to the cave this man was in deep despair. Bill was a man who if he was made a fool of, it was twice a fool. And he'd been made a fool of. So maybe down in that cave he had a grand recuperation. That's the only thing that I can think he'd stay there a month or two for. I don't think he did much in that cave, except that he had plenty of books and papers and magazines. He could absolutely relax and read, could Bill, and just act like he'd never done anything else in his life. He had that way of doing when he wanted to relax. And besides, he probably had three or four bottles of good liquor with him."

"I didn't find any bottles in the cave."

"No liquor bottles at all?"

"None."

"Hm," said Mrs. Mazeris.

But that, I said, need not mean much. Over the years, our habits change. And it sounded to me as though the cave could have marked a watershed in Bill's life.

Mrs. Mazeris nodded. "When he went down into that place Bill was *a-borning*—that's what he was doing. He was getting born to a new life. The Bill Simmons I knew was *born* down in that cave. . . . But after a while he suddenly said, 'I can't stay here. I've got to go.' Bill was like that. If we were somewhere and he wanted to go, we went. And he figured on coming back for that trunk because there were things in it that he wanted to keep. But . . . time . . . Well, you know how it is. You have things you think you couldn't live without—and in five years you never know you had 'em. And Bill was very much that way."

Mrs. Mazeris finished her story quickly. She slid over her departure from Bill and the rock house, and I asked no questions. She apparently bought a ranch near Garnet and spent the next several years "fighting to save it." Again, I held my tongue.

During that period she and Bill remained good friends. But after she had left the desert for good somebody sent her a newspaper clipping. That was probably in late 1937, certainly no later than 1939. The report said Bill Simmons had been found three miles out of Indio. "He had his back up against a mesquite tree—some kind of tree, anyway—and he had water and he had whiskey . . . and he died. Heart failure."

Mrs. Mazeris swallowed. She had done so several times as she told of Bill's death. "It's costing me to tell you all this," she said with a weak smile. "I wasn't even going to tell. . . . Oh, but what the heck?"

We sat silent for a moment.

"Almost everything you tell me about Bill," I said, "is consistent with my man."

The leprechauns leaped into Mrs. Mazeris' eyes. "He wasn't *your* man," she said in mock outrage. "He was *my* man."

And we killed our drinks.

Soon afterward we went out to dinner. While we demolished a huge platter of Chinese food and a bottle of Riesling I began to learn more about Bill Simmons, the man—and about Grace Mazeris, the woman.

"I've been trying to remember where Bill was born," said Mrs. Mazeris, sipping her wine. It was some small place in Pennsylvania, probably just outside Scranton—or maybe Pittsburgh. She would remember if she could see a map. I promised to send her one.

"Although Bill was always called Bill Simmons—or Chuckawalla Bill—he told me several times that his real name was not Simmons but Simone. French, he said. French Canadian. But he had Indian eyes. And the way he could make things with just a knife! 'You *are* an Indian,' I'd say to him. But when I told him about my Indian blood—I'm a sixteenth Indian myself—he used to pooh-pooh it. I'm sure he had Indian blood in him, though."

"Maybe that's why you two got along."

"Maybe. We certainly got on well. For one thing, we were both great talkers. And both good listeners. I loved to listen to Uncle Bill because I can only write when it has happened to me and I had it in the back of my head that someday I'd write a book about him. I did write a book once, about Alaska, and a publisher was interested—but they wanted me to *pay* for printing it! . . . Mostly, Bill and I talked about his past. Mine wasn't so interesting to him because he thought, 'Oh, the damn fool's wasted her life. All she's got is a couple of kids for it and she's never been out in the hills.' And here was I, a well-raised girl but I'd gotten in the theatrical profession because I had an exquisite voice and because I made money out of it and because I had two kids to support. All my life I've been a money scraper, ever since I was nineteen—mostly for my kids, with no husband to look after them. But Bill . . . I knew him for four years and I never knew him to work for anyone. Only for himself. But Bill toiled and he spun. And actually he made more money than people who worked for salaries in banks. He made the money but he didn't care. . . ."

"You mean he wasn't terribly interested?"

"That's right. He wasn't after money. What he was after was what Bill Simmons could do. He was after . . ."

"Satisfaction?"

"Yes, satisfaction. That people respected him was a great thing to Bill—though sometimes he used to get little spells of thinking, 'Why am I here? I could have done bigger and better things.' Because he *had* done better things. Bill's one thing in life was, I think, he had a sort of superiority complex. That he could do 'most anything. And between you and I, I think he could. Except for fixing cars. He couldn't abide fiddling with them, and if one'd get bad on him he'd take it down and sell it and get another one. In the two years I was with him he had three different cars. But that was Uncle Bill, too. Anything he did, he wanted to do well. Otherwise it wasn't worth doing. The old perfection kid, you know."

"I know. And oh, I feel for him."

"Are you that way? Well, I'm not that way, so Bill was constantly having someone to correct and teach, and that was what he wanted in life. I fitted him, because I was so damned dumb about the things he knew. And he had to have a woman around, because that was Uncle Bill. I mean, he liked women. He liked . . . to be around them. And he was a *nice* person to be around. I was never ashamed of Bill. If some dudes come riding up the canyon to the rock house he knew how to handle them. He knew good people from bad people. And if a real person got ahold of Bill they liked him tremendously, always, because he had something of profit and benefit to talk about. I'll tell you. One night I come into the de Courselles' bar in Garnet—this was after that awful Prohibition was over—and Bill is sitting over in the corner with two of the biggest surveyors up there. And they're *listening* to him. They were *enjoying* him. I said, 'Oh, Bill has found his own, thank heavens!' Something to take him off of me, you know. . . . Say, this is a good wine. . . .

"Yes, Bill was a smart man, honey. Never a desert rat. Oh boy, how he hated that word! And he had a shrewd intelligence. Shrewd. He was a trader, too. When we sold that mine to the German undertaker in Banning, Bill helped me, of course. He took the undertaker and his son out to see the mine, and then we met together and laid all our cards on the table. The German didn't have all the money so Bill says, 'I'm sure Miss Mason will take property or what-have-you.' The German said, 'Well, I've got a new car.' And right away I hitched on to that. So we got twenty-five hundred dollars and a brand-new car. Or maybe it was two thousand dollars."

"I see. And you got half?"

"Oh-ho, I got three-quarters. I sure did. Bill had his pension, you see. It probably wasn't enough but he took five hundred dollars where I took fifteen hundred. I was a woman. And I needed it. Bill was a gallant man, you know. Very gallant. Yes, he was a good man. I've had two, three husbands, honey, but I've never had anyone I really *cared* to *live* with like I did Bill Simmons. No one. He had the most unique personality. No, I've never had another . . . friend that had the personality Bill had."

"Mason was your maiden name?"

Mrs. Mazeris made a tiny, choking sound. Once again, her face almost crumpled.

"I'm sorry," I said.

But her voice, when it came, was strong and under control. "No, not my maiden name. Another of those short-lived things I did. We were married 1918 to '19. . . . You've probably never met a woman like me, have you? You know, half wacky?"

"Oh, I think most reasonable people are half wacky."

"I should have written a book," said Mrs. Mazeris. "I was born in Kentucky, like I told you. August 31, 1891. My father was a horse trainer and trader. . . ." While she was still at school they—or at least she and her mother—moved West. Her sister had married "a *multi*millionaire" but had no children. She herself had married very young and had two children before she was nineteen. Separated from her husband, she had worked as a singer, then in motion pictures, and later had started up an interior decorating business. "I gave them so much when I was young. I worked so hard for them. I saw that he got his college and she got her musical training. . . ." Her voice, suddenly weak and sad, even plaintive, tailed away. Then: "Do you have children?"

"No."

"No? You've missed something." Then the battling voice and the tough, half-cynical smile took over again. "But I can't exactly tell you what you've missed. Just a lot of hell and damnation. . . ." She gestured, all bravado, and knocked over her empty wineglass. I refilled it. "All my spoutings off," said Mrs. Mazeris. "Sounds like Agnew."

She sighed, then resumed her life story. Over the years she had worked at a lot of things. In Garnet she worked in the de Courselles' bar for a while, at the counter. "And then in the evening I'd sing for them, and Martha played the piano. Poor Martha! She and her husband both committed suicide. . . . But then, in the bar, it was fun. . . ."

At one time, she said, Walt Disney had been interested in buying the ranch she had owned near Garnet, but in the end she sold it to Warner Baxter, the movie star. And then she had left the desert for good. "Sand in my soup, darling. Couldn't stand it any more. No, I'm a sea urchin, Colin. Just give me the beach. Not even mountains—just the beach. I went down to the Salton *Sea,* not the desert. . . ."

After that, she spent several years in Alaska, writing for a newspaper, but mostly she had lived around Los Angeles. She still had many friends there. "Just the other day" she had had lunch with Anita Loos. "I like all new things to come to me. I intend to have them as long as I'm alive. I don't want to be mundane. To sink, you know. Sink. A vegetable. . . . I've always said I'd live to be a hundred, and so far I've had such perfect health it scares me. There's nothing the matter with me now but . . . well, sometimes I think I'm living too long, maybe. Boring people, huh?"

"Far from it. What hope would I have of finding . . . this . . . without you?"

"Thank you. I only wish I could tell you more about Bill." Mrs. Mazeris sipped her wine, looked past me down long corridors of memory. "He had the keenest eyes, Bill did. I remember that. Real snappy eyes, they were. And he could look right into me and read me like a book. I tried to lie to him a couple of times—just little white lies, you know—and he'd look right at me with those eyes of his and say, 'Now tell me the truth.' I gave up in despair. I *knew* him—knew him well—but I could never read him like that. If he wanted to keep something from me, he could. Yes, I knew him, all right. Knew his tempers. . . . He was a secretive type, a soldier type, a don't-tell-unless-you're-sure type. He was never a bigmouth. Bill hated a bigmouth. And he couldn't abide fools. He'd tell them off with a sort of 'Don't take up my time, I'm a very busy man'— which he wasn't. No, he had no patience with stupidity. I remember once he was pouring water into his Ford's radiator and the wind was blowing a gale, the way it usually did around Garnet, and he was holding his ten-gallon hat on with one hand and holding the hose with the other and the water was spraying all over him, and just then a car drove up alongside and a woman leaned out and hollered at Bill, 'Does it always blow like this, here?' And Bill took a quick look at her and said, 'No, madam. Not always. Sometimes it comes straight down.' That tells Bill better than anything. Because . . . Let me tell you something, honey. Bill Simmons never demeaned himself in any way. Gesture or anything. He was *always Bill Simmons.*"

"But he could laugh at himself?"

"Occasionally. If he did the laughing first."

"Even you couldn't laugh at him first?"

"Who? Me? I wouldn't risk my neck."

I laughed. "Would he understand what you said about his having been reborn in the cave?"

"Bill? Not on your life. He knew he'd been born perfect, so how could he possibly change? But don't get me wrong. Bill stood tall, always. In every way. He was really quite a small man but he always stood like a ramrod, shoulders back like this—from the Army, that was—so that people thought of him as taller than he was. And he stood tall in his actions. I never knew one act of his that wasn't honorable. Some were kinda skrimish and kinda mean in a way. . . ."

"Really?"

"Well, in this way. If he thought someone was trying to twist his elbow they never had a chance. He twisted it the other way."

"Oh, that's different. I'm with him there."

"That's what I mean. Yes, Bill hated villainy in anybody. And he was a truthful man. Oh, he had a certain amount of braggadocio about him. Did you ever see a little man that didn't have?"

"You mean he might embellish things?"

"Yes. Like his poker playing. But he wasn't an out-and-out liar. Never."

"Hm. So he was a poker player?"

"Very much so."

"I found a corner of a playing card in the cave. At the time, I thought of it as somehow out of character. But . . ."

"Oh no! Bill was a great one for poker. A born gambler. He'd gamble his last nickel away. But he'd never cheat. Never dream of it. Not Bill. You know what he taught me most? The ethics. You can go to college and take ethics but you could never learn like I learned from Bill. He was a gentleman. Inborn. He always treated me with great respect. Never too familiar. You know what I mean? Yes, he was nice. I wish one of my husbands had been as nice as he. . . .

"Oh, Bill asked me to marry him twenty times. Twenty times a month, I think. But I never wanted to marry him because I knew that then he would have a victory over me, entirely, and no one had ever had one over little Gracie.

"And he would have. He had that magnetism. And by making me so darned comfortable he'd make me love him. . . . He never pretended he was in love with me. Oh, for the longest time . . . I'd known him two years before he even said anything to me like that. Then, when he thought I was going to leave him he said, 'Well, you know we could get married.' "

Mrs. Mazeris sighed again. We had finished the platter of Chinese food. The bottle, too.

"He was such a nice thing, was Bill. You don't know what a man can become when he lives alone like that and searches himself. He can be a very fine person. They don't go to hell. They don't go to the dogs. They find themselves. And I think Bill had found himself."

A waiter came and cleared the table.

"I could never raise a monument high enough for Bill Simmons, really. He had something very, very fine in him. And he was a good lover, too. Not like some men you meet on the road. No, that wasn't any trouble at all with Bill. But he didn't give himself up easily. I always felt he thought he was giving more than he got. But that man, he didn't have any . . . any lewdness about him. And he was one of the tenderest men you could imagine. I've never known a man could be so tender. But because of the gentleman Bill was, that was the slowest-developing affair that ever took place on God's earth. I can't remember how long it was before I crawled into his bed or he crawled into mine, whichever it was. I sometimes think he did it out of pity, even then. Perhaps he'd never met such an unsexy-looking thing."

The waiter brought our fortune cookies. Mrs. Mazeris opened hers, read the strip of blue paper and pushed it across the table.

I read it: "He who teaches me for one day is my father for life."

"Dear Bill!" said Mrs. Mazeris. Behind the glasses, her eyes were misty again.

We went out onto the street and began the one-block walk back to the hotel.

"He was the great love of your life, wasn't he?"

"Bill? No. Not the great love—the great experiment. Bill was a stile to me. His way of living was a complete change, and way out of character for me. It was that time of my life, I guess. I had all those psychological flibbertigibbeties that go with that kind of thing, you know. Many women went into rest homes and insane asylums, and yet . . . Oh, people talk a lot of nonsense about it, you know. My friends used to say, 'But Grace, what about your menopause?' And I'd say, 'Yeah, one afternoon in Riverside.' "

Back in the hotel I wrote out the check for a hundred dollars. "I guess I'm about ninety-two percent sure Bill is Trunkman," I heard myself say.

"Oh, I'm a hundred and two percent sure. And if you need any more information, I'll be here. I hope I'm going to see you again, anyway."

Before I left she gave me the two snapshots, her scribbled-on copy of the newspaper article and a sheaf of notes she had written. She also suggested I visit Garnet. "Between there and Indio you should find . . . well, there must be at least two or three people still alive who knew Bill and me, and they'll tell you that everything I say is true." She smiled. "I get a funny kind of feeling that you'll do all right down there. You and Bill— I've never seen two people so alike in so many ways."

Two weeks later, on the eve of a quick trip to Garnet, I returned to Santa Cruz.

On the drive down I tried to assess my doubt quotient. I felt fairly sure, now, that Grace was not a deliberate, calculating liar. For one thing, she often seemed genuinely unsure of what did and did not appear in my newspaper article. But she was obviously a spontaneous and perhaps compulsive embroiderer of plain fact—witness the escalating price she said the German undertaker had paid for the Eagle Mountain mine, and her inconsistent versions of how often Bill asked her to marry him. Sometimes, too, the lady did protest her veracity too much. I also remained pricklishly aware of her hundred-dollar motivation for lying. But every time I found myself in serious doubt I remembered how her face had crumpled when she saw the photo of the Dutch oven hanging from its tripod; remembered the way her features had fallen apart. On balance, then, I retained a healthy and carefully stoked skepticism—yet found myself leaning strongly toward belief in her story.

But was Bill Simmons my Trunkman? That very different question still hung—and would likely hang for some time yet. The two men certainly meshed, quite remarkably. If you allowed for changes in Bill's camping practices between 1916, when he was a desert tyro, and 1933, when he was a veteran, then nothing I had heard could be said to weigh against him as a Trunkman candidate. Nothing. Absolutely nothing. And the more I thought about that, the heavier it weighed. By the time I drove into Santa Cruz I was seeing it as perhaps the most important fruit of our first talk.

Grace was sorting through a box of papers and photographs, a glass at her side, very relaxed. "I've already spent the hundred dollars, darling. Bad bills and so on. But I'm seeing what else I can find to help you."

Still hunting through papers, she began to fill in gaps in the story of her desert life.

First, she went back to meeting Bill at Eilers' Place on the Salton Sea. The script was vivid. Pass by pass. Yet strictly family stuff. It featured a careful and reluctant Grace agreeing to go "on safari" only after three weeks of Bill's blandishments and on strict conditions of "no funny stuff." I had an idea Bill's camera might have captured the action from a rather different angle.

Suddenly Grace pulled a paper from her box. *"Here* we are! That letter from Walt Disney. I told you he kept pestering me to sell him the ranch."

The photostat looked genuine enough. Disney explained that he and his wife thought the ranch "a lovely spot" but had decided they would be able to spend too little time there to justify buying it.

"I see the letter is addressed to, uh, Mrs. Stenderup."

"Yes, I made a very poor marriage there. He was the cause of me selling the ranch, damn him." She had met Nils Stenderup while working at the de Courselles' bar but still living with Bill. Stenderup was a Dane, an engineer working on the aqueduct then being built near Garnet. "We got married in one mad day. Just got in the car and went to Arizona. . . . What's that border town?"

"Yuma?"

"Yes, Yuma, Arizona. It's on record down there." Grace sighed. "You see, I saw no future with Bill. It wasn't what I wanted, naturally. The wilderness was fading into the background, money was coming to the fore, I knew that pretty soon I'd have to face reality. I'd been living in a . . . a cave, really."

We both laughed.

After the Stenderup marriage, Bill had stayed on up at the rock house. At first, he was "just broken up." "But he got over it," said Grace. "You know how men are."

"It can take four years."

"Not me! Never longer than overnight."

Around this time, Grace got her ranch. But details of how she got it remained unclear. "I bought it from Mr. Knox," she said at one point. And then, later, "I got it in part on trading—got it for almost nothing because

63

the party I got it from was nearer collapse than I ever was—and those were collapsible days, honey."

After the first shock of the Stenderup marriage, she and Bill had remained good friends. He often visited them at the ranch. "He had the triumph of knowing I had done something foolish, which made him very kind to me. He was that sort of person." Bill had brought "bags and bags of silver ore" for building the ranch fireplace: if I went there, I would see that. And I would see that it had been a showplace. Grace had given tea to Greta Garbo on the veranda.

The marriage to Nils Stenderup lasted quick. He turned out to be a bully and "only after the ranch." "He had a raptious brother who got to be a *multi*millionaire. But he's dead now, and so is Nils."

Grace sighed, switched. "Oh, I forgot! That map you sent me. Of Pennsylvania. It jogged my memory all right. Braddock! That's where Bill came from. Braddock, Pennsylvania. Near Pittsburgh." She leaned back, stared at the box of papers and began to pluck random, unconnected memories of Bill from the mists of time. They were mere shivereens of recollection, really. Inconsiderable trifles. Yet they were also shards of life—the kind of warm pulsating snippets that can, in big enough sum, convert a pasteboard figure into the joyful, erring, cantankerously unpredictable organism, rich in slant and foible, that is your ordinary human being. And slowly, grain by grain, the recollections focused my pale picture of this Bill Simmons who was beginning to look as if he really might be my Trunkman.

Bill had "the reflex and temperament of youth," and young actions, too. . . . He would walk miles to get sweet-smelling firewood. . . . He always carried binoculars. . . . He had disliked San Francisco because it was cold and he had to wear an overcoat and sweater, and he hated heavy clothing. . . . He used lotions, and bars of pure Castille soap. Always had a big bath- or beach-size towel. Hand towels, too. And liked sponges for cleaning: they lasted longer than rags, he said. . . . It seemed to Grace that he trusted a woman more than he did a man. . . . She always kept a square of chocolate around because he liked to pinch off a small piece for dessert. . . .

I smiled at that. For me, too, no dinner is complete without "a little bit of something sweet to finish up with."

Bill, said Grace, was a born diplomat. Take the story he told her of how he got his name of Chuckawalla Bill. A Catholic priest had visited his camp one Friday. Bill, lacking fish, had trapped a chuckwalla—a large desert lizard—and served it as fish to the holy and wholly unsuspecting man. The story got around. And the name stuck. (Although "chuckwalla" is the correct spelling, almost all desert people say "chuckawalla.")

When the flood of Grace's memories began to subside, I asked whom I should see in Garnet. "Naturally, I'm hoping to find someone Bill told about a trunk or cave or cache in Nevada. After all, the whole Trunkman connection depends on that. Do you know if he ever talked to anyone about it?"

Twice, said Grace. Once to a stranger in a bar in Indio. And once to Rose, the waitress at Garnet. "By the way, I've found a snap of Garnet back then, with Rolly's Place, where Rose worked."

Garnet had not been much of a place, said Grace. A roadside gas station, a store and a post office. Later, a bar. "In those days, darling, Garnet was a long ways from anywhere. But I liked it. There were some hot springs up the road but they didn't amount to much. . . ." She gave me the names of several local people who had known Bill, then drew a map with directions to the rock house.

I began to explain other lines of inquiry I had started. I had found a man in Los Angeles who often went to the National Archives in Washington, D.C., and he thought we might be able to find Bill's army pension file. The file might prove that Bill was in Las Vegas in 1916. "Look," I said, "if this fellow goes to Washington next week and he . . ."

"Let's have a highball," said Grace.

Just for a moment, I hesitated. Then: "Yeah, let's have a highball. . . .

My God, I've gone all this time without bumming a cigarette from you!"

And that was the end of business.

When I left, Grace kissed me like a girl of twenty—or rather, come to think of it, like a woman of thirty-four. Afterward she looked up and said, "What a pity I'm not thirty years younger! We could have had fun together, you and me. . . . You're so much like Bill. In so many ways."

Moments later, as I began to walk away down the hotel corridor, she called out, "Do have a trunkful of scandal about me when you come back from Garnet."

And I only just heard her add, softly and rather sadly, "You will."

# 4  Garnet

THE PLACE that was once Garnet lies a hundred miles east of Los Angeles, in low desert.

The country is not the kind to send you into rhapsodies. Not at first, anyway. Not even if you are a desert aficionado. Not even if you arrive, as I did, in springtime.

Barren, sun-battered hills. A broad, stony plain. The plain now can-kered by freeways and rampant concrete. But wilderness, too—the other, manforsaken kind—waiting in the wings. And wind. Always, it seems, the wind—funneling down canyons, sand-blasting across the plain.

So at first you are unlikely to see the Coachella Valley as God's own garden.

You soon concede, though, that the place has its points.

You live in desert light, under desert sky—if the smog is not lining out from Dodgerville. You enjoy balmy days and cool nights—in springtime, that is, not summer. You delight in snowcapped San Jacinto towering ten thousand feet above—instantly delectable, even if too remote to satisfy for long. Perhaps you savor, if it is your cup of brine, the Salton Sea—a huge natural sink, man-filled by mistake. And eventually, with luck, you dis-cover the valley's pearls: its rare unraped oases. They are green groves of swaying palms—rich, secret sanctuaries, all shade and coolness, calm and rustle, birdsong and silence.

Before the concrete came, there was an oasis six miles from Garnet, at the place still called Palm Springs. Not far away, another still stands invio-late. This is where Peter Williams lives, and where I began my three-day search.

As I drove down the little dirt road that led to Williams' oasis I ruminated on the quirkiness of fate.

The day after my second visit to Grace I had dined with a man I see about once every five years and a woman I had never met. When I told them the story of Trunkman and his Garnet connection the lady said, "Then you must talk to Peter Williams. He's lived near Garnet since the flood and knows everybody." I wrote to Williams, enclosed a copy of my newspaper article, outlined Grace's story and asked if he could confirm any details. There was no time for an answer before I left home, so I asked him to leave a message at his local post office. And at the post office I had found a card with directions to his oasis.

The car plunged from sun-drenched desert into tall, dark palms. Into a different world. Inside, the road softened to a track that wound and humped its way forward over sandy, unimproved soil, shielded from the sun's glare by walls of greenery. That is, the track came about as close as any vehicleway can to being in harmony with earth and vegetation. But before long it ended; just petered out. A few yards ahead, nestling so naturally among the palms that at first my eye hardly registered it, stood a thatched-roof cabin. Or perhaps the right word is "shanty." For the place had a definite South Sea Island air. The big stars-and-stripes hanging from a flagpole seemed almost colonial.

The house turned out to be twice as big as it had looked. Williams—a small man, mid-fiftyish—led me into the cool, dark sitting room. On a table lay my letter and the Trunkman article.

Williams picked up the papers. "This Trunkman you wrote about—before you had ever heard the name 'Bill Simmons,' you say. . . . Well, I met Bill Simmons—met him twice—and I find it interesting that your Trunkman is absolutely consistent with the man I knew."

I began to smile, stopped. First, I must make sure. I produced Grace's two snapshots of Bill.

Williams nodded. "That's him. No doubt at all."

I let out a long breath. I had come south primarily to find out whether Grace told the truth—but halfway hoping for some kind of dramatic revelation that would halfway clinch Bill Simmons' Trunkman candidacy—such as proof that he had been in Las Vegas in the fall of 1916. I had all along been painfully aware, though, that I was much more likely to sink the candidacy. A single incontrovertible negative, such as proof that Bill had *not* been in Nevada in 1916, would do it. And almost as fatal would be reports of a man with traits markedly different from those I had discerned in Trunkman. But now, on that score alone, the trip was already a success.

Peter Williams motioned me into an easy chair and settled into another, alongside. He still held Grace's two snapshots of Bill. "Funny," he said, smiling, "I had almost forgotten how he looked. I didn't know him well, you understand. And it was all thirty-five years ago. But he was the kind of man you remember."

He had first met Bill at the camp of Johann Samuelson, an old Swedish prospector who lived in the mountains above the oasis. One of Samuelson's tall stories—about being shipwrecked in Africa—had earned him the lead in a chapter of Erle Stanley Gardner's book *Neighborhood Frontiers*. Later he had killed two men in a Los Angeles bar, avoided trial on grounds of insanity and then escaped from the asylum—forever. But in the mid-thirties he was still Peter Williams' neighbor.

Williams, though barely twenty, was already living alone at the oasis. "By the time I was eight I knew exactly what I wanted in life—a place way out in the desert where I'd find peace and solitude. And when I was fourteen I came to this oasis with my dad and fell in love with it. My dad said, 'You'd better finish school first, son. And go through college. Then, if you still want to, you can come out here.' And I did. All three. And except for four years in the Army in World War II, I've been here ever since."

In those early years Williams would often take groceries, mining equipment or warm winter clothing up to his old Swedish neighbor, and it was on one of these visits that he met Bill Simmons. "They were both eating this great big potful of lima beans and salt pork, I remember, and the house smelled beautiful. I guess Bill had cooked it. . . . You could see that Johann was enjoying this man—and that was unusual. Johann didn't like anyone around his place; he only tolerated me up there because I could sometimes divine what he wanted in the way of groceries and so on. But he had taken to Bill. Although they were quite different kinds of men, they spoke the same language. It seems to me Johann even called him 'pard' once.

"That first time, I didn't talk to Bill much. Johann wanted his few friends loyal to him, and anyway, when you were with Johann he did all the talking. But Bill was very easy to get along with. He had a good voice, I remember. He talked right from in here." Williams tapped his chest. "No, no French accent. Southern? Yes, you'd take him . . . Well, he spoke methodically and, in a way, low. I remember him chuckling a lot, and I've always found that chucklers are . . . oh, I don't know, after you get to know a chuckler there's something rich about them. They have a sort of a depth of humor. And they're content. Yes, I'd say Bill Simmons was a contented man."

Bill had not stayed long at Samuelson's camp. There was apparently a falling out, because Samuelson spoke of the departed Bill as "an old scarecrow."

"But he was no scarecrow," said Williams. "As I say, they were quite different kinds of men. Johann was a show-off, a clown. Bill struck me as shy, almost timid, especially when it came to revealing his feelings to a stranger. I thought of him as a combination of mountain man, recluse and mystic. He was sensitive. Attuned to nature. Ahead of his time. He loved to hear a fox bark, for example. So did Johann, in his way—but they went about things differently. Johann was always trying to woo the fox in, you know, and the only way that he could do it was to catch him in a trap and then put him in chains. And at nighttime when I'd stay up there I'd hear these chains dragging around on the rocks. I'd call out, 'Johann, what's that?' 'That's my fox. Go back to sleep.' Now Bill wouldn't do that. He would . . . oh, golly, he would attract them. They would come there and I'd bet two bits they would just *be* there right with him."

Williams picked up the snapshots again. "D'you know, I think Bill was one of the original hippies—a love child, before his time. He loved everything. Yes, in his way he was one of the first of the flower children. He was gentle, kind, good. . . ."

"You seem to have been very impressed by him."

"I was. You see, I'd been living the same kind of life he was living. Mentally, I mean. In complete harmony with all things. So much so that when the Indians come back to this oasis—to them it's a sacred 'spirit place'—they quite naturally include me in their sings and rituals and healing ceremonies. Indians can feel these things. They follow earth laws, and if a person's attuned, they know. And Bill was like that, I feel sure. Of course, people often don't understand. They'd just dismiss him as odd—like they do now with a nephew of mine who talks to trees and holds a stone up and says, 'Look at the fire in that!' Bill wasn't that far out, but for his time he was way, way out."

A few months after Bill's brief stay with Johann Samuelson, Peter Williams had run into him again—at the rock house in the hills behind Garnet. It was pure accident. Williams had no idea Bill lived there. He had simply walked up the canyon with a friend called Mabel. ("Not a girlfriend, really. She was at least ten years older than me.")

That would have been in the spring of 1935. "I know it was springtime because the apricot mallow was in bloom. I can remember the scent of junipers, too, as we walked up the canyon. And suddenly there was this little cabin, looking much the way it does in your snapshot here. There was a spring up above, I remember, and a little pool with a willow growing beside it. And a man with a goatee beard came out of the cabin.

" 'May we bring our sandwiches in and have a kind of meal with you?' asked Mabel.

"It was only after we had gone inside and begun to talk that I recognized Bill. Up at Johann's he hadn't worn a beard.

"Inside, the cabin was very neat. There were charms or talismans hanging about the place, I remember. Bells, little images, figurines, that kind of thing. I think old Cabot Yrkza, who used to live near the hot springs, had given them to him. They were horrible-looking things, most of them, and I got the idea that Bill only accepted them and hung them up because he didn't want to hurt Cabot's feelings. He was that sort of a man.

"I can't remember too well what we talked about that day, but I do recall asking Bill if he was always going to live in the rock house. And he quoted something from Emerson about a man who had gone into the mountains and been happy but who knew that 'peace and happiness are inside a man, not in a place,' and that 'there's fine men living in the city, too.' Soon after that, we left. And I never saw Bill again."

No, there had been no sign of a woman's presence at the rock house. And Williams had never met or even heard of Grace. He smiled. "In fact, I remember that after we left the rock house Mabel said, 'That man needs a woman.' 'But he's an old man,' I said. 'Maybe,' said Mabel, 'but he had a gleer in his eyes and compared with you he's *muy macho*—much more the man.' As I say, she wasn't really my girlfriend—though if she'd been ten years younger we'd likely to have married. And afterward, when I stopped to think about it, I realized that Bill had had a gleer in his eye all right. A definite gleer."

Williams did not remember Bill's having a car either at the rock house or at Johann Samuelson's camp. No, Bill had not mentioned a trunk or cache in Nevada. In fact, he had not spoken of his past at all. But I might learn more from other old-timers still around. Before I left, Williams gave me a list of several who might have known Bill.

That afternoon I visited Grace's old ranch, a couple of miles from the place that had been Garnet.

The ranch house was squat and ugly. I failed to picture Grace serving tea to Greta Garbo on its veranda. But the caretaker for the absentee owner assured me that it "looked nothing like the old one": successive owners, beginning with Warner Baxter, had remodeled it, "to make it more livable." The original fireplace had long since been taken out or at least bricked over.

The caretaker had a talent for gossip and a vision of the universe bounded by the real estate market. She had arrived years after Grace left but knew the history of house and property down to the last lien, the faintest smear. The story she told had nothing to do with Bill, but it sounded right. Though only gossip that would require careful checking, it essentially jibed with Grace's version. It even confirmed the Disney offer. And it explained, fully, why Grace, who seemed ashamed of nothing, had slid over the business of "fighting to save the ranch," and had been softly sad at the knowledge that I would come back from Garnet with a trunkful of scandal.

Two miles beyond the ranch I came to an intersection and turned left toward the freeway cloverleaf that had, my map suggested, flowered on the site of Garnet. Five minutes later I was on the brink of assuming that the cloverleaf and pendant gas stations had canceled Garnet when I discovered, off to one side of the rank new growth, its remains.

A line of wind-bent tamarisk trees. Two concrete building foundations, stripped clean. And the shell of a typical, unlovely, 1930's commercial building. Across its pockmarked walls, still clear, rode two superimposed legends: MILT'S GARAGE, GARNET GARAGE. That was all. That and the wind.

The wind still streamed the tamarisk trees out like smoke. And after I had stood in their lee for a while I half imagined I could see, out beside one concrete foundation, the wraith of a man filling the radiator of his Model T Ford with a hose. In the car sat a dumpy, familiar-looking woman of forty. A car pulled alongside and a woman leaned out and hollered, "Does it always blow like this, here?" The man replied, "No, madam, not always. Sometimes it comes straight down." In his car, the dumpy, fortyish woman smiled.

I drove back under the freeway, toward Desert Hot Springs.

In Bill Simmons' time, when Garnet was the local hub, Desert Hot Springs did not exist. Today it is a town of 5,500 souls and 115 motels—12,000 souls in winter—that has all too successfully avoided the rather plastic charm of rival Palm Springs. The buildings that line its gaunt, treeless streets are square and prisonlike. The few that bid for architecture achieve only frozen Muzak. Everywhere, the half-dollar rules. So the place thrives, economically, but remains sterile, soulless, curiously embattled.

I spent most of the next two days in and around Desert Hot Springs, hunting down old-timers.

Few had been there in Bill and Grace's time, and most of these remembered them only as characters they saw occasionally or would pass the time of day with. "Yes, I knew Bill Simmons," said one man. "But not well. Nobody did. Kind of a recluse, he was."

In the end, I hit two small veins of memory.

The first surfaced in a pillar of local rectitude.

"Well, I'd never say anything really against the man, because I don't know a thing against him. If I thought he was a . . . a rotter, I'd tell you. But I don't know enough. I never had a conversation with him, even—though we did exchange a few words once when I found him on the road with a flat tire on his old truck. Yes, it probably was a Model T. No, I can't really remember anything about the man himself, but I'd heard about him and this woman he was living with, up Long Canyon, and I knew we didn't have anything in common.

"We're not prudes, my wife and I, but we just don't cotton to those kind of people. There were too many good people around who had their feet on the ground and did something for the community—who had a history of helping others with their wells and roads and all that. But this fellow here was . . . just apart."

"Sure."

"So I didn't give a continental about him and he didn't give a continental about me. We had nothing in common. And he wasn't the kind of man, and she wasn't the kind of woman, that you'd cultivate or ask into your home."

The second vein of memory I struck was Rollin Proebstel's—the Rolly of Rolly's Place in the snapshot Grace had given me of Garnet. A small, wiry man, now almost seventy, he still rode horseback all over his "cow outfit" back in the mountains. The evening I talked to him in his house at the head of a big canyon, he had just come in from a long day in the saddle.

Rolly had built Rolly's Place at just the right time. "What made that corner was the aqueduct. They'd just begun to build, see, and the road that joins the highway there went out to all those construction camps and sometimes on payday I'd cash fifteen, twenty thousand dollars' worth of payroll checks. Jeez, it was a big deal for me. I'd have 'em lined up at the gas pump—fifteen, twenty cars waiting to cash their checks and fill up with gas. There was a lot of wind and sand, see, between over there and Palm Springs."

Rolly had known Grace well, Bill only a little. "I just figured he was a good old rounder that had been to a lot of places and done a lot of things. There used to be lots of 'em around."

I brought out the snapshots of Bill.

"That's him. I'd kinda forgotten what he looked like. Yeah, he tried to Buffalo Bill 'em, you know, with that goatee of his and the whole thing." Rolly did not recognize Rose, the waitress, or even remember her name. But she could well have been there before his time.

He had first met Bill and Grace in about August 1934, just before he bought the corner. They were living up Long Canyon, back in the hills, and would often drive down into Garnet. "They had some little old wreck of some kind that they pedaled around up and down the backcountry there with. Yes, it could have been a Model T. They were right together all the time—'Chuckawalla Bill' and 'Desert Grace.' She passed herself off as his niece, I remember; it was always 'Uncle Bill.' But hell, everybody that knew them or anything just took it for granted that that was a gag. And then, the next thing I knew, she was with Stenderup. It caused a person to wonder what was going on. After that, I'd still see Bill around—kinda just 'There he is and there he isn't.' Could have been for as much as a couple of years, I guess. And then I didn't see him no more.

"But Grace, she stayed around. Before long I had her pretty well sized up, and I wasn't wrong because . . . well, it turned out that way." And Rolly launched into a series of stories about Grace and the ranch and, especially, her way with money. By the time I left he had fully confirmed the caretaker's messages: Grace embroidered; she slid around inconvenient facts; she had indeed left a trunkful of scandal cached in Garnet; but once you allowed for all that, she told the essential truth.

Next day I went looking for the rock house.

It might, I knew, no longer exist. Peter Williams had told me that when he went back a few years after he and Mabel ate their sandwich lunch with Bill, he had found the spring dry, the house deserted. Its walls still stood but the roof was gone. And since then, he said, several big floods had scoured those hills. The topo map, dated 1955, showed neither spring nor building.

But that third and final morning of my Garnet visit, I drove out of Desert Hot Springs with high hopes.

Vehicles are no longer permitted up Long Canyon beyond the boundary of Joshua Tree National Monument, and I parked my car just above the aqueduct. I had walked up the canyon for almost two hours before terrain and vegetation began to match the clues I was looking for.

Peter Williams, like Grace, had been able to dig up no clear recollection of just how you got to the rock house. Grace remembered no forks: "You just kept going up." But there were junipers nearby, she recalled, from which they made gin. And her snapshot of the rock house showed a moderately steep slope behind it, with scattered clumps of vegetation, including one unmistakable Spanish bayonet yucca. So as I walked I kept an eye on the slopes and their vegetation.

By the time I stopped for my second hourly halt the canyon's flanks sloped almost the way the one in the snapshot did. And junipers and Spanish bayonets now dotted them. For the hundredth time, I scanned the way ahead through binoculars: no hint that man existed. But in the wash, all around me, spring flowers bloomed thick and rich.

Fifteen minutes later I stopped to examine a flurry of tracks in the sand. The sand was still moist from an overnight shower and the tracks, sidelit by morning sunshine, stood out dark and distinct. The deer had been running, fast. A pawed animal, also traveling fast, had pursued it. The action recorded in the sunlit sand was so vivid that I looked up, almost expecting to see a bobcat or cougar ahead, still chasing the frightened deer. Nothing. Yet in that moment elation flooded through me. It was not simply that the canyon's slopes now looked exactly right and that junipers and Spanish bayonets clustered on them, dense. It was, I think, more a matter of the light. For the desert morning had reached its peak of vividness. And all at once—as so often happens at moments when you see the physical world amplified by some special light—my senses knife-edged. The flowers at my feet bloomed thicker and richer than they had done a moment earlier. The cool, almost liquid air vibrated with sudden birdsong and splashed me with the scent of junipers. And as I stood there, taut and expectant, a hummingbird scouted my beard—tiny, eager, iridescent, trembling, inches from my eyes.

I strode on. The rock house, I knew, would be around the next corner. It was not.

Nor around the next corner.

Soon, the canyon forked. I climbed the ridge between its two arms, surveyed them both. Nothing. I followed one fork far beyond the point at which sheer narrowness would have halted a Model T, let alone a Buick. More nothing. I had followed the other fork for less than a mile when I came to a sheer rock bluff. It would have stopped a tank.

I sat down, slowly, on a scoured rock ledge and unpacked my sandwich lunch.

I had been searching for more than just a rock-walled desert cabin: I had been hoping and expecting to find what might well be the only home of Trunkman's, other than the cave, that I would ever see—the only other place, perhaps, that he lived in and made uniquely his own. But now this rock bluff marked the mocking terminus of my hopes. I cannot pretend the disappointment did not cut.

After lunch I dozed, and about two o'clock I began the long walk back down the canyon. By then the cutting edge had blunted. I halfway accepted that the tide of change—in this case, probably, the tide of a flash flood—had washed over the rock house and obliterated it. The flood had left behind no stick or stone or even scar, only sandy wash. And those flat and level sands of time no longer bore any human record. They bore only the traces—the even more temporary traces—of the deer and bobcat that now kept the canyon where Bill once gloried, laughed and wept. But then, that was what always happened in the end.

I am inclined to think—though I can no longer be sure—that I was just opposite the place I had seen the vivid tracks of deer and bobcat, over on the far side of the wash, when I noticed a certain side canyon. Beyond its narrow and easily overlooked entrance it seemed to broaden out. I stopped; considered. If you were following a well-defined vehicle track, it would be easy to angle up that side canyon countless times but remember, years later, only that you "just kept going." I walked through the narrow entrance, into the side canyon.

The soil underfoot was no longer sandy and eroded bare; it was gravel-based and firm and thickly vegetated. And I had walked no more than a few paces before I saw the road. It was just a faint double track, worn hard and flat by wheels a long time ago, but it set my heart pounding. I strode along it, up the canyon. Almost at once I saw, beside the road, a sheet of corrugated iron, as from a roof, half buried in gravel. Soon there was a piece of wire screening, as from a window, its wooden frame badly buckled. Then more corrugated iron. Then some ancient lumber. I bet my bottom dollar, out loud, to the gravel and bushes.

Soon, more rusty sheeting, more ancient and weathered lumber. Then, leaning jauntily against a bush, a frying pan. I picked it up. BB shot had perforated much of the metal and left it bared to rust; but sides and handle still bore gray enamel, streaked and blotched in the pattern known as Graniteware.

I hurried on. The wash narrowed. At a sharp corner, an odd little block of compressed and buckled sediment in the rock wall set me thinking that it had probably signaled "Almost home!" to Bill. I turned the corner.

"There she is!" I shouted to the rock walls and the years.

In that first moment, it all looked the way it had been when someone took the snap of Bill and Grace, forty years before. The rock house stood square and strong on a little shelf. Rock walls flared back to gentler gravel slopes. The slopes were green with greasebush, junipers and scattered Spanish bayonets.

I walked up onto the shelf.

Close up, the rock house was a shell: no roof, no doors, no windows. Inside its still-solid walls the sun beat down on scattered refuse. But the fireplace remained intact. And it had a cement superstructure that bore the bold inscription CHUCKAWALLA BILL. Beneath the name, less clear but undeniable, was "1933" and, probably, the letters "A.D."

I unslung from my shoulder the little tape recorder on which I had been taking notes and put it down on the cement mantelpiece. Then I hesitated, hand in midair, looking at shiny black machine resting on weathered gray cement. The machine had recently captured the voices of people pouring out their memories of Bill—messages that the machine had inscribed on time in a richer if less conscious and less lasting way than that inscribed by Bill himself in the wet gray cement, forty years earlier. And there seemed something fit, something harmonic, about plastic machine and cemented word coming together like that. But there was something not quite right about it, too—something rather like invasion of privacy. I reached out and lifted the tape recorder from the mantelpiece and set it down on a sheet of rusty corrugated iron that lay in front of the fireplace.

After a while I went back outside.

The stretch of canyon that the rock house commanded was not what you would call beautiful. To the uninitiated, anyway, it would seem a bare and rocky backwater—almost stark, close to intimidating.

I walked to the lip of the shelf.

Down below, the wash supported two clumped orchestras of purple, yellow-stamened trumpets, half a dozen to each slender stem.

I knelt down. In spite of several drought years, the shelf still had its filigrees. The desert's most delicate spring flowers still carpeted it—the gauzelike under-membrane, so fine that when you are standing up you rarely see it.

I remained kneeling, there in front of the rock house, listening to the calm, cloistered silence. In spite of its starkness, the place would grow on you. Like the cave—like Grand Canyon, like almost any desert—all it needed was time.

But time was not something I could afford right then. Even if I left immediately, I would hardly be back at the car by dark. On this first reconnaissance, though, just finding the rock house had been the thing. I would be coming back.

Before I left I took a couple of hurried photographs and made a quick survey. Old lumber and rusty furnishings lay scattered around the rock house. And off to one side, a few feet up the slope, stood the remains of what seemed to have been a strange and decidedly fancy structure.

In among the branches of a small juniper, so commingled as to be almost a part of the tree, there had been nailed, haphazardly it seemed, a motley of unlikely components: a stripped yucca pole, two cut branches from another tree, a small rectangle of wood that was resistant to description but bore a series of complicated incisions along one edge, and a slender and curiously carved handle or beam that looked as if it came from a scythe or other old-style agricultural hand implement. The general effect suggested the remnants, half a century crumbled, of a piece of democratic, free-form sculpture—the kind that today sprouts overnight on wasteland beside freeways. Yet sculpture hardly seemed the right description. I could not really picture what the structure had looked like when Bill built it—as I immediately felt sure he had.

Three hours later, I phoned Peter Williams.

"That's right," he said. "I'd forgotten all about it. It was the first thing I saw when Mabel and I turned the corner. It was a bit of a shock, somehow. Kind of out of place there. Oddly enough, I don't actually remember giving it more than a passing glance. Maybe we saw Bill right away, up at the rock house, and began talking to him. I know he didn't mention it and he'd obviously taken a lot of pains over building it and somehow it seemed private and not a thing to talk about. . . . Yes, 'fancy' is just the right word. What was it for? Well . . . I think it was a place to contemplate. A place to go and just look, and meditate. A place to sit and be happy. I guess you could call it a gazebo . . . but there was a sort of aery fairy feeling about it . . . like a miniature teahouse. . . . Yes, that's it. Later on, I saw a beautiful little teahouse in Imperial Valley, about forty feet across, and I remember thinking that Bill's little place up above the rock house had been like a miniature of it. But I'd really call it a gazebo, a miniature gazebo, right there in the juniper tree. A place just to go and sit and be happy."

"That sounds like Bill, all right."

"Oh yes, it was pure Bill. Pure Bill."

And as I began the long drive home, Peter Williams' words kept running through my mind.

The Garnet visit had been a greater success than I had dared hope. Its prime aim had been to confirm that Grace told the truth. In essence, she clearly had. Yet her apparent reliability did not even begin to prove that Bill Simmons was Trunkman. Only solid facts could do that. And I had found none of relevance. On the other hand, I had turned up nothing at odds with what I knew of Trunkman. So far, every sliver of evidence had the right feel. And such glimpses of Bill as I had caught—reflected through the lingering human memories that were the only echoes time had really preserved of the place that was once Garnet—all suggested an intriguing individual of just the kind I had pictured Trunkman to be. A man I found myself wanting to know better.

I knew I could not yet go full tilt at the job of assembling the necessary proofs. Another major project was consuming my days and weeks and months. But I would continue to snatch such time as I could spare. And in the end I would get this job tidied away, this tracking down of Trunkman. It might take a little longer than I had thought, that was all.


WHAT ACTUALLY HAPPENED was that in the next three years I did precious little searching and even less finding.

The basic reason for the three-year hiatus was simple enough: I come equipped with blinkers. Once I have put my hand to a plow I tend to look only ahead, down my chosen furrow. I focus all my energies on overcoming such obstacles as stand between me and wherever I think I'm going. To that end I block out all else and go at it like—if you will let me mix mammals in mid-metaphor—a bull at a gate. This is, of course, both a strength and a weakness. But it is in me. And for three years after my Garnet visit I plowed—head down, blinkers firmly in place—the furrow of that other project. I always knew that once I got Trunkman firmly and singly in my tunnel vision, the blinkers would work in his favor. But for the time being they virtually blocked him out.

There is one other thing about the three-year hiatus. In telling the Trunkman story I could simply oil past it: could just ignore it, and leave you none the wiser. But doing so would leave me feeling uncomfortable. Besides, the hiatus in a sense proved the strength of my resolve. During those three years the idea had plenty of time to die. But it did not. When the time came, I simply realigned my blinkers and, without question, began to plow. I do not think I had yet asked myself why I felt so driven.

Now I do not want to suggest that during those three hiatus years my Trunkman research ground to a total halt. At intervals I chased leads in person, by letter and phone—and even through the published word. I had the original newspaper article, plus a paragraph giving Bill's name and background, published in *True West Magazine*. My hope was that the magazine's treasure-hunting and Western Americana contents were the kind that just might attract the Vandals—whom I discreetly relabeled "The Discoverers." But the article raised no response. Nor did a couple of paragraphs in Las Vegas papers giving Bill's name and background.

During this time I came up against a more serious dead end. My Los Angeles friend who often visited the National Archives in Washington, D.C., reported: "There is a general index to the pension applications filed between 1861 and 1934. In it there are literally hundreds of men named William Simmons." Did I know a middle initial? Was I sure Bill had not spelled his name Simmonds, Symons, or even Simon? Could he have enlisted under his reputed French-Canadian name—Simone? I phoned Grace. No joy on any score. Was she sure, I asked, that Bill had died near Indio, and in the late 1930's? Yes. Not later than the mid-1940's, anyway. So I began to look for a written record. I searched in old Garnet and Indio newspapers. I wrote to the coroner of Riverside County, which included both places, and to the California Office of Vital Statistics in Sacramento. Everywhere, I drew blanks.

Soon after the Garnet visit I also sent letters to many old-time residents who had moved away. One of these letters generated my most promising lead. A Leslie Moore replied from Palm Springs that he "knew Bill real well in the 30s, and it could well be the man you are researching—he spoke about prospecting in Nevada and Arizona many times as he and I were going through the mountains here." I wrote asking some specific questions. Mr. Moore replied that Bill had "never mentioned a trunk or cave or cache. He said he had been in Vegas, though; in fact, had been there many times—but I don't remember what year or years." I arranged to visit Mr. Moore as soon as time permitted.

Meanwhile, soon after the Garnet trip, before I had a chance to see Grace again, I lost touch with her. Then I got a letter. She was staying with a niece near Los Angeles. And soon she had moved into her own apartment in Hollywood, apparently financed by the niece. It was a great apartment, she told me on the phone, "and right across the road is the best goddam liquor store you ever saw." Her letters, like her talk, were fun seamed with sadness. "I made the eighty mark last week. Ha!" Once, she sent me a pale pink card with pressed flowers on its front and, inside, the message "Greetings—Dried up flower of the desert—Grace. (A pun intended.)" Later she wrote, "Today I'm fired with ambition to write a book about my stay in the desert with Bill, and how I tried to save the ranch. On the foreleaf I'll put: *I am gone away from my own bosom: I have left my strong identity, my real self, somewhere between the throne and where I sit, here on this spot of earth.* Keats—Hyperion."

In late 1973, before leaving on a trip that would take several months, I phoned Grace and arranged to have dinner with her in Los Angeles when I got back.

"Well, don't be too long about it," she said. "I won't live forever, you know."

"Oh, come on! You've always said you were going to live to be a hundred. And the way you're going, you'll probably outlast me."

Grace laughed.

Soon after returning home I called to fix a date for our dinner. The phone rang a couple of times, gave a familiar little hiccup; and then the impersonal recorded voice was telling me that Grace's phone had been disconnected and that there was no new number. I searched frantically through her papers for the phone number of the niece with whom she had stayed near Los Angeles. As I searched I kept telling myself that there could be a dozen explanations. But the room had grown gray, icy. I found the number, dialed it. The niece answered. Yes, Grace had died a month earlier.

When I put down the phone I sat still. It was difficult to think of Grace as dead. For all her years, she was one of the most inextinguishable people I had known. And her death had left a wider gap than if I had lost only my prime source of Trunkman information. We had, even more firmly than I knew, become friends.

Grace's death should have alerted me. But two months passed before I grasped the truth. Then, in reply to a letter I had sent Leslie Moore saying I hoped to visit him shortly, I learned that he, too, had died.

And at last I saw what should always have been obvious: in the tracking down of Trunkman I faced a natural statute of limitations. One by one, the memories of him were flickering out—those memories on which I would, above all, have to rely. I must buckle down, fast, and as tightly as I could. Otherwise, the tide of slow, inevitable events would obliterate such faint tracks as my man had left on the shifting sands of time.

# 5   Breakthrough

I BEGAN by plowing the most fertile field in sight.

From the start I told myself, firmly, that I would not be seduced into the dulcet but impossible task of trying to pin down the butterfly that had been Grace. I would simply check some known facts of her life against the colorful version she had fed me. That should be enough for a final fix on her reliability as a witness—on which hung the whole Bill Simmons Connection.

My prime sources turned out to be a novelist friend—"Dear old Gracie. One of my most memorable characters. I wouldn't have missed her for anything"—and the niece that lived near Los Angeles.

"Oh sure," said the niece. "She was kind of loose with men and that, but she was a good person too, in many ways—and she did everything with flair. Always the grande dame, the grand old lady. She had this thing, you know, about traveling first-class, money or no. She'd live high on the hog even when there wasn't a hog within miles."

The niece and novelist and other friends validated many autobiographical crumbs that Gracie had scattered. She had indeed rolled her own cigarettes. No matter whom she was with, she did the driving—so it would have been natural enough for Bill to ask her to drive him up to Nevada. She had definitely run an interior decorating business in Los Angeles ("She did everything like that exquisitely. . . . Another time she raised goats—and that was in L.A., too"). The singing career also proved genuine, and the movie stunt-riding almost certainly so (though Anita Loos was unable to confirm or deny friendship: "I meet so many people, you must understand"). And it emerged that Grace had actually played down one feature of her life: she had had not "two or three" husbands but

Grace, high on the hog,
in her early fifties.

"around about eight"—though it was uncertain which couplings had actually gone legal. (I had now confirmed the one marriage featured in the Trunkman case: from the County Recorder at Yuma, Arizona, I had extracted a marriage certificate dated November 24, 1934, conjoining Nils P. Stenderup and Grace Lucille Mason, both of Garnet.) Another coupling, probably unlegalized, shed unexpected light. About 1946, Grace had "married" a Basque named Mazeris and lived with him on a sheep ranch in Idaho. A box of Grace's papers that the niece gave me included a handwritten will signed by this man. It bequeathed all his "real and personal property" to "Grace Stenderup . . . known as Grace O. Mazeris . . . because of my love for her and her kindness and devotion to me."

Grace's papers yielded other confirmations. A rambling account of her meeting with Bill at the Salton Sea—probably intended for the book she had been "fired with ambition to write"—essentially echoed what she had told me. So did brief annotations about the first forty years of her life. And letters from Vantage Press—a New York vanity publisher—dated 1951, indeed offered to publish her book, *Ace Me Away—An Alaska Interlude,* on a "shared" basis. But best of all were a sheaf of chatty newspaper columns by Grace O. Mazeris from the Wrangell, Alaska, *Sentinel* of 1949. For from one of them a paragraph leaped out: "The winds remind me of a time past when I was visiting a crusty old uncle of mine at the windiest place in the world—the desert near Palm Springs, California. We had an old Ford jalopy and Unc was trying to pour some gasoline from a can into the tank. The wind kept blowing it back in his face. . . ." And the column went on to tell the familiar "Sometimes-it-comes-straight-down" story.

At this point I brought myself up short. I had learned what I needed to know. All Grace's friends, when asked, had said that although she might embroider facts with relish and artistry, she told the essential truth. A graphologist friend of mine who analyzed Grace's handwriting echoed that verdict: "A little white lie will sometimes be used to escape an unpleasant truth, but for the most part she will tell it like it is." And when I went back and listened to the tape we had made three years before in her Santa Cruz hotel room I found, sure enough, that I could now tell, or thought I could tell, when she was Hollywooding it up. None of the script tinkering seemed important: it was mostly just money stuff. So the final verdict was now in: Grace had been a reliable witness blessed with an astonishing memory. And it was time to call a halt to that line of research.

But in the course of getting my fix on Grace's reliability I had come to recognize that her Trunkman role had been more than that of straight informant. In her, one of the puzzle's jigsaw pieces had come alive, had upped and danced—and danced so delightfully that I now found myself asking, "Would I still be chasing Trunkman if some dull slob had answered my newspaper article?" On the whole, I thought the answer was probably yes. But Grace, just by being Grace, had added a dimension to my picture of Bill. After all, he had mated with her, briefly—with Grace, not with some dull slob. And that said something about him.

But while remembering Grace—remembering her with gratitude and affection—I must now accept that the time had come to switch tracks. My mystery was not Grace; it was Bill. And what I now had to do was lay hands on some solid information about him.

In late June I drove down to his corner of the California desert.

I was looking, above all, for a name.

My friend who often visited the National Archives had discussed with me the impasse we had run into: literally hundreds of pensioners indexed under the name William Simmons. "It's a good thing," he had said, "that you seem pretty determined. Because I'd have to say at this point that you seem to have dedicated yourself to looking for the proverbial needle in a haystack. What you need is a fact. Preferably your man's full name. But anyway at least one good, fat, solid fact. Then, if he's in that list of pensioners, maybe we can identify him."

So I went down to Bill's desert looking for a fact. Looking, above all, for his full name.

I went, as I say, in late June—into the maw of summer. And when, early one Friday morning, I pulled into the parking lot of the Riverside County offices—a bleak parking lot, gray yet already glaring—the skies sparkled like lentil soup in a preheated oven.

Yet I walked into the County Coroner's office with high hopes. Correspondence had failed to raise any record of Bill's death, but the Law of Bureaucratic Returns has it that "results come in direct proportion to pressure applied," and I now meant to apply pressure.

Seven hours later—seven hours of attempting to apply pressure, then of hunting through scores of dusty tomes—I had come up with nothing. No death listed under Simmons, 1935 through 1946, that had a tendril of a chance of being Bill's. Nothing under Simmonds, either. Or Symonds. Or Simon or Simone or any other reasonable variation. And nothing under John Doe that remotely resembled Grace's description of Bill's death: under a tree, three miles out of Indio. Nothing anywhere else in Riverside County, three miles out of anywhere. Nor five miles. Or fifteen.

At 4:40, reeling from seven hours of eyestrain and overloaded air conditioning but suddenly realizing that the bureaucratic week was almost dead, I moved from the main Recorder's Office—to which I had migrated some hours earlier, in search of death records—to a sterile, stifling, shelf-and-cabinet corner that housed the mining claim records.

I started in at 1932: that seemed the most likely year for Bill and Grace's sale of the Eagle Mountain claim to the German undertaker. Almost at once I discovered that the claim locators listed in the index under "Si" included a number of Simmonses. And in 1932 and 1933 an "Anthony W. Simmons" had staked several claims. Down in my stomach, a small ribbon began to flutter. "W." could stand for "William." But almost at once I saw that in two of these entries the name was bracketed with "Pearl and George A. Simmons"; then, a page later, with "L. B. and Sue M. Simmons." And that seemed to rule the man out. He clearly belonged to a sizable family—and Grace had several times said that Bill had had no relatives in California and had cut all ties with his family back East. So I hurried on through the pages, ignoring several more "Anthony W. Simmons" entries. Soon, the clock struck the bureaucratic witching hour.

Outside in the gray parking lot it was still 106 degrees. Overhead, the lentil soup had thickened toward mulligatawny.

The week that followed hangs in my memory as a sun-baked blur. It consisted of a slow, irregular, southerly drift toward the Mexican border.

First, Garnet—at 117 degrees. Nothing else new.

Next, two days in Indio, fourteen feet below sea level. The oven now at

120 degrees. My brain poached; addled. Nothing about Bill's death in local newspaper or cemetery records. From the county Historical Society, a list of old-time residents. Face-to-face interviews. At least twenty calls from macrowave-oven coin boxes—handkerchief wrapped around receivers to make them holdable. Results: none.

Next, in the "cool" of evening, a hundred-mile drive along the eastern shore of the Salton Sea to El Centro—not only because it was the county seat of Imperial County, neighbor to Riverside and the next-best chance, but also because in the margin of Grace's copy of my San Francisco *Chronicle* Trunkman article I had found penciled: "He died in desert . . . found against a tree or cactus—dead . . . out of El Centro." Grace, questioned, had stuck with Indio: El Centro, she thought, was a mistake, made before all her memories flooded back. But still . . .

It was dark by the time I drove through the string of little towns that outlie El Centro: Niland, Calipatria, Brawley. My headlights yielded only a thin impression of deserted streets and bleak, dilapidated buildings. The Imperial Valley hardly looked like Bill Simmons' kind of country. I sped on through the hot and heavy dark.

In El Centro, my first stroke of luck: a cold snap. Opening day, the mercury never rose above 108 degrees. The car's air conditioner virtually worked. My brain, too. Almost.

Otherwise, a familiar script.

First, official sources. Coroner's Office: nothing. Recorder's Office, for mining claims: blank. Post office for old records: forget it. Police station for arrest records: no records. County Clerk's Office, for censuses, voters' rolls: not a flicker. Library, for old newspapers: dead loss. Cemetery: dead end.

Lunch.

Next, people. A 1930's sheriff. A prospector, son of another old-time sheriff. A writer specializing in local history. Visits with sundry miscellaneous old-timers. Phone calls unending.

Dinner.

More old-timers. More phone calls. Lead leading to lead leading to lead leading to nothing.

Bed.

Breakfast.

By midmorning of the second day, all leads exhausted. Me too. And the sum total: zilch.

I retreated to a coffee shop, felt back for leads left dangling—and touched the mining claim records at Riverside. I could see now that they demanded more than twenty minutes at the butt end of a Friday afternoon. The Eagle Mountain claims sold to the German undertaker had to be there, somewhere. And maybe more. Bill was supposed to have staked a lot of claims.

En route for Riverside, I at last notched a minor success. At least, I rather thought I did.

In Thermal, where it was 112 degrees and deadly, I met Iron Jaw, a half-breed Sioux who was ninety-two and very much alive. From the first, he was both friendly and helpful. Quite extraordinarily helpful.

Yes, he had known Chuckawalla Bill Simmons. But he was dead. Long dead. Without doubt, that was him in my snapshots. Yes, he had known Bill for a number of years. Not well, though. He wished he could help me more.

Hoping to jog old memories, I asked how he had liked Bill.

"Oh, I liked him well enough. Except that he smelled like a skunk."

"But people tell me he was a very clean man!"

"About right. Very clean. A smart man too. A very smart man. But he always stunk like some kind of a rose."

"A rose? But you said like a skunk!"

Iron Jaw scratched his nose and smiled. "Well, I meant a skunk. He always had some kind of stinko on him—for the girls."

"Oh, perfume?"

"That's right. Some kind of skunk oil."

"A real lady's man, eh?"

Iron Jaw's pale eyes twinkled. "Yes, a very bad man. Always women and gambling. I met him in Winnemucca once, up in Nevada. I went into the Ferris Club and there he was, gambling."

"Winnemucca? You didn't meet him in Las Vegas too, by any chance?"

"No, but I remember he talked about being there."

A little breathlessly, I asked if Bill had ever spoken of living in a cave or having a trunk or cache up in that country.

"No, he never said anything about that. . . . I wish I could help you more."

Mostly, Iron Jaw had met Bill in the Coachella Valley, within about fifty miles of Indio. Yes, he had several times passed the rock house in the hills behind Garnet and met Bill there. Yes, Bill had a rifle, a .30–30, but no shotgun. No, he had never seen Grace there—though Bill had girls all over, including Winnemucca. There had been no Model T Ford at the rock house when he was there, but Bill used to drive one. "He come to Winnemucca in a bus, though."

When I tried to get a description of the rock house, Iron Jaw became curiously vague. Quite extraordinarily vague. And after saying that Bill usually walked places, he added, "But he must have had a car that he used to hide—because of the way he got around." Then it emerged that Iron Jaw had never actually seen Bill with a Model T.

That brought me up short. I had, trustingly, been asking leading questions, and anyone could with a little imagination have fed me just the answers he thought I wanted to hear—the way amiable people, eager to help, will sometimes do.

I stopped asking leading questions. The flow of information dried up. My suspicions hardened.

When I left I thanked Iron Jaw for his help.

"I wish I could have helped you more," he said again.

Before leaving Thermal I made inquiries. And my suspicions set: Iron Jaw had a reputation for tending to go along with what he thought people wanted to hear. But as I drove on toward Riverside I decided that although I would have to regard his confirmatory evidence as suspect, going on phantasmal, the perfume and Winnemucca bits, which had come spontaneously, were probably accurate.

That evening I moteled in Beaumont, twenty miles short of Riverside but two thousand feet higher and ten degrees cooler. The motel room's air conditioner did a discernible job of conditioning the air. It and the swimming pool gradually unaddled my brain. And once I was unaddled I saw that my possible success with Iron Jaw meant nothing. After a week in an inferno, I had failed. Failed totally. Failed to discover Bill's real name. Failed to turn up a single hard fact even remotely like the kind my friend said we needed to get the show off the ground.

But do not get the idea that I abandoned hope, that evening in the air-conditioned Beaumont motel room. If ever there was a point at which to give up my Trunkman search, I suppose that was it. Yet I am pretty sure the idea did not even occur to me. For by now I had my blinkers firmly in place. And although it is no longer possible to be sure, I think the frustrating week had left me more determined than ever.

When I speak of blinkers I do not mean that during those early days I never stood outside the search. On occasion I became aware that there was something illogical, even ludicrous, about my solemn pursuit of this obscure man who had been dead for a quarter of a century. And from time to time I was struck by further shafts of the fear that such lamps as he had left burning in human memory might gutter out before I pinned down my proof. But such moments remained small and transitory chinks in a general absorption. Mostly, I plowed my furrow and saw nothing else, left or right.

Looking back, I rather wonder at my tenacity. Perhaps I wondered even then, just a little. I can no longer be sure. But it occurs to me now that perhaps I had already begun—had just begun, that cool evening of respite in the Beaumont motel room—to question whether some hidden spur drove me on. To ask if my plow were not pulled by something I did not yet fully recognize, and might never focus.

Early next morning I drove to Riverside.

First, I searched for records of tenure to the land on which the rock house stood. I searched in several county departments, in various buildings spread around town. But by 11:30 I was back at the mining claims records I had checked so hurriedly at the butt end of the previous Friday—back in the same sterile, gray, shelf-and-cabinet corner of the Recorder's Office. It was a strangely detached corner, half screened-off by tall storage shelves from the clack of voices and typewriters out in the main office. A little wearily, I laid out my notebook and tape recorder, the way I always did now when searching records, ready for written and verbal notes of what had been checked and what found.

I opened the big ledger that included the index for claim locators with names beginning "Si."

Once again, I started at 1932. This time I took things more slowly and my eye kept coming up short at entries for the Anthony W. Simmons whom I had felt obliged to rule out because he was three times bracketed with other Simmonses and therefore must have had local relatives.

Each mining entry had its locator's name in the first column, the claim's name in the second. Because Grace had been unable to remember any claim names, I ignored the second column. I simply ran my eye down the first column, page after handwritten page, carefully checking all entries under "Simmons"—except "Anthony W."—and variations on it. I had scanned only two pages when, just after my eye had been briefly arrested yet again by "Simmons, Anthony W.," it was stopped, before ever quite moving on, by an entry in the second column. I only noticed it, I think, because the "Anthony W." entry was almost at the foot of a left-hand page in the index and my eye, quickly rejecting the lone entry below it and beginning to swing right and upward to the top of the next page, was still traveling slowly enough to catch a familiar name.

Now mining claims formed only a small percentage of the index entries. Deeds and other transactions predominated. So the second column held mostly the names of people. And it was the name of a person that caught my eye—on the same line as "Simmons, Anthony W." The name was "Mason, Grace L."

I stood there in front of the ledger, staring down at the two adjacent names that now shrieked up at me from the white page. I stood there, back still bent, breath blocked, heart sledgehammering. And in that first moment, even before I read the notation "Mining Claim Deed," I knew that "Anthony W. Simmons" must after all be Bill.

But I did not know it beyond shadow of doubt.

I ran my eye up the page until I found a certain three-line entry. There it was: "Simmons" ditto-marked, and the names "George A.," "Pearl" and "Anthony W." bracketed together. At least, so it seemed. But then, looking closely, I saw that what I had taken for a three-line parenthesis was in fact a two-line parenthesis coupling "George A." and "Pearl"; it appeared to extend downward for another line only because a letter "l" at the end of the third entry—"Anthony W. et al."—ran up and joined it.

At once, I understood. The three entries actually represented two separate transactions. George A. and Pearl Simmons had recorded a deed. Two days later, Anthony W. Simmons had recorded a claim. The entry clerk, to save time, had simply ditto-marked "Simmons"—and by chance had run the "l" up into the two-line parenthesis.

I straightened my back. So it had been sheer coincidence that . . .

And then I was once more leaning forward, flicking back one page.

There it was again: the same unlikely chance. The entries a week apart this time; but once again the clerk had ditto-marked the family name and run the "1" up into the two-line parenthesis.

I began to restraighten my back; stopped.

One more shadow still lurked. Lightning had surely not struck thrice.

I flicked the page forward, found the third bracketed entry: "L. B., Sue M. and Anthony W. Simmons." It was the same again. Exactly the same: two separate entries; dittoed family name; and the "1" of "et al." running up into a two-line parenthesis.

And then I knew, beyond shadow of doubt, that I had my fact, my name.

I stood and let the news sink in.

After a while—a minute, perhaps, or three minutes—I believed. Believed freely and fearlessly. And standing there among the sterile shelves and cabinets in that gray corner of the Recorder's Office with the voices and typewriters still clacking away up front just as if nothing had happened, I knew how Archimedes had felt when he rushed naked from his bath into the streets of Syracuse crying *"Eureka! Eureka!"*

There in Riverside I stayed put and kept my clothes on. And when I opened my mouth at last all I said into the waiting tape recorder was "My God! We've hit him!" I said it very quietly. But the moment had released, rapturously, all the pent-up frustrations of the long hot week—had dissolved them instantly, absolutely, as if they had never existed. I knew, of course, that having Bill's name did not make him Trunkman. But it meant that with luck we could now get our show off the ground. It meant I could at last begin collecting evidence of a kind that might eventually jigsaw into the proof I wanted.

My MEMORY of that first major visit to Bill's desert has the "Eureka" moment thrusting up as its high point, and therefore its culmination. But my notes advise me that I gumshoed around for almost another week.

The Eureka morning, in the Riverside County Recorder's Office, I found sixteen mining entries for 1932–33 under either "Anthony W. Simmons" or "A. W. Simmons."

At first I could not be sure that both forms of the name belonged to the same man: the microfilm records that the index led me to were only typed copies of the original claims and deeds, with no handwritten signatures. But all spelling mistakes had been meticulously copied and then underlined, and I noticed that certain distinctive misspellings appeared in claims signed by both "Anthony W." and plain "A. W." Simmons: "highway" always appeared as "heighway," for example; and sometimes, though not always, "April" became "Aprial." Eventually I found two documents signed by Grace L. Mason that dissolved my last doubts: in one, the cosignatory was "Anthony W. Simmons"; in the other, "A. W. Simmons."

Of Bill's sixteen entries in 1932–33, eleven were for mining claims and five for sales, transfers or agreements. Three of the claims, staked in early 1933, covered the immediate rock-house area. The remaining eight had been staked in March or April 1932, in the Eagle Mountains. Although various people appeared along with Bill as co-locators of different claims, Grace was not one of them. But in August 1932 a mining claim deed—the one that had first caught my eye in the index—certified that Bill had sold the entire group of claims to Grace as the Trail's End Mining Company. The price: three hundred dollars—with one dollar down payment and the balance "to be paid in eleven equal consecutive payments, whenever the property becomes productive." In other words it was, just as Grace had said, a gift.

The last of the deeds and transfers showed that on September 10, 1932, in Banning, Grace sold the Trail's End Mining Company to a Frank J. Wiefels.

The moment I read the German-sounding name I knew the man would turn out to have been an undertaker. And seconds later I was reading: ". . . for the following consideration: one 1928 Chevrolet Coupe Automobile and the sum of $300, payable in ten monthly installments of $30."

I think I laughed out loud, there in the tight little microfilm reading room of the Riverside County Recorder's Office. For the words did much more than nail down as truth the sale that Grace had told me about.

First, there was the car. Grace's mistake in remembering the Chevy as a Dodge somehow made her story truer: that is just the kind of trick memory pulls on you, given enough years. Then there was the money: the exaggeration fortified my conviction that, although a mistress of embroidery, Grace wove her stories from whole, dependable cloth. And sitting there in the dim cubbyhole of a microfilm reading room I found I could almost see Grace and Bill as they whooped it up after Frank Wiefels had finally signed. Pulling off this deal—their first together—would be a big thing, there in the maw of the Depression. And I could feel their elation. Could share it. Taste it. Because I had known Grace, that single microfilmed document recording a flat, forty-year-dead mercenary transaction evoked for me a pulsating, three-dimensional world—a world populated by warm, breathing, sweating, scheming, boozing, screwing people. A round and real world. And now, looking back, I believe that in that moment, sitting in front of the microfilm reader, I caught a glimpse of what I already half wanted to find out about Bill Simmons—if he indeed turned out to be my Trunkman.

That Eureka morning in the Riverside Recorder's Office I checked a few years back and forward and found two more of Bill's claims. Both lay near "Chuckawalla Peak." One was staked in 1931. The other, located on "the 17*n*th day of Apr*i*al, 1939," proved that Bill had lived at least four-and-a-half years after Grace left him to marry Stenderup.

From Riverside I drove ten miles north to San Bernardino and checked the mining records for San Bernardino County. I found two more of Bill's claims, both staked in 1931, just over the county line. I also found something that I had a hunch might turn out to be further evidence.

To be on the safe side, I backpedaled down the San Bernardino mining claims records for half a dozen years before 1931. Just as I was about to stop, the name "Simoyne" came leaping up from the page. It caught my eye because for a week I had been searching records for all variations on "Simmons," including the "Simone" that Grace had said was Bill's real name. This "Simoyne" had recorded more than twenty claims in 1925–26, with his typed signature appearing in three forms: "William Ashee Simoyne," "William Asher Simoyne" and "W. A. Simoyne." Now people who change names tend to play no more than variations on the original. Why Bill should have changed the name under which he recorded claims was beyond me, but "W. A. Simoyne" certainly qualified as a variation on "A. W. Simmons." So I tried to establish a connection. I could find no names among co-locators or witnesses that were common to any Simmons and Simoyne claims. And although Simoyne's spelling was as sublimely capricious as Bill's, the only shared error I could detect was "be-gi*n*ing"—and that, I discovered, was a frequent one in the copiously mis-spelled claims of that time. The claims' location proved inconclusive too: they lay on the north slope of the San Bernardino Mountains—rather beyond Bill's territory as I presently knew it, yet only thirty straight-line miles north of Banning. So in the end I was left with no more than suspi-cion tinged by hunch. But I tucked the name into my memory and copies of a couple of "Simoyne" claim notices into my briefcase.

While in the San Bernardino County offices I also checked, unsuccess-fully, for a death record for Anthony W. Simmons—and for William A. Simoyne. And for the rest of that second sweltering week in the desert I kept searching for such a record.

The Frank J. Wiefels to whom Grace had sold the claims indeed turned out to have been an undertaker in Banning. His mortuary was still there—though both Wiefels and his only son were long dead, and the family no longer ran the business. But the mortuary records, 1939–49, featured no Anthony W. Simmons—and no Simoyne at all.

For a while, then, I found myself back on the treadmill. I spent long, stifling hours in libraries and newspaper morgues, checking 1940's issues of *Desert Magazine* and of local papers in Banning, Palm Springs and Desert Hot Springs. Nothing. Finally, because I now had a full name, I went back to Riverside to recheck county death records. I checked under both Anthony W. Simmons and W. A. Simoyne. No change.

I also rechecked the Riverside mining indexes for the 1920's: on my previous visit I had, because of Grace's impression that Bill was "new to the country" when she met him, taken 1930 as my cutoff point. This time I searched very carefully. I had almost given up when I found a claim recorded by Simoyne in 1921. I saw this as some slight support for my hunch that A. W. Simmons and W. A. Simoyne were the same man: neither in Riverside nor next door in San Bernardino County had I found any claims earlier than 1930 for Simmons, or later for Simoyne. So perhaps, I thought, it was around 1930 that Bill had chosen, for reasons unknown, to switch from his original name.

I continued to search, back down the years. Almost at once I found half a dozen more claims recorded by Simoyne in late 1917 and early 1918. The earliest, called Black Horse Mine, had been staked on December 9, 1917.

And as I stood looking down at this entry in the index I saw, suddenly and blindingly, that I faced a cusp. When I made my next move—the move I knew I had to make—I might uncover precisely the kind of damning detail that I had all along been fearing. If I found a single claim recorded by A. W. Simmons in the fall of 1916, when Trunkman was living in his cave, that would torpedo Bill's candidacy. One recorded by W. A. Simoyne might be as bad. And if Grace's story of what Bill had done in the years just before 1916 was true, any claims staked before that would be equally damning.

Breathing fast, I went back to the mining indexes.

Slowly, meticulously, I worked backward from the December 1917 entry. Back to the beginning of 1916: no Simmons; no Simoyne. My lungs stabilized. I kept checking, all the way back to 1902. Still nothing. I leaned away from the index, warm with the relaxation that floods through you after a cusp has been negotiated and fears banished.

Half an hour later I had a copy of the December 1917 Black Horse claim in my hand. Like the other half dozen staked about the same time, it had been located "near McCoy Springs." I checked a map. McCoy Springs was in the McCoy Mountains in eastern Riverside County, near the Colorado River.

I studied the map more carefully. And all at once I saw that my search of the indexes before 1916 had, like a true cusp, offered two poles. And the outcome had not merely failed to torpedo Bill's Trunkman candidacy: by being negative it had become positive. For I now had a man named Simoyne, who could very easily turn out to be Bill, pinned down on contemporary official paper as staking his first claim in California barely a year after Trunkman had probably left his cave—staking it in a place only a hundred and fifty miles due south of the cave, along the Colorado River. Huge doubts about identities remained, of course; but if my hunch proved out, then I had myself a new, important and neatly fitting jigsaw piece.

Now as you may have heard tell, there comes a time in all open-ended journeys when a little monkey gets up on your shoulder and whispers, "Go home!" I emerged from the Riverside County offices that day into the oven of noontime and onto the same bleak, gray, glaring parking lot at which I had begun my research, two weeks earlier; and as I did so, a monkey that I had been glimpsing in the wings for several days at last made it up onto my shoulder.

"There are things that need doing at home," he whispered in my ear.

I said nothing, kept walking toward the car.

"You've got your name. In fact, maybe you've got two. Why not go back home and exploit them? That's the way to get this show on the road."

I could not argue with that. I unlocked the car.

"Anyway, it's too damned hot down here—for man or beast."

I did not argue with that, either. I opened the car doors and stood waiting for the furnace inside them to cool.

"Besides, even you can see that we've about come to the end of the useful things we can do here. For the present, anyway."

I nodded. Nodded again. And then me and my monkey got into the car and pulled out of the parking lot.

I headed for the freeway. And as I drove I looked back in my mirror of memory at what had happened in the two weeks since I first pulled into the bleak, gray Riverside County parking lot.

About the high point there could be no doubt: the name Anthony W. Simmons. That was my prime and shining pumpkin. But now that I had time for perspective I saw that perhaps it was just as important that this visit, like the one to Garnet, had in the end turned up nothing irrevocably negative. After all, if Bill were not Trunkman, then the more I found out about him, the greater grew the danger of discovering a jigsaw piece that did not fit—that misfit severely enough to kill the whole case.

And that led to another thought. If one of the names I had unearthed indeed led me to Bill's pension file, and if the file proved that a check had been sent to him in Vegas in late 1916, or if it yielded some other clincher, then that would sew things up, neatly and finally. But I was beginning to see that I might have to build a different kind of Trunkman case: not a cast-iron, documented, all-*i*'s-dotted kind of case, but rather a mass of detail, an edifice of fact and suggestion, assembled piece by laborious piece until in the end, as at a jury trial, the weight of evidence grew too great to resist—until the thing became certain beyond all reasonable doubt, until any twelve good persons and true would accept it with an enduring conviction. That, I had begun to suspect, was how my Trunkman mystery would turn out. And if so, it was going to be an even longer job than I had thought.

I stopped for a traffic light.

If it was going to be that kind of verdict, one thing would be easier to accept. For two weeks I had mostly been chasing flat, recorded facts. The high point had certainly been a "fact." Yet perhaps the most luminous moment had been the start of my talk with Iron Jaw—before I began to doubt him. And it always seemed to be like that: what excited me most, whether I liked it or not, was harvesting little human glimpses of Bill Simmons. Bill perfumed, smelling like a skunk-rose. Bill arriving by bus in Winnemucca to wench and gamble. Bill refilling his Model T in a Garnet gale and pausing to inform the woman leaning out of her car that sometimes the local wind blew straight down. Those were the things, after all, that had allowed me to begin assembling from the past, out of fallible but vivid human memories, the first faint lineaments of a living, breathing man. An obscure man. An ordinary man. And yet, somehow, not an ordinary man. Not by any means an ordinary man. Perhaps that was what really intrigued me.

The traffic light turned green.

In a vague sort of way I had fought against getting too wrapped up in this business of wanting to know Trunkman for his own sake. Perhaps I had worried about losing sight of my real target. But if I was going to have to settle for a weight-of-detail verdict, then the road lay clear for me to indulge myself. Understanding the kind of man Bill had been—understanding him as intricately as possible, so that I could fit all elements of him into the final verdict—might in the end turn out to be the weightiest contribution of all toward solving my Trunkman mystery.

I hit the freeway and turned westward, homeward.

Anyway, true or not, the idea was at least a fetching bit of rationalization.

IN THE WEEKS that followed I prodded at stalled lines of inquiry, launched some new ones—down such alleys as Bill's reputed Pennsylvania origins—and kept sieving all the evidence through my memory so that it would be on instant tap to help me recognize and then assess new clues.

I soon pocketed a prime payoff from Bill's real name. I had already tried, by mail, to pin down his death, through state records in California, Nevada and Arizona. But I raised nothing, anywhere, for Anthony W. Simmons, 1939–49, or for William A. Simoyne, 1926–49. Then, one September afternoon I found myself in Sacramento with an hour to spare, and drove to the California Office of Vital Statistics.

Death records for 1940–48 were stored in a Soundex system open only to staff. While the staff rechecked those years I sat at a little table and worked the 1939 and 1949 indexes. Entries were computer-arranged in precise alphabetical order and the job took all of two minutes: no Anthony W. Simmons; no Simoynes at all.

As I slid the blue-bound 1949 index back into its place on the shelf in front of me I felt surprisingly deflated. I had not really expected success; yet now, in the face of failure, I had to ask, "Where do I go from here?" At first I could glimpse no hint of an answer. But as I sat there, elbows on table, head in hands, staring ahead, I saw one open-ended route I could take: it stood barely a foot from my eyes. Grace had felt sure that Bill died no later than the mid-forties, and 1949 more than covered that; but Grace, for all her astonishing memory, had occasionally been wrong. Anyway, until the staff finished rechecking, I had nothing to do. I reached out, slid the blue 1950 index from its shelf and opened it to "S."

Almost at once, leaping up from the page, came "Simmons, Anthony W." Breathlessly, I decoded the line of computer numbers that followed: male, aged 81, died Los Angeles 11th January 1950.

Ten minutes later, a Xerox copy of the death certificate silenced all but my most mulish doubts.

The key entries, of course, were "William," "Pennsylvania," and "Spanish American." Yet the one that intrigued me most was "Palos

CERTIFICATE OF DEATH — STATE FILE NO. 50-004350

REGISTRATION DISTRICT NO. — 1992 — REGISTRAR'S NUMBER 24

1a. NAME OF DECEASED—FIRST NAME: Anthony — 1b. MIDDLE NAME: William — 1c. LAST NAME: SIMMONS

2a. DATE OF DEATH—MONTH, DAY, YEAR: January 11, 1950 — 2b. HOUR: 1 PM

DECEDENT PERSONAL DATA

3. SEX: Male — 4. COLOR OR RACE: White — 5. MARRIED, NEVER MARRIED, WIDOWED: Never Married — 6. DATE OF BIRTH: August 2, 1868 — 7. AGE (LAST BIRTHDAY): 81 yrs.

8a. USUAL OCCUPATION: Unknown — 8b. KIND OF BUSINESS OR INDUSTRY: Unknown — 9. BIRTHPLACE: Pennsylvania — 10. CITIZEN OF WHAT COUNTRY?: United States

11. NAME OF FATHER: Pierre Simmons — 12. MAIDEN NAME OF MOTHER: Anita Armour — 13. NAME OF SPOUSE (IF MARRIED)

14. WAS DECEASED EVER IN U.S. ARMED FORCES?: Yes — SPECIFY YES, NO, UNKNOWN; IF YES, WAR OR DATES OF SERVICE: Spanish American — 15. SOCIAL SECURITY NUMBER — 16. INFORMANT: Records of Veterans Administration Center

17a. PLACE OF DEATH—CITY OR TOWN: Rural West Los Angeles — 17a. LENGTH OF STAY (IN THIS PLACE): 2 months 9 days — 17c. COUNTY: Los Angeles

17b. FULL NAME AND ADDRESS OF HOSPITAL OR INSTITUTION: Veterans Administration Hospital, Wilshire & Sawtelle Blvds.

USUAL RESIDENCE — 18a. STREET ADDRESS: General Delivery — 18b. CITY OR TOWN: Palos Verdes — 18c. COUNTY: Los Angeles — 18d. STATE: California

CAUSE OF DEATH

19-I. DISEASE OR CONDITION DIRECTLY LEADING TO DEATH: Infarction of myocardium — Over 1 yr. — APPROXIMATE INTERVAL BETWEEN ONSET AND DEATH

ANTECEDENT CAUSES — 19-Ib. DUE TO: Arteriosclerotic coronary thrombosis — Over 1 yr.

19-Ic. DUE TO

19-II. OTHER SIGNIFICANT CONDITIONS: Encephalomalacia of brain due to arteriosclerosis — Over 1 yr.

20a. DATE OF OPERATION — 20b. MAJOR FINDINGS OF OPERATION — 21. AUTOPSY: Yes ☒ NO ☐

22a. ACCIDENT, SUICIDE, HOMICIDE — 22b. PLACE OF INJURY — 22c. LOCATION CITY OR TOWN, COUNTY, STATE

22b. TIME MONTH DAY YEAR HOUR — 22c. INJURY OCCURRED ☐ WHILE AT WORK ☐ NOT WHILE AT WORK — 22d. HOW DID INJURY OCCUR?

23a. CORONER'S: I HEREBY CERTIFY THAT I HAVE HELD AN ☐ AUTOPSY, OR ☐ INQUEST, OR ☐ INVESTIGATION ON THE REMAINS OF THE DECEASED AND FIND THAT THE DECEASED CAME TO DEATH AT THE HOUR AND DATE STATED ABOVE. — January 11, 1950

23b. PHYSICIAN'S: I HEREBY CERTIFY THAT I ATTENDED THE DECEASED FROM November 2, 49 THAT I LAST SAW THE DECEASED ALIVE ON January 11, 50 AND THAT DEATH OCCURRED FROM THE CAUSES AND AT THE HOUR STATED ABOVE.

23c. SIGNATURE: Ward Samuel, M.D. (S.D. Samuels) — 23d. ADDRESS: V.A. Center, Los Angeles, California — 23e. DATE SIGNED: 1-14-50

24. BURIAL — 24a. DATE: 1-17-50 — 24c. CEMETERY OR CREMATORY: Veterans Administration Cemetery — 25. SIGNATURE OF EMBALMER: John C. Vondin — LICENSE NUMBER: 3317

27. DATE RECEIVED BY LOCAL REGISTRAR: January 14, 1950 — 28. SIGNATURE OF LOCAL REGISTRAR — 29. SIGNATURE OF FUNERAL DIRECTOR: F. K. Breezeale, V.A. Center, L.A., Calif

STATE OF CALIFORNIA — By ___ — DEPARTMENT OF PUBLIC HEALTH

---

Verdes." For Palos Verdes is a slightly snazzy shoreline suburb of Los Angeles and not Bill's kind of place at all. But out in the desert, only a hundred airline miles from Garnet, there stands a sleepy little backwater village called Palo Verde. It is not a place that many Californians have even heard of. But I happened to have spent a little time there. And the moment I read "Palos Verdes" I placed a short-odds bet with myself that some insular Los Angeles clerk had made an understandable mistake, and that Bill Simmons had actually lived his last days in Palo Verde.

That evening I phoned my friend who often visited the National Archives. "I've got another fact," I told him. "A big, fat, juicy one with lots of little ones in it."

My friend was just back from Washington. At the Archives he had found an "Anthony W. Simmons" in the army pension file index. But his request for the file had come back marked "Not Here." He had asked the Archives to obtain the file and send him Xeroxes of its contents. They undoubtedly would—in their own good time. But for the moment all we could do was wait.

Ten days later I got a letter from my friend. The Archives had found the file and sent him Xeroxes of half-a-dozen documents from it. They did not amount to much: another copy of Bill's death certificate; a couple of forms concerning his pension. There was, wrote my friend, no way of knowing whether the Archives had sent the whole file. There might be a whole lot more. The only way to find out was to go and dig for oneself.

I beamed down at this letter. An hour earlier I had finally confirmed that, just as I had been hoping, tag ends of the project that still kept interrupting Trunkman research would take me to Washington. That business would not take long. And afterward I would be free to dig for buried treasure in the National Archives.

# 6   The Archives

THE HUB OF WASHINGTON, D.C.—the stately, radiating pattern that re-
volves around White House and Capitol, beaming its symbols through
space and head and heart across nation and now planet—was planned to
trumpet the power of man. And mostly it succeeds. If you stand on the
Capitol steps and look down across the Mall to the Washington Monument and then turn half right and gaze toward the White House down the
furrow of Pennsylvania Avenue—that prime, deforested axis—you can
hardly miss the message. Geometry, landscaping and architecture bugle it
in unison: power to control. Explicitly, the power of man controlling man.
But also, implicitly, the ancient and consecrated conviction, untainted by
whiff of doubt, that man shall have dominion.

When I stood on the Capitol steps, after three days of non-Trunkman
activities in town, I was briefly and obediently impressed. For a spell I forgot that during the course of those three days I had felt no danger of being
overwhelmed by efficiency or drowned in the milk of human kindness. I
even forgot certain insights I had gained—that if you are dumb enough,
for example, to walk after dark in this hub and nub of our nation and are
born lucky, then nothing worse may befall you than a patrol car pulling up
alongside and a weary, semi-suspicious cop inquiring if everything is all
right. Standing there on the steps of our Capitol, I temporarily forgot
these things. Geometry, landscaping, architecture—I saw and heard them
all, in unison. And for perhaps three minutes I embraced their message,
their illusions.

Then I came back down to earth.

Early next morning—the Monday of election week, in a year still quivering from Watergate—I entered the rather forbidding portals of the Na-

tional Archives, midway on Pennsylvania Avenue between Capitol and White House. I went in without great ecstasy, or even very sanguine hope.

Now I do not mean that I had lost eagerness for my Trunkman quest or confidence in ultimate success. Far from it. But I went into the Archives wearing a cynic's hat: I carried no truly great expectations concerning the heart and sinew of that institution.

I am no longer talking politics. The rhythms of authentic bureaucracies reverberate on planes beyond the puny reach of mere individuals, such as Presidents. They move, relentlessly, to basic human cadences. Among their more devastating if minor measures is the *rallentando,* or perhaps I mean *lamentabile.* And in due course of creeping time just such a deadly slackening infects almost any institution designed to serve the public with a flow of information, person to person, face to face, and transforms it into an armadillo of a place crewed by ornery ignoramuses. In any specific case the mechanics may remain obscure; but the sad statistical tendency is about unarguable.

So I entered the Archives without radiance.

In the lobby I obtained a "Researcher Information Card" and an information sheet. Both were written in clear, concise English. Rebounding from this shock, I went upstairs.

"A lot will depend on the archivist you draw," my researcher friend from Los Angeles had said. An archivist, it seemed, was a guy who showed the ropes to greenhorns like me.

I drew James D. Walker—a small, finely built man, black, highly strung. He listened to my Trunkman story, glinted a bit, got on the phone, glinted a bit more—and began to counsel me with grace and precision.

The Anthony W. Simmons file was now in the Archives, he said. And I could Xerox almost anything I found in it, or elsewhere. The only taboos: no information "of a derogatory nature" could be released until it was fifty years old; and no original medical document less than seventy-five years old could be Xeroxed—though I could take what notes I pleased. With luck, the pension file would suggest other sources within the Archives and he, Walker, would do all he could to help me locate them.

He did, beyond the call of duty.

He piloted me deftly through the Archives' labyrinthine resources—reconnoitering new leads, pondering possibilities, culling no-nos, red-flagging potential pitfalls. And slowly, Xerox by Xerox, I amassed an Anthony William Simmons portfolio.

Looking back, I find the collecting process oddly episodic. The spacious central research room. My first glimpse of Bill's promisingly thick pension file. Corridors. Tiny elevators. Huge stacks, solid with papers. Microfilm rolls in neat little boxes. Rows of glass-fronted microfilm readers. An unexpected wad of peacetime cavalry papers pressed flat and precious in a yellowing envelope. The ready help of pleasant, knowledgeable assistants. These were my lodestuff and galleries, and for three days I mined.

From the start, I knew I had struck it rich. And I followed, meticulously, the advice my Los Angeles researcher friend had offered: "In gathering information, go for overkill. Collect every scrap of information you can, because in the end one apparently insignificant item may prove vital."

The documents came haphazardly, in batches, from various corners of the Archives, and I had no time to study and assimilate details. But I soon grasped the basic facts about two periods of Bill's life.

Between 1898 and 1908 he had served four times in the U.S. Army: a short tour during the Spanish-American War; a longer one, as first sergeant, on active service in the Philippines during the Insurrection; a peacetime stint with the cavalry; and a curiously brief repeat in 1908.

He did not apply for a pension until 1929. It was granted in 1930. For the rest of his life he received a monthly check, at various addresses in southern California.

Now the outlines I have given you were only the crude ore. Out from stern gray forms and reports kept popping a live, chuckling, boozing Bill Simmons. At first I struggled against seduction by these fascinating glimpses: because of the years the documents covered, they seemed unlikely to contribute to my Trunkman research. Then I discovered that even from a narrow sleuthing standpoint there was gold in them thar papers. Embedded in items peripheral to the army and pension records lay many nuggets—in the form of promising leads that could prove central to my search.

Mostly, these nuggets lay in Bill's answers to the questions that armies and other octopi delight in asking you: date and place of birth; names and birthplaces of parents; religious persuasion; marital status; next of kin; residence; previous occupations. But I soon ran into a difficulty. Bill had an engaging disrespect for bureaucracies. In answering their questions, he played fast and loose.

When he gave his date of birth, for example, the day was always August 2; but the year oscillated between 1868 and 1876, with way-stops. Sometimes the choice seemed to have been made because Bill wanted to appear more mature than he really was, or more youthful. Sometimes he seemed to select on whim, and sometimes, perhaps, because of genuine uncertainty. In the end, anyway, I was left with no firm date, only the eight-year bracket.

Bill also ran option plays on his birthplace. In all military records it appeared as "Twin Lakes, Colorado"; in all pension records, as "Turtle Creek, Pennsylvania." And he was just as fickle with parental backgrounds. Father—Peter or Pierre—born in France or Kentucky, take your pick. Mother—Anna Marie or Anita Armour—born in France or Alsace or Louisiana.

On religion, Bill stood firm: "Catholic." He never admitted to having children. And his marital status remained "single"—until near the end, on admission to the Los Angeles Veterans Hospital in which he died, he proclaimed himself "divorced." (In those last months, though, Bill's responses had to be suspect: the hospital reports showed that he was in bad shape, mentally as well as physically.) His death certificate stated: "Never married."

Other mutations sounded marginally legitimate. Deaths in the family could account for only some of the discrepant next-of-kin answers at successive army enlistments: mother, of Braddock, Pennsylvania; Peter Nau (or perhaps Nan—script unclear), of Homestead, Pennsylvania; father, also of Braddock; and then, once again, mother, still of Braddock. His residences changed, understandably enough: Mobile, Alabama; Twin Lakes, Colorado; and then Braddock, twice. So did his occupations: mechanic, machinist and cook; and also, much later, chef and laborer (both 1929) and retired miner and prospector (1949).

I saw all these entries, whether factual or fictional, as glistening, high-grade leads.

Among the richest in potential were the addresses to which Bill's pension checks and other correspondence had been sent from 1930 to 1949. All were in the California desert. They included Garnet. All but one—"c/o Mr. J. M. Roper, Cherry Valley, Beaumont"—were general delivery addresses or post office boxes. The last of them intrigued me most. It was not Palos Verdes, as Bill's death certificate had maintained, but, just as I had guessed, Palo Verde. And Bill had apparently lived there for his final thirteen years.

Now Palo Verde was a sleepy little backwater of a village. At least, it had been when I stopped over for two days and nights in what was my first sample of "civilization" since just after leaving the Mexican border a week earlier at the start of a thousand-mile, summer-long walk to Oregon. And sleepy backwaters on the edge of wilderness rarely change very fast. So although seventeen years had passed since my visit and twenty-five since Bill had lived there, I thought I might well find several Palo Verde old-timers who had known him.

But perhaps the most intriguing lead was Braddock, Pennsylvania. That was the place Grace remembered Bill speaking of as "home." There had also been the letter in response to my San Francisco *Chronicle* article from a man who owned a trunk almost identical to Trunkman's—a trunk that came, he said, "from somewhere in the Midwest." And now I had a street address in Braddock, admittedly almost seventy years old, at which Bill's mother had lived. Obviously I had to visit the place. With luck, I might still be able to trace his family. One of them might just have heard of his living in a cave—or even be able to identify the trunk.

But during the three days I spent at the Archives there was, by and large, little time for such planning ahead—and no time to sift what I had extracted, let alone to assay it. I had my hands full simply mining the ore.

Throughout the three days, James Walker remained my guide. I do not mean that he literally led me by the hand; in fact, I rarely saw him. But every time I needed help, he helped. And while guiding me around a block I had hit he would often place in perspective some item of information I had misinterpreted. Bill's slidings into and out of the Army, for example, far from being marks of shiftlessness, were perfectly normal at that time. Again, men known to be married could not in those days join the Army, so I should not necessarily accept "marital status—single" as fact. And I should not take too literally the vivid death's-door doctors' reports that I had been copying from the pension file. The 1930's pension system was "a game." The services leaned over backward to give older wartime veterans something to make life easier, and most doctors played along.

Walker was also responsible for my most surprising find, on the third and final day.

After shepherding me through intricate channels to a certain roll of microfilm, he came and watched while I fed it into the reader—which he had never done before. I cranked the film to a reference number apparently connected with Bill's final army tour.

All at once I stepped back. "My God!" I said. "He deserted! How on earth did he manage to get a pension after that?"

Walker smiled. "Now that you know about the desertion," he said, "I can show you something else." He handed me a sheet of handwritten notes. "At this point I can't lay hands on the original documents, but it is now perfectly in order for me to pass along these items."

Among the notes was a report that Bill, who deserted in October 1908, had in May 1918 obtained a "deserter's release." At the same time he apparently tried to re-enlist but was rejected.

The deserter's release, said Walker, was normal practice. During a war the Army tended to look forgivingly on old peacetime desertions. And the release would remove any barrier to a pension.

I was explaining that this new information lent sudden and surprising support to my wild early theory that perhaps Trunkman had gone to live in the cave because he was a deserter—just as Grace's story of the Seattle marriage had seemed to confirm my equally long-shot "woman trouble" theory—when I saw another entry on Walker's handwritten sheet: "Nov 1, 1907 to Apr 6, 1908, in employ Frank Heather, Burlington, Washington." And I had hardly registered that Burlington was somewhere up near Seattle when my eye caught yet another entry: "Also known as William Simoyus."

"Now if that 'u' is a clerical error for 'n,' " I said, "we may really be onto something." And I explained.

Neither "Simoyus" nor "Simoyns" cropped up again. Nor did "Simoyne" or "Simone" or any other variation on Simmons. But before long I unearthed a desertion poster. Bill in his thirties was frankly unrecognizable as the man in Grace's rock-house snap. And you would hardly call him handsome. But then, how many of us come out recognizable, let alone handsome, in mug shots?

The poster turned out to be my last big find. Late in the afternoon of that third day, James Walker confirmed my suspicion that further searching would probably yield few if any Xeroxes to add to the wad that now barely fitted into my briefcase. But I should, he said, keep probing by mail. If more documents existed they were probably scattered around outside the Archives. In army and V.A. records, particularly. That often happened. And when it did, you had to allow time for wheels to turn.

I thanked Walker for all his help, then went out through the now familiar and therefore less forbidding Archives portals onto Pennsylvania Avenue.

As I walked across the Mall to my hotel I realized—for the first time, strange as it may seem—that because Bill drew no pension until 1930 I could not possibly find the dated-check evidence I had long hoped might link him, cast-iron, to Las Vegas in late 1916. In fact, except for James Walker's handwritten notes about the 1918 deserter's release I had hit a blank for the two decades ending in 1929.

Yet that hardly seemed to matter. My briefcase bulged with the kind of evidence I had known I would probably have to rely on: the jury-trial kind

# $50.00 REWARD

### FOR THE ARREST AND DELIVERY OF

# ANTHONY W. SIMMONS,

### CHARGED WITH BEING A

## DESERTER FROM THE ARMY.

ANTHONY W. SIMMONS, cook, Troop D, 14th Cavalry, who was enlisted May 3, 1908, is reported to have deserted at Fort Walla Walla, Wash., October 14, 1908. At enlistment he gave his residence as Lobinger and Coalmont avenues, Braddock, Pa., and the name and address of person to be notified in his behalf in case of emergency as Anna Simmons (mother), corner of Lobinger and Coohounts streets, Braddock, Pa.

DESCRIPTION (at date of enlistment): White; born in Twin Lakes, Colo.; age, 31½ years; occupation, cook; eyes, brown; hair, dark brown; complexion, fair; height, 5 feet 6 inches; weight, 158 pounds. Prominent scars and marks: Front view—tattoo marks, hinge and keystone on left forearm; scar on right cheek, left palm, and left thumb. Back view—tattoo marks, anchor on left forearm; scar on upper right side of back, lower right thigh, left thumb, and left hand.

A REWARD OF $50.00 is payable for the apprehension of this man, and for his delivery to the military authorities, at any time within five years from the date of his enlistment. The reward is payable at any United States Army post to any civil officer or other civilian who delivers the man there. If he is apprehended he should be delivered at, and the reward claimed at, the nearest Army post.

The act of Congress approved June 18, 1898, provides "That it shall be lawful for any civil officer having authority under the laws of the United States, or of any State, Territory, or District, to arrest offenders, to summarily arrest a deserter from the military service of the United States and deliver him into the custody of the military authority of the General Government."

Any information that may be secured as to the whereabouts of this man should be communicated to

**THE ADJUTANT GENERAL OF THE ARMY,**

**WASHINGTON, D. C.**

November 5, 1908.                    [273]

that could build block by block into an edifice of fact and suggestion until in the end its weight grew too great to resist.

Before I reached the hotel I realized something else—something I was always inclined to overlook. At the Archives I had turned up nothing that stood at odds with what I already knew of Trunkman. And that unspectacular fact could once again turn out to be the most compelling of all.

Yet I knew I must not start counting unhatched chicks. The Archives visit had been a success all right. It had probably been pivotal—but only in what it promised. I had not collected any evidence that in itself helped prove that Bill Simmons had been Trunkman. I had quarried a rich carload of leads, that was all. But on future research trips I should be spared the sweaty, lineman-battle kind of grind I had fought for more than two weeks around the Salton Sea. I would know exactly where to go. Even who to talk to first. For the Archives had sprung me loose. From now on my research would be broken-field running, with a good chance that I might at any moment break free and go all the way. And that sounded like fun.

Not until next morning, on the drive to Friendship Airport, did it occur to me that the National Archives had in one sense crossed me up. It was no armadillo of a place, crewed by ornery ignoramuses. Instead, it had turned out to be a phenomenon: nothing less than a long-established bureaucracy that was designed to serve the public and yet actually operated, face to face, as if the reason for its existence was to serve the public.

An hour later, briefcase tucked safely under seat and the jet already sucking me westward, I found myself looking down onto the stately, radiating complex that is the symbolic hub of our nation. It stood out, clear and impressive, in the winter sunshine. And it occurred to me that if I had at that moment been standing on the Capitol steps, exactly where I had been four days earlier, looking down past the National Archives toward the White House, considering prospect and symbols and illusion, I might have looked on man's aims and achievements with greater charity—or at least with a touch less jaundiced eye.

Nothing succeeds like success.


BACK HOME, a few days later, I had a conversation with a friend.

Dave Taylor is an ecologist by doctorate, an airline captain by paycheck, a father by avocation and a general, all-around perceptive sonofabitch. We had dined at his house, and his wife and children had left us alone as usual with the last of the wine.

Dave refilled our glasses. "But you got your big apple when you found Grace, didn't you?"

"Not really."

"How come?"

"Well, Grace had her hundred-dollar motive, you know."

"You mean to invent the bit about Bill's asking her to drive him up to Nevada for his cache?"

"Yes. And that's the vital link."

"And you don't really think she was telling the truth?"

I hesitated. "Well, it's a funny thing. Mostly, I'm pretty well convinced she was. On any given Monday I'll likely feel ninety-five percent sure. But come Tuesday, the whole Bill Simmons connection may look thin as hell. Not necessarily untrue, but hopelessly fragile. And that's not enough. I've got to *prove* it—beyond all reasonable doubt."

"Do you think you can?"

"I don't know."

"But what about this new stuff from the Archives?"

"It looks good. About two hundred documents—and more leads than you could shake a map at. The most likely of them are . . . Oh, that reminds me. This little place Palo Verde, where Bill lived at the end of his life and where I stopped over on the California walk—it's barely two hundred miles from the cave, straight down the Colorado. And that's no distance, in that country."

"Certainly isn't. So no doubt you'll soon be visiting Palo Verde?"

"Sure. But the logical starting place is Pennsylvania."

"Will you go there too?"

"I guess so. If I get a chance. After all, I just might track down his family. The odds against finding someone who actually knew him look pretty long, but hell, I might well hear a lingering story of a maverick uncle who went out West and was never heard of again. Family legends like that often live on. Anyway, I might get some kind of a line on the boy who was, well, father to the man. And . . ." I sipped my wine. "You remember how this started out looking like a kind of amateur archaeological project?"

"Sure."

"Well, it keeps changing. Evolving. Now, it's beginning to feel more like a detective mystery. And maybe something more, too."

"Frankly, I never did quite see you as an archaeologist."

"Hell, I once had a drink with Louis Leakey."

"Name dropper! Anyway, he was an anthropologist. But I'm still intrigued about why you keep at it. I mean, is there something exceptional about this man Simmons?"

"No, he seems to have been a very ordinary kind of a guy. In the ordinary sense. But also, in his ordinary way, extraordinary."

"Now just what do you mean by that?"

"I guess I don't really know. But I mean it."

Dave leaned back and clasped his hands behind his head. "Well, from what you've told me, it at least sounds as if he got caught up in some of the broad events of our time. As a small cog, I mean. In our first imperialistic war, for instance. As a kid, probably, in the industrialization of the Midwest. As a young man, you say, in building the railroads that brought about the final opening up of the West. And later on in the large-scale human occupation of the California desert. I guess that makes him kind of interesting."

"Maybe that's a part of it."

"Hm."

I had heard the falseness too.

Dave leaned forward again. "Is there something more?"

"I don't think so."

"Are you sure?"

"No."

Dave twirled his glass. "You don't by any chance think you're being lured on by the research itself? Sort of seduced? It happens, you know."

"I know it does. In fact, I was warned against just that. But I don't think it's really happening in this case—even though I admit the research can be fun."

"But no one except you would still be at it. I mean, any normal guy, any man with any sense, would by this time have decided he'd gone far enough and let it go at that. So I guess I'll have to assume it's just an ordinary, simple, straightforward case of obsession."

I smiled. "Maybe it looks like that from the outside. But I see it differently. For one thing, especially with all this stuff from the Archives, I feel, as I say, that I've got to *prove* that Bill was Trunkman. Or come pretty close. And for another thing . . ." I heard my voice trail away.

"Yes?"

"Oh, I don't know. Perhaps it doesn't make much logical sense, but although proof is what I've been after all along, it's somehow been just as important to try to understand Bill, to see things through his eyes, to . . . to . . ."

Dave was smiling his slow, airline-captain smile. "You don't think a part of it might be that Bill Simmons is a lot like you?"

"Like me?"

"Yes, you mentioned that Grace kept saying so."

"But it hardly seems likely, does it?"

"I'd say it was very likely indeed. A great deal of natural selective process obviously went into getting Bill to that cave, and then you, fifty years later. After all, humans seemed to have reached it only once in between. So I'd be rather surprised if the two of you didn't have a lot in common."

"I hadn't thought of that."

"In fact, I'd be surprised if you don't uncover other . . . convergences."

I drained the last of my wine. "Come to think of it, there do seem to be some traits that Bill and I have in common. I guess you could say that I'm sometimes overmeticulous too . . ."

"Could and would."

"Bastard!"

"You brought it up."

"And as far as I can see, Bill didn't discover the desert until he was in his thirties or early forties—and promptly fell in love with it. Ditto me. There are other things too. But . . . oh hell, we're also opposites in some ways. He seems to have been an inveterate gambler, but gambling frankly bores me—for money, that is. And Bill seems to have talked less than I do. . . ."

"I can believe that."

"Bastard again! . . . Then there are some odd coincidences. Like Palo Verde—if you call it a coincidence that it was my first stop on the California walk."

"Well, you could see that as another product of natural selection."

"And I've just remembered that I once lived in a Cornish fishing village in an odd little house that had been built as a sail-drying shed and was known locally as 'The Cave.' "

"Now that's really stretching it!"

"I know, I know. But don't let's get too serious. Even if there turns out to be some truth in this business of my being a bit like Bill, it'll just be an intriguing bonus, that's all."

"Maybe," said Dave. "And maybe not."

# 7    Pittsburgh, Pa.

MY CHANCE to visit Pennsylvania came sooner than expected. I had to make a quick trip to New York, and on the way home I stopped off in Pittsburgh. I would just stay two or three days, I told myself, and see if one of my clues would lead, if not to Bill's family, then perhaps to a church or government record of his birth.

I rented a car at the airport, drove through a humid mid-June midday to the downtown Recorder's Office for Allegheny County—which includes both Turtle Creek and Braddock, neighboring eastern suburbs of Pittsburgh—and landed on my feet.

The Recorder's Office had advised me by letter that no county birth records existed before 1893—two decades too late for Bill. I quickly confirmed that there were no other useful records readily available. But within five minutes I had—because that happened to be her weekly research day—met the president of the West Pennsylvania Genealogical Society.

From the start, Helen Harriss seemed fascinated by the Trunkman story. She insisted on helping. And her research expertise made the difference. Without her I would have floundered helplessly among the Recorder's arcane filing systems and would probably never have gone, as we soon did, to the Carnegie Library. For hour after hour—that first afternoon, and then again next morning—we scanned ledgers and microfilms for likely-looking entries in Turtle Creek or Braddock records under Simmons or Simoyne or such other variations as Simon, which Mrs. Harriss thought might well turn out to be Bill's real name. And at last, in mid-morning of the second day, we found in the 1880 Turtle Creek census the entry for a certain Simon family that we had been trying to track down. From the start, the names looked right:

| Name | Age | Relationship | Occupation | Where Born |
|------|-----|--------------|------------|------------|
| Peter | 46 | | Miner | Prussia |
| Annie | 43 | Wife | Keeps house | Prussia |
| Anthony | 19 | Son | Miner | Prussia |
| Mary | 13 | Daughter | at home | Pa. |
| Joe | 11 | Son | at home | Pa. |
| Peter | 8 | Son | | Pa. |
| Wm. | 6 | Son | | Pa. |
| Annie | 4 | Daughter | | Pa. |
| Hellen | 1 | Daughter | | Pa. |

"William!" I whispered.

"Yes," breathed Mrs. Harriss.

We shook hands, silently, solemnly, unsolemnly. And in that first moment, although my logical sector knew that doubts would linger for a while, I felt sure, deep down, that I had at last pinned Bill to Pennsylvania.

When we found that the 1870 census showed the Simon family living in the same place, it seemed safe to assume that Bill—or at least a William Simon who also had a father named Peter and a mother named Annie—had indeed been born in Turtle Creek in 1874, give or take a year. But we could not follow the family after 1880: the 1890 census records for almost the entire United States were destroyed by a fire in Washington, D.C., in 1921; and because census details are not made public for seventy-five years, the 1900 lists were still under wraps.

The Carnegie Library opened one other window into the Simon family. An 1876 map of Turtle Creek showing individual lots with owners' names included one labeled "P. Symonds," and comparison of neighbors' names with those listed in the census records made it clear that this was our "Peter Simon." In those days, said Mrs. Harriss, spelling tended to be erratic.

The map was our last success, and late on that second day in Pittsburgh I drove out to Turtle Creek. All I had to do now was pick up Bill's trail and keep going.

That was when the frustrations began.

Turtle Creek was a gray little nineteenth-century town, sternly stagnating beside a muddy waterway of the same name, two miles above its junction with the Monongahela River. It nestled at the foot of a steep side valley, once heavily mined but with its scars now greened over. A thousand yards up this valley I located the lot on which, I confidently assumed, Bill had been born.

I had no difficulty pinpointing the lot, on Larimer Avenue. The 1876 map showed that when Bill was born there ran along its north boundary some kind of mining feeder line known as "Oak Hill No. 2 Incline" that debouched over Larimer Avenue and Thompson's Run—the creek that tumbled down the valley—onto the tracks of the New York and Cleveland Railroad Company. The eroded gully, now softly overgrown, down which the "incline" once ran was easily identifiable.

But the place remained curiously elusive. Though little more than an acre, the lot straddled a bluff thirty or forty feet high, and I found that because of the six frame houses that now stood at the foot of the bluff and the eight that lined the terrace above, and because of the trees in their gardens, there was nowhere I could stand back and see the property as a whole. So I never really managed to visualize the way it must have looked a century before. I even failed to find a trace of the two buildings shown on the lot on the 1876 map—inside one of which Bill had presumably come bawling onto our stage.

I spent two days in Turtle Creek—forty-eight long, hot hours of sleuthing and sweating in midwestern midsummer humidity. But I dug up only one faint hint and two small snippets of hardish information.

On the first day, an elderly man living in one of the houses on the old Simon property pointed down into the gulley where No. 2 Incline once ran. "There used to be caves down there," he said.

Later, a woman born a Simon, though not related to Bill, recalled that her grandfather, one of the family's original immigrants, was always known as Simone rather than Simon, "because that was how they pronounced it in Germany."

The final item came from the baptism records of St. Colman's Roman Catholic Church, established 1882. An entry on the first page featured Edward Simon, born July 23, 1883, son of Peter and Anna (nee Débold) Simon. Tentatively, I assumed that Edward was Bill's brother, and that Bill had therefore lived in Turtle Creek until he was at least eight.

St. Colman's records indicated that there had been two or more separate Simon families in Turtle Creek, and I spent most of my two days there trying to untangle a nightmare's nest of bloodlines. Finally, from the one remaining person to have lived locally since before the turn of the century, I raised a faint and rather uncertain recollection of a Simon family in which the mother had been short and heavyset and there was a daughter, Mary, and maybe a son, Bill. Yes, it seemed like there'd been a Bill. And it seemed like that family had moved to Braddock.

By this time I had untangled the Simon lines as much as I seemed likely to untangle them. All ended at brick walls. And on the afternoon of the second day—my fourth in Pittsburgh—I drove three miles over the hill to Braddock.

Braddock was once a pulsating industrial hive, swarming around the huge Edgar Thomson Steel Works. Today, it is a husk, cast up like a slag heap on the banks of "progress." When you look east along Braddock Avenue, the town's tattered main drag, you still see through gray haze the massive bulk and towering stacks of the Edgar Thomson Works. But the vitality that built works and town has drained away.

For more than twenty-four hours I scoured the mean streets and stern, gray buildings of Braddock—along with neighboring North Braddock and Rankin—striving to root out some trace of Bill's family.

At the steep, cobbled corner of Lobinger Street and Coalmont Avenue stood an old frame house, gaunt and pale green and peeling, that was probably where Bill's mother lived in 1908—if you chose to believe his desertion poster. But I failed to establish any Simon connection with the house. In fact, I could pin down none of its history: a big fire at city hall in 1934 destroyed all records. I soon confirmed that, as I had expected, the "Coohounts" Street of the desertion poster could only have been a clerical error for Coalmont.

No local newspapers, I discovered, had filed copies earlier than 1920. But in the records of Braddock's three huge Roman Catholic churches I finally found three hints that Bill's family had indeed moved to the town before century's end. Tucked among whole shoals of Simon entries were marriage records for two young men and a young woman—Peter, Joseph and Annie—who were probably Bill's siblings. The Latin entry for Annie's marriage—on April 24, 1899, during the brief interval between Bill's first and second army tours—seemed to confirm something I had long suspected: that Bill had been christened "William Anthony." One of Annie's sponsors was "Giulielmus Antonius Simon."

It was late at night when I turned up these faint but welcome encouragements. Next morning I caught my first warm glimpse of Bill's family—on cold stone.

Monongahela Catholic Cemetery stands high above Braddock, among folds of rolling, still-green hills. It, too, had netted shoals of Simons. Among them I found the grave of an Anton Simon who died in August 1935 at age seventy-four. Bill's brother Anthony, nineteen on the 1880 census, would in 1935 have been exactly that age.

I visited what I felt sure was his grave.

The square sandstone pillar stood on a gentle, grassy slope, clean and gleaming in bright sunlight. Its inscriptions, though already eroded into softness, stood clear: ANTON SIMON, 1861–1935, Father ... JOSEPHINE SIMON, 1870–1935, Mother ... VALERIE B. STANLEY, 1898–1916 ... DAVID A. STANLEY, 1916–1916. And this poignant little capsule history worked an unexpected sea-change on the way I looked at the family Bill had left behind in Pennsylvania—the family he seemed to have rejected. Perhaps the assumed rejection had prejudiced me. Anyway, I had until that moment, without really thinking about it, seen Bill's parents and siblings and collateral descendants as mere bits of information to fit into my Trunkman jigsaw. But now, standing before brother Anton's grave with my feet on the soft green grass and my body bathed in warm, living sunshine, I grasped for the first time—for the first time, I mean, in any living sense—that Bill's family was made up of people who, like all of us, had danced their little dance. They had been born and had worked and played and rejoiced and suffered and perhaps, before they died, had borne children who in their turn worked and played and rejoiced and suffered—except, of course, when a child died at birth, in 1916 or some other sad year, killing the young mother and thereby cutting off at the roots a barely begun sub-lineage that at joyful marriage moments, and others too, had shone bright with hope and a quiet, unquestioned sense of continuity.

The cemetery records, read along with those from the churches and from a funeral parlor— sole survivor of five that once parlored Braddock's dead—had shown that at least four local families were descended from four different Peter Simons, all immigrants. Each family shimmered with Josephs and Anthonys and Williams and Marys, and I spent the rest of that second day in Braddock—it was a Saturday—trying to sort them out.

A long, hot afternoon of Simon-house to Simon-house canvassing raised no whisper that sounded like Bill's family. Hot and humid afternoon eased over into hot and humid evening. I followed a lead across town to a little hill in western Braddock. Evening greased over into hot and humid night. By ten o'clock, only one lead remained on that little hill. I trudged through narrow, dimly lit streets toward yet another house.

Now I do not want you to think of me, tired though I was by then, as tottering on the brink of defeat. Excitement still drove me—the excitement that had been there almost every minute of the five days since I landed in Pittsburgh. But I have to admit that as I walked wearily up that little hill I began to wonder whether I had achieved all I could reasonably hope for in Pittsburgh. Chasing further details might be sheer needle-and-haystacking. And as I turned into the street I was looking for it occurred to me, not the first time, that perhaps I should give up on this octopus of

Braddock Simons and try a new tack across the river in Homestead—searching for traces of the Peter Nau (or perhaps Nan) whom Bill had, at one army enlistment, designated his next of kin.

I think I was still considering a move to Homestead when I found the house I was looking for—or, to be more accurate, the house I thought I was looking for.

Only later did I discover that I should have been higher on the hill: the number I went to was right but the street one block wrong. And that seems to suggest the existence of an anti-Murphy's Law. For as I walked wearily up the steps of the little frame house that in the tenuous light of the streetlamps looked much the same as all the other little frame houses for blocks around, there came leaping out at me, double-barreled, from aluminum screen door and neat black mailbox, the black-on-silver-decal name of the occupant. The name was "Nau."

For a moment I froze in mid-step. Then I had reached out and knocked on the aluminum door.

Silence.

I waited, knocked again. And again. And again. At last I turned away and began to walk back down the steps.

"Can I help you?" The voice came out of the darkness, off to my left.

I peered. Two houses away, dim in the street lighting, a man and woman were sitting on a stoop. I walked to the foot of their steps and explained, capsule-form.

The woman had been born a Nau and was aunt to the young couple on whose house door I had been knocking. Yes, she had cousins in Homestead. They still pronounced the name "Now," but here on this side of the river they all called it "Gnaw." Why, yes, she could just remember from back when she was a child in the early twenties an old man they called Uncle Peter. "He was a little fat man who sat and made knots in a kind of rope that unraveled. Maybe he was senile, but they were clever, them knots. . . . Yes, seems to me I remember hearing there was Simons living in North Braddock that was related to us. . . . Oh no, your Bill Simon couldn't have been married to a Nau and divorced her or deserted her. Nothing like that, or I'd have heard about it."

I learned no more that night. But next morning the young Naus were at home, and they referred me to "Uncle Charlie" who lived just around the corner.

Charlie Nau was small, gray-haired. Yes, he knew the Naus and Simons were related in some way. His father had told him that his old Uncle Anton used to say, "A whole bunch of us came over together from Germany"; and he, Charlie, had an idea the Simons might have been in that bunch. Come to think of it, he rather thought he remembered seeing the name Simon on the family grave, up in the Catholic cemetery. He insisted on driving me up there.

The Nau grave stood barely fifty yards from Anton Simon's, on the same grassy slope. It, too, was soft sandstone, and some of the lettering had already weathered away.

First: HIER RUHET BERNARD NAU GEB. JU(?) 27, 1833(?) GEST. MAY 13, 1885.

Below, only two words of a separate inscription remained legible. But they read: CATHERINE SIMON . . .

"Ah!" said Charlie Nau. He muttered something about remembering another grave and drifted up the hill, half right. I moved left.

The next gravestone was hard black granite and its lettering still stood clear. I had barely begun to walk toward it when I saw the single word inscribed on its base: SIMON.

Two quick paces, and I could read the main inscription—only one of the other three sides bore lettering:

And standing there in front of a Simon grave for the second time in two days, in warm summer sunlight with the green grass growing all around me, I again knew that something had changed: the two family graves, paces apart; the two fathers born a year apart; the Nau mother nee Simon; Charlie's "a whole bunch of us came over together"; in sum, these clues virtually clinched the Nau Connection.

I called Charlie. In his quiet way, he seemed to share my excitement. "Yes, I remember now," he said, pointing at the name MARY ALGER. "The Simons and Algers was hooked up somehow, though I don't know how. And the Algers was related to Honus Wagner, the baseball player. They had money, too—even during the Depression, when elderberry jelly and potatoes was a meal. In those days, nobody bought bread—that was cake. . . . Yes, the Algers lived in a big house up on the hill and I remember going to see my Aunt Mary there. That must be her, there on the grave. . . . I can remember where the house was, too. I'll take you there."

The house, though bigger than most in Braddock, fell short of grandeur.

"No," said the owner. "The Algers sold out long ago. Lord knows what became of them. . . . But wait a minute. . . . Yes, that's right, there's an Alger daughter still lives in Braddock. Down on Locust Street. She's married to a man called . . . Now what *was* his name? . . . Gross, that's it. Yes, she's Mrs. Gross. I can tell you how to find their house. . . ."

Ten minutes later a tall, white-haired woman wearing glasses opened the door of the house on Locust Street.

Yes, she was Mrs. Gross. And yes, she had been born an Alger.

Charlie explained their relationship.

"Won't you come in?"

I had hardly begun telling my story to Mrs. Gross and her husband when she exclaimed, "Why, that'll be Uncle Bill! I've heard about him all my life. My father had met him before I was born and was very struck by him. He'd often tell stories about old Uncle Bill who'd gone out West and was never heard of again."

I leaned back in my chair. At last, on that quiet Sunday morning, after six days' travail, I had found what I had hardly dared hope for.

"My dad apparently looked *very* like Uncle Bill. I often heard that. Same little brown eyes that could sparkle. . . . Oh, they could sparkle! And I know my dad thought a lot of Bill. Toward the end, he got interested in writing up the family history. He was sports editor of the Pittsburgh *Post-Gazette*, you see. And scholastic editor, too. *His* father—he spelled his name the German way, 'Arhelger'—was a professor at Heidelberg University in Germany before he came over and married Bill's sister, Mary. . . . Anyway, after he retired, my dad was always going to write up the family history. . . ."

"Yes," said Mr. Gross. "And I've just remembered that Bible. Isn't it still downstairs?"

It seemed that around 1960, five years before her father's death, "somebody on that side of the family" had died, and survivors had come to visit him. Later, they had sent him the family Bible. Fred Alger had always meant to use it in his write-up of the family history but he never got around to it and for years the Bible had just been gathering dust in the basement.

Mr. Gross went down to look for it.

No, his wife said, the Wagners were not actually related to the Algers, but through his work her father had gotten to know all the sports people, and he had been a great friend of Honus Wagner—and of Art Rooney, present owner of the Pittsburgh Steelers.

Her husband came back into the room carrying a big box, still partly wrapped in the brown paper in which it had been mailed. He put it down on a table and with great care lifted from it a massive, gray-covered tome.

The "Bible" was actually a collection of "Catholic Gems or Treasures of the Church: A repository of Catholic Instruction and Devotion," copyrighted in 1887. Both covers and most of the flyleaves and contents pages had broken free from the binding. One by one, Mr. Gross turned them over.

The front flyleaves bore only two handwritten inscriptions: "RANKIN, JULY 27th, 1887" and "MR. PETTER SIMON." But pasted on the back cover were two undated newspaper cuttings and two small sheets of handwritten German.

Mr. and Mrs. Gross kindly offered to let me take the loose covers and flyleaves home for careful study and to get a translation made of the German script of the handwritten sheets. I wrapped them all up and also copied the return address on the brown paper in which the box had been mailed: "Marlene A. Simons, General Delivery, Yorkville, Ohio, 4B."

Meanwhile, Mrs. Gross was on the phone.

Each time I had asked a question about some item in the newspaper cuttings she had said, "Aunt Marie will know." Her Aunt Marie, she explained, was Mrs. John Schuster, daughter of Mary Alger—and therefore a niece of Bill's. She lived just across town, in Dormont, a southern suburb. "She was always the nosy one of the family—and her mother before her. Nothing much happened in the family that they didn't know about,

## ...ate a Thrilling Scene at a Funeral, Wrecking

# HEARSE AND CARRIAGES.

### The Casket Had Just Been Removed, and Mourners Had Entered the Church.

## AWFUL CATASTROPHE AVERTED.

A frightened horse created much excitement this morning at the funeral of Edward Simon, the young son of Capt. Peter Simon, killed on Wednesday afternoon by jumping from the Derry express at Copeland. The hearse and two carriages with the funeral procession, were badly wrecked.

The procession had drawn up in a long line of carriages on both sides of George street, after the mourners had entered St. Joseph's German Catholic church, where the funeral services were held. The mourners and friends of the deceased had entered the church but a few moments, when the thrilling accident, which was a sad one in its connection, occurred.

A carriage owned by Milo McAnulty with a colored man named Johnson as driver, was at the head of the line of carriages near the church and in front of the hearse. A train on the P. R. R. passed, and the engine blew off steam. Johnson, the driver, had left his seat, and was attending to some portion of the harness.

The horse took fright and whirled the carriage around. One of the wheels struck the hearse and smashed the glass windows. A carriage of Joseph Walton was in the center of the street, and the McAnulty carriage collided with it. The wheels of both carriages became entangled, and the Walton carriage was thrown over and wrecked. The McAnulty coach was badly damaged.

A carriage belonging to Liveryman Null, was in line with the others on the west side of the street. The horse quickly jumped out of the way and moved up the hill, giving the frightened horses an open space in which they were brought to subjection. Had the McAnulty carriage struck the first in line owned by Null, the runaways would have wrecked every carriage on both sides of the street, on their flight down the hill, which could not have been stayed.

The damage to the carriage and hearse will be quite large, and will fall upon Mr. McAnulty. Undertaker Joseph Flannery was director of the funeral.

Another hearse and other carriages were secured by the time services were concluded, and the sad procession, doubly saddened by the thrilling event, moved on to the Monongahela cemetery where the interment took place.

## EARLY RANKIN SETTLER DIED THIS MORNING

### Peter Simon, Among The First Business Men in That Borough, Died After Long Illness.

Mr. Peter Simon, one of the early settlers of Rankin, died this morning at 12:30 o'clock, at his home on Baltimore street, near the Baltimore and Ohio railroad station, where he had lived for more than 20 years. His death was the result of rheumatism and general debility. He has been ill for several months.

Mr. Simon was born in Germany in 1834, and came to America with his wife in 1865. He settled in Turtle Creek, and remained there for a number of years, then came to Braddock. He was in the liquor business while in Braddock. About 20 years ago he went to Rankin, and built one of the first houses in what is now the lower part of Rankin. He conducted a large grocery and general store for some 18 years.

Mr. Simon was a member of St. Joseph's German Catholic church, George street, this city, and is survived by his wife and a family of grown children, four sons and two daughters: Messrs. Joseph and Peter, of Rankin, employed in the Rankin plant of the American Steel & Wire company; Anthony Simon, of Penn street, fireman of the Braddock water works plant; and William E. Simon, first sergeant of Company E, Twenty-eighth Infantry, now in the Philippines; Mrs. Mary Arhelger, of Rankin, and Mrs. Frank Abels, of Homestead.

The funeral services will be held on Wednesday morning at 9 o'clock, in St. Joseph's German Catholic church, and the burial will be in St. Joseph's division of Monongahela cemetery, under the direction of Undertaker Flannery.

and then they'd talk about it for years afterward. If we want to know any family history we always go to Aunt Marie. I'll call her right now."

Before long she handed me the phone.

"Why, of course I knew Uncle Bill," said Aunt Marie. "He was a real wanderer, that one, but when he come back after being over there in the first war he stopped for a couple of days on his way back to California and stayed with me and my husband. We was just married, then. That was the last time Uncle Bill come to P.A., but he wrote once, soon after that, from the Black Hills. Sent five dollars, he did, to buy shoes for Rosemary— that's our first daughter, who was just about due."

"The Black Hills?"

"Yes, he said he was living all alone in a cabin in the desert with his little black cat. Oh, he'd been wandering all his life. He should have been an explorer, that one. They couldn't keep him at home. First time he took off was right after he left school. He was only about sixteen then. . . ." Details kept pouring out, and I knew that I had finally hit my Pittsburgh jillpot.

We arranged that I should visit Mrs. Schuster and her husband next afternoon at their apartment.


AUNT MARIE was small and brown-eyed and seventy-six, and she twinkled. But geography was not her bag.

"Yes, he said he was back in the desert, that time he sent the five dollars for Rosemary's shoes. In the Black Hills, he was. North Dakota."

"North Dakota?"

"Well, somebody told me the Black Hills was in North Dakota. Maybe Bill had to go there to pick up his mail. Anyways, I know he said he was writing from the Black Hills. Black Horse Mine Number Two, his address was."

"That's right, Black Horse Mine Number Two," said John Schuster. He was a tall, gaunt man, a year or two older than Aunt Marie, and ailing.

"Black Horse?" I fumbled for the connection. "Let's see, there was a claim staked by . . . Tell me, do you know if Bill ever used any name other than 'Simon'?"

"Well, he spelled it different," said Aunt Marie. "He always said it was really 'Simone,' not 'Simon.' He was the one that was *vicious* about the name. He'd get real angry. And he put a 'y' in there, someplace. He was the only one that did it. Funny name it was, the way he had it, and that 'y' always got me for pronunciation. . . ."

Off to Aunt Marie's left, white blinds half-covered the windows. They muted the traffic noise and mollified the hot June sunlight. It seemed an unlikely place, this rather bare little walk-up apartment in suburban Pittsburgh, for me to prove at last, beyond reasonable doubt, that my hunch had been right: that Bill Simmons/Simon was indeed the same man as the William Ashee or Asher Simoyne who had staked mining claims in the California desert before 1930, beginning with Black Horse Mine in the McCoy Mountains in December 1917.

Aunt Marie had never heard of the name Ashee, or Asher. "Maybe he just didn't like the name 'Tony' and changed it himself. He always wanted his own way, that one. And he'd get it too. I remember when he stayed with us that time, after he came back from the First War—he was over there with the Canadian Army, you know—he was mad at the Canadians because they wouldn't pay him, after all he'd gone through. So he throwed his bundle in the ocean and told them to 'go to h.' But our Fred—that's my brother, Fred Alger—he knowed Clyde Kelly, the congressman or legislature or whatever he was, and Bill said he was going after Clyde Kelly to see if he couldn't get the money. And he got it, quick. No flies under Uncle Bill's feet."

"How long did he stay with you?"

"Two, three days. That's all. Our boys was all coming home at that time. And Bill, his teeth was all loose. Beautiful teeth, he had—like pearls—but every one of them was loose in the socket from that mustard gas. He'd been wounded in the leg, too. Shrapnel. They was digging under the lines, and when they come up out of the hole the Germans was there, and that was when the shrapnel got him. But he'd been wounded in other wars, so he was used to that. In the Spanish-American War he had a sword run straight through his back. . . ."

"Well, actually his records say . . ." I stopped. It did not really seem necessary to tell Bill's niece that his army records showed that the only "wound" he had sustained was from falling onto a stake while searching a Filipino hut.

"Yes, Bill was always after war, all the time. As long as there was a fight, he was in it. He only joined the Canadians because he was too old for the American Army, and when they wouldn't pay him he went after Clyde Kelly and he got the money for him right off. And as soon as Bill had it he went and bought a beautiful dress for me and a lovely thin Georgian waist for my mother."

A waist, it seemed, was a blouse.

" 'I might never see you again, Mary,' he said to my mother. 'And this is to remember me by.' Yes, all Bill would talk about was California. 'You just don't know what living is till you live out where I am,' he said. 'It is just wonderful. Death Valley and Imperial Valley and places like that—you've never seen anything until you've seen those places. I have to get back so I can breathe good fresh air again. The air is so pure there, not all smoky like it is here. . . . Oh, I don't know how you people can live here.' No, Uncle Bill, he didn't like it around here—oh my God no. He hated Braddock. Thought it was terrible. 'I'm going right back out to the desert,' he said. And he got ready and went. And the last we heard from him was when he sent the five dollars for us 'to buy a pair of shoes for the new baby.' Rosemary was born just after he left, you know.

"No, we didn't answer his letter. With him always on the go like that, we figured he'd never get it. And we thought maybe he'd keep in touch. But we never heard of him again. Never. We often talked about him, though, and wondered if he'd found his cat and his shack. A desolate place, he said it was—just him all by himself, him and his little old black cat. He was a mining prospector, and he'd just discovered this place when he had to go off to war. Of course, none of us could see him living like that. What they'd call a hermit, I guess. He'd cooked in the Army, though, so he knowed how to cook, all right. And he liked it that way. You never had nobody around to watch you, he said, and you was your own boss and you could come and go when you felt like it, and that was the way he liked to live, see. 'The free life,' he'd say. 'That's my life.' He liked to work in his cave and . . ."

"His cave? Did he say he lived in a cave?"

"No, I think he worked in his cave and lived in his shack, outside of the cave. His little old shack, and his cat. But we never paid too much attention to all his stories from out West because we never really knew what to believe. And of course, I'd just keep my mouth shut because we didn't want to get in trouble with him, you know."

"But he definitely used the word 'cave'?"

"Oh yes, he talked about a cave right enough. No doubt about that."

I tried to establish whether the cave was really in the McCoy Mountains or two hundred miles north, in Nevada.

"No, I don't know the name of it," said Aunt Marie. "Unless it was the Black Horse Mine. Is there a difference, now, between a mine and a cave?"

And I had to leave it at that.

Neither Aunt Marie nor her husband seemed at first to have any vivid recollection of what Bill had looked like. But when I showed them the 1908 desertion poster mug shots Aunt Marie said, "Oh, *that* looks like him. Those eyes! Snappy, they were. Real snappy. Yes, he'd got the Simon eyes, right enough. But he looked better than that. A fine-looking man, he was. No, I'm not surprised he deserted. That would be Bill, to run away."

John Schuster also examined the photograph. "Yeah, that's Bill, all right."

"I don't think he wore his hair like that all the time, though," said Aunt Marie. "Seems like he had brown hair. Dark brown."

"Yes, that's what his army records say."

I brought out the snap of Bill standing beside Grace outside the rock house. Aunt Marie held it up close to her snappy brown Simonized eyes, then out at a distance. "I can't really see but . . . Why, it looks like he wore a beard! I don't know . . . He used to have more of a puffed-out face, Bill did, when he was younger."

I handed her the snap of Bill standing beside Rose, the waitress.

"Oh yes, I see his features there. Right here, below the hat. . . . Yes, he was nice-looking, Bill was."

"I get the impression that he had an eye for the girls."

"I never heard that," said Aunt Marie. "He just didn't seem that kind."

I asked about the Pennsylvania wife and child that Grace had spoken of. But Aunt Marie had never heard of them and thought it very unlikely that Bill married locally. For one thing, he started wandering too young. The family never understood his wanderlust, said Aunt Marie, but they never forgot him. " 'I wonder where Bill is now,' my mother would say. And I'd say, 'Oh, out West someplace, I guess, with the cowboys.' Because he'd talked about Montana too, and how the boys all went into town once a week."

When I tried to trigger Aunt Marie's memory with place names—Las Vegas, Seattle and others—I drew a blank: no, he was just interested in California.

"What about the Colorado River?" I asked.

"No. . . . But wait a minute. The Colorado River . . . let's see, Colorado. . . . My mother had an uncle—and so did Bill—that lived up near Pike's Peak in Colorado. And he was a mining prospector. . . ."

"Oh, was he? This could be Twin Lakes."

"His name was Tony. Anthony Simon. He'd have been my grandpap's brother, I think. They come over together from Germany. . . . And he was murdered."

"Murdered?"

"Yes, he was married one or two times, and his wife murdered him. He was wealthy, too. Lovely stones and stuff he used to send home to us young nephews and nieces. Horseshoes and inkwells and things like that. When was he murdered? Oh, I was very little then. If Annie was living, she could tell you. She went out there to see Uncle Tony and they went up Pike's Peak and she fell off and broke her arm and they had to go up with burros and bring her down to the hospital. No, I'm afraid I don't know the name of the place Uncle Tony lived. All I can remember is Pike's Peak. . . . Oh yes, Bill got along fine with Annie. In fact . . . didn't Mother tell me that he stood for her when she was married?"

"Ah!" I said. "So it *was* Bill." I told her of the church marriage record showing "Giulielmus Antonius Simon" as a witness.

"I thought so," said Aunt Marie. "She married Frank Abels, did Annie."

I voiced my long-held assumption that Bill had quarreled with his parents and perhaps with the rest of the family.

Aunt Marie felt sure I was wrong. During his brief reappearances, Bill didn't bother anybody. He was a self-minded man, right enough, but he was never around long enough for anyone to fight with. Oh yes, he got along pretty well with the family. They all liked him. And his parents weren't the kind to drive him out West. They were independent people and they'd hoped he would do better than he did, but that was all. In his last years, Bill's father had been very sick with painter's colic and couldn't stand the climate in Rankin, where they lived then, and used to spend a lot of time in Mobile, Alabama. Oh yes, it was quite possible that Bill could have stayed with him before he enlisted in Mobile in 1898, though Aunt Marie couldn't actually remember hearing of that. But Peter, Sr., had died in Rankin: "I guess he just had a feeling that he wasn't going to live or something and came home to die."

I put forward an idea Helen Harriss, the genealogist, had suggested: that Bill had gone down to Mobile from Pittsburgh by river—the normal route at that time—and had given his parents' birthplaces as Kentucky and Louisiana because he had just passed through those states on his river journey.

"Oh, he'd do that," said Aunt Marie. "A regular jokester, that one was." But both parents had actually been born in Germany. "Grandpap died when I was only two or three, but I can remember my grandma well. A little old French lady . . ."

"French?"

"Yes. Her name was Deeborn or something. I don't know just where she was born, but they had a war or something over there and soldiers snuck the brides from the other side of the line. Oh yes, I remember my grandmother well. Short and stout, she was. They say I take after her, being a shorty—but I don't want to get as fat as her."

At a guess, Aunt Marie, soaking wet, weighed all of ninety-nine pounds.

"Why, I was right there with my grandma when she died. I was only eleven or twelve then. My grandma, she was sitting up at the table and peeling green beans for my mother and I had just gave her a glass of water. . . ."

Soon, Aunt Marie was in full flood of reminiscence. I let her cascade. And there in that little suburban apartment, with the sun beating on the white blinds that muffled the traffic noise, she handed down the history of the Simon family in the way family history has been handed down since long before man learned to write.

By the time she tired the sun had set, traffic had tapered off for the evening and a hint of coolness was floating in through the open window.

I SPENT two more busy days in Pittsburgh, confirming and rounding out what Aunt Marie had told me. I went to Rankin and Homestead, revisited Braddock and Turtle Creek. And I saw and heard and grasped many things that helped me reconstruct a picture of Bill's earliest years—a picture that even in outline suggested an explanation for the way he lived his later life.

At last, ten days after arriving in Pittsburgh, I caught an early flight out.

The jet banked over the murk that half-hid the city, then leveled off— carrying me westward faster than Bill had ever gone but bearing me along with the same warm sense of going home that he had felt when he left Braddock for the last time in April of 1919. I knew how he had felt, that day. I knew it exactly, just by consulting my own feelings. For both Bill and I had been lucky.

In that April of 1919, California was already Bill's adopted home. And your homing instinct can be just as strong, just as warm, for an adopted as for an ancestral home. It can be stronger, in fact, and warmer. For such a home is no accident of birth: you have built it—by and large, and if you were lucky—by free, unfettered choice.

It was important, I had begun to grasp, that I often seemed to know how Bill felt simply by consulting my own feelings. You could call it natural selection or whatever you wanted to; but on a practical level the empathy meant that I now felt curiously confident of being able to reconstruct a great deal of Bill's life. For in Pittsburgh I had found far more than I had expected—far more than the sum of Peter and Anna and Anton and Mary and the other children. I had found Bill's roots. And no matter how happily and firmly you transfer your allegiances to an adopted home, your roots remain attached to the being you eventually become, and affect that new being's actions.

All I had left to do now, with luck, was follow the leads I had tucked away in brain and briefcase. Then, using empathy as my diviner, I could begin to assemble the jigsaw pieces into a coherent life—into a history fashioned from such a weight of detail that any impartial jury would in the end accept it as proof that Bill Simon/Simoyne/Simmons was indeed, beyond all reasonable doubt, my cave-dwelling Nevada Trunkman.


NOW LOOK, I want to be as honest as I can—as straightforward as circumstances permit. But they make it curiously difficult.

I have implied that when I left Pittsburgh my ruling itch was still to solve the Trunkman mystery. Perhaps it was. But I am not sure. It could well be that my Trunkman sleuthing had already become a mere excuse for going ahead with what I wanted to do—much as Bill's prospecting seems to have been an excuse for him to wander around the California desert.

What I really wanted to do, apparently, was get to know Bill. The more I saw of this man I was chasing, the more I liked him—and by now I wanted for some reason to rebuild his life as fully and accurately as I could, for its own sake.

But perhaps that is not wholly true either.

In the months and then years that followed my Pittsburgh visit I was able to devote myself almost full-time to Bill, for I had at last silenced the lingering echoes of the project that had so long kept me away from him. And I know that throughout those months and years I continued to search as eagerly as ever for proof that he was Trunkman. I even constructed a buttress for the convenient rationalization that I was amassing evidence of a kind that would convince a jury.

When the Warren Commission investigated the motives of Lee Harvey Oswald they examined every penetrable crevice of his life: parental and environmental influences, friends, politics, sex life, quirks, frustrations and fantasies. And in the end they concluded that "out of these and the many other factors which may have molded the character of Lee Harvey Oswald there emerged a man capable of assassinating President Kennedy." Whether you agree with the Warren Commission's overall conclusions or not, I think you must admit that the method they used in this particular sector of their research has merit. Anyway, I applied their method. And I offered the need for jury-convincing proof as my reason for going ahead and digging for intimate details—often offered it to other people, and sometimes to myself.

Now if all this sounds enigmatical—as if I still did not quite understand what I wanted when I came home from Pittsburgh, nearly seven years after finding the Trunkman cave—I am not surprised. I think that is about how things stood. But I feel I must at least do my best to come clean: to present the obfuscation clearly. At a guess, I would say that the one sure statement about the Trunkman project at the time I flew out of Pittsburgh is that it had taken another quantum step forward in its ongoing evolution.

There is another kind of change that I must tell you about, too.

For months after I came home from Pittsburgh, information about Bill's life kept flooding in—from people who had known him and also through the written word. A year after my National Archives visit, for example, there appeared in my mailbox one day, unheralded, a bulky envelope bearing the name of that non-armadillic organization. It held Xeroxes of 114 army documents, and they opened new windows on Bill's military career. That same red-letter mail brought more than twenty documents from another country's army, and they illuminated a hitherto shadowy chapter of Bill's life during which he . . . But that story can wait. For the moment, the important thing about this later information is the way it reached me.

It came in fits and starts—in sudden spurts; in a disorder that bordered on randomness. And if I continued to feed it to you in the order it reached me you would soon become hopelessly confused.

So from here on in I will be telling you of events not, as I have been doing, in the order in which they became known to me but in the order they happened to Bill. After all, that is "what happened"; that is the life. Once you get a jigsaw puzzle started, the sequence in which you assemble its pieces becomes immaterial.

There is one other thing.

Bill's life is—like everybody's, in retrospect—seamed with uncertainties. I will try not to harp on them. Sometimes, when the element of doubt is important, I will state it explicitly. I will also do so occasionally just to keep the general tone honest. But where doubt seems commonsensically obvious I will often make flat statements. Otherwise we would soon find ourselves bogging down in a morass of "may haves" and "must haves" and "likelys" and "probablys." The uncertainties lie heaviest, of course, on his early life: details are necessarily sparse, sketchy, speculative. But patterns emerge. And in later years the rich treasury of surviving human memories builds a sure and satisfying roundness.

In unfolding the story of Bill's life I will try to heft some of the daily, ongoing loads of prejudice and temperament and folly and wisdom and other internal verities of the kind that indelibly color all our little lives. If I succeed, then when I have finished telling this story to you, my jury, you will not only have heard enough to conclude from the weight of accumulated evidence that out of the many factors which may have molded the character of William Anthony Simon there emerges a man capable of choosing to live in a cave in Nevada in the fall of 1916; you will not only have heard enough circumstantial evidence to conclude that he in fact did so; you will also, I hope, have heard a good deal more.

# PART II

# 8   Early Years

WHEN WILLIAM ANTHONY SIMON came bawling onto our stage on August 2, 1875, in Turtle Creek, Pennsylvania, near the point at which Oak Hill No. 2 Incline crossed Larimer Avenue, Ulysses S. Grant was President of a nation still mending from civil war but now rip-roaring toward its centennial, Otto von Bismarck ruled with an iron chancellorship the German Empire he had built less than five years earlier around the Prussian homeland of young Bill's proud parents, and Victoria—by the Grace of God, of the United Kingdom of Great Britain and Ireland, Queen, Defender of the Faith, etc., etc. (but not yet Empress of India)—was midway through giving the age her name; the human population of the United States stood at 45 million and booming, of the planet at about 1.3 billion and beginning to ditto; *The Origin of Species* had been published sixteen years earlier but evolution was taught in schools almost nowhere, let alone in Tennessee; the first volume of *Das Kapital* had been published eight years earlier but no red revolutions had yet taken place, anywhere; during the previous decade, Alaska had been purchased and Colorado, Nevada, Arizona, Idaho, Montana and Wyoming had been organized as territories, but the West, though six years Golden-Spiked, was hardly what you could call Won (six months were to pass before the registration of patents for the barbed wire that would subdue the Great Plains and for the telephone that would subdue distance, and eleven months later Colonel Custer would bite the Little Bighorn dust); as part of the price for its helter-skelter transition from a country of extractive industries into one of the great manufacturing nations of the world, the United States kept bouncing from boom to bust and back—and the Panic of 1873 had just subsided sufficiently for the huge Edgar Thomson Steel Works, over the hill in Braddock, to have been completed after a brief hiatus; Henry Ford was twelve years old, Orville Wright four, Guglielmo Marconi one and Albert Einstein minus four; meanwhile, on that unflagged Monday in a quiet and tumultuous period that was as usual the best and the worst of times, the weather all over the world remained unpredictable.

On that first of the 27,191 days that William Anthony Simon was to spend on earth, the sun set in Turtle Creek, technically speaking, at 7:15 p.m. But no one saw it sink behind the steep hills west of Larimer Avenue. For three days, a huge and unseasonable storm had been lashing the Middle States. Swollen rivers had swept away bridges and buildings. Dark clouds still lowered, decanting the last of their loads. The rain had scrubbed away most of the pollutants that booming industry was already belching into God's own skies.

TODAY'S COPIOUS record-keeping and corner-drugstore photography mean that few modern childhoods pass without lasting chronicle. But young William Simon lived an obscure life in an era with a much more spartan cast, and except for a handwritten birth entry in the family Bible, his first seventeen years seem to have generated no verifiable personal tracks. So I cannot construct a hard, historical playback of those years in Turtle Creek and Braddock. But perhaps it is no great loss. Childhood, even more than adulthood, is something other than an accretion of hard, historical facts: its internal realities are a warm and shifting pageant, all color and shading. Naturally, it will take time to convey the colors and shades. In Bill's case, the very elements that cast them are now shadows. For his childhood, like most, was governed by—aside from fickle chance—the nature of his stage, the characters of other players, and such light as his roots and the pulse of history projected onto his scene.

Young William's roots reached back across the Atlantic into the valleys of the Mosel and Saar. His father and mother were born less than forty miles apart, in 1834 and 1837, in what was then western Prussia, near the Luxembourg border. Their birthplaces, Kantenbach on the Mosel and Besseringen on the Saar, lie about equidistant from the rivers' confluence near Trier, in a heavily Catholic and largely pastoral region of rolling green hills.

Bill's parents probably married in 1858. Peter was then twenty-four, Anna twenty-one. When they emigrated—the year a silence fell at Appomattox—they were older not only by six years but also, most likely, by four living children. Anton, now four, was the oldest. The "whole bunch" of them that crossed the Atlantic—including Peter's sister, Catherine, wife of Bernhard Nau—formed a small drop in what would become a great postbellum flood of immigrants from Central and Southern Europe.

Once in America, they followed a pattern often discernible among immigrants, worldwide: they chose a new home that echoed the old. They settled close to a big city standing at the confluence of two major rivers (the Allegheny and Monongahela join at Pittsburgh to form the Ohio) in what was then a largely pastoral region of rolling green hills. A Nau family legend (committed to paper a century later by a daughter of one of the immigrant children) has the party completing the last leg of its journey by floating downriver on a raft to "a little place called New Town, near Turtle Creek, Pa." By 1870 the Simon family had leased and moved onto the Larimer Avenue lot in Turtle Creek.

From many sources, but especially from four tattered and crumbling gray pages of "births, deaths and marriages" that Mrs. Gross found in the family "Bible" after I left Pittsburgh and was good enough to send me, I have managed to compile the bare-bones statistics of this immigrant family with a background that was, for its place and time, almost archetypical. (See the table on the next page.)

You will see that, as was normal at the time, a distressing number of the many children died before reaching maturity. So Bill arrived in a household of six: a father just turned forty-one who worked in a nearby coal mine; a mother of thirty-eight who had already borne eight children; and the four surviving children—Anton, fourteen; Mary, eight; Joseph, six; and Peter, almost three.

Peter, Sr., was clearly a good provider. Two years before Bill's birth he had bought the Larimer Avenue lot. Soon, he would become a family grocer and a builder and contractor. He was also an active churchman: a history of St. Joseph's, Braddock, lists him among those "through whose sacrifice and efforts" the church was organized in 1877 "and made to flourish."

My only glimpse of a flesh-and-blood man came from a daughter of Peter, Jr. Her grandfather, she said, was "a great gambler" who had a boat—"a trade ship, they called it"—which he used for trading merchandise, especially from Cuba. "Every so often he'd have to make a trip with his boat, and when he came back he came back broke—from gambling. Grandmother Simon got money from him as she could, and she ran the store and put it into property in North Braddock. . . ."

| NAME | BORN | | DIED | | |
| | Date | Place | Age | Date | Place |
| --- | --- | --- | --- | --- | --- |
| Peter | 7.13.34 | Prussia | 68 | 10.20.02 | Rankin, Pa. |
| Anna (nee Dibong) | 6.16.37 | Prussia | 74 | 7.29.11* | Braddock Park, Pa. |

*Their children:*

| NAME | Date | Place | Age | Date | Place |
| --- | --- | --- | --- | --- | --- |
| †Margareta | ca.1859 | Prob. Prussia | at birth | ca.1859 | Prob. Prussia |
| †Anton | 1.17.61 | Luxembourg | 74 | 8.24.35 | Braddock, Pa. |
| †Nichola | ?1862 | ?Prussia | 7 | ?ca.1869 | ?Pennsylvania |
| †Ingel | ca.1863 | Prussia | 9 | ca.1872 | ?Turtle Creek, Pa. |
| †Albert | ?ca.1864 | ?Prussia | 4 | ?ca.1868 | ?Pennsylvania |
| Mary | 6.13.67 | Pennsylvania | 58 | 11.22.25 | Braddock, Pa. |

(=Fred Arhelger. Children: Fred Alger, 1891–1965; Marie [=John Schuster], 1899–1979)

| NAME | Date | Place | Age | Date | Place |
| --- | --- | --- | --- | --- | --- |
| Joseph | 3.16.69 | Pennsylvania | ca.65 | ?Mid-1930's | Pennsylvania |
| Peter | 10.28.72 | Turtle Creek | 40 | 1.7.13 | Michigan |
| William | 8.2.75‡ | Turtle Creek | 74 | 1.11.50 | Los Angeles, Cal. |
| Annie | 7.2.77 | Turtle Creek | ? | ? | ?California |
| Herman | ?1878 | Turtle Creek | 2 mos. | ?1878 | Turtle Creek, Pa. |
| Helena | 6.14.79* | Turtle Creek | 7½ | 1886 or 7* | Prob. Rankin, Pa. |
| Edward | 7.23.83* | Turtle Creek | 9½ | 1892 or 3* | Braddock, Pa. |

* These dates differ from those on the family grave (see p. 116). But gravestone dates are often wrong and in these cases were definitely so.

† Irresoluble doubts exist about the order of birth of these children.

‡ A tiny cloudlet of a question mark hangs over the year: though almost certainly 1875, it could just possibly be 1874. Doubt persists because on the page from the family Bible the figure for the year of Bill's birth is unclear, and because neither Bill nor Annie, unlike the other Simon children, appears in church baptism records. (No baptisms were recorded at St. Joseph's, Braddock, until August 1877. And the third pastor of St. Thomas' died in 1879 after a long and debilitating illness that had prevented him from keeping abreast of his paperwork, and his baptism records for 1874 and 1875 are incomplete and those for the next three years nonexistent.) But it would probably be unwise to undermine your trust in me by admitting even a twinge of doubt, so we had better stick solemnly and unwaveringly with 1875.

Bill's mother remains an even more shadowy character than her husband, but I did unearth one photograph of her.

My only report on parental influence exercised by Peter and Anna came
from Aunt Marie: they both worked hard at losing their German accents,
she said, and did not teach their New World children the Old World language. But then, that was—and remains—par for the immigrant course.

Nothing, of course, would have colored Bill's childhood more than the
swirling, day-by-day, I-love-you-but-goddam-him relationships with his
brothers and sisters: that would be a horizon-filling reality with long-last-
ing echoes. But the other children's characters have left little imprint on
time. I know that Mary became a strong-minded, practical woman as well
as a gossip. And the adult Peter emerges faintly from the mists. Once, in
his early days at the Wire Mill, "a hot steel rod wrapped itself around his
legs and he was badly burned." And he grew up to be "a spindly little
man, very active, who didn't live long enough to enjoy life." Essentially,
though, our only solid fact about the geometry of Bill's sibling web is that
he was lowish kid on the family totem pole.

I have now talked to many scores of people who knew Bill well as an
adult. Some of them were children at the time. Yet the only person to

whom Bill seems to have mentioned his childhood was Grace. I realize that I must not lean too heavily on this apparent reluctance of Bill to discuss his early years: received at second hand like that, it may not be real; and if real, it could have had many causes. But it raises questions. The only relevant item that Grace passed on was that he had gone to a Catholic parochial school: "He'd tell me how he didn't have any use for Catholics any more and if it hadn't been for the damned Catholics what he could have done and so forth." The suspicions this raised in my mind were fueled by the graphologist friend who examined Bill's handwriting and reported, among other things: "A man of tremendous potential. The fears caused by the pain he experienced early in life kept him from realizing all he was capable of accomplishing. . . . Somewhere along the way was made to feel inadequate and rejected."

I certainly see Bill's early years as somewhat unhappy. I do not mean miserable—or even, perhaps, very consciously unhappy. But I see an unsatisfied and puzzled child surfacing periodically to look around at a bleak world and ask quietly, "Can this be all there is?" I see him asking the question more and more often, less and less quietly—until at last, as he emerges from the chrysalis of childhood, he wanders off on his own to search for an answer.

Bill's family certainly had something to do with this state of affairs. Later in life his feelings toward them became, at best, ambivalent. And his memories of his schooling hardly seem to have been what you would call "fond." But in the end I see the wellspring of his discontent stemming from a separate element—though in his mind that element may have been inextricably connected with both school and family.

Our nests leave marks on all of us, and in Bill's case the places in which he spent his formative years would have imposed a deep and lasting imprint: all his life—clear through to the end, the very end—he was a man to whom place meant a lot. And though Turtle Creek and Braddock may not have predetermined the paths he trod, they certainly flagged these paths pretty heavily.

Bill's birthplace occupies a small but significant niche in early American history. In 1742 a certain John Frazier came west from Philadelphia and obtained a grant of several hundred acres of land from Queen Alliquippa of the Delaware tribe. The queen ruled from a royal wigwam just above the mouth of what is now called Turtle Creek, close to an old-established and important cross-country trail that followed roughly the line of today's Larimer Avenue. On his nearby land grant John Frazier built a cabin— and so became the first white settler west of the Alleghenies.

Frazier built his cabin in the same kind of rich "sylvania" that William Penn had found further east. And when Bill was born more than a century later the pastoral land outside the main valleys, which were already succumbing to the Industrial Revolution, still retained something of their original, soft, wooded richness.

Bill lived in Turtle Creek for eight years. It so happens that I lived in the place of my earliest memories for the same span. So I think I have some idea of how the adult Bill remembered Turtle Creek—an idea, I mean, of the size and shapes it retained in the layered fabric of his long-haul memory; an idea of each lingering memory's flavor. And our earliest recollections come loaded. They are among the quirky little daubs that distinguish us from each other and, in aggregate, color and so in a sense create the idiosyncratic internal world we each of us build from the reputedly objective universe.

I was lucky enough to record some firsthand impressions of how things were in Turtle Creek when it was still the coal-mining town of Bill's childhood.

Mary Sholder Yost, aged seventy-eight and affectionately known to everyone as "Grandma," had the alert and probing mind of a thirty-year-old. She had moved to Turtle Creek in 1899, aged two, and had lived there ever since.

"Oh no," she said. "The coal miners certainly weren't oppressed. Or depressed, either. Not at all. They were very proud people. Why, not one of them would wear working clothes on a Sunday, nor fix a fence, or anything like that. People were happier in those days than they are now, you know. Very happy and kind. Everybody helped everybody else." "Grandma" paused; dug for memories. "They took the kids down the mines when they had whooping cough, I remember.

"Of course, life was rougher in some ways, back then. Larimer Avenue had ruts four feet deep, so wagons would often follow the bed of the creek. When it was low, I mean. Mostly, the creek ran deeper than it does now.

"Oh no, it wasn't at all ugly. Not even when it was still all coal mining. It was a beautiful place, really. Yes, that's right, at one time there were four inclines in town." The inclines, she explained, were overhead hawsers that slanted down the hill bearing coal-laden tip cars that were operated by engines up at the mines, high above. "No, I can't actually remember No. 2 Incline. But now that you mention it, I recollect that when I was very young there were still slag heaps in the gully that ran down beside what you say was the Simon property. Heaps of coal, I mean, that had spilled out of the cars.

"Oh no, it wasn't a noisy place, either. Not noisy at all. Much quieter than now, what with all this traffic. The only noise, really, was when a load of coal came down one of the inclines and was tipped into a railroad car on the line over beyond Larimer Avenue." Mrs. Yost sat silent for a moment, listening back down the years. "And even that noise was only at the beginning of each load," she said. "As soon as the coal covered the floor of the wagon, you wouldn't hardly hear it."

And afterward, when I had let this item nod around for a while among the recollections of my own childhood in Wales, I knew that the sound of coal emptying from a tip car at the foot of No. 2 Incline into a waiting railroad car on the far side of Larimer Avenue was something that would have been imprinted on Bill's mind.

I knew it with a certainty that went far beyond having watched the sound come welling up from Mrs. Yost's seventy-year-old imprint. For a short block down the street from the house in which I lived until I was eight stood two big gray doors with writing on them. And from the cavern behind these doors—a place that we kids called "Knocksanwells"—there used to come, intermittently, a sound with a certain specific pitch and timbre and rhythm. It was an all-pervading sound—a sound you could hear, vaguely, without really registering it, whether you were indoors or out, anywhere within our little universe. I know now that this high-pitched sound with its metallic timbre and irregular rising and falling rhythm, was a circular saw, cutting lumber. I am not sure whether I knew this, fully, when we lived down the road from Knox and Wells. But I know the sound is still there in my mind, faint yet sure. It is not a bad sound or a good sound. It is just a fact sound—a sound that gets triggered up into the open, to be greeted with a small inner nod of recognition, whenever I hear a circular saw cutting lumber.

That is why I knew about Bill and the sound of coal tumbling out of a tip car into a railroad car—a sound loud at first, then tailing away as coal covered the floor of the wagon. Until he was eight, Bill lived with that sound, intermittently. It was an all-pervading sound that he could hear, indoors or out, anywhere within his Larimer Avenue universe. And whenever the adult Bill heard a similar sound—once a year, or once in five or ten years—he would greet it with a little inner nod of amused recognition, and for an expanding moment would recall the round reality of how it had felt to be a young lad in Turtle Creek, before the family moved to Braddock.

Even during the Turtle Creek days, Braddock had been a part of Bill's life—over the hill but not far away. Until St. Colman's opened in Turtle

Creek in 1882, when he was seven, he was surely carted over the hill, Sunday after Sunday, to the new St. Joseph's Church on George Street, Braddock, for interminable, incomprehensible purgatories on long, hard wooden benches.

And then, eventually, there was school.

In September 1881 there at last arrived the long-awaited, nerve-racking day on which the six-year-old Bill joined the older children on their daily pilgrimage to St. Joseph's. The small wooden school building in back of the frame church, completed only six months earlier, fostered thirty or forty children. A history of the school sheds a little light on how it was for them—including Bill:

"The desks and benches were long, with about a half dozen children sitting at each desk. . . . In the front of the room stood a large heating stove, and when cold weather came the children near the stove were uncomfortably hot, while those in the back of the room shivered beneath heavy topcoats.

"Every evening, after school, it was the duty of a few of the children to remain and sweep and dust the school room and church. Those were the days of hardship for the children, many of whom came a great distance over steep, muddy paths and roads. In the winter, many of them had to break paths through deep snowdrifts and pick their way over slippery trails."

For two years Bill was one of these stalwart foot-slogging commuters. Then, in 1883, the Simons moved to Braddock—and St. Joseph's school and church became twin poles of towering influence.

The interminable, twice-sabbathly church services, intoned in Latin, would at best have been marginally comprehensible to Bill. But St. Joseph's was the town's "German parish." Sermons there seem to have been in German. And that raises a language question—and more.

St. Joseph's was a social as well as religious and educational consortium. There were church and school picnics, for example, and a drama society. And according to the church history, the drama society's "plays and entertainments [were] given entirely in German." Even if the Simon family did not attend such performances—because they chose not to teach the children their native tongue—it is difficult to believe that Bill did not one way and another, in school and church and streets and houses, hear a lot of German spoken around Braddock. At that age, he would surely have picked up a good deal. At a guess, he knew considerably more than the *"Abend ist rot, Morgen ist gut"* that Grace remembered. It may even have been German that he spoke when he took her to the Los Angeles

"French" restaurant: Grace recalled it as "nothing like my boarding school French and the little bit I got abroad." Yet I have never heard of Bill's mentioning any command of the language to anyone. And he certainly disowned his German antecedents: he was always "French Canadian." This denial of his German roots may have carried political overtones, particularly after World War I. But it more likely reflects a rejection of everything Braddock stood for.

Municipally speaking, Bill did not actually live in Braddock. When his family moved over the hill from Turtle Creek they soon moved to Rankin, and for twenty years they lived in a house Peter had built on Baltimore Street, near the Baltimore and Ohio Railroad Station, opposite his grocery business and the Rankin Wire Works. Fire long ago consumed both store and wire works. Although there is today no railroad station, not even a Baltimore Street, it was in Bill's time a busy place. It stood just within Rankin's city limits, but it was less than a mile down Braddock Avenue from St. Joseph's church and school. So throughout the years Bill lived there, Braddock remained the core of his life. And those years—1883 to 1891—saw him grow from eight to sixteen.

Braddock—a modern name contracted progressively from "The Field of Braddock's Defeat," "Braddock's Field," and "Braddock's"—was then a new town. "In 1850," says a local history, "the Monongahela at Braddock's Field rolled through a quiet scene of sylvan beauty. Thickly wooded hills shaded her peaceful waters on the south, while on the Braddock side long grassy swards dipped to the river's brim.

"The low land along the river, now filled in with cinder, ash and slag, and usurped by belching steel plants, was the home of the bullfrog and the meadowlark, while on a summer's night a thousand glow worms swung their lanterns in the swamp land and gave the first faint prophesy of the myriad electric arcs that later were to change night into day upon that ground. . . .

"But not for Braddock was the lure of green fields and running waters. Hers was to be a life of action and achievement, hers was no Lotus land of dreams. Already the faint tapping of a hammer and musical song of a distant saw-mill come at intervals on the quiet air: her industrial history is beginning. . . ."

About 1865—the year the Simons and Naus arrived—three coal mines opened on the hill up which there now climbs the street called, very explicably, Coalmont. Soon, pits were operating as far out as Turtle Creek—and giving Bill's father an early American living. But what transformed the scene was not coal but "the most wonderful system of iron

works the world has ever known." Beside the Monongahela, at the mouth
of Turtle Creek—on land granted to John Frazier 130 years earlier by
Queen Alliquippa, and in fact on the very site of his log cabin—Andrew
Carnegie built the huge Edgar Thomson Steel Works. They opened the
month Bill was born.

Bill and the steel works arrived at the end of the greatest burst of business development America had ever known. Soon, Pittsburgh was called
"Smoky City."

The local history book—published in 1917 but looking at a world essentially unchanged since Bill's childhood—reports the transformation:

"Far indeed is the Braddock of today from the Braddock of 1850. Silent
is the kingfisher and the bobolink, gone are the green fields, the shady
groves, and running brooks. . . . The city's natural life is a spasm of human
effort, and the thunder of her forges marks her heart beats. All day the
clang of steel assails the ear, and at night a hundred lurid flames set up the
pillar of fire that is the core of Pittsburgh's Steel district, itself the steel
center of the world . . ."

In those days, "Braddock had much the aspect of a Western Mining
Camp. Women seldom went on Braddock Avenue on Saturday night.
Street fighting seemed to be a favorite and universal diversion." The community therefore became a cockpit for whose soul God and the Devil
fought cross and horn: at the mouth of the Edgar Thomson Steel Works,
the downtown strip, thirteen blocks by four, embraced forty-eight
churches (including St. Joseph's) and eighty-nine bars that ran "full blast
twenty-four hours in the day."

This, then, was the setting for Bill's daily commutes to St. Joseph's and
for the short, tentative, wing-strengthening walks that the fledgling wanderer made along gray but bustling streets and also, I am convinced, into
green, bordering backways.

Yet perhaps the heaviest legacy that Braddock laid on Bill was not this
ever-present nineteenth-century setting but a theme that thumps through
its early history—from back before it became "the home of . . . the meadowlark," from back before white settlers cleared meadows for the mead-
owlarks, from back when the whole Monongahela Valley was forest, was
wilderness.

"The Battle of the Wilderness" is another name for "Braddock's Defeat"—the famous military engagement that took place on the site of modern Braddock. Some authorities attribute heavy historical significance to
the battle; but that is not why I see it as casting a tenuous yet also fundamental shadow across the history of William Anthony Simon.

The engagement occurred more than a century before Bill was born, but he certainly knew all about it. There is a long tradition, remembered by the oldest living Sisters of Divine Providence—the order that has been running St. Joseph's since Bill was nine—that its students were taught not only the story of Braddock's Defeat but also its relationship to the town in which they lived. In addition, the school stood on the site of the battle's focus. And just across the railroad tracks from the church stands a commemorative monument, surmounted by a statue of its most famous survivor.

The battle took place on July 9, 1755. That morning, a column of about 1,400 British regulars and Virginia militia crossed the Monongahela River near the log cabin that John Frazier had built a dozen years earlier, on land granted by Queen Alliquippa. The General-in-Chief of His Majesty's Forces in America, General Edward Braddock, commanded the column. His aide-de-camp and colonial adviser was a certain Lieutenant Colonel George Washington, aged twenty-three. And driving one of the column's thirty-four wagons was a youth whose name would also go into the history books: Daniel Boone.

Braddock's objective was Fort Duquesne, recently built by the French at the junction of the Allegheny and Monongahela rivers, where Pittsburgh would soon grow: the British saw Duquesne and other forts as threats to their claimed sovereignty over the Ohio Valley. To make the hauling of the expedition's wagons and heavy guns possible, the column's pioneer battalion of axmen had already hewn a crude road—"a twelve foot clearing between green ramparts"—through more than a hundred miles of primeval wilderness.

When the column forded the Monongahela that sunlit July morning, Duquesne lay only seven miles ahead, and it promised to be a sitting duck for the expedition's eight cannon and four howitzers. As a member of the column later wrote: "[We] hugged [ourselves] with joy at our good luck in having surmounted our greatest difficultys & too hastily concluded the enemy never wou'd dare oppose us."

The column's fording of the Monongahela was an act that would rumble down the future, and the young George Washington, in spite of a fever—or perhaps because of his fever—may have caught a faint pre-echo. Late in life he would recall the sight: "Scarlet-coated regulars and blue-coated Virginians in columns of four, mounted officers and light cavalry, horse-drawn artillery and wagons, and dozens of packhorses, splashed through the rippling shallows under a brilliant summer sun into the green-clothed forest." It was, said the mature Washington, the most beautiful spectacle he had ever seen.

The beauty would not last, even in the short haul.

Beyond the Monongahela, the column looped around John Frazier's cabin, then angled up and away from the river, through what is now the Edgar Thomson Steel Works. Behind a small vanguard, the axmen continued to hew the twelve-foot clearing between green ramparts. By noon the rearguard was across the ford. When the vanguard had reached a point that Washington estimated as "about six hundred perches," or two miles, from the river, it entered a narrow defile—a defile that would later house the Pennsylvania Railroad's Copeland Station, where Bill's young brother Edward would fall and be killed. In the defile, the forest thinned and became, says a contemporary account, "free from underwood . . . so open that carridges could have been drove in any part of it." And there, with the suddenly pleasant landscape no doubt reinforcing the vanguard's overconfidence, the enemy sprang an ambush.

The combined force of French and Indians attacked first from a hill off to the left—the hill on which the name "Nau" would, two centuries later, come double-barreling out at me from door and mailbox. The vanguard, caught by surprise, fell back into denser forest down the twelve-foot-wide swath—and erupted in panic among the main body, which was hurrying up to help. Meanwhile, the enemy had fanned out into a broad "U" that enveloped the column. Soon they began pouring musket fire into the mass of milling bodies.

For more than two hours the British and colonial troops held their ground—"with little or no order, but endeavoring to make fronts toward ye enemies fire." Throughout those two hours of midday heat, their flanks were harried by "French and Indians skulking behind trees." The lower flank of the milling mass of trapped soldiery lay along a line that the Pennsylvania Railroad would later take, a dozen yards above St. Joseph's church and school.

During the two hours of bloody confusion, General Braddock fell mortally wounded. Soon afterward the main body withdrew in a "retreat [that] was full of confusion and hurry." Of the column's original 1,459 officers and men, 977 had been killed or wounded. The survivors withdrew to Philadelphia.

The military setback proved temporary: three years later, the British captured Fort Duquesne and secured the Ohio Valley. But some authorities regard Braddock's Defeat as carrying heavy historical significance because of its impact on the mind of the young George Washington. It seems that during the engagement and retreat his Virginia militiamen, operating under conditions familiar to them, fought far more valiantly than the British regulars; and that disastrous afternoon in the forest seems to have convinced Washington that his militiamen were, at least in certain circumstances, more than the equal of British redcoats. This conviction became crucial to history when, twenty years later, he took command of the combined colonial militiamen—now called the Continental Army.

But Braddock's Defeat left another, larger, even more lasting historical legacy.

The beauty George Washington saw that fateful morning—the beauty of green-clothed forest bathed in clear summer sunlight—would not last in the long haul, either.

In a sense, the hundred-mile-long, twelve-foot-wide swath that the axmen had hewn through Pennsylvania's green, primeval wilderness had, by inducing Braddock's surprised and demoralized troops to huddle within its confines, led to the military defeat. But it also led to a great deal more. It became known as "Braddock's Road." Soon it was being used for Indian raids. Later it developed into a highway for the western migration that would lead—step by inevitable step, from Indian raider through home-steading immigrant and Andrew Carnegie—to Pittsburgh and Braddock and the Edgar Thomson Steel Works.

When I suggested that Braddock's Defeat cast a shadow across the history of William Anthony Simon, I did not of course mean only that he was taught the story of Defeat and Road in the St. Joseph's schoolroom. He learned deeper and surer lessons outside. And I do not mean only from the commemorative monument, just across the railroad tracks, with its statue of the young George Washington. It may well have been at the monument, though, or close by, that Bill learned his deeper lessons.

Beside the railroad tracks, a dozen yards above St. Joseph's, there grows today a little thicket of rather stunted trees and bushes, and among them fireflies sometimes dance. I made this discovery late on one of my warm June evenings in Braddock. Now fireflies have always spelled magic for me. And as I stood waist-deep in the pulsating carpet of aery mini-lanterns I found myself transported into a world of the kind you rarely enter once you have passed through the eye of the needle called puberty, and I saw, suddenly and clearly, that even in the Braddock of the 1880's—even in the gray, blinkered, unmagical, industrial artifact that had overrun the land—there would be green sanctuaries a boy could escape to. Soft, leafy places that in summer daylight gave coolness and shadow and birdsong and silence. Dark, leafy places that on warm summer evenings might suddenly stage magic firefly dances. Places that a certain kind of boy would go to dream—and so, unknowing, "learn" his lessons and plot out his life.

Note "unknowing." Because I came to understand the grown man, I find it difficult to avoid the conclusion that young Bill sat and dreamed in such Braddock places—perhaps among those very trees and bushes; dreamed, as I did, of other trees that had grown there a century earlier— thicker, healthier trees among which French and Indians skulked as they volleyed musket balls into Braddock's demoralized column. Such dreams could have sparked Bill's lifelong fascination with war. But I doubt that at the time, still chained to Braddock, he "knew" the deeper lessons he had learned. After all, he was, at most, fifteen or sixteen. But he was puzzled and unsatisfied. When he stood back and contemplated the Edgar Thomson Steel Works and its tailings—the "pillar of fire," the pall of smoke, the forty-eight churches and eighty-nine bars and all the sprawling gray bleakness—he surely asked, more and more often, "Can this be all there is?"

The lessons we are taught in youth often lie dormant for years. Bill may not, at sixteen, have understood the connection between the Edgar Thomson Steel Works and what it had replaced: the "green-clothed for- est" of Washington's primeval wilderness, with "rippling shallows under a brilliant summer sun." He may not even have known about the "long grassy swards [that] dipped to the river's brim," "home of the bullfrog and the meadowlark," where on warm summer nights "a thousand glow worms swung their lanterns"—and moved toward becoming fireflies. But the broad history of his nest surely worked on him. The germ of under- standing had been planted. It would lie there, waiting. And a quarter of a century later, at a cusp in Bill's life, it would germinate and burst into full flower. The child is father to the man.

"I FIGURE he was only sixteen or seventeen when he set out for the first time," Aunt Marie had said.

She was probably right.

I have certainly detected hints that the spring of 1893—which found Bill a few months past his seventeenth birthday—was a likely moment for him to have attained traveler's puberty and abandoned himself, big, to wanderlust.

A growing and growingly unsatisfied child would probably have seen life in Braddock of the late 1880's and early 1890's mostly as an ongoing disaster. Even a cursory glance at history reveals events that would in their various ways have reverberated around Braddock with cumulative and depressing effect.

Industry was already exhibiting simple, natural flaws. The morning of June 1, 1889, brought news from barely fifty miles away that a wave of water from a broken dam had swept through Johnstown, another steel town, with huge loss of life. And industrial labor relations of that time were hardly a feather bed. In 1887, when Bill was twelve, twenty leaders of the Molly McGuires—a secret organization of Irishmen dedicated to combating oppressive industrial conditions by violent means—had been hanged. On July 6, 1892, across the river in Homestead, where the Nau cousins lived, a 143-day holdout at the Carnegie Steel Works culminated in the arrival of two hundred Pinkerton detectives—and riots in which seven men were killed and twenty or more wounded; to restore order, the governor sent in the entire state militia; afterward, Henry C. Frick reduced wages and re-established an eighty-four-hour week. Economically, boom still alternated with bust. And that spring when Bill was seventeen there began the Panic of 1893 that would plunge the whole country, very much including Braddock, into a deep four-year depression.

Meanwhile, the Simon family had suffered its own disasters. And Bill, because of his age, perhaps suffered more than others. In those days, barely 50 percent of children lived beyond the age of ten; but when his sister Helena died at seven and a half he was eleven or twelve, and the bereavement may have left indelible scars. Edward's death came without warning: older boys had coaxed him into riding home on a boxcar, Aunt Marie told me, to save the walk; "but Eddie fell down between cars and the last car hit him and just caved his skull in." The second fragment of poetry pasted onto the back cover of the Simon Bible attests to the family's desolation—or at least to the mother's. She almost certainly did not compose the poem; but she copied it out, probably from memory, in her characteristic Gothic-script hand. Insofar as poems are translatable, it reads:

*He died, oh died, too soon for us,*
*Too soon for all who loved him,*
*And bitterly we weep for him,*
*Weep bitterly before his grave.*
*In pain and suffering he died;*
*And now we wish him quiet sleep*
*Until that hour we meet again—*
*When all in triumph rise.*

Edward died in late 1892 or early 1893. Bill was seventeen. It is difficult to visualize him as anything but emotionally mutilated.

Around about that time, too, he had begun working—as had all his brothers, at their due moments—in the Rankin Wire Mill, across the tracks from the house on Baltimore Street. But Bill "wouldn't knuckle down like the rest of the boys," Aunt Marie had said. "They couldn't keep him at home."

No wonder.

One way and another, then, the spring of 1893 seems a singularly apt season for Bill to have escaped from Braddock and all it stood for: the huge, gaunt, belching Edgar Thomson Steel Works that had always been there, down at the end of Braddock Avenue; its smaller cousin, the Rankin Wire Mill, that had always been there across the tracks from home but had now become a daily prison; all the mean gray streets and mean, money-grubbing horizons; and other things, too.

Anyway, whatever the year and whatever the agents provocateurs, Bill took off.

# 9 First Wanderings

THE YOUNG MAN went west—at once, or soon after.

Given his times and his character, it was written.

His times, alone, practically dictated the move. Horace Greeley was just twenty years dead, and the West still empty enough to suck up like a vacuum cleaner any wanderer with "the old American idea that all mistakes are canceled by the horizon, by more room, by moving out." Come to think of it, this is by no means an exclusively American idea: it has been acted on by whole bunches of us from Prussia and South Wales and a hundred other once-green valley-lands of the planet.

The character of the new-fledged wanderer went with the flow. At seventeen, Bill must have been, in embryo, the man he would become, the man I would come to know well: dreamer, star follower, flower child before his time; above all, foot-loose fantasist to whom the grass on the far side of almost any fence looked irresistibly greener.

There was also, I eventually discovered, a specific westering magnet in his family.

With one exception though, the places the wanderer went and the things he did during his first five post-Braddock years are now unpinnable.

According to Aunt Marie, Bill kept returning to Braddock. And that fits his later pattern: he always tended to establish bases, wander far and wide, then return for a spell. Grace recollected that Bill "worked on the Harriman railroad"; but the Panic of 1893 brought a temporary halt to railroad construction, and Edward Harriman did not begin his western railroading until 1898, when the economic recovery had begun. So if Bill indeed worked on the railroads he did so, at least principally, in later years.

But the railroads almost certainly transported him: in those pre-comfort-at-any-cost days, they were "the only way to go." For that was the heyday of the "hoboes."

The urge to hobo, according to one authority, "had its place in the American dream: to keep on the move, to stay independent, to scorn security and routine. [But] the heroic image of the free, self-sufficient 'knight of the road' was very different from the facts." Typically, these "Weary Willies" and "Tired Tims," "who added a picturesque feature to the countryside like the Gypsies of old, . . . roamed the northern part of the country, catching rides on freight trains, stealing or begging their food, and spending cold winters in local jails." I like to picture Bill adopting only the best folkways of this popular public transportation system. That may be mere wishful thinking. But the experience can hardly have failed to educate him about his fellow men. And it showed him for the first time, from the doors and roofs and perhaps even undercarriages of freight trains, the wide plains and towering mountains of the West.

Of all the things he learned on those plains and in those mountains, none was to bear more heavily on his life than what he found in a western place I am almost sure he visited at least once sometime before 1898.

Aunt Marie had mentioned Bill's Uncle Tony—his father's brother, who had been one of "the whole bunch" that crossed the Atlantic together and whom Aunt Annie had been visiting in Colorado when she fell on the way up Pike's Peak and broke her arm. Tony, said Aunt Marie, was a mining prospector who had been "murdered by his wife" in the early 1900's. At the time, I had wondered whether he could be Bill's link with Twin Lakes, Lake County, Colorado—the town Bill gave as his birthplace on all his army enlistments. When Twin Lakes turned out to be only seventy miles from Pike's Peak and to have been served by a railroad after 1888, I set about trying to establish an Uncle Tony connection.

From a mortuary in the county seat of Leadville I eventually obtained the death certificate of an Anton Simon, a white married male aged sixty-eight who on March 6, 1909, had been "found dead in bed with obstruction of bowel and peritonitis." Most other details fitted Bill's Uncle Tony: occupation, miner; father and mother both born in Germany. His birthplace, given as Pennsylvania, seemed like an understandable error. And the natural death did not necessarily mean I had the wrong man: the "murder" could well be lurid family folklore. Anton Simon was buried in Leadville in a single-grave space of a kind "usually reserved for single persons with no family ties in the region, but *not* a potter's field." Tax records and deeds and other documents suggested that he had come to Twin

Lakes quite on his own. But funeral records showed an expense of one dollar for "Telegram to Mrs. Simon and telephone."

The informant listed as supplying the details on Anton's death certificate was a certain George Lane of Leadville, and I managed to talk on the phone with two of his sons.

Teddy Lane, now seventy-four, had been seven when Anton died. All he could remember was that he had been "a nice old gentleman and us kids all liked him."

Harry Lane, now eighty-eight but with mind and memory sharp as yesterday, had been twenty-one when Anton Simon died. "Oh, yes, I knew him well. He was a hell of a good guy. How did he look? Well, he was short and heavyset. Weighed maybe a hundred and sixty or seventy pounds. And he stood up straight and had a brisk walk to him. Sometimes he grew bushy gray whiskers and sometimes he'd shave them off.

"You're right, he must have been born in Germany, not Pennsylvania, because he talked pretty broken English and him and my father used to talk for hours in German. They'd often go off prospecting together—they had a gold mine, one time, up in Eagle County, with an ore mill, and I spent a summer up there."

By this time I felt fairly sure I had the right man. And when I began to describe Aunt Annie's trip, Harry Lane broke in: "Yes, that's right—I heard about some trip up Pike's Peak when a niece of Anton's from back East fell and broke something. I remember it as a leg, though, not an arm. . . . And Anton talked about a nephew from Pittsburgh, too. I'm not sure of the name. . . . Yes, it could have been Bill—or Jack. Come to think of it, the nephew had been badly burned in the steel mill when some rods wrapped themselves around his legs."

"Oh, that was Peter, Bill's brother," I said.

"That's right, Peter. Or Pete. I remember now. Sure, there could have been another nephew, too. And he could well have visited with Anton earlier. I was just a kid back then, you know."

When Anton Simon died, Harry Lane had just been married for the first time and he bought the house Anton had lived and died in. A pretty nice little house it was, and still much the way it had been when Anton lived there. Twin Lakes hadn't changed too much either. Back then, it was just a little mining town with a population of maybe five or six hundred where everybody knew everybody. But even in those days it had been a tourist place in a small way: it was on the main road to Aspen and had good fishing around about. Unfortunately, I wasn't likely to find anyone else who had known Anton. Just about all the old-timers were dead now.

No, Anton's wife had not come into the sale of the house. It wasn't in her name. Hell no, nothing at all to the murder story. She was definitely not there when Anton died. He was just found dead in bed. No, he couldn't recall her name. They were married a couple of years at most; then she left him and went back to the Black Hills in South Dakota.

"The Black Hills?"

"Yes, she was a waitress at Holt's Hotel."

"A waitress?"

"Yes."

"In a restaurant?"

"In a hotel restaurant. Holt's Hotel, in Twin Lakes. That's where Anton met her. He used to hang out there when he went into town. Oh no, he was no heavy drinker. Maybe an occasional beer, like on the Fourth of July, but that's all. I never saw him in a saloon. The hotel? Well, it became Andersen's for a while, but it's been gone these twenty-five years."

"And she was a waitress there?"

"Yes, and he married her."

And after I put down the phone it was the waitress story that hung in my mind, sharp and edged—the story of a shadowy waitress who had become Uncle Anton's wife and then left him. Uncle Anton, obviously, had meant more than I knew. Had meant more to Bill, I mean. So it was indeed no accident that Bill had chosen Twin Lakes as his fictitious birthplace for army purposes. He had chosen it, I felt sure, because at least once and probably more often during his five years of wandering before he joined the Army in 1898, he had visited his Uncle Anton. His Uncle Anton who was short and sturdy. His Uncle Anton who sometimes wore a beard and sometimes shaved it off. His Uncle Anton who liked kids and was liked by them. His Uncle Anton who was "a hell of a good guy." His Uncle Anton who probably went to Colorado in the 1870's, when it had a big mining boom and who spent a lot of his time back in the hills, prospecting. His Uncle Anton who lived a life that was the very antithesis of the lives being lived by the rest of the family the impressible young Bill had left back in Braddock. His Uncle Anton who above all had married a waitress who soon done him wrong. His Uncle Anton who, I now saw, had stamped himself on young Bill's mind almost like a template, so that a description of the uncle fitted, word for word, many descriptions I had by that time heard of the later Bill Simon.

I sat looking at the now silent phone.

Uncle Anton of Twin Lakes had loomed large in Bill's life—had, whether Bill knew it or not, become an enduring dream. It was even possible that the "facts" about Bill's having married a waitress in Seattle might turn out to have their roots in Colorado. That whole story could be a fantasy that Bill had built, with typical embroidery, around his model, his template.

I smiled at the phone.

And I had just been lucky enough to stumble on what was probably the last remaining record that connected these fantasy-facts—a record imprinted in the bright, untarnished memory of a remarkable, eighty-eight-year-old man who lived a thousand miles from Seattle. Clearly, a serendipitous anti-Murphy Law indeed governed my sleuthings.

Until that moment I had assumed that in trying to pin down Bill's life I was chasing facts. But now I saw that I must also look for his fantasies—or for what might, in poetic cases, be more fittingly called "dreameries." They might not crop up too often, but I must keep my eyes open, always.

For a while I worried about the apparent incompatibility between the Uncle Anton fantasy and Bill's fundamental honesty. But a psychiatrist friend reassured me. "Oh, that's very common," he said. "A person who's totally honest in everyday life will often embroider stories and indulge in extravagant, way-out fantasies." And another friend said, "Oh yes, some people seem to prefer living lives of fantasy rather than fact—in part, anyway." It is probably a matter of degree. I guess none of us lives a reality constructed solely of raw fact, unrelieved by fantasies that color our lives and make them bearable.

Now I may seem to have had very little evidence on which to base the sweeping assumptions I made about Bill and his Uncle Anton. Certainly, such sudden glimpses of "truth" do not always hold up. Time often undermines them. It can do so overnight. But once the notion of Bill's Uncle Anton fantasy had struck me, it stuck. I still see no reason to doubt it.


MY FIRST fully pinnable, post-Braddock, footloose-years fact—and the earliest written evidence of an Uncle Anton fantasy—is dated May 9, 1898. That was the day Bill first joined the Army.

By enlisting, he crossed a threshold. He closed the door on five years of apparently unfettered wandering and at the age of twenty-two stepped into a checkered, intermittent, ten-year soldiering career.

# 10 The Army

WHEN HE ENLISTED, that second Monday in May, Bill was flowing with the tide of the hour.

Two weeks earlier, President McKinley had formally declared war against Spain. The following weekend, Commodore Dewey had sailed into Manila Bay and "without losing a single man had reduced the Spanish fleet to junk." His victory raised to fever pitch the patriotic fervor of "a nation more nearly unanimous than in any war in her history." Under banners proclaiming "Free Cuba!" "bands crashed out the chords of Sousa's 'Stars and Stripes Forever,' and everyone sang 'There'll Be a Hot Time in the Old Town Tonight'." Congress authorized a volunteer army, 200,000 strong, for what the Secretary of State would soon call "the splendid little war." Clear across the country, young men flocked to the colors.

Bill enlisted in Mobile, Alabama, probably because he was visiting his father—who at that time, Aunt Marie had said, was "very sick with painter's colic and couldn't stand the climate in Rankin . . . and used to spend a lot of time in Mobile." If Bill indeed visited his father—and one entry in his enlistment papers gives his residence as Mobile and his mileage to place of rendezvous as zero—the meeting seems to have gone badly. It was not uncommon at that time for enlistees to give false names and backgrounds, but Bill's papers hint at a rejection of the father in favor of the uncle. He enlisted as Anthony William Simmons. That is, he not only changed the family name but also switched his given names so that the uncle's came first. And he fictionalized his birthplace to Twin Lakes, Colorado.

Bill signed on to serve "for the term of two years from date of enrollment, unless sooner discharged," and quickly became a private soldier in

Company C of the 2nd Regiment of Alabama Volunteer Infantry.

For seven weeks the regiment remained in Mobile, presumably training. During those weeks, an American expedition assembled in Florida and waited for the tropical Caribbean rains to end. On June 27, the day after that expedition finally got ashore in Cuba and stood ready to march on Santiago, where the Spanish fleet lay, Bill's regiment left Mobile and covered "a total distance of 1185 miles in 62½ hours, arriving at Miami, Fla., at 2:30 p.m., June 30, 1898." They went "into Camp at a point about one mile from Miami."

That Thursday evening in the new camp, anticipation must have run high among the eager volunteers. With luck, they would be in Cuba within a week.

But events were moving fast. Next day, Teddy Roosevelt's Rough Riders charged up San Juan Hill. By evening the Americans commanded heights from which they could bombard Santiago and the Spanish fleet. On Sunday morning that fleet tried to escape through the U.S. Navy's blockade—and was destroyed. The war was virtually over. Two weeks later, Santiago surrendered. July 30, McKinley dictated the peace terms.

By August 4, sickness was so rampant among army units in Cuba and in camps back in the United States—largely due to poor sanitation practices (5,462 men died during the war, but only 379 in battle)—that the Cuban force was ordered withdrawn, and certain home camps closed. On that date, the 2nd Alabama Volunteers left Miami by rail at 1:30 p.m., "arrived at Jacksonville, Fla., at 6:30 p.m., August 5/98, covering a distance of 366 miles," and encamped at "Camp Cuba Libra."

This final and irrevocable withdrawal from what had seemed the very brink of combat must have left its mark on the men. And you should not underestimate the sincerity or depth of their frustration. It seems to be a fact, like it or not, that a man who has engaged in military combat to his own reasonable satisfaction finds a big monkey taken off his back. He is freed from a load he did not even know about: now, if he so chooses, he can quit worrying about the gallantry crap and get on with other things. But a man who has lived through a war and for some reason has failed to get into combat is liable—especially if he has tried like hell and been thwarted on the brink—to suffer for the rest of his life submerged feelings of possible masculine inadequacy.

You can, with a little out-on-a-limb imagination, detect a letdown and possible need to prove something in the sub-glorious recorded deeds of Private Anthony W. Simmons during his stay in Camp Cuba Libra, Jacksonville. August 9–11 he was sick with malaria. August 16 and 17 he suffered acute diarrhea. August 19—one week after the signing of the Peace Protocol—he went AWOL for three days and was fined one dollar.

A month later the company returned to Mobile and went on thirty days' furlough. October 31, it was "mustered out," or disbanded. Bill's service had been "honest and faithful."

Except for his presence in Braddock as a witness at sister Annie's wedding in April 1899—a presence confirmed by papers from the family Bible that Mrs. Gross had sent me—no record remains of Bill's doings during the civilian interlude that followed. But seven and a half months after his discharge, he re-enlisted.

The Treaty of Paris that formally ended the Spanish-American War ceded the Philippines to the United States. But Emilio Aguinaldo, the young insurrectionist leader the United States had supported against Spain, had already declared the islands independent. In February he began a revolt against U.S. rule with a fierce but unsuccessful attack on Manila. In March, Congress passed an act authorizing more volunteers to fight the insurrection. And on July 13, in Harrisburg, Pennsylvania, Bill joined a unit being formed under that act.

Now Bill was, a later friend told me, "very patriotic." That may have been his prime reason for re-enlisting. In addition, he may have decided that there was something attractive about army life—at least when seen from the civilian side of the fence; and also that in the insurrection he could resolve, after all, his frustration at having been denied the chance to prove himself in combat. But he may also have been trying to put distance between himself and his family. For this time he gave Twin Lakes, Colorado, as residence as well as birthplace, and as next of kin he nominated not his mother but Peter Nau of Homestead.

He re-enlisted "for the period ending June 30, 1901, unless discharged sooner by proper authority "—and so began the army tour that although not his longest was certainly the best documented and probably the most significant.

In Harrisburg he was assigned to Company E of the 28th U.S. Volunteer Infantry. Within three weeks he had been promoted to sergeant, and two months later the company entrained for California. The eight-day journey carried Bill along a route that echoed and pre-echoed. The train passed through Pittsburgh and also Denver, Colorado—terminus of the railroad that served nearby Twin Lakes; and Bill's company commander concluded his monthly Record of Events with the words: "On train near Winnemucca, Nevada, midnight September 30. Health of company good. Discipline good."

After three weeks in the San Francisco Presidio the company embarked on the U.S. Army transport *Tartar* at the Folsom Street Wharf and on "Thursday, October 26, 1899, at eleven a.m. . . . steamed out to sea." For the first recorded time, Bill had wandered beyond his native shores. He went aboard a military transport—the way I would also travel the first time I wandered from mine.

Except for a two-day stopover in Honolulu, where the ships received coal and the troops "were taken off and exercised"—just as I took off and exercised when my civilian ship made a two-day stopover there, the year before I found the cave—the voyage seems to have been your standard, rhythmic, open-sea procession. It lasted a month. On Wednesday, November 22, "at 6:30 p.m., [after] traveling 6832 miles by water," the *Tartar* sailed past Corregidor and dropped anchor in the Manila Bay that Commodore Dewey had eighteen months earlier rendered safe for Americans. Bill had finally arrived in a theater of war. With enemy-held mountains looming close to starboard he must have felt that at last he stood on the brink of combat.

But Aguinaldo's battered army had just switched from pitched battles to guerrilla warfare, and Bill's 28th Volunteer Infantry, after "marching 12 miles by water," hunkered down for what turned out to be six weeks of inaction in Bacoor, south of Manila. Two days before Christmas—when only four of the six weeks had passed—divisional special orders carried this paragraph: "Sergeant Anthony W. Simmons Company E 28th Infantry U.S.V. is detailed on special duty, as overseer, to have charge of native laborers, unloading cascoes and handling public property, and will report without delay to Captain W. M. Elkin, Brigade Quartermaster. . . . By command of Colonel Birkhimer."

The first discernible result of this posting was, when it ended, to place Bill in an invidious position.

He spent almost two months with the Q.M.'s department, while the century turned. Presumably he oversaw Filipinos as they unloaded cascoes—big, flat-bottomed, bargelike boats fitted with outriggers. But two weeks after he left his company it "took the field with [an] expeditionary force under General Wheaton through Southern Luzon." At least one platoon had its baptism of fire. Others brushed with the enemy. And the entire company covered a lot of ground under threat of attack. When Bill at last rejoined them on February 19, 1900, they were resting "in vacated houses" after a three-day, sixty-nine-mile march.

It must have been a delicate moment for Bill. He remained green and untried. But he was back in charge of men now five weeks toughened and

practiced—and no doubt pretty damned pleased with themselves. A good
NCO could cope; but he would need character.

For three weeks the company rested. Then, at 6 a.m. on March 6, they
moved again—into the mountains that had loomed south of the *Tartar*
when she dropped anchor. Two days later they marched into the plaza of
the coastal town of Nasugbu, having covered "40 miles over very rough
trails."

In Nasugbu the company rested, then began to probe back into the
mountains in a series of the patrols or "scouts" that would form the core of
the company's role. The first two scouts netted an insurgent company
commander and twenty-seven of his men. Then, on April 7, Bill's company commander led an innocent-sounding little foray back into the
mountains: "Captain Coasmun with small detachment from Co.'s E, F and
G left camp at dark on scout to vicinity of Utud and Tubingen . . . to
search for arms of the Insurgent Company . . . returned to camp 5 p.m. on
the 8th. Distance traveled 14 miles." Bill went on that scout. And I am
sure he never forgot a moment of pain and humiliation in an enclosed,
dimly lit place. For when the party returned to camp on the 8th, Bill was
admitted into the hospital with "severe incised wound of back, center right
of spinal column. . . . Accidentally injured by falling on stake while
searching Filipino house for arms, April 7."

For three weeks Bill languished "sick in quarters." The company's
quarters at that time were "Conical Wall Tents which are elevated three
feet from the ground and placed upon bamboo floors which were built by
natives at a cost of four dollars per tent, the expense being borne by the
men who occupy the tent."

Bill returned to duty the day the company moved a few miles south, into
old Spanish barracks in the town of Balayan. They were to spend six
months quartered in those barracks. Throughout those months they
mounted scouts back into the mountains.

The scouts covered rough terrain. One difficulty was that Filipino dogs
always barked when the Americans approached a village, no matter how
silently they moved. And although engagements became increasingly rare,
the patrols had to be on the alert, every minute, against surprise attack.
Not all the patrols were peaceful, either. On one three-day, seventy-five-
mile patrol in mid-June, a party from Bill's company, led by Captain
Coasmun, "met the enemy near Presna, 3 miles from Liau and in slight
skirmish routed them. No casualties. Reported by the natives 6 of the
enemy killed and 12 wounded. Sent in 7 prisoners." Bill may or may not
have been present.

Most of these operations were pure foot-sloggery. An exception was one in which Bill definitely took part. "July 12, Lt. Porter, Sgts. Simmons and McDonald with 37 men left Qrs. at 11 p.m. Proceeded to Taal [on far side of Balayan Bay] via Gunboat to reinforce garrison at that place, arriving at Taal at 1:45 a.m. Bivouacked for the night on Taal side of Lemery Bridge. Morning of 13th assigned to Qrs. in church." Four days later, the detachment went on a normal, foot-slogging scout. It "accompanied expedition under Capt. Bickham via Gunboat to Jno Jno and proceeded towards Taal passing through several small barrios and bivouacked for night in small barrio in the mountains where captured one Mauser rifle and 100 rds. Ammunition and several bolos. . . ."

Bill's discharge papers credit him with having "participated in scouts 36 days on island of Luzon in 1900." Even if you deduct five calendar days for the first two forays from Nasugbu—on the second of which he fell on the stake in the Filipino hut—then Bill went on scouts on thirty-one days out of Balayan. Yet the total number of days the company spent on scouts from Balayan amounted to no more than forty; and since its contribution often consisted only of an officer and half-a-dozen men, part of a multi-company detachment, no individual would have been expected to go on each of the forty days' scouting. That makes Bill, at the very least, a veritable workhorse of a sergeant. So his officers clearly held him in high regard: you do not select a weak NCO to go on so many combat missions. It therefore seems safe to say that Bill overcame his early setbacks and won his spurs.

This conclusion is reinforced by the number of times he features in the company Record of Events. The names of six sergeants appear, and Bill, with five mentions—which, significantly, grow more frequent toward the end of the campaign—ranks second. Also, the top-ranker and Bill and the quartermaster sergeant are the only senior NCO's not named in a burial party for two men, probably from another company, who had been killed in combat near Balayan—and a burial party is just the sort of duty you would spare your workhorse combat NCO's.

By the time the company left Balayan, then, it seems that Bill had proved himself—to his officers' satisfaction, and probably to his own. And I have caught one glimpse of the kind of NCO he was, or at least liked to think he had been. Thirty years later, he told a friend about a private who said he would "beat the shit out of" Bill if he had not got those stripes on his arm. Bill, by his own account, took off his coat, said "Now I'm a private," and duly beat the shit out of the insubordinate subordinate.

It is clear that these operations in which Bill won his combat spurs were, though strenuous, not hideously hazardous. Company E's reports for the entire Philippine campaign mention only six American casualties—two killed and four wounded, all in a single engagement—and even they seem to have been members of another unit to which a few men from the company had been attached. Their scouts did the job, though; as the weeks passed, the company made less and less contact with the enemy.

The fight against disease was being won, too. The company had learned the lesson of the Cuban campaign. Its records, especially at the beginning, stress health precautions: "The company still continues to use boiled water for drinking purposes and the number of Sick has been very small. The company has dug a well which affords an abundance of clear pure water." There was some sickness, of course. From May through August, Bill himself was hospitalized three times with malaria, three or four days each time, and once, for ten days, with "diarrhoea, acute." But thereafter he stayed healthy.

In other words, the insurrection was no apocalypse. And the six months Bill spent at Balayan turned out to be the worst of it.

In late October his company moved to Los Banos, north of Manila, but after a restful month there was rushed back to Manila and boarded the transport *Garonne*, ready to sail south to the unsubdued island of Mindanao.

Next day, Bill boobooed.

Only the bare bones of the story emerge from his trial. Having been granted a shore pass that expired at 6 p.m., he at some unspecified place "failed to obey an order of a non-commissioned officer" in that at about 3 p.m., "having received a lawful order from 1st Sergeant Franklin Acocks, Co. E 28th Inf. U.S.V. to go with him and get on-board the Steam launch 'Boston' and return to the U.S. Army Transport Grone [*sic*], then at anchor in Manila Bay, P.I. [he] did fail to obey the same." He did not turn up again until "about 6 p.m." the following day.

What actually happened, no doubt, was that Bill, once ashore, wasted no time and was by three o'clock that Monday afternoon awash to his gunwales. The confrontation with First Sergeant Acocks must have been something to behold and audit. And I smell a feud. It is difficult to imagine two senior NCO's from the same company letting things get to such a pitch out of clean and friendly air a full three hours before the liberty boat's last trip. Acocks' name appears only once in Company E's Record of Events—he was detailed for the burial party—and I suspect he was the mess sergeant (the only other witnesses at Bill's trial were Cook Carrier Thompson and Cook Edward Abplanalp, both of Company E). But the important thing that emerges is apparent confirmation that Bill's officers thought highly of him. For a week, at anchor in Manila Bay and then sailing south, they let Bill soak in his sins. Then, at a summary court that seems to have consisted of the adjutant of the 2nd Battalion, he was fined ten dollars. Had Bill been a weak NCO, they would surely have busted him.

The trial took place aboard the *Garonne* on December 6, 1900, the day she anchored off Cagayan in northern Mindanao; and ten days later the company took the field as part of a force consisting of the entire regiment under its commanding officer, Colonel William E. Birkhimer. The expedition proved strenuous rather than savage. "From Dec 16 when took the field until last day of month, Company was on the march about every day and assisted in destroying two different Strongholds but did not encounter any large bands of Insurgents." By early January the big sweep was over, and Bill's company settled down in a place called Villa Nueva. For two months they mounted scouts and "furnished escorts for a wagon train." But the insurrection was petering out. Insurgents began to surrender and take oaths of allegiance. By this time, a survivor remembers, there were "even some school people who brought textbooks with pictures and pidgin English and pidgin Spanish" and distributed them among the Filipino children, who were now made to go to school.

The troops' duties became more peaceful, too. Bill helped repair a bridge and almost certainly was in on a series of small scouting parties that "made [a] map of town and surrounding country"—a chore that may have been the root of Grace's report that "Bill learned his surveying out there, with the Army." Bill could have done some photography, too: Aunt Marie remembered that when she was still a child he showed them "a big roll of film from the Philippines. . . . The women out there, and how they lived, you know. They were so curious-looking—very big girls running around with half no clothes on. Well, now they all do it around here, but in them days it seemed funny to us. Real savages, with just these little wraparounds on them. Rough country it was, too. And they were fighting or something at that time."

Anyway, at Villa Nueva Bill read the peacetime writing on the wall— and made his move. In late January he applied for discharge from the service. His given reason: "the fact that I wish to remain in these islands; for the purpose of engaging in mercantile persuits." By that time, the grass on the far side of the military fence must have been getting to look entrancingly green. Bill had, after all, stuck with soldiering for eighteen months, straight, and that was something: as far as careers go, no one would accuse Bill, before he reached forty, of excessive staying power.

The company and battalion commanders recommended approval of Bill's request and rated his character "good." But Colonel Birkhimer disapproved: "No man who does not receive the character 'excellent' from his immediate commander will be recommended for a discharge, with a view of remaining in these islands. I have seen too many ex-soldiers hanging around the streets of Manila to favor any other course, men who had no evident means of support and who only brought reproach on the name of ex-soldier and upon American character generally."

But, by means unrecorded, Bill got his way. In early March he sailed with the company back to Manila Bay. March 13, he was promoted to first sergeant, and next day—my minus twenty-first birthday—was granted his discharge. Bill left with a character now rated "very good," service again judged "honest and faithful"—and with a final pay settlement of $202.51.

Two days later the company sailed for the United States. It was mustered out, at San Francisco Presidio, on May 7.

When Bill walked ashore, free, onto the streets of Manila, he had crossed another threshold: at twenty-five—the precise age at which I would pass through that same door—he found himself for the first time a civilian in a distant land. The keenest and most lasting military echoes he carried across this new threshold were for his ears alone: he knew he had participated to the hilt, if not beyond, in what his unit had been called on to do. But there is more than that to combat memories. A man remembers, all his life, the way he responded to moments of life-or-death crisis. It seems unlikely that Bill ever came eyeball to eyeball with such a test. He therefore left himself prey to the third, last and most ludicrous of all forms of combat-as-test neurosis: the notion that, through no fault of your own, you were never thrust into a crucible quite hot enough to test your true mettle. Tinges of such a regret are, I suspect, not only common but damned near inevitable for all except genuine blue-riband heroes, and on this score Bill looks distinctly vulnerable. Stories he told later in life certainly suggest that he dreamed of gory and glorious engagements in which the only wonder was that he received no Congressional Medal of Honor. But please do not see all this as criticism of Bill—only as one explanation of occasionally discernible rifts in his self-confidence, and as a sort of *amicus curiae* brief for some latter-day romanticizing. The whole thing is passing crazy, anyway. Given what he found on his plate, young Bill had more than done his stuff.

Although this photograph has been so airbrushed that details other than the face are fuzzy and unreliable, it was definitely taken sometime during Bill's second army tour: inscribed on his hat—or perhaps on the photograph—is "28th, E."

Despite Aunt Marie's recollection that Bill when young had "a fuller face," I could at first see in this likeness nothing of the Bill I knew from later photographs. Then I realized that the face was very similar to that in the 1908 desertion poster, and astonishingly like the mother's. And when I failed to reconcile it with Grace's snaps of Bill in his fifties, I went to a scrapbook, found a photograph of another young man in his twenties and uniform, took it to a mirror—and found no connection there, either.

BILL'S CIVILIAN STINT in the Philippines lasted a month longer than had his second army tour.

During those twenty-one months the insurrection ebbed away. Emilio Aguinaldo was captured a week after Bill's discharge—he promptly swore allegiance to the United States and went on to live until 1964 and the age of ninety-five—and the last Filipino resisters surrendered in April 1902. Meanwhile, President McKinley had been assassinated; Teddy Roosevelt reigned.

Only three facts, or probable facts, emerge from this period of Bill's history. They appear in statements he made later, on bureaucratic documents.

For eight months (or possibly three months—the figure is unclear) he worked "for I.P.A. Maj. Shield's Com."—presumably some kind of "mercantile persuit."

In June 1901 or 1902, in Manila, he contracted cholera.

On September 24, 1902, he went to work for the "Depot Quartermaster, Calamba Laguna, P.I."

Then on Friday, December 12, 1902, at Santo Tomas in Batangas Province—still in that part of southern Luzon in which he had served with the 28th—he re-enlisted, in a regular unit.

By that time Bill was due, if not overdue, to covet the grass on the far side of some damned fence or other. But mostly I see him in need of a travel agent.

The islands had not worked out too well. At a guess, he now had roughly $202.51 less in his pocket than twenty-one months earlier. And the cholera, if that is what it was, had shaken him: not too many people survived it, and even they took time to recover. So now Bill wanted to go home—and thought he saw a way to have the Army take him there, then set him free.

Back in Pennsylvania, two months earlier, his father had died.

The newspaper obituary shows that the family knew where Bill was, even if not just what he was up to; and there is a strong suggestion that they informed him of Peter's death. For in answering the standard enlistment questions he made two significant changes and one addition. His residence reverts to "Braddock." His next of kin becomes, for the first time, "Father." And when asked if any brothers or sisters had died he states that one brother had died at birth and two in accidents. I can only view this quintessentially Billish fantasy—convenient, credible and loosely based on fact—as designed to create a family history that would, once the news of his father's death became official, leave his poor mother grief-stricken and unsupportable by anyone except her long-lost only son, who would surely deserve to be released by a responsive Army so that he could go home and do the supporting.

M TROOP, 6TH CAVALRY, SAN PUEBLA, P.I., 1902.

Because Bill did not join the 6th Cavalry until December 12, 1902, the odds against his being in this photograph—if its date is correct—would seem to be rather long. But the man one from the left in the last row but one is the spitting image of the sergeant sitting on the trunk—if you shave off the sergeant's mustache—and also of the rather older, clean-shaven Bill of the desertion poster. Unfortunately, no names came with the photograph from the Army Research Collection at Carlisle, Pennsylvania.

For six months, Private Anthony William Simmons of Troop M, 6th U.S. Cavalry, had to sit around and wait. But by August 31, 1903, both the troop and Bill—still a private—are at Fort Keogh, Montana. In September, sure enough, "an acquaintance" in Elco, Pennsylvania, writes to the local congressman asking for help in getting Bill's discharge because his father has died "since his enlistment" and his mother is still living. In spite of the congressman, though, and in spite of the aging-mother-in-dire-need-of-support tear-jerker, the game develops into an ongoing bureaucratic struggle. And it ongoes far longer than Bill had intended.

In December he is home on thirty days' furlough, getting a thirty-day extension through a Homestead doctor because of dysentery, and no doubt plucking at strings. But in October 1904 he is still at Fort Keogh, though now a corporal. By April 20, 1905, he is a sergeant again. Then, a week later, out of the undocumented blue, on Thursday, April 27, two years and four months after he re-enlisted and only eight months before he would have been routinely released, he gets his discharge "by purchase" and is at last free to sample once more, as he approaches his thirtieth birthday, the grass on the civilian side of the fence.

He grazed that field for almost three years.

Much later, he spoke of having lived—probably during those years—in Butte, Montana (which he always called "Boot," as the locals often did), and also in Boise and Warren, Idaho, and Spokane, Washington. It certainly makes logistical sense: all these places lay on Northern Pacific or Union Pacific lines, directly connecting with Fort Keogh. In them, Bill may have worked as a miner or as cook or bartender. But this is also probably the period when, according to Grace, he "signed on with the Harriman railroad"—even though she probably got him wrong as "prospector and mineralogist for survey of roads": those years, 1905–8, saw Edward Harriman at his zenith, with control or part control of both Union Pacific and Northern Pacific. And I have one possible confirmation. A friend's curiously unverifiable account has Bill working at this time out of Denver on "the Moffet railroad, Denver to Salt Lake City." That line runs not far north of Twin Lakes, Colorado, and if there is one person I would bet on Bill's having visited at least once during those years it is his Uncle Anton—at that time probably married, briefly, to a waitress. Anyway, it seems overwhelmingly likely that during the three years after his discharge from Fort Keogh Bill peripateted around Rocky Mountain railroads and drifted slowly west, toward Seattle.

He certainly ended up in Seattle.

At the National Archives, James Walker had handed me a sheet of paper with the handwritten notation: "Nov 1, 1907 to Apr 6, 1908, in employ Frank Heather, Burlington, Washington." Later, I found the questionnaire including this information. In it, Bill gave his occupation as "cook"—and also admitted that about January 1, 1908, he had been treated for gonorrhea.

Burlington is a small town sixty miles north of Seattle. Its 1909 directory carries a one-line entry: "Heather, Frank L., Restaurant." Frank Heather was long dead: he fell from the gangplank of a moored tug in Seattle harbor and drowned November 14, 1949—just ten days after Bill went into the Los Angeles VA hospital from which he would never emerge. But eventually I spoke on the phone to Frank's son, Russell, in Seattle. He had no recollection of hearing family mention of a Bill Simoyne or Simmons or Simon. Indeed, his parents always operated small mom-and-pop places that they ran strictly themselves. But then it emerged that Russell Heather was born just three weeks after Bill went to work for his father—and born in Seattle, where his mother had traveled to stay with her parents for the birth. So Bill had clearly been a temporary replacement cook for Mrs. Heather. If we accept Bill's questionnaire answer, he stayed seven months. When he left on April 6 he went south—no doubt pausing in Seattle, and perhaps joining the crowds that welcomed the newly arrived competitors in the New York–Paris automobile race. A month after leaving Burlington he was sixty miles south of Seattle, in Centralia. There, on Thursday, April 30, barely three years after buying his way out of the Army, he asked back in. And that Sunday, at Vancouver Barracks, across the Columbia River from Portland, Oregon, he signed on for another three years with the cavalry.

Perhaps he was broke again: 1907 had brought yet another financial panic. But he may have had something going inside the Army. A month after his enlistment, a telegram went out from Yosemite National Park, California, to the Adjutant General, U.S. Army, in Washington, D.C.: "Request that recruit Anthony W. Simmons unassigned Vancouver Barracks be assigned Troop M Fourteenth Cavalry and ordered to this station. (Signed) Benson, Commanding." Now Colonel Harry Coupland Benson was not only commanding military officer of the park but also its energetic acting superintendent (a lake and pass are named after him); and I find it difficult to avoid the conclusion that he or one of his officers had known Bill during his 6th Cavalry days and had, at Bill's urging, before or after he enlisted, asked to have him assigned. The C.O. at Vancouver Barracks gave his approval to the posting; but a fortnight later the Adjutant General advised Colonel Benson, without explanation, that the request was "not approved." So Bill found himself a cook with Troop D, 14th Cavalry, in Tacoma, thirty miles south of Seattle. There, ten days after his thirty-third birthday, fate took a hand—or, rather, a leg: he was admitted to the post hospital at Fort Lawton, Seattle, with a broken tibia, "incurred by stepping on loose stone while wrestling with comrade in camp." Seven weeks later he returned to his troop, now stationed at Fort Walla Walla, Washington, two hundred miles inland. And seventeen days later, on October 25, the troop commander reported that Bill had deserted.

Forty years later, Bill gave a friend a convincing account of what happened. "Sure he told me about having deserted," recalled this man. "But he didn't run off, you know. He just got on a drunk when he was on furlough, him and a couple more guys. They was riding freight trains and drinking, and when he came to he was in Kansas City or St. Louis or some damn place and three weeks over. AWOL. So he says the hell with the Army, and just didn't go back."

But there were probably other, underlying reasons. A sergeant of several years' standing who had hoped for a posting to Yosemite finds himself wintering in barracks on a cold, windswept plain, as a private soldier and cook. A veteran fence-hopper finds that the taste of promised grass fails yet again to live up to its billing. And this time there is also the age question: men in their thirties often find old certainties dissolving, new questions looming.

At a guess, then, Bill got swiftly and sourly fed up. And the facts are clear. In Kansas City or St. Louis or Walla Walla or someplace else, the thirty-three-year-old Bill went over the hill. He vamoosed. For the last time, more or less, he stepped across the threshold of the U.S. Army—into a new chapter of his life.

# 11 Back to Seattle

THIRTY-THREE. Over the hill. New chapter.

Now I am not quite saying that when Bill went militarily over the hill he thought of himself as being over the chronological hill. And I am certainly not suggesting that a man of thirty-three is in fact over that hump. But despite a popular assumption that forty marks the big watershed, a man in his mid-thirties often begins to sense that time is no longer flowing his way. At first he may not be fully aware of the new currents tugging at his moorings—or in a case like Bill's, at the patterns that for him serve as moorings. I am by no means sure, for example, that I was aware of any solemn intimations when, at thirty-one, near the end of a fairly extensive wandering, I in my turn scuttered through Spokane en route for the Pacific Coast. But now, equipped with hindsight, I can detect in that period a great deal that was still iceberged down and away. So when Bill deserted he may well, without quite knowing it, have been beginning to harbor suspicions that he was beyond his prime, had moved over the hump. If so, it must have hurt. For he could not yet have learned that "prime" and "hump" are merciful, almost indefinitely extensible terms that can, with care, be redefined to meet your revised needs almost every time a new decade ticks past.

To this point in Bill's life I have patched together from his sparse early history only the outline of a fairly straightforward, more or less run-of-the-mill young fellow. The reason is simple enough: human life-spans being what they are, I have been unable to speak to anyone who met him before he was forty—with the very marginal exception of the friend who passed on that curiously unverifiable account of meeting him when he was working on a railroad "out of Denver." So I have gained no radiant insights into the mind of this immature Bill. But because I have been able to

168

talk at length with several people who, like Grace but in different ways, were fairly intimate with him in his later years, I feel I know the older man well. And I find him almost a different individual from the earlier version. At times, I am hard put to reconcile the two. I suppose that should not really surprise me: I detect the same dichotomy in myself. But with Bill it compounds an information slump—the longest period in his adult life for which I have been able to gather neither written evidence of his doings nor insights from people who knew him well. And the slump, 1909 through 1917, straddles those years during which he negotiated perhaps the straitest of the hoops called "growing up"—that period during which most people who are going to mature finally do so.

Fortunately, the information slump is not a bottomless pit. I have several touchpoints.

A fortnight after he deserted, Bill may have been picked up by Braddock police. His army file contains a report that he was. But the report concludes: "it is evident that the deserter in question was never delivered to the military authorities by the police officials who were reported to have him in custody." Because all Braddock's records were burned in a city hall fire in 1934, there is no way of discovering just what went on, if anything did, between Bill and the Braddock police. But Bill's quick return to Braddock seems a highly likely event. It would fit his pattern. And the date of his reported arrest is November 2, 1908—the eve of the election in which William Jennings Bryan, in his third and final bid for the presidency, lost out to William H. Taft. Although I have never heard anyone accuse Bill of being politically active, he could well have homed to vote. In those days, with feelings running high and a dry day looming, the pre-election warm-up tended to be soggy, and it seems a likely time for booze and bragging to have helped land Bill in the civilian brig. If so, he somehow slithered out again.

In the years that followed, Bill went back to Braddock at least once and probably several times.

Around 1910 or 1911, Aunt Marie had told me, he stayed for a spell with his sister Annie. "My mother and grandma and me was staying with her too, up at Parker's Landing, near Oil City. Annie was in the hotel business then, and Bill was tending bar or something with her. They liked each other O.K., though Annie used to get angry because Bill wanted to live so far away. 'I don't see what's the matter with Bill that he wants to be a wanderer like that,' she'd say. But while we was there, him and Annie was into some kind of a scrap. Well, they didn't exactly fight, but they must have had a . . . a little difference some way or another, and away he went. Flew the coop again. The instinct got into him and he just had to go.

When he'd go, he'd never say where he was going—he never knowed himself, I don't think. . . . Come to think of it, I imagine that time up at Annie's must have been the last time Bill saw his mother. . . ."

Annie Simon did not die in the big green house at the corner of Lobinger and Coalmont, said Aunt Marie. She bought that house soon after her husband died, in 1902, and lived there for several years. But then she grew too old to live alone. Among other things, she lost the sight of one eye. So she sold the house and spent her time staying with one or another of her daughters, Annie and Mary. When she died she was staying with Mary, Aunt Marie's mother, at their place in Braddock Park, up in the hills above Braddock. She died—of apoplexy, says the death certificate—in July 1910.

Two entries in the final accounting of her estate—which totaled $1,069.64—suggest that Bill may soon have returned to Braddock: "27 Oct 1910—William Simon, loan, $65; 17 Feb 1911—W. A. Simon, loan, $200." These loans could be genuine. But they may merely mean that the family hit on a way to write off sums that would be very, very difficult to trace. Bill's loans are the only straight payments to family members. The rest goes in expenses. And that hardly rings true.

All the same, I know that his mother's estate drew Bill back at least once to the banks of the Monongahela—sixty miles south of Pittsburgh, in West Virginia.

I made the West Virginia connection by way of Ohio.

The name on the brown paper that had wrapped the family Bible—Marlene A. Simons of Yorkville, Ohio—eventually led me to Mrs. Edna Simon, mother of Marlene and widow of a William Simon, son of Bill's brother Peter. And through correspondence and phone calls with her I established contact with two new branches of the family.

On the phone, Joseph's son, who farmed thirty miles south of Pittsburgh, was abrupt and uninformative. But when I called Mrs. Virginia Tabron, daughter of Peter, Jr., in Morgantown, West Virginia, she was from the start open and helpful.

Certainly she knew about Uncle Bill, the maverick who had gone West and disappeared: she was quite a family bug—sort of an unofficial historian. No, she was afraid she had never met Bill, but she had heard a lot about him from her mother and from her brother. Bill didn't die until 1950? Then it was a shame he didn't contact the family again, because he was wondered about.

The last time Bill came to West Virginia, she said, was in 1913. Oh yes, the year was definite. Bill came to find out about his share of his mother's estate. He knew that she had died and that his brother Peter was administrator, but not that Peter had died in January 1913 and that Tony, or Anton, had taken over as administrator. It was 1913 all right because he came the year before the estate was settled, and it was settled in 1914.

The nature of the settlement turned out to be revealing.

"There was a lot of friction over the estate," said Mrs. Tabron. "The rest of the family didn't get along so well, you know. They didn't treat my mother very good after my father died. After he died, Mother turned the papers over to Uncle Tony and Aunt Annie—they was the two oldest— and then when they went on to make a settlement they come onto her for several thousand dollars, and there was a lawsuit. But without telling them, Mother had had the papers recorded in Pittsburgh. So she could prove she hadn't done what they said. And she won. For a long time after that the two sides of the family held apart. But Mother always said they'd come back. And they did. Uncle Tony came and stayed for about a week before he died. Aunt Annie, too, I think."

Bill's 1913 visit was probably brief, said Mrs. Tabron. He was going back West "because the country air suited him better than here." But first he was going up to Pittsburgh to see Tony and Annie about the estate— even though he did not get on well with Tony.

Mrs. Tabron sighed. "Family affairs! Yes, there was a lot of friction. There were always stories going around. Like between Bill and Joseph. But my father was Uncle Bill's favorite brother. He named one of his sons after him, you know. Yes, Uncle Bill got on well with my mother, too. He must have done, because when he went away he left his discharge papers with her. Then there's the picture of Uncle Bill in uniform, up in the old house. . . ."

"A photograph?"

"Yes."

In the old family home that Peter had built in 1900, up in the mountains, there had been an almost complete set of family photographs. They had very nearly been lost. For some years the house passed out of family hands. Then Mrs. Tabron and her husband bought it back, along with forty acres of the land—and she found all the pictures stashed away in an outbuilding that they used to call "the grainery." She had cleaned them up and now they were hanging on the living-room wall. But the photo of Grandpa Simon, Bill's father, was missing. "And all I really know about my grandfather," said Mrs. Tabron, "is that he was the original immigrant and . . ." She told me of his "trade ship" and gambling instincts. "The only other thing I know about him is that he was a German Jew."

"He was *Jewish?*"

"Yes, a German Jew. The name was spelled S-I-M-O-N, you know."

"Yes, I've got the family Bible."

"And it's written in Gideon, isn't it?"

"In what?"

"Gideon . . . you know, a language between Jewish and German."

"Oh, Yiddish?"

"Yes, that's right."

I explained that the text had been English, the family entries written in an old German Gothic script.

Mrs. Tabron sounded surprised. In the family, she said, it had always been understood that her grandfather had been Jewish and his wife French.

"Why, yes. I suppose I could have a copy of Uncle Bill's photo made. And of his mother's. Hers is an ordinary portrait, but Uncle Bill, he's sitting down. On a trunk."

"On a *what?*"

"A trunk."

For a moment I sat silent, fingering this new, ancient reverberation that had just come down the line from West Virginia at the speed of light. Then I outlined the Trunkman story. "I still haven't *proved* that it was Bill who lived in that cave," I concluded. "But I'm virtually sure it . . ."

"Oh, without doubt it was him. Because when he came here for that last time in 1913 he said he had been sick and had lived in a cave and Indians had found him and nursed him back to health. At least, that's what he told my brothers, Ed and Joe. Or so they said. The family thought it was all lies, of course. But now it looks like it was true after all! No, he didn't say what he was sick with. Nor where the cave was. At least, not to my knowledge. But he talked about a cave all right. They all said that. My mother, too."

And when I put the phone down it was this new cave story, dated 1913, that kept roiling around my mind. It could mean, I decided, any one of three things.

The least likely was that Bill had lived in "my" cave in Nevada on two separate occasions, the first of them not later than 1913. The fragments of the September 1912 *Young's Magazine* lent some support to that hypothesis—but also remained consistent with 1916. On the other hand, a 1913 occupation did not fit Grace's story.

The second possibility was that when Bill visited West Virginia he was talking about a different cave. And the Indians nursing Bill back to health could have been real; or they could have lived only in one of his romantic fantasies, perhaps dating back to childhood in caves that used to exist in the gully down which slanted No. 2 Incline.

My third alternative had the 1913 cave story as pure fantasy.

Whichever alternative I picked, though, I came up with Trunkman support: a solid cave-dwelling record; or a stated fantasy just waiting to be realized.

Then there was the trunk in Bill's photograph.

Mrs. Tabron could not remember what it looked like, and I knew that until the photograph arrived all I could do was dream of it as a Rosebud clue that had hung there all the time on the wall of an old house in West Virginia, with a dusty interlude in the granary; a clue that had hung there waiting to emerge, long after I had given up hope of solid proof, as a final and irrevocable clincher.

I had to sweat it out for almost a month. The photograph turned out, of course, to be the one taken when Bill was with the 28th Volunteer Infantry, and I could see at once, even through its heavy airbrushing, that the trunk—apparently the standard army field type of that period—could not possibly be the one I had found outside the cave. All the same, a photograph of Bill sitting on any trunk carried a pleasing kind of illogical, symbolic, second-clockworks connotation.

During this time I learned from the diocese of Trier, Germany, that Peter Simon, Sr., had been born of two apparently Catholic parents—John Peter Simon and Margarita Anna Janz; and also that "in our area there were Jews by the name of Simon but many more Christians bearing the name." For a while I flirted with the idea that the Simon family might have followed a known local precedent: in 1824, just ten years before Peter Simon's birth, in the same diocese of Trier, the father of young Karl Marx, aged six, converted from Judaism to Christianity. But this beguiling hypothesis eventually foundered. I made inquiries through Mrs. Gross, Fred Alger's daughter, and she advised me that her father's closest friend, himself Jewish, when asked about the matter had laughed and said, "No one named Peter at that place and time was ever Jewish."

Meanwhile, I had phoned Aunt Marie.

"Well, yes," she admitted. "I guess you could say that the Joseph and Peter branches of the family more or less broke away from our side. After Peter died, his widow married a farmhand. That may have had something to do with it."

And in the end I decided that Aunt Marie's rather reluctant admission confirmed what was really the heaviest news to have come out of West Virginia: that I had been right after all in my more-or-less discarded intuition that family hassling was at least a part of the reason for Bill's rejection of Pennsylvania.

After his 1913 West Virginia visit—and, no doubt, a meeting with brother Anton that can hardly have dripped honey (Mrs. Simon's estate balance now stood at $6.65)—Bill went back West.

Given his lifelong pattern of fence-hopping back to old haunts, returning to Seattle was a natural enough move. And I harbor no real doubts that sometime between 1914 and 1916 he lived there for a considerable spell. Yet I have failed to find any hard, incontrovertible evidence that he did so.

The most promising take-off point for turning up such evidence looked like the marriage and restaurant in Grace's cuckolding story. Bill and "the head waitress called Marge" might not have been legally married, of course. And I suspected that the winning of the restaurant in a poker game had been Graceful embroidery: in the margin of her copy of my San Francisco *Chronicle* Trunkman article she had scribbled "bought restaurant." But there seemed to be both a woman and a restaurant in it somewhere— each hinting at a new settling-down trend in Bill's life; and I had a Seattle genealogist search local marriage and restaurant ownership records, 1908 through 1910, for entries under all Bill's names and variations. He found nothing.

By now, though, I had an alternate Seattle scenario.

It came—secondhand and conflicting, yet also curiously corroborative—from the man who, of all those I have talked to, probably knew Bill best. He remembered very clearly that chapter of Bill's history, as retailed by Bill twenty years later.

"Then before he came to California," this young man told me, "he was up in Washington State. Do you have any readings on him in Spokane? I knew he'd been up in Spokane. Seattle? Sure. He went there meaning to go up to Alaska, but never did. He was cooking for some fellow in a restaurant and got kind of chummy with his daughter and she got pregnant. The father was ready with his shotgun but the girl tipped Bill off and he got out just in time. The father came after him but Bill ran down a railroad track and soon outdistanced him. That's what he told me, anyway. . . . Oh, I remember he said he had seventeen hundred dollars when he left Seattle and took the train on down to San Francisco. That was a lot of money in those days."

In those days it certainly was a lot of money, especially for a wanderer like Bill. Fifty years later, when I came down from Canada to Seattle to start my American life at age thirty-four with almost the identical amount, it still seemed like a lot of money.

Now one answer to the question of where Bill got such a sum could be "by clearing out a restaurant bank account." And that is not the only way in which the shotgun scenario, though conflicting with Grace's denser restaurant story, in a sense corroborates it. The smoke from the two sources may smell different, but it comes from the same kind of fire.

Naturally, I tried to tie the shotgun scenario to Frank L. Heather—the man Bill cooked for in Burlington in 1907. His son, Russell, told me that by 1915 the family had indeed moved down to Seattle, and at one time ran a restaurant there. But by then Russell was eight and he could still remember the restaurant clearly and he was sure no one called Bill Simoyne or anything remotely like that had been connected with it. When I told him both the Grace and shotgun versions of Bill's reputed restaurant romance he roared with laughter. He had certainly heard no whisper of such interesting events. He had a sister, right enough, but in 1915 she was two years old.

Finally, I tried to reconcile all this with the Uncle Tony fantasy. It could have worked two ways, I decided. Events that had actually taken place in Twin Lakes—Uncle Tony, templating for Bill, marries a waitress who does him wrong—may have tinged Bill's later accounts of his own amatory adventures in Seattle. Or the template may have functioned as a self-fulfilling prophecy. That can certainly happen: events start unfurling and you recognize echoes from long-standing dreameries and say, "There! It is written!"—and tend to take the signposted path.

From the start I had felt inclined to accept Grace's Seattle script: a man is unlikely to invent a tale of cuckolding, especially with vivid details of finding his wife in bed with a "friend." And the diluted and mildly comic shotgun-and-railroad-track variation is just the kind Bill might feed a twenty-year-old friend many years later, when the pain had ebbed.

In time I became more and more convinced that Grace's script was the true one, and that it concerned the love of Bill's life. But whatever the details, we are left with three presumptive circumstances: In Seattle, Bill suffered some kind of romantic, restaurantic entanglement that ended in trauma. He went by train to San Francisco. He carried what was for him an unusually thick roll of money.

It also stands clear, beyond doubt, that when Bill left Seattle he approached the most fateful watershed of his life.

He seems to have reached San Francisco about November 1915: Grace said he visited "The World's Fair" there just before it ended—and the Panama-Pacific Exhibition closed on December 4.

By that time, the war in Europe was more than a year old. The *Lusitania* had been sunk. The Western Front, scene of appalling carnage, had bogged down into grinding stalemate. Woodrow Wilson dreamed of becoming the ultimate peacemaker. And Bill was forty—and counting.

# 12    Metamorphosis

WHEN BILL LEFT SEATTLE he entered the cusp of his life. For a year, or even longer, he existed in a huge gray envelope that tyrannized and distorted and almost annulled his days and nights.

The trauma that brought on this depression was, I believe, essentially the one reported by Grace. The picture Bill painted for her certainly suggests severe shock. His first impulse, he said, was to shoot the policeman and beat the hell out of his wife. "The only reason I didn't do anything was because I walked and I talked to myself. Otherwise I'd have been a murderer."

There is, of course, a pattern to these things. The loss the victim suffers is bad enough. The wound inflicted on pride may hurt even more. But what cut and gouge and eviscerate are the shattering of trust—and the rejection. These can destroy you, not just for a year, but for three or four. If you survive, though, you emerge with a clearer vision, and toughened.

In Bill's case it all fits. In fact, one reason I came to favor Grace's version of the trauma is that it provides the only reasonable explanation for what Bill did in the year or so after he left Seattle.

He did not stay long in San Francisco, that winter of 1915. Its streets no doubt failed to live up to his nostalgic memories of nights of liberty from the Presidio, sixteen years earlier: the gray envelope that cut him off from the world would take care of that. He would now see events in Seattle as final and irrevocable confirmation that cities were not for him, and before long he would be ready to take off again.

But first he visited the Panama-Pacific Exhibition.

"He spent days in the mineral exhibit rooms," Grace had said. That seems very likely. A man I know who also did so, as a child, still remembered, sixty years later, "big mineral and metallurgical exhibits . . . with a lot of mining procedures." Now chance encounters often divert our lives down new channels, and it is easy to picture Bill returning time and again to certain imaginative exhibits and eventually deciding, there at the nadir of his depression, that the time had come for him to act out the fantasies he had constructed around his template, Uncle Anton, the prospector.

One particularly striking exhibit may have funneled Bill down the next momentous leg of his physical wanderings. A letter published in a contemporary Las Vegas newspaper, from a local man who had visited the Exhibition, reported that the mineral representation for Clark County, which includes Las Vegas, was "fine enough to warm the cockles of your heart."

Names may also have helped lure Bill to Nevada. He was, as we shall learn, big on names. He heard music in simple syllables. And Nevada serenaded him with distant siren songs—with Las Vegas and Tonapah for starters, and Searchlight and Pioche. And further north, perhaps still echoing in Bill's mind from his company's railroad journey to San Francisco in 1899, sang Winnemucca.

We residents of today are likely to assume that the newly bankrolled Bill must have been drawn to Las Vegas like a moth. There could be truth in the notion. They gambled in Vegas then, as they did in most towns. But gambling was certainly not chamber-of-commerced. A January 1916 headline in a local newspaper announced: "First Gambling Case Results in Conviction."

The town, founded only eleven years earlier, when the railroad reached that point, remained essentially a rail center—a raw, down-to-earth, dirt-and-gravel place, worlds removed from today's glittering yet sleazy vortex of slots and sluts. As a natural livestock shipping center for a thriving ranch community, it featured a long line of sheep corrals flanking the railroad freight yards. But the year Bill arrived, sidewalks came to the main street and the city fathers passed a muffler ordinance that "silenced at one blow all the particular brands of Gatling guns, seventy fives, Big Berthas and other fiendish devices attached to Overlands, Dodges, Maxwells and Pierce Arrows which people of the city have been enduring for the past several years." The suddenly popular automobiles were also opening new avenues and reweaving the fabric of society. "Many auto stages [now] reach Nelson daily with freight and passengers." Nelson and Searchlight, both within fifty miles of Vegas, were centers of a strong mining industry, and Vegas had become the natural hub to spin men and supplies out to them and other communities.

At first, Bill does not seem to have done any mining or prospecting. No records exist of claims staked in Clark County in any of his names, 1916 through 1918. At a guess, he soon gambled away most of his money. And I think he also lost his way. When you live in a huge gray envelope it is difficult enough to discern a way ahead, let alone follow it.

According to Grace, Bill spent "several months" in Vegas, "living with a woman." Another friend has him around about this time "living with an Indian woman" in Pioche, a hundred miles north of Vegas. But whatever Bill did to keep body and soul together during the first eight months of 1916—cooking or tending bar or plain living on his wad—he seems to have lived in a town and done more-or-less conventional things. And I do not believe that conventional things were what Bill wanted to do at that time. What he really wanted was a radical change that would help him shake off old shackles.

So in the fall he went to live in a cave.

Given his cusp, the act made sense: his needs were time and space and peace in which to think, absorb, decide.

One minor distraction also preyed on his mind. America, though still adamantly eschewing the European war, looked by no means safe from involvement. And a campaign against Mexico seemed to be brewing. During July, the city of Las Vegas began enlisting volunteers for a local company, and two troops of Nevada cavalry were mobilized. "Where are the men who want to whip Mexico?" trumpeted the papers. "Battery A of the Utah National Guard passed through Vegas Wednesday evening under orders to proceed to Nogales, Arizona. The battery was under command of Captain William C. Webb, a veteran of the Philippines Insurrection." Such reports could hardly have done anything but confuse Bill's already distraught mind. Wars had always attracted him. And although he would know that peacetime desertion was a largely technical offense, his pride would be hurt.

But overshadowing all else that September, muting the distant rumbles of war, hung the huge gray envelope. That, above all, is why the cave makes sense. At times of wounding woman trouble, the desert exerts a powerful pull on a man.

Many years ago, the man I know better than any other was lying awake at three o'clock one February morning in his San Francisco apartment, wondering whether he should marry the girl he was living with, when it came to him out of nowhere that what he wanted most in life just then was to walk from one end of California to the other: if he could do that, he would know what he wanted. A month later he took his first step northward from the Mexican border—out into desert. He was thirty-five, going on thirty-six. His walk took six months. And it was a turning point in his life: in ways both connected and unconnected with the girl, things were never again quite the same for him.

That was not the end of his desert therapy, either. Several years later, bogged down in a deep, gray depression brought on by the traumatic results of answering "Yes" to the question that had sent him walking up California, he stood for the first time on the rim of Grand Canyon and saw in a flash of enlightenment that the solution to all his problems lay in walking the length of the Canyon. A year later he began a two-month journey through that huge desert chasm carved by the Colorado River. By the time he completed it he had at last cast off his four-year depression. And in his new freedom he exulted that "life begins at forty-one."

When Bill went down to his cave in that other desert canyon carved by the Colorado River, he too was forty-one—an age at which, even in our Western culture, many men regear their lives; an age at which wise men in the East often renounce Mammon and retire into seclusion before launching out in new directions.

Perhaps Bill stumbled on the cave while prospecting, far out in the desert. Perhaps he was still walking and talking to himself, as he had done the night he found his wife in bed with the policeman. Barely a year had passed, so that is not unlikely. Anyway, he was no doubt moving across the almost level plain when he came to the edge of the drop-off and found himself looking down into that gigantic two-mile-wide rubble hole. If he was prospecting, perhaps he went down into it because he was a tyro and did not know that the "hot" volcanic rock would hold no minerals. But he may already have understood that he was less interested in minerals than in the desert itself.

In due course he made the same route choices that I would make, walked up the same canyon—and found the little cave at the foot of the dark, overhanging cliff.

He saw the petroglyph on the rock. When he walked up the cave's natural ramp he probably saw the metate and several tortoise shells and other signs of Indian occupation. And after he had stood there for a while, gazing up and down the wash and beyond it at the soaring walls of the canyon, he knew—exactly as I had known at three o'clock one February morning in my San Francisco apartment and again on the rim of Grand Canyon—that he must act out the idea that had just leaped into his mind. Doing so, he saw, would solve all his problems. And the more he thought about it, the sounder and more inevitable it seemed: what he needed most in life just then was to live for a while in precisely the sort of place he had stumbled on. If he did that he would discover what he wanted to do with the rest of his days.

The place he had stumbled on—this man to whom place had always been important—was both very unlike the canyon I would find fifty years later and yet also essentially the same.

It was unlike the place I would find because, as official records confirm, it received twice as much annual rainfall. That January, in particular, had brought what local papers called "the heaviest rain in years." So it was a different world. The place was green. And because grass and other vegetation grew thick and rich, so did the animals that fed on them—the deer mice and wood rats and ground squirrels and jackrabbits and tortoises and deer and bighorn sheep; and the animals that in turn fed on them also flourished—the coyotes and foxes and bobcats and mountain lions. The rain meant running water, too. Most likely, a miniature creek flowed over the natural spout outside the cave—the spout beneath which I would find the end of a yellow measuring tape and the three spent .22 shell cases that would date the Vandals.

Yet the place Bill found was also essentially the same as the one I would find. Beneath the soft green beauty then clothing the canyon lay bare-bone desert—the stark simplicity, the cleanness, the ribbed magnificence and barren majesty that strip away human fiffle-faffle and force humility on you, and perspective—and so allow you, given time and solitude, to come to terms with yourself, and thereby with the rest of the world.

I do not say that Bill understood all this in the first moment he stood in the mouth of the cave, at the head of the ramp. But once the idea had surfaced, it felt right. And the minutes and hours and days confirmed its rightness, its inevitableness.

After that moment of decision, Bill went back to Vegas.

He went back the same way he had come the twenty miles out of town—on foot or by burro or horse or wagon or automobile. And in Vegas he outfitted. Everything he bought—Dutch oven and sheepherder's stove and Graniteware utensils and all the rest—he chose carefully, by his own special criteria. Because names meant a lot to him, for example, he selected with a wry smile two mousetraps made by the Simmons Hardware Company of St. Louis and—unless he had brought it with him from Seattle—a fifty-foot yellow fabric measuring tape in a metal case bearing the name of the maker that had emerged when, knowing Bill's name, I scraped away the corrosion: E. O. Simmons. It seems likely that he did not buy any booze. Perhaps he recognized by now that booze was a weakness in him and decided against taking any down to a place in which, he sensed, he would be making pivotal decisions.

And then—not earlier than Sunday, September 10, and probably a few days later—with all his gear packed neatly in wooden boxes and in the new trunk that he had brought with him from Seattle (if Grace was telling the truth and not just striving to convince me), he went back to the cave.

To carry the gear he bought or rented a burro or burros, or hired a packer with burros or an automobile. (There were burro outfits in Vegas at that time; and a story in the May issue of one Vegas paper mentions a man who "hired an automobile for a prospecting trip.") Or perhaps he had the gear brought out to the edge of the plain and then ferried it down to the cave himself, by burro or backpacking.

And then he began to set up camp.

He collected firewood and cut grass for his bed. He found stones for his fireplace—or used the fireplace the Indians had left. He chose other, flatter stones to make a level base for his trunk—maybe at the foot of his bed, where I would put it, fifty years later, or maybe someplace else. He set up mirror and washbasin in, or maybe not in, the obvious place I would set them up—at the head of the ramp. When he had unpacked the first of the food he set up the sheepherder's stove and the Dutch oven. And at some point he walked fifty paces up the wash and built his garbage dump.

At first he clung to his habits from the outside world. He played patience or other solitary card games. He read a lot too, in those first days at the cave, the way he had always done. The fat Sunday issue of the Los Angeles *Times* kept his fingers on the pulse of the outside world. The copy of *Young's Magazine*, which he often carried folded in his back pants pocket, kept him supplied with the kind of romantic stories he had always liked and always would. And the November 1915 *Popular Mechanics* turned out to have several articles, other than "Piano Transported up Mountain by Burros," that must have intrigued him: "Secret of a Simple Card Trick"; "A New Kind of Mousetrap"; "Motor Road to Summit of Pike's Peak"; and, most beguiling of all, "Bearing Made of a Brass Cartridge." He could not resist making a few of these bearings; and then a few more. What he wanted them for, I do not know. Perhaps he just liked making them. Anyway, he spent a good deal of time cutting, very neatly, a variety of brass rifle cartridges. He also wired a rickety old folding chair so expertly that it felt rock-solid when he sat on it; wired it so that it would stay rock-solid for longer than he knew. And in time, as he got around to other odd jobs, he began to assemble in a natural pocket on the cave's inner wall a little repair shop of washers and nails and carpet tacks and grommets.

He also spent a lot of time whittling away at two kinds of stick for deadfall traps. And that raises a question.

In my scenario, he lives alone. And in all probability that is how it was. But one friend of his remembers that years later Bill spoke of living in a cave somewhere with an Indian woman, and a few shreds of evidence lend support to his story. An Indian woman could account for the very small green shoes, for there being both a chair and a stool in the cave, and even for the metate. And it could account for the thin-and-toggle sticks for deadfall traps—whether Bill actually made them or not. For such traps were originally of Indian design, and it is easy to imagine a local Indian woman teaching Bill how to make them. Perhaps, then, such a woman stayed briefly in the cave. But I still see Bill living alone, at least most of the time. That was an essential part of his cure, of his rebirth. Only in solitude can you slow down enough to rechart your life.

Even then, it takes time.

At first, Bill's inner life no doubt followed many of the patterns it had always followed. His thoughts would still be shaped by human coordinates. And reading did more than keep him in touch with recent events in the outside world: it held him to the habit of words. As time passed, though, he would find himself reading less and less—and not only because he was running out of material. Slowly, new rhythms began to permeate his days.

When you live alone in a place like the cave, time does more than simply slow down: it becomes more of a piece. Live the life long enough, and on occasion you find that past, present and future seem to cohabit. Their meanings mingle.

That is one reason I see Bill spending a lot of time making such items as brass bearings and little sticks for deadfall traps, whether he wanted the end products or not. Handiwork, especially with wood, does more for him than just make and mend physical things. It gives him the chance to sit and whittle, whittle and think, mull and cull, drift and dream. It gives him a chance to replay recent events, over and over. A chance to assess and master them. A chance to step back and, by standing still, to catch up. As Murl Emery knew, a man can be on the run from many things, including himself.

And now Bill had the time and the eyes to learn from the world around him.

A pair of ravens patrol the canyon, swinging high past dark pinnacles, craaking. Finches and phoebes come to share his water supply; they land in a little pool below the natural rock spout, out in the wash, and drink and then bathe—body-shaking halos of spray into the sunlight, then studiously refitting all feathers. Wood rats and deer mice on nighttime forays nibble at food and paper and almost anything left lying around; Bill curses them and puts out traps—but in time finds himself on stroking terms with a deer mouse family that comes regularly to his dinner table, scurrying under his wrist to reach their breakfast.

As time passes, other relationships change.

The deer that at first took off whenever he appeared now begin browsing closer to the cave—though they still monitor him with their soft, warm eyes. The bighorn sheep begin to accept him too, sometimes moving directly down the slope toward the cave when they leave their resting place, just below the canyon's far rim.

The beat and timbre and taste and wholeness of this quiet life in the canyon are new to Bill. Most of his roaming years, he has lived communally—in the Army or with railroad gangs; he has never before spent any protracted spell cut off from other people in a place so remote that it teaches you, slowly, the ways of the world as it was in the time before man gained dominion. And he finds those ways a revelation.

The animal visitors write only the primer.

Although the canyon had fascinated him from the start, it seemed at first, in spite of the grass and bushes greening its floor, too stark and barren to be called beautiful. It was closer, perhaps, to an ugly-attractive woman. At least, so he thought. But now his sense of beauty has moved into full harmony with the place.

He runs his eyes lovingly over curving lines of rock—and sees the earth's story laid bare, back down immense chapters of geologic time. He traces the swirls and convergences of dry watercourses—and grasps, tight, the way this canyon was cut. Close-up, he relishes the patterns of pitted boulders, the life that sunlight brushes onto scattered seed heads.

One morning, perhaps, when he has at last freed himself from the coordinates of the outside world, he wanders up the canyon's easy west slope, toward the ledge on which he knows the bighorns have a resting place. Standing beside the little hollowed-out patch of bare earth, he finds himself looking out over a panoramic view of the rubble hole's jagged peaks. As he looks, sunlight breaks through the morning's clouds. And it transforms the peaks from dark, glowering sentinels into pink and smiling guardians that shine with a clean, new-day purity. As the sunlight moves forward, embracing ridge after angled ridge and spur after echeloned spur, touching rock into life, it builds behind each ridge and spur a somber black shadow. Bill acknowledges the shadows. He knows that they keep you honest; remind you that in the end, everywhere, a night must fall.

For long moments the vivid light holds. Then, slowly, its intensity fades.

Bill glances down at the cave. It looks very small. He begins to walk back down the talus slope.

It was such moments as this that "taught" him, eventually, a lesson he had "learned" a quarter of a century earlier—the lesson that stemmed from all he had seen and heard and smelled and felt during his early years in Braddock. Then, he had known only that something was wrong. "Can this be all there is?" he had asked. In the end, as he emerged from the chrysalis of childhood, he had wandered off to find an answer. And at last he had found it. Now, sensing the linkages between all life elements in his unspoiled canyon wilderness, he could see, clearly and devastatingly, connections between the Edgar Thomson Steel Works and what it had replaced—"the long grassy swards . . . home of the bullfrog and the meadowlark"; and connections with what they had replaced—the "green-clothed forest" of George Washington's primeval wilderness with "rippling shallows under a brilliant summer sun." For now he had "learned" what he had always recognized: the flaws of industrialization—defects so deep that they could cause the whole pulsating experiment to self-destruct.

Now I cannot be sure that Bill recognized these flaws openly and consciously. Had he lived another twenty years he would still not have talked about "changing evolutionary paradigms" or even "a post-industrial society." He was not that kind of man. But he did something more important, more committed. He lived his life as if he understood the flaws. I think that is what Peter Williams discerned when he called him "the first of the flower children." For Bill's life in the cave had crystallized his vision. There, he had sorted out his priorities and got himself firmly on track. He had grasped the continuities. He now understood, for example, the Defeat inflicted on Braddock by the Edgar Thomson Steel Works and its gray, smoke-filled battlements. Perhaps he even understood that this victory, too, was only temporary. But one thing is certain: from that time on he chose to live and work in places that were the very antithesis of Braddock and all it stood for. He lived in the rock house and in many other quiet places I came to know. He lived in places that his family back in Braddock would have been "ashamed of"—but in places that were all, in their own ways, beautiful; places that were open and unfettered, even when enclosed by rock; places never at all restricted in the way Braddock was restricted; places that had one thing in common—an absence of man-crud. He chose such places to the end. To the very end.

So there at the cave, although Bill may not yet have known it, the die was cast.

At sunrise and sunset, now, he is always ready for the magic that light can paint on desert canvas; always ready to stand and watch the colors go on; to heed the way they hold briefly, then fade. He will pause at any time of the day to watch the sky—to study cloud shadows creating abstract patterns that flow smoothly across rock and talus and rich green grass. And at night, in the cave, he is content to sit and smoke his pipe and watch firelight flicker across the furnishings and build deep, dancing shadows. All around him, the rock glows red; its bumps and bubukles pulsate. At such moments, his new home comes alive with hint and mystery.

He revels in the silence, too, and the way his spoon resonates against the Graniteware cup. He smiles to himself as he wonders what the bighorns, high on the far slope, make of that sound.

He gets up and goes down the ramp and crosses to the far side of the little wash and urinates. Overhead soar familiar black rock walls and a wedge of less than black, star-spangled sky. He takes a deep breath. It is good and clean out here in the desert—bitingly real, honed to essentials. And the cave, back there over his right shoulder, is the best home he has ever had. He will never leave it.

He goes back up the ramp, fetches some more firewood from the wood-shed-annex, and sits down again on his little folding chair.

He leans forward, prods the fire, leans back again.

That was ridiculous, thinking he would never leave the cave. Of course he will. For the first time in more than a year there are once again places to go—things he wants to do, not just things to run from. Down here in the canyon he can see everything more clearly. The war in Europe seems very far away; ditto the war in Mexico that is perhaps being waged this very night. Even Vegas with its dust and sheep corrals and new sidewalks seems far away. Seattle, too.

He kicks a half-burned log back into the fire.

Down here in the canyon, now, the grayness no longer overshadows everything. The ache and hurt are still there, of course, and always will be. He will never be able to forget the look on Marge's face when he opened the bedroom door, and the way she . . . But that is all in the past now. Already the pain is a little less agonizing. In just these last few weeks the world has regained color and roundness—and even things that are worth doing. . . . Things that are worth doing. . . . Not for money, but for other reasons, out here in the desert. It will have to be out in the desert, some-where—like the place down in California that the old graybeard told him about when he was tending bar in Vegas. But wherever he goes, things will be different now. Different in many ways from what they have ever been.

Bill smiles. Perhaps they are right when they say that life begins at forty-one.

He looks around at the walls of the cave, at the bumps and bubukles, glowing red, dancing to the firelight.

That was a surprise—thinking about leaving. But come to think of it, he probably will. And maybe fairly soon.

He gets up, kicks the fire again, stands looking out into the darkness.

He will come back, of course, sometime. So he can leave all his gear behind. That little alcove up in the woodshed will be a great place to cache it. Yes, now he has faced the prospect, there is not much doubt. Before long he will be out and doing again.

He goes to bed. For a while he lies listening to the canyon's canopy of silence.


WHEN BILL LEFT the cave he went south.

Among his reasons for leaving, up on the surface, could have been need for money or a simple response to his normal other-side-of-the-fence itch. It often happens that way: mundane matters seem to push and tug and jostle you into a move—but deep down you know you go because the time is right.

I believe that Bill knew, on some level, that in leaving the cave he was moving away from a place that had been the turning point in his life. Grace's intuition that he was "a-borning" there did not materialize from thin air; Bill must have planted the seed. There is certainly no doubt that the man who gradually emerges in the years that follow is markedly different from the one who went down into the cave.

Patterns persist, of course. That is inevitable. But at last the wanderer has found a chart.

For the first forty years of his life Bill performed like a vessel swirled rudderless on stormy seas of chance. His voyages, though fun, lacked destination. But the man who emerges from the cave knows what he wants— and what he does not want.

He does not want to live in a city. He does not want heavy moneymaking deals, like running a restaurant. He does not want heavy organizations, like armies (he goes against that grain once, but regrets it). And he has apparently decided—just as I did, very consciously, at thirty—that he no longer wants to lead any son of a bitch, anywhere: he likes life and himself a whole lot better when he is leading only himself.

His new rudder, though, is the knowledge of what he does want to do.

What he wants to do is wander around the desert on foot and watch what is happening in that subtle world: after the cave, his vision will never again be restricted to the merely human scene. And although he steadfastly masks his new avocation with the pseudo-vocation of prospecting, and although he at first has to take time out for the nuisance business of making just enough money to keep body and soul conjoined, wandering around the desert on foot is essentially what he does for the rest of his life.

In other words, when he left the cave he was set safe and sure on the course that would eventually make him Chuckawalla Bill of the California desert. And although he did not know it, he was already close to sighting his harbor.

After he left the cave, I think he paused in Searchlight, barely forty miles south. Later, he told several people he spent time there; and it was then the big town in those parts, with three square blocks of buildings— "the place a man would gravitate to if he was interested in mining or wanted work as a cook." But the pause in Searchlight was a false start to Bill's new life—a page from an old pattern book. And it did not last. Soon, he moved on, downriver.

He may have ridden the rails. Or perhaps he followed one of the growing number of tracks through the desert—by car, adventurously, or, more conventionally, on foot. If he walked, then he pre-traced in reverse a hundred miles of the route I would follow forty years later, at the start of my walk up California. But he may have traveled by river. At the time, according to Murl Emery, that was "the natural way to go—by raft or whatever." And I like the thought of Bill's having gone by raft. He would surely have heard the Nau legend of the family's first immigrants rafting down to their journey's end in Turtle Creek, Homestead and Braddock; and he would revel in reliving the legend. If he rafted, he played the game to the hilt. For at his journey's end he found the Palo Verde Valley.

By whatever method Bill made his journey south from the cave, it was over by the second week of December 1917.

By then, eight months had passed since America declared war on Germany. U.S. troops were arriving in France. In Washington, President Wilson was putting the final touches to his Fourteen Points for peace. And on December 7, 1917, in the McCoy Mountains, barely twenty miles north of the Palo Verde Valley, the forty-two-year-old Bill, using the name William A. Simoyne, staked a claim that he called the Black Horse Mine.

# 13   Black Horse

IN THE McCOY MOUNTAINS, at the Black Horse Mine, Bill at last began his new life. As at the cave, he lived alone, in peace and quiet. A year later he would tell Aunt Marie how it had been: "A desolate place, it was—just him all by himself, him and his little old shack and his black cat. . . . What you'd call a hermit, I guess. . . . But he liked it that way. You never had nobody around to watch you, he said, and you was your own boss and you could come and go when you felt like it, and that was the way he liked to live, see. 'The free life,' he'd say. 'That's my life. . . .' "

That, he meant, was his new life. He also meant, clearly, that it had been a very good time.

Two islands of information, uneroded by the years, tend to confirm that judgment.

The first is the place itself.

The ridge of barren brown rock known as the McCoy Mountains humps northwestward from Blythe and the Palo Verde Valley like a twenty-mile-long, two-thousand-foot-tall caterpillar. Its northern tip tapers abruptly away. But beyond the main massif stand two small, round hills. They protrude from the surrounding plain the way islands protruding from the sea often show you that a rocky promontory persists, down there below the waves.

The larger of those two hills at the tip of the McCoys is almost certainly where Bill built the little old shack in which he lived with his little old black cat.

By now he could look at landscape with understanding, and he knew it was no accident that the two small hills looked like islands protruding from the sea. For he would have seen that the plain surrounding the

McCoys—and the other rocky ridges that caterpillar across it—is essentially a sloping sea formed by the drainage of detritus from the ridges. Year after year, century after century, millennium after millennium, wind and rain, heat and cold, plant roots and gravity have eaten away at the upthrust rock. Slowly, grudgingly, it yields boulders, pebbles, particles. In the due course of time, rain and wind and gravity wash them all down into the troughs between the ridges. That is why the dry, sandy watercourses that drain from desert mountains are called "washes."

The washes, flowing in the tortoise creep of 'geologic time, fan out and blend into broad, sloping plains that surround the mountains. And these constantly fed plains slowly rise, burying the mountains' foothills—burying, in time, more than the foothills. Soon, the mountains stand awash in their own sand.

This is, of course, how all landscape is formed: as soon as rock thrusts up into mountain it begins eroding toward ultimate plain. But in desert the bone structure stands naked, undraped with conventional folds of greenery.

It is no accident, then, that the two small hills at the head of the McCoy caterpillar look like islands protruding from the sea, showing you that a rocky promontory persists, down there below the waves. They *are* islands. And the ridge does persist, down there below the wash. In much the same way, a few salient facts from a man's history, standing uneroded by the years, can, if you look with empathetic eyes, reveal the submerged and ongoing realities of his life.

By the time Bill came to live in the McCoys he understood that to see the naked beauty of desert landscape your eye has to be tuned: when he told Aunt Marie it was "a desolate place" he was surely trying to compensate for the knowledge that its beauty might be hidden from a homebody niece tuned only to green Pennsylvania lushness. Yet the panorama you command from the northern tip of the McCoys is not, by desert standards, really stark. The sheer size and openness of the plain, sloping away to impossible distances, might daunt a stranger. And the brown caterpillar-ridges that crawl across the landscape can at times turn into immense battleships, built to curve with the planet. But across this stage, light and shadow play, and other desert magics. Above all, though, there is space and silence. If you climb onto any eminence, such as a small round hill, you feel that you are master of all you survey. And you seem to survey a hell of a lot, going on the universe.

It is still that way. Today, several jeep trails cut across the plain. But they are hardly what you would call heavily traveled: on a busy weekend day you may, between sunrise and sunset, see two or three slow-moving dust clouds tracing the paths of adventurous souls on four driven wheels. But that is not too different from how it was in Bill's time. Even then, occasional traffic passed.

There is no doubt, though, that Bill found, there at the tip of the McCoys, a sense of freedom.

I can see him wandering around the flanks of the larger of the two terminal hills and finding a small natural cave; can picture him standing in front of it, smiling at the way its shape has jogged his memory of another cave, barely twelve months and two hundred miles away. I can see him strolling out onto the plain and looking south toward a line of distant jagged mountains; can feel him being drawn toward them, even though he does not yet know they are called the Chuckwalla Mountains.

Given such moments, it is easy to accept that the days and weeks and months Bill spent at his Black Horse Mine were a very good time indeed.

A second uneroded island of information tends to confirm that judgment: there, at the start of his new life, Bill had as partner a man of stature.

Within two months of staking Black Horse Mine, Bill had added seven more claims to form a solid group at the northern tip of the McCoy Mountains. The names of the claims were Social #1 and 2, Northerner #1 & 2, Billy Wright, Darling Sisters and Core. Sometimes, Bill was the lone locator. When other men signed, Bill's name headed the list. The co-locators were P. H. Bray, Frank Goldsberry, Harry Powers, Jim Harrington—and Floyd Brown.

Brown was clearly Bill's prime co-partner. None of the other names appears on more than half the claim forms; Brown's is on all but one, as co-locator or witness. And in those days Floyd Brown was a big name around Blythe, the main town in the Palo Verde Valley.

He appears frequently in a book about the valley's early days: "Floyd Brown was one of the best men I have ever met. He was a big man, six feet four inches tall and broad shouldered. He was easy to work for because he never seemed to be standing off and giving orders but working with us. . . . I believe Brown did more for Blythe than any other one man. . . . In business he was a hard worker but he was very scrupulous. In the pursuit of women he had no scruples at all."

The people I met who had known Brown would say only good of him: "Quite a boy, quite a boy. A drinker and a carouser, but he never let it interfere with his work. A good man. . . . Only educated up to the fourth grade—but a born engineer. . . . A producing son of a gun. . . . A man whose ideas stayed young. . . . He seemed to have everybody's welfare at heart. . . . If there were four people standing together and he was one of them, you knew who to talk to, because he dressed a little better—or perhaps because he wore his clothes better. You know how it is—some people wear clothes, some people just put 'em on."

Floyd Brown, then, was a man after Bill's heart.

The two men may have been partners in another venture too. Grace mentioned an isinglass mine: "he showed me the papers where he sold it to the government in 1918." Black Horse Mine was purely a manganese prospect, but around that time Brown also had a hand in a nearby mica mine—and isinglass is a thin-sheet form of mica.

But Bill did not regard Brown, who was his own age or a little older, only as a business partner. Before long he would testify, in writing, that he thought of him as a friend. And it must have been comforting, during those months at the end of 1917 and the beginning of 1918, to have a man like Floyd Brown around.

But it would not last—this almost idyllic opening act in Bill's new life. He had not yet totally discarded his old patterns.

The brute demands of commerce and war—the demands that always inject a worm of irony into the peaceful pursuit of prospecting—were tunneling in.

By June of 1918, the Germans' great March offensive had brought them to within thirty-seven miles of Paris. American forces, in decisive combat for the first time at Château-Thierry, had helped the French hold. Back in the United States, industry was gearing up fast to full war production. Among other things, that meant a sudden demand for alloys—and manganese. So these events reverberated as far afield as the McCoys.

The Blythe *Herald* began to report activities out there. P. H. Bray— co-locator with Bill on some of the Black Horse group—"brought in some fine specimens." Claims changed hands. A June 20 page-one story had a government geologist from Washington, D.C., visiting the McCoys: "Among the active mines visited by him were . . . the Social and Dioxide group which are being operated by Floyd Brown, J. Harrington, Harry Powers, Frank Goldsberry [and others]."

Now the Social claims, #1 and 2, were part of the group that Bill and these men had staked around Black Horse Mine. But Bill does not feature in the newspaper report. And I know why. By then he had once again climbed over a fence—and was about to go far away.

# 14   Imperial Valley

HALF A DOZEN PEACOCKS patrolled the ranch yard. Off to our right, one
of them displayed. Spring sunlight dazzle-glinted off sumptuous plumes.

"Just look at that!" said Joe Bowers, softly.

Joe was eighty-four, and one of the Imperial Valley's oldest-timers.
After nearly fifty years as a bucket dredge operator on the valley's irrigation canals he had retired to his little ranch midway between Calipatria and
the Salton Sea. He had raised peacocks, he told me, ever since he bought
the ranch, thirty years earlier. Sometimes he had had two or three dozen
running around. Why? Joe smiled. "Oh, just to get a kick out of looking at
'em." Shoeless, he led me into the simple ranch house.

Joe's memory, I found, tended to flicker. But when something stayed
still long enough for him to grab it, he held on. No, he was sorry, he had
never heard of a Bill Simmons or Chuckawalla Bill in the valley. Nor a Bill
Simoyne. "Now if it was Blackie Simoynes you was talking about, I could
have helped you."

"Blackie *who?*"

"Simoynes. Blackie Simoynes. Old Blackie, he was a cook with the
water company that I dredged for, and like all them cooks, when he got
stakey he'd quit and either get drunk and gamble or he'd go prospecting."

Could his name have been Simoyne? Without an 's'?"

Joe Bowers scratched the crown of the stained blue Chevy dealer's cap
that he wore indoors and out. "Well, I guess so. I never seen it written or
nothing. But I always called him Blackie Simoynes."

"Did you ever hear him called anything except Blackie?"

"No. Just Blackie."

"Never Bill?"

"No."

Joe had met Blackie not too long after he, Joe, had moved to the Imperial Valley in 1916. "Yes, I knowed him before and after World War I, both. He'd go and come, you know. And finally he didn't come, and I guess he died and was buried, see. But when I knowed him he was a happy old son of a gun. Hell of a fine guy, too. He wasn't no bum, either. A goddam good cook and a good egg all around."

I put some leading questions.

Goddamnit, yes, seemed like Blackie had been in the Army. Maybe in the war between the United States and Spain—in Cuba and then in the Philippines. "And then in World War I he went and joined the English Army because the American Army wouldn't take him for some reason. . . ."

"The English Army?"

"Yes."

"Not the Canadian Army?"

"No. 'Least, I don't think so. They had a place here you could sign up, see, and they'd take you over there. . . . No, I don't know what else Blackie done. He was a smart son of a gun, and he'd done everything. I was a mule skinner by trade and it seems to me like Blackie had cooked around mule skinner camps all over Nevada and California. He was a working man, and I don't know but whether he may have skun mules himself."

Blackie had tended bar, that was for sure. Because that was how come four of them went out once and filed on a mining claim up in the mountains north of Niland.

Blackie had been tending bar somewhere up in Nevada—no, Joe couldn't remember the name of the place—when he heard about the claim. "There was this old gray-whisker who used to come to the bar regular, Blackie said. He kind of liked Blackie, I guess, and he was getting ready to die, so he told him about this prospect in the mountains down here. I believed Blackie about that, and still do. He wasn't no bullshitter. . . . Well, Blackie knowed his stuff about prospecting, and he'd walked all over them goddam mountains. Walking didn't bother him at all. And he found the place right away. So the four of us went up there—Blackie and me and Henry Law and Fred Hansen. . . ."

"Do you remember what year that was?"

"Well, let's see. We drove up to the mine in my 1919 Model T, and I bought that car new. So it couldn't have been before 1919. And in 1923 I bought a two-seater Dodge. The first closed car around these parts, it was, and they used to call me Lord Bowers on account of it. There's one guy in town still does. So it must have been before 1923. The water companies consolidated that year, and I know it was a while before that. So it must have been 1920, or maybe 1921."

"Did you record the claim?"

"Sure we did. Fred Hansen was a careful businessman and wouldn't have had nothing to do with it if it hadn't been filed. Green Bay Mine, we called it, on account of Fred and me both coming from there. Old Blackie was smart and he knew how to file a claim, so I'm sure we filed it right enough, up in Riverside. . . . But in the end it didn't assay out. Why, it's years now since I even thought about that claim."

I leaned back in my chair. It was a pity I had passed through Riverside on a Sunday on the way down and had not been able to stop as I had intended and get copies of all the Simoyne claims instead of just the sample few I had taken when I first suspected that Bill was William A. Simoyne. But at least I could check on the way back. A recorded Green Bay Mine would nail down Blackie Simoynes as William A. Simoyne.

No, Blackie had not been real tall, said Joe Bowers. But he stood very straight. Husky, but not heavy—oh, maybe 160 pounds. His eyes? Hm . . . Maybe brown. He was a great talker, was Blackie, but not the sort of guy to tell a lot of goddam lies. How did he talk? Well, you could understand him all right. No, no idea why they called him Blackie: he wasn't particularly dark-looking. Seems like his hair was black when Joe first knew him, but later on it was gray. No, never did see him drive a car—but not too many people owned a car in them days. No, didn't know if he was ever married, either. One for the girls? Well, no doubt he'd go down and get his Peter once in a while, but never heard of him going with any steady girl.

"Last time I seen old Blackie? Playing poker, he was, in a gambling joint run by Johnny and Edna, over in Westmorland. What year? Oh, maybe 1923 or '24. Someplace in there. Could be wrong about that, though. . . . No, most of the people from back then are dead and gone now. Why, I remember . . ."

Joe launched into rambling reminiscences about his years as bucket dredge operator.

I went out to the car and brought in my photographs of Bill.

We began with the pair from the 1908 desertion poster. Joe held the print close to his tape-repaired eyeglasses. "No, that's not him. This guy looks like he's a little younger than Blackie. . . . Blackie was a little older than that."

With Grace's two snaps, the man was "too old." And I failed, utterly, in my efforts to persuade Joe to make any allowance for the passage of years.

Finally I handed him a snap I had by this time obtained of Bill sometime during the thirties, sporting a full beard. Joe held it up close, then at arm's length. "This one standing up there? By God, it does look something like him, at that. Just about his build, too. But he didn't have no mustache. Nor a beard. Why, I imagine that if old Blackie come in here with all them whiskers on, I wouldn't know him. . . . He was an interesting character, though, or I wouldn't have remembered him."

Soon afterward I drove away, leaving Joe Bowers, dredge operator and poet, standing barefoot at eighty-four among his peacocks.

For several days, then, I drew a blank. I found no one in the Imperial Valley who had known Bill during his early days there, either as Blackie Simoynes or under some surer name—though I did get the addresses of several old-timers who had moved away. The local water company had no records before 1923, no Simoyne or Simoynes or Simon or Simmons on pay lists dating back to that year. And the El Centro Recorder's Office, rechecked for mining claims by a Simoyne or Simoynes—even though I felt sure I would have picked up the name on my first, sweltering visit—yielded nothing. But on the way north I stopped in Riverside and found the record for the Green Bay Mine: the claim had been staked by Joseph Bower, Fred Hansen—and W. A. Simoyne. And soon afterward, back home, I found among Grace's notations in the margins of my San Francisco *Chronicle* Trunkman article one I had overlooked. It was a single word, standing on its own: "Simoines."

One morning several weeks later, my phone rang and a voice said, "I'm Arden Harlan, calling from Kelseyville. You wrote asking about Blackie Simoyne."

After a moment's blank, my memory dug up the name: it had been low on the list I had collected of old-time Imperial Valley residents who had moved away. I had almost not bothered to write.

"Sure I knew him—from about 1917 on through 1928." The voice was that of an old man, yet full of vigor—curiously forced, as if fighting something. "Did I know him well? Better than anyone in the world, that's all."

A few mornings later I drove into Kelseyville, a hundred miles north of San Francisco.

Arden Harlan lived, or at least was domiciled, in a rest home for the elderly. An ordinary private house, it stood among thin pine trees, relaxed as a box-girder bridge, bristling with prohibitions: QUIET! NO SMOKING!! Visitors 9–11 and 2–4 ONLY!! Heavy summer heat beat down.

Harlan lay on a divan on the back porch. He was gaunt, cadaverous. His face, and especially the jaw muscles, had atrophied almost to a death mask. Periodically, his emaciated arms would begin an uncontrolled quivering. Yet he had a shock of white, healthy hair; and in spite of his fighting-against-extinction voice and coughing bouts and gaspings for breath and intermittent dribblings from a corner of the mouth and the Kleenexes that coped with that degradation, this shadow of a man still managed to summon up a spirit that strove to deny the odds.

"That's him, all right," he said when his faded blue eyes had absorbed my photographs. "That's Blackie. That's Bill. . . . Yeah, lots of people called him Bill. Hell, he had all kinds of goddam names and nicknames. Signed two or three different ways. Sure, I remember one of them was this 'William Ashee Simoyne.' " Harlan put the accent on the last syllable of "Ashee."

"Something to do with France that was. But all the names meant the same thing. Frenchmen got their own way of describing things, you know."

He restudied the photographs.

"Yeah, sometimes he grew a beard, sometimes he shaved. But always a short, heavyset fellow like that, solidly built—a perfect man, physically, except for his teeth. All the time he was working for me he didn't have any teeth. So he'd just get a good big mouthful of meat and swallow it whole. Apart from that, though, I never saw anybody in finer shape. Good-looking too. . . ."

I produced a photograph I now had of Bill in the last year of his life.

"That's him with the cane? Wouldn't have recognized him. He's sure lost a lot of weight. He was seventy-five then? Died in 1950, eh? Yes, he'd have been twenty years older than me. And I'm eighty now."

They had first met in 1917, over on the west side of the Salton Sea, where Bill was staying with a local Indian chief known as Fig Tree John. Harlan was a foreman with Number Three Water Company in Calipatria and had signed Bill on as cook. Bill would have been forty-two then; Harlan, twenty-two. For the next six years Bill had worked intermittently for the young foreman. "A good cook won't stay anywhere, that's the hell of it. And I always had a hell of a time with cooks. They're a breed on their own."

"Yes, I know. Go into a kitchen in a mining camp, outside of mealtimes, and you risk your life."

Harlan smiled. "That's right. But Blackie was a damned good cook, don't think he wasn't. He couldn't work only just so long at a time, though. Get a little money, and he'd quit. Had to take a trip some goddam place. So he'd pick up and go and we wouldn't see him for three or four months, or maybe six. Then he'd come back with his hind end sticking out, and why, he had a job."

"His hind end sticking out?"

"Sure, worn his pants out."

"Oh. Do you know what he did when he wasn't working?"

"Prospecting, I guess. That's what he'd talk about. A lot of those guys had a habit of going mining, you know—prospecting, and stuff like that. Have something to talk about, to get people to listen to 'em. No, I don't remember what he said. Didn't pay too much attention."

I tried a few names.

"Black Horse Mine? Yes, I heard him mention that two or three times. 'Blackie Black Horse' was one of his names. But I didn't know what it meant. Well, yes, that *could* have been where he got this name Blackie. But hell, he was just a dark-complexioned Frenchman."

On at least one occasion that Bill worked for Harlan, he had owned a Model T Ford.

"One of those old square brass radiator things with no top on it. A bad driver? Hell, no one was much of a driver then. But he was the damnedest guy I ever saw with that car. You could get in it in town and drive all the way out to camp without ever touching the throttle, and old Bill he'd laugh and holler and swear up and down that because you didn't have to touch the throttle his car didn't use any gas. Hell, we just laughed, and never told him anything."

It was the first piece of sheer stupidity I had heard attributed to Bill. But it rang true: Grace had also remembered his obtuseness with automobiles.

"Yeah, I found an old picture of Bill standing beside that car." Harlan reached down beside his divan, handed me a small snapshot. "You can see that I wrote his name on the side. We'd come through a rainstorm, driving back to camp that day, and there was mud sticking all over the car."

For a moment I felt I was looking at a stranger. I could make no connection between this bespectacled man in his early forties, hamming it up beside the car, and the Bill, fifteen years older, in Grace's snaps. Then I saw that the features were the same as those of the man standing beside Rose, the waitress at Garnet. But I still could not reconcile this new Bill with the rather callow, unformed thirty-three-year-old who stared out from his desertion poster. Here, only ten or a dozen years later, he looked

a much more solid citizen—sure of himself, and reasonably content with what he found there. After a while I realized that the metamorphosis at the cave had worked on body as well as mind.

"Bill always had a Kodak," said Harlan. "And he liked to take pictures. For some reason he had somebody else take that one, but as a rule he took the damn pictures himself. Here, I got some others from that time, and most of them must have come out of Bill's camera."

There were two more shots of the mud-caked car and several others from those days when Bill cooked for Arden Harlan's gangs in portable camps around Calipatria. One snap showed four mules pulling the double-roofed cookhouse that had, intermittently, been Bill's. It had side flaps that opened up to form windows, said Harlan. A counter ran around inside, and you could seat up to twenty-five men at a time. Sometimes there'd be as many as thirty-five, fed in two sittings.

Although Harlan thought most of the photographs had been taken by Bill, he couldn't be sure. "Christ, I can't remember back there, all that stuff. . . . But if you want 'em, take 'em. Oh, hell no. You don't have to pay me. Get what you can out of 'em. I'm not going to be around here much longer." He dissolved into one of his terrible coughing bouts. It left him gasping for breath.

When he had recovered I probed for more details.

"Oh, in hot weather he'd wear just as little as he could put on. No shirt, often. Just a pair of shorts. But on Saturday nights he'd take a bath and get a shave or haircut like all the rest of us and dress up and go into town.

"Yes, he always dressed up when we went into town. He looked good, too. All he had was a ten-dollar suit from a junk store but he'd look better than I did in my hundred-dollar tailor-made. Hell, he had me skinned to death. But back in camp he was easy. What he liked to do Sundays, in the latter part of the season when we had the crew cut down, was to go picnicking. 'Harlan,' he'd say, 'you get us some chicken and I'll fry it up.' So I'd get the goddam chicken and we'd all go out. Just go out on the desert. The whole crew. All the white fellows, anyway. . . . Oh sure, he got on O.K. with the men—though a lot of 'em got tired of him hollering. You see, he was a damn peculiar guy, was Blackie. One of the finest guys in the world when he was in a good humor. But he'd get nasty spells. He'd get mad over something—anything—and raise hell. Maybe in a couple of hours he'd be fine again. But sometimes he'd stay mad at everybody for three, four days.

"The only time he didn't get any spells like that was once when he brought a woman from San Diego back to camp. Homely as hell she was, but a good woman. And Bill, he was a different guy altogether. You'd be surprised. She was there about two months, and he was happy all the time. Hell, I didn't care a damn about feeding her and all that. Suited me. I knew that as long as she was there I'd have a happy cook. But one day the superintendent come to camp and said she'd have to go. It was a mutual company, see, with all the farmers in it, and he said the farmers were talk-

ing, asking questions, and one of the big bosses was hollering his head off, and I'd have to get rid of her. There was nothing I could do about it, and she went. And Bill got real mad at that. Didn't stay much longer, that time. And it always stuck in his craw."

I began to probe for the kind of insights to be expected from someone who said he had known Bill "better than anyone in the world."

"Oh yeah, he had a sense of humor all right. Laughed at lots of things. Sure, he liked to read. Had a lot of goddam time on his hands and he'd just lay there, reading. Books, magazines, anything laying around. But hell, he'd read a story and then when we came in at night he'd put it on himself. Tell the damned story back as if it had happened to him. He'd be laughing and hollering and having a hell of a time. For a little while he got away with that 'cause we didn't know it. Then we found out later, and we just laughed and didn't pay any attention any more.

"Yeah, like I said, he was a damned peculiar guy, was Blackie. A nut on wars, for example. If there was a war going on, he was going to get into it, one way or the other. He'd been fifteen years in the cavalry, you know. . . . Sure I saw him ride horses. Dozens of times. Rode well, too. Yeah, he'd been a mess sergeant in the Philippines."

"A mess sergeant?"

"So he said. And he liked to put on the dog, you know. So he had a whole bunch of these guys, these little Filipinos, running around there with fans—a-fanning him while he was laying in a hammock. He'd talk about that. Yes, he liked to go to wars all right. And when the war come off in 1918 he was all set to go. So when my vacation came up in September I took him with me to Los Angeles. He went every day to the military there—the U.S. Army, I mean—but for some reason they wouldn't take him back. Well, Bill, he meets up with some guy he knew and of course they get to drinking. And in the end he goes down to the English, who had some kind of program there for miners to dig tunnels under the ground to blow up things. And do you know he went over there and worked in them damned things until the war was over! . . . No, it was the British Army— even though he hated the British. He was always a Frenchman. And when he come back after the war he hated them worse. Yeah, he was always one for wars, Blackie was."

Delighted as I was with the new information, I realized long before I left that "knew him better than anyone in the world" had been sheer non-sense. Bill had worked for Harlan perhaps half a dozen times, never for more than a few months at a time. Harlan had never seen him during his absences and apparently never inquired what he had been doing. And after

Bill's last stint as a cook the two men had met only once, years later, for a few hours.

I confess I felt disappointed. But Arden Harlan did all he could to help. Before I left he had two beers brought from the refrigerator, and while we drank them—with him sitting propped up now, on his divan—he tried to think of other people who had known Bill. But everyone he could remember was dead. At the very end, I asked about a man connected with the water company whom several people had mentioned.

"Charlie Guest?" said Harlan. "No, he died before . . ." He broke off. He was looking very tired now—even more drawn and cadaverous. Impatiently, yet with a certain dignity, he Kleenexed away a trickle of saliva from the side of his mouth.

I stood up.

It was a difficult parting: we both knew we would almost certainly never meet again. At such moments it is not easy to avoid insincerities. As I walked away around the jutting corner of the house that was now Arden Harlan's home, would be his last home, he began another of his rasping, wrenching coughing spells.

He died five weeks later.

THE RECORDED DETAILS of Bill's attempt to enlist for a fifth time in the U.S. Army went up in smoke during a fire at the National Personnel Records Center in St. Louis in 1973, a year before I visited the National Archives. All the history that remains is the bare statement James Walker found for me at the Archives: Bill obtained a deserter's release in May 1918 and tried to re-enlist but was rejected.

A friend from twenty years later remembers that Bill told him it happened at Fort MacArthur in San Pedro, Los Angeles. "They said that if he done thirty or sixty days or something, then he'd get an honorable discharge and all his benefits. And that's what he done. That's how he got his pension."

The official record of what Bill did after the U.S. Army rejected him very nearly went up in smoke, too.

Soon after talking to Arden Harlan I wrote to the British Ministry of Defence—and also, just in case, to the Canadian equivalent. The Canadians reported no record under any of Bill's names. The British Ministry opened with a classic bureaucratic gambit: Simon and Simmons were very common names, they wrote, and it was not possible to help me without the man's army number or at least regiment. I parried by pointing out that I had given Simoyne as the most likely name for him to have used, and that it was a very unusual one. The Ministry quickly capitulated. Within a month they replied that they had located the records of 370731 Sapper William Ashe Simoyne. And within another month I had everything that was apparently to be had: Xeroxes of twenty-two documents that "although rather charred around the edges evidently survived the World War II blitz fire [at] . . . the Army Records Centre."

The documents consisted of twenty-one forms that outlined the barebone facts of two hundred and thirty-six days in Bill's life—and one full-blooded letter.

When Bill applied for enlistment in the British Army at Los Angeles—not in September, as Arden Harlan had remembered, but on August 6, when it remained uncertain whether the great German offensive toward Paris had indeed been broken—he played his usual whimsical-pragmatic game with the inevitable deluge of bureaucratic forms. He signed the application form "William A. C. Simoyne." (Later, he rounded out the "A" to "Ashe." The "C" never reappeared.) He trimmed his true age of forty-three to a more acceptable thirty-eight. His nationality became "British" ("born of French parents on board a British ship crossing to the US"). And he gave his occupation as "miner and prospector," his address as "Blytha Ironwood, Mimatora, Riverside County, California," and his next of kin as "Mr. Floyd Brown (friend), of Blythe, Paloverde Valley."

Naming Floyd Brown as next of kin is hardly surprising: as a colleague of Brown's commented, "His friends trusted him." But Bill apparently decided that although the British Army might as well have someone to inform should anything happen to him, giving them an address that would pin him down was a different matter—and an opportunity for fun. "Ironwood" is an old name for the McCoy Mountains that Bill used on all his claim forms for the Black Horse group; but the rest of the address seems to be word play in Latin—a language Bill would have been exposed to during those interminable services at St. Joseph's, and probably at school, too. "Blytha" can hardly be anything but a Latinized "Blythe." And an old-timer, still living in Blythe, suggested that "Mimatora" might be a corrupt form of "Mini Terra," meaning "small country"—"because in those days this was a small place, right enough."

On August 8, 1918—the day the British attacked near Amiens with 450 tanks, and so began what turned out to be the final Allied offensive—the British Army shipped Bill to Chicago. There, nine days later, he signed a form of attestation for Short Service (For the Duration of the War) and took an oath. He swore by Almighty God that he would be faithful and bear true Allegiance to His Majesty King George the Fifth, His Heirs, and Successors, and that he would, as in duty bound, honestly and faithfully defend His Majesty, His Heirs, and Successors, in person, Crown and Dignity against all enemies, and would observe and obey all orders of His Majesty, His Heirs, and Successors, and of the Generals and Officers set over him. So help him God. At a guess, Bill indeed implored some god or other to help him forget this heresy. Three days later he was at the Imperial Recruits Depot in Windsor, Nova Scotia, declaring—after he had been duly cautioned that he was liable to severe penalties if he gave false answers to the questions—that he was born on 2 Aug 1880, was a British citizen, and was not a citizen of the United States. And on 10 September, with these lies and comedies all tidied away, he sailed aboard S.S. *Themocles* for Tilbury, London, England. In France, the Allied offensive was now moving forward over a broad front. Two days later, the American ground forces made their first big contribution to the Allied cause when they attacked at St. Mihiel.

By the last day of September, when Sapper Simoyne arrived for training as a Tunneller at the Royal Engineers' Tunnelling Depot Company in Chatham (rate of pay: one shilling and sixpence a day), the Central Powers were crumbling. The day before, Bulgaria had signed an armistice. Austria was suing for peace. With the Allied offensive in France gaining momentum, Germany seemed about to follow suit.

But the war dragged on through October. The Allied armies continued to advance toward Germany. Bill, still at Chatham, passed a trade test as Tunneller's Mate. He was still at Chatham and still training to mine under the enemy's trenches when, at the eleventh hour of the eleventh day of the eleventh month, the guns on the Western Front at last fell silent.

Very slowly, the world began to readjust.

On 2 February 1919, Sapper Simoyne—who now judged it propitious to proclaim his age as forty-six and his address as Calipatria, Imperial County—formally applied for repatriation in order that he might "return to work on Manganese Mines." And nine weeks later, on 9 April, he achieved demobilization and was repatriated.

En route for California he stopped off in Braddock and stayed for two or three days with his niece, Marie, daughter of his sister Mary. Marie was then twenty-one, newly married and very pregnant.

"He tried to coax us all to go back to California with him," Aunt Marie had told me, fifty years later. "But my mother, she wouldn't have none of it. She liked Bill well enough but she knowed him, too. 'He might be here one day and gone the next,' she said. 'And where would we be then?' "

Bill knew he might be making his last visit to Braddock, and he made the social rounds. "He went up to see Tony," Aunt Marie said, "as well as some of the fellows he'd been at school with and had worked with in the wire mill when he was young."

Above all, he went to see Fred Alger.

"He spent a whole afternoon with Fred," Aunt Marie's husband told me. "I took him up there."

That postwar spring of 1919, Fred was twenty-eight, and it is easy to see Bill and him hitting it off. For although Fred still lived in Braddock he, too, through his newspaper work, had escaped the Simon treadmill. And he had the Bill spark in him. Art Rooney, owner of the Pittsburgh Steelers, wrote me: "Fred Alger was a very good friend of mine and I can confirm that he was also a longtime friend of Honus Wagner's. Like his uncle, he too was a maverick. . . . He always chewed tobacco and in the press boxes at Pitt Stadium and Forbes Field they always had a special spittoon for Fred. . . . I never heard about Uncle Bill Simon but he couldn't have been a greater character than Fred."

So Bill went up to see Fred, that spring of 1919, partly because he just plain wanted to see him.

But he also had something on his mind.

Through his newspaper work, Fred knew the local congressman, Clyde Kelly, who owned the Braddock *Daily News*. And Bill wanted Kelly as an ally in a skirmish with the British Army. Now in this matter of what Bill had on his mind, Aunt Marie got two important facts wrong, in addition to the country the army came from: Bill was not actually fighting for pay; and Kelly did not really bring victory before Bill left Braddock for the last time.

That final departure from Braddock occurred shortly before April 28, when Bill's great-niece was born; and five months later Bill was still skirmishing with His Majesty's War Office in London. By now he was definitely not amused:

> Calapatria,
> Imperial Valley
> California
> USA
> 9-21-19

Sir. I herein Enclose one form "Z" 21 which was forwarded to me Instead of My Discharge. I want it distinctly understood that I am NOT AN ENGLISHMAN nor an ENGLISH

SUBJECT but an American Citizen who tryed to do his duty as he saw it during the World War and Who Was Considered to Old to Enlist in his own Countrys Army & who th[r]o an over Abundance of Patriotism joined the British Over Seas Expeditionary Forces thro Misrepresentation on the Part of his B.M. Recruiting Officer. But I was game to go thro With the *farce* But since the War has Ended I *want* My Discharge and I want it By Return Mail, do not Return this form Z "21" as i haven't any use for it and if you do Return the same I will Hang it in the *Toilet* I have had Enough of you Hot Air Excuses for you have sent some of My Comrades their discharges and I see No Reason why you will not send Mine. Hoping you do this I sighn Myself

W. A. Simoyne

American Citizen

When this letter reached London, bureaucrats entered due notations in Bill's file. Although their prose is more polished than Bill's, its meanings remain far less clear. And meanings, after all, are what prose is about. But justice seems to have been done. I think Bill got what he wanted. I can certainly detect no hint that in the years that followed he ever suffered any impediment from a lingering allegiance, real or imagined, to His Majesty King George the Fifth, His Heirs, or Successors.

But then, that is hardly surprising. Bill's mind soon moved on to other matters.

# 15  The Twenties

WHEN BILL GOT BACK to California from England and Braddock he apparently returned to his Black Horse Mine: that was his address when he sent Aunt Marie five dollars to buy shoes for her new baby. But things had changed, out there at the tip of the McCoy Mountains. The world had begun to readjust to peace. The government no longer needed manganese, and at a guess the mining operations had already closed down. That may be why Bill does not seem to have stayed at Black Horse for long: he simply needed money.

But there may be a very different reason.

Although Bill was born in a mining village and for eight years lived beside No. 2 Incline—and its repetitious sound reminder, whenever coal poured into a waiting wagon, that there was a mine just up the hill—he had not until this time had thrust on him, brutally and unduckably, that edgy irony inherent in the peaceful pursuit of prospecting: if you succeed, you wreck the place. But when he went back to his little old shack and little old black cat that he had carried so fondly in his memory he found that the short, sharp, war-generated burst of mining activity, though minor in modern terms, had crucified the desert. Even today, sixty years later, open pits and tailings still scar the foothills. And roads cut across the plain, wind up washes and, on one dark slope, radiate into an ugly swastika. In 1919 there would have been fuel drums and rusted machinery and other alluvial man-crud, too. And Bill would have grieved at what his quiet, idyllic months of freedom out there in the unspoiled desert had done. He never again lived by choice in a place where the hand of man had fallen harsh and ugly.

By September of that year he was back in the Imperial Valley, mailing off from Calipatria his final salvo at the British War Office. And for the first half of the twenties—the decade that pedaled him along from forty-four to fifty-four—he went back to the Imperial Valley whenever he needed a few dollars to reclothe his rear end and build a small stake.

For four years he continued to cook, intermittently, for Arden Harlan and the water company.

It was during one such stint—on March 21, 1921—that he staked Green Bay Mine with Joe Bowers—the bucket dredge operator and poet who kept peacocks—and Fred Hansen.

"Fred was in on it because he grubstaked us," Joe Bowers had told me. "He was a friend from Green Bay, Wisconsin, where I came from, and he used to come down here for the winters sometimes and work at some roustabout job. Fred had the old folding money, though. Always did have. Born with it—his folks had a brickyard. Yeah, Fred was a different kind of an egg. Made his money with his head, some way. So when the four of us went up there, he grubstaked us. I had an interest in the mine on account of I was the only one with a car. And Henry Law was in on it, too. He was my stepbrother and a trapper by trade. Lost in Alaska, years ago now. . . ."

Later, I talked on the phone with Fred Hansen. He was eighty-one and still living in Green Bay. He remembered the events and the actors with clarity and affection.

"If ever there was a good fellow," he said, "it is Joe Bowers." They had been school friends and neighbors and had always stayed in touch. "Joe is as honest as they come, never harmed anybody, and always worked hard. Did a lot of night dredging, you know, because it was too hot, days."

Henry Law had been a good, honest fellow, too. They were all about twenty then, and they all worked for Number Three Water Company, and they would often look up from the flats of the Imperial Valley and wonder what lay back in the Chocolate Mountains, to the east. Blackie, the cook—no, Hansen had never heard him called Bill—would often talk about the minerals up there. So one weekend the four of them drove up into the mountains in Joe's Model T and found this prospect that Blackie knew about, and staked it. Sure, they had recorded it. In fact, he still had the original. Yes, it was in Blackie's handwriting. And he would be happy to let me have it to get a good photograph made.

The ore from the "mine" had been colorful stuff with gold and silver and copper in it, and Hansen and Henry Law spent two weeks working the site. After the first time, when they staked the claim, Blackie did not

# Notice of Location
## QUARTZ CLAIM

**Notice is Hereby Given:** That _We_ the undersigned citizens of the United States, having made discovery of mineral and rock in place, do locate and claim by right of discovery and location, the within mentioned Quartz Mining Claim, and upon the discovery monument have posted a duplicate notice and do hereby give Notice of its location in accordance with the U. S. Revised Statutes, and with local laws and customs, and with the rules and regulations of this Mining District. The measurement of this claim is _1500_ linear feet, in length, on the vein. The _North_ erly end line is _1100_ feet _North_ erly from the discovery monument, and the _South_ erly end line is _400_ feet _South_ erly from the discovery monument, and said end lines are parallel. The general course of the vein is _North_ erly and _South_ erly. The width _300_ feet on the _East_ erly side, and _300_ feet on the _West_ erly side, measuring from the center of the said quartz lode, vein, ledge or deposit, and it is more particularly described as follows:

**Commencing** at _Southwest Corner Monument of Stone_ in a _S. West_ erly direction from the discovery monument, _400_ feet therefrom, and _thence in a Northerly direction 1500 feet to a Monument of Stone thence 600 feet in an Easterly direction to a Monument of Stone thence 1500 feet in a Southerly direction to a Monument of stone thence 600 feet in a Westerly direction to a Monument of stone thence 400 feet in a North Easterly direction to discovery Monument the Point of beginning. this Claim is in the What is known as the Dos Palmas Mountains at the Southern End 6 Miles from Dos Palmas Springs and 2 Miles S.W. of the Cofer Ore Mine_

And all the dips, variations, spurs, angles, and all veins, ledges, lodes or deposits within the lines of this claim, together with all water and timber and any rights appurtenant, allowed by law, are hereby claimed.

The **Name** is the _Gran Bay No 1_ Mining Claim.
Said claim is situated in the _Dos Palmas_ Mining District,
County of _Riverside_ State of _California_
Located this _21_ day of _March_, 19 _21_. This discovery is made and this notice is posted this _21_ day of _March_ 19 _21_

**Locators** _Witness_

_Joseph Powers_
_Fred Hansen_
_W. A. Simoyne_
_Henry Saw_

_Billie Van Andale_
_Wm E Collins_
_Roy F Leonard_

The exterior boundaries of a Quartz Claim cannot be limited by any local mining regulation to less than 25x1500 feet, measuring from the center of vein on either side.
If the rules of the District require it, a duplicate of the location notice should be recorded with the District Recorder; and whether the local rules require it or not, it is safer to record also with the County Recorder because the County records are less liable to be destroyed by fire or otherwise. If possible have the signatures witnessed.
The above Form conforms to the requirement of the U. S. Statutes. See Wolcott's Mining Manual, pages 74, 75 and 76.

1500. LOCATION NOTICE—Quartz—Wolcott's Mining Blank. 1915

go up again. They had sent in some samples of the ore, but it assayed out very low and mining it would not have paid. So they had never done any more with it.

Hansen had known Blackie for only four months in that spring of 1921, but he remembered him vividly. "He was just a little different from other people, I guess. It wouldn't surprise me at all to hear that he had a kind of secret life.

"In a way, I guess I didn't know how to take him. I regarded him as a man who'd been around, but he was a bit of a windjammer—he'd talk a lot. Still, we got a kick out of him, even though we didn't always know whether to believe it all. You thought he was kinda romancing a lot, with his stories. And he could be kinda moody. Not always the same fellow. Sometimes he'd be very jolly—and sometimes not so jolly. I liked him, though. He wasn't just an average fellow. He liked to bear respect and show a little dignity when he was dressed up. . . . Why, I remember meeting him in a pool hall in Calipatria one evening. Calipatria has gone down some since those days, what with big business taking over all the little farms and so on, but back then it wasn't a bad place. There was a little picture show at that time—and this pool hall. Blackie liked to shoot pool, and he was pretty good at it. But that evening . . . God, I didn't know the man hardly. He was all dressed up in a nice dark suit. He was a pretty nice-looking man, and that evening he had an air. He had glasses on, I think—maybe dark-rimmed—and I didn't know he wore them. Anyway, at first I didn't recognize him. He was a different man, and I was impressed. He looked like a . . . well, you wouldn't have thought of him as cooking for us. And he saw the funny side of it—the way I didn't recognize him. He laughed right away, I remember. Not that he was stuck-up at all, don't think that.

"Come to think of it, I must have liked the man. Because after the water company shut down for the hot weather I heard he was cooking for a big ranch and I went to see him. It was five or six miles out of town, maybe more, and I walked all the way out there. And he was glad to see me, and everything like that. When it came around to mealtime he was alone, all the others were away, and he said, 'I can't give meals to people and I'll have to charge you. So let's call it thirty-five cents.' With some people you'd think they just wanted to pocket the money, but I regarded it as honest on his part, and I was glad to pay. Yeah, he was nice to me. . . . And that was the last time I saw him. When? Well, let's see. It must have been May or June of 1921, because in June I left and came back to Green Bay."

My only other glimpses of Bill in the Imperial Valley during the first half of the twenties find him with a pack on his back.

When I met Eusibio Savalha he was seventy and lying in a Brawley hospital, weak and faded, cobwebbed ignominiously to the bed by intravenous feeding tubes. But in the fall of 1922 he was seventeen—digging and maintaining irrigation ditches just outside Calipatria at the start of what turned out to be a forty-year stint with the water company. And at seventy he still remembered, vividly, his first meeting with a man named Blackie —second name unknown—who was probably, but not quite certainly, the man in my photographs. Savalha's eyesight, as well as his Spanish accent, at first left me questioning whether this Blackie was indeed Bill Simmons. But everything fitted too neatly for any real doubt to linger.

Every fall for four or five years in the early twenties, beginning in 1922, a man carrying a pack used to come walking down from the north.

"Ah, here comes old Blackie," the other ditch workers would say. The man was not tall but he stood very upright. He wore a goatee beard. He had intense brown eyes. And he smoked a curve-stemmed pipe. His pack was a simple affair with shoulder straps, for "pots and pans and things." And he always carried a walking staff.

Every year, he would stop for an hour or two and chat with Savalha. He would talk of prospecting back in the red hills beyond Niland and bring out some of the rock samples he carried in gunny sacks. And always, at some stage, he would say it was a shame the young Mexican was wasting his life there with the water company.

Savalha would say, "But what can I do? I need steady work or I'll be sunk."

And Blackie would say, "No. All a man needs is to work for a while and then go out and do what he wants to."

Half a century later, lying in bed in a Brawley hospital, the seventy-year-old Savalha smiled up at me and said, "You know, that man he talked pretty good. Talked like a guy with plenty sense. But sometimes young guys like me, that time, you know, we think, 'That man is crazy.' But he wasn't no bum. No, no, no. So I listen to him. I talk to him. . . . And now, sometimes, I think he's pretty smart man."

In those early years of the twenties, Niland and Calipatria seem to have been the towns that drew Bill. And at first that puzzled me. Close up, they had lived down to the hints picked out by my headlights, that hot June night I drove south for the first time along the Salton shoreline: a string of rabbit-hutch communities, dilapidated and sad. The dominant sound along their soulless streets, I later discovered, was the rattle of tin cans tumbling before the wind to bang against discarded lumber, oil drums and boilers. In Calipatria, a rash of signs chamber-of-commerced the town's sole claim to distinction: "The lowest down city in the Western Hemisphere—184 feet below sea level."

But in the twenties things were different.

Since then, Niland has actually moved.

The old town of that name—contracted from "Nile-land," a reference to the Imperial Valley's fertile alluvial soil—stood a mile east of the present highway. It was a solid sort of place, centered on a wedge of dignified and almost stately buildings with a bank at its core.

But old Niland has died. Today, the bank and all but one store stand shuttered tight. The town was killed in the 1940's, by a real estate developer. Thwarted in development plans by the owner of the solid central complex, who refused to sell out to him, he vowed to "get even" by building "a new town." And a mile away, on the new highway that paralleled the Salton shoreline, he strung a line of small commercial buildings. They had never quite been filled, all at one time, I was told; but they had throttled the old Niland. The timbre of the new town was inevitable: something done purely for money or sustained only by spite rarely turns out beautiful.

But the old Niland that Bill knew, though defeated now, retains its dignity. The pillared colonnade of the central complex stands clean and gleaming in the desert sunlight—still impressive, for all the shuttered sadness. In its time, it must have lent the place distinction. And looking at it with half-closed eyes, I could see why Bill had kept returning there.

Calipatria, eight miles down the highway, did not die. But it has sickened.

In the twenties, several old-timers assured me, their town was "real pretty." At least one of the streets now abandoned to windblown tin cans was bordered by palm trees, oleanders and roses, all sustained by an irrigation canal. But the trees and shrubs "went down" in the early 1930's, when the Depression hit.

Before the Depression, though, the whole valley hummed. Hundreds of small farmers raised flourishing crops of tomatoes, green peas and other crops. There was even an ostrich farm. The Calipatria railroad depot served a big, bustling stockyard, and the town itself had "lots of stores—so many buildings, you wouldn't believe today." Beer and gambling joints abounded. The place pulsated with warm human purpose and vibrant human folly. "A real Wild West town," one old-timer told me.

So I understood, now, that the towns of the Imperial Valley would appeal to the unquiet part of Bill—the sector that loved war and pool and poker. They would draw him back in the fall of each year, when he needed money, and hold him for several months.

During the rest of each year, all through the twenties, Bill wandered widely. Reports from people who knew him later put him in the Mother Lode country, up in the western foothills of the Sierra Nevada; in Bodie, an old gold-mining town below the eastern escarpment of the same range; in Death Valley, meeting Death Valley Scotty; and cooking for the mule skinners that hauled borax out of Trona with the famous twenty-mule teams. Other reports, less firmly tied to the twenties, have him in the Superstition Mountains near Phoenix, Arizona, and in a string of Nevada mining towns—Tonapah and Goldfield and Beatty. If Iron Jaw spoke the truth, then about this time Bill also bused into Winnemucca.

Uncertainty clouds all these events. But on August 2, 1923, Bill celebrated his forty-eighth birthday, Warren Harding died and Calvin Coolidge succeeded him. I also know that from April 1925 until March 1926 Bill spent most if not all of his time prospecting in the short, steep canyon of Crystal Creek, on the northern escarpment of the San Bernardino Mountains. These claims were in San Bernardino County, the largest county in the United States—going on half the size of England or New York State, more than twice as big as Wales or Vermont; and this fact at first seems to suggest at least a broadening of Bill's known southern California territory, hitherto restricted to Imperial and Riverside counties. It does. But only just. The claims lie barely forty straight-line miles from Garnet. So Bill was still stomping his old grounds. A decade later, he told a friend that "there was a back road into that country from near Garnet, and he had always wanted to go back for a summer."

During those twelve months of 1925 and 1926, Bill and a fluctuating crew of half-a-dozen cosignatories recorded no less than thirty contiguous or almost contiguous claims in Crystal Creek Canyon. This is by far the largest group I know Bill to have recorded. And the claim forms constitute our longest more-or-less continuous written fix on his civilian doings. Yet I know very little about those twelve months. I have failed to find anyone who knew Bill then. And the claim forms themselves tell us almost nothing, even by implication, of how the year went for him, beyond his merely physical acts of staking and recording. It seems likely, though, that he sold the claims to a man named Delameder, who operated some small gold workings there in the late twenties and early thirties. And this sale could lie at the root of Grace's story, placed at about that point in time, that he "made lots of money and decided to go back to Pennsylvania in style" by buying a Cadillac, filling it with food and liquor and hiring a driver—only to "sober up" in New Mexico, sell the car and dismiss the driver, then head back West. In the late twenties Bill certainly seems to have broken his earlier pattern of regular commuting to and from the Imperial Valley—where he made such money as he needed to cover his rear end—and other places in which he did the things he wanted to do.

By this time he had established one place in particular as counterpoint to the Imperial Valley. It had replaced Braddock, which he hated, as "home." It was a place he loved; and he kept returning to it for the rest of his life. It was the place he may have first reached by floating downriver on a raft, just as his parents may have reached their first New World home in Turtle Creek.


THE FLAT, ALLUVIAL PLAIN that we modern men call the Palo Verde Valley was built down thousands and hundreds of thousands and probably millions of slow, eventful years by the deposit of mud from intermittent Colorado River floods. During the last few ticks of the plain-building clock—the last couple of thousand years, perhaps—humans began to settle locally. We now call these first known settlers Chemehuevi Indians.

In the year we call 1875—the year Bill came bawling on stage—an English-born San Francisco millionaire, Thomas Blythe, "bought" the plain to develop it for human agriculture under irrigation. Blythe soon died of a heart attack, and for years his irrigation plan languished. But by 1903 enough homesteaders had settled at the southern end of the valley to justify a post office. Its name: Paloverde—soon changed to Palo Verde. Four years later, Palo Verde was still the only place in the valley that could be called a town. But Blythe, established in 1908, soon outstripped it.

In 1912 one of the intermittent Colorado floods, creators of the valley, broke through levees that humans had fondly imagined would control the river. The flood threatened the whole north end of the valley. Only heroic efforts led by a go-getting engineer named Floyd Brown beat back the tide.

The turning point for the valley—in human economic terms and in others—came in August 1916 when a railroad pushed down from the north to Blythe. The railroad made economically feasible such projects as mining and large-scale agriculture. A human tide began to pour in. It included an obscure pseudo-prospector known as William A. Simoyne, who drifted down from the north and soon staked, just north of the valley, a manganese claim in partnership with the successful flood-control engineer

Floyd Brown. By that time the valley had begun its transformation from a desert prairie of grassland and scrub and arrowweed and mesquite and paloverde trees into a tamed checkerboard of levees and ditches and squared-off cotton and alfalfa fields.

In 1921 a spur of the Atchison, Topeka and Santa Fe reached down to the center of the valley. Its terminus, ten miles northeast of Palo Verde, was named Ripley, after a former president of the railroad. And in Ripley, believe it or not, the railroad built a palatial, two-story $100,000 hotel, heated by electricity and cooled by electric fans and fitted with carpets into which "you sank up to your ankles." The following year, another of the Colorado floods swept over levees south of Blythe. For weeks, five feet of muddy water covered the southern half of the valley, including Palo Verde and the new Ripley hotel and its ground-floor carpets. The hotel never reopened. For more than twenty years it stood as a mud-caked shell, lacking doors and windows, used only by itinerant bums and their allies—no doubt including, on occasion, one William A. Simoyne.

So Ripley never really made it in the struggle for supremacy among the towns of the developing valley. But at least Ripley survived. Other small communities budded, thrust out a few leaves, then faded and died. And in the late twenties more floods and the Depression beset the valley. Its fortunes slumped. The human population dwindled. The place slowed down, rested. The tiny village of Palo Verde at its southern end, twenty miles from the now dominant Blythe, slumbered.

In other words, the early human history of the Palo Verde Valley echoes that of many other California desert communities which have struggled into existence, then paused and pushed and paused again before peaking and finally succumbing to decline and fall—the way countless human communities have waxed and waned, all over the planet, ever since man first set up shop beside Yangtze and Euphrates.

I do not know just when Bill discovered Palo Verde, but it was sometime between 1917 and the mid-twenties; and after that he kept going back.

On his first visit he camped close to the cluster of two or three buildings that were "town." He pitched his tent less than twenty paces north of the Imperial-Riverside county line. Later, he favored a site a quarter of a mile south, between the road and the Colorado backwater that was always called "the lagoon." There, to provide shade for his camp, he planted half a dozen tamarisk trees. For years he watered and tended these trees. They flourished. And being a man who took pride in whatever he did, he never forgot them.

Bill spent many of his early Palo Verde days with a Scotsman, Byron Strauss, who was about his age and called everyone "lad" or "lassie." They would go out prospecting for weeks at a stretch with Strauss's burros and when they came back they would throw a big party, everyone invited. Nobody had heard of Bill's having burros of his own. Perhaps he had learned his lesson.

Bill did not lack congenial company in Palo Verde. Other old-timers used to camp, permanently or periodically, in and around the village. But at that time Bill also counted among his friends two young fellows who remember him well.

"He was a wonderful old man, Chuck was," said Bob Stallard, who now lives and drinks deeply of life near Indio. "Not so damned old either. . . . Yeah, a wonderful guy—you should have known him. A-one. Right on. . . ."

Bob paused to reconsult his current can of beer. "I was only nineteen then, or maybe twenty, and he was over fifty, but we were buddies, good friends. We went to L.A. together once. . . . He used to tell me things he never told anyone else. But hell, I can't recall 'em now. Had no reason to, so they didn't make a dent in my idiot brain.

"We used to go prospecting sometimes in my old Model T. We staked some uranium claims once, out of Glamis, before uranium became a big deal. They just used it for some kind of health gag then. . . . No, Bill wasn't much of a prospector. Not really. Just liked to cruise around the hills. Hell, if he'd run onto a gold nugget he'd have thought it was a horse turd. . . . Yeah, Bill and I, we drank more goddam beer than you ever saw. Barrels of beer. No, all he drank was beer. . . . Oh, maybe some moonshine once in a while. . . . He'd come and stay with me down at my place for two, three weeks at a time. A wonderful old guy. Never ill-tempered. Yeah, we were good friends. . . . He'd tell me things. Told me the whole history of his life. No, like I say, I can't recall much of it. I'm too goddam dense, that's all.

"Sure he told me he lived in a cave. No, nothing about a trunk. But he lived in a cave, he told me that. The way it came up was when he first came to stay with me. I said, 'Jesus Christ, Bill, don't you mind coming down here and roughing it with me?' I'm down in the damned jungle below Palo Verde then. 'I'm used to that,' he said. 'I lived in a cave once.' I don't know how long it was he said he lived there—maybe six months or a year or a year and a half. And I don't know where it was. But I know he told me he lived in a cave."

"You're sure I didn't put the idea in your head?"

"Hell no. He told me. I think he had an Indian woman with him there
. . . but don't quote me on that."

Bob broke out two new cans of beer and handed me one. "Then we
used to go burro hunting together. It was against the law, but the burros
tasted good. I'd shoot one and we'd skin it and hang it up and jerk it. No,
Bill never shot them. Never shot anything. But he liked to eat them all
right. Went to hell and gone, we did, in that old Model T, way back into
the mountains.

"Yeah, a good-looking old gentleman, Bill was. Stood up there straight
as a goddam colonel. Why, the last time I saw him, he was a hell of a lot
better man than I was. . . ." Bob's voice blurred off. He took another long,
strengthening pull at his beer. "Hell, I wish I could help you more, I really
do. But I'm just too goddam dense, that's all."

Sam Faubian, who now lives in Ripley and is married to Bob Stallard's
sister, echoed his brother-in-law, with variations.

"I was only twenty-one then," he said. "But Bill and me, we had a lot of
fun together. He was a hell of a good sport, I tell you. Why, everybody
liked him—except maybe some of the young girls, because he was always
wanting to get in their pants. Yeah, he was a cocksman, was Bill. Just
woman-crazy. And the older he got, the more it'd get on his mind. Always
wanted a woman to take care of him, but he lived in old cabins and the
like, so he never had no place for a woman to stay.

"But every once in a while he'd dress up in a blue serge suit and a tie
and a big hat, and when he did he looked real fancy. I remember he was
wearing that suit one day when we was fishing in the lagoon—it was the
Fourth of July, that's why he was all dressed up—and old Bill was drunk
and he just fell off a tree stump into the lagoon. He got water in his lungs
and hollered for help. Someone went after him but Bill went the other
way, swimming underwater half the time. When we fished him out he
looked like a drowned cat, but after he'd pressed it, that suit was O.K.
again. A damned nice suit, it must have been.

"A trunk? Sure, he'd got a trunk cached away someplace. Told me
about it more than once. There was something in that trunk real valuable
to him, and he was always going to get it. Had it on his mind all the time.
Yeah, it could have been as far away as Vegas. Could have been—though
he never said where it was. No, I can't be sure he ever said anything about
a cave. But there's no question about the trunk. None at all. Like I say, he
had it on his mind."

Connie Talley went to live in Palo Verde in 1928, and Bill had been
there for some time, off and on, when he arrived. Talley did not know him

well but would meet him occasionally when he went up to play pitch and penny ante in the old, raised-up store. Back then, the floods still came, and both store and post office stood high and safe on stilts.

Bill was still pretty active, said Talley. He could walk like hell and would often go out prospecting. Talley owned a 1927 Chevrolet, pretty well stripped down, and he would sometimes take Bill and a couple of the other old-timers, along with their dry washers and picks and other equipment, out into the Chuckwalla Mountains, west of Palo Verde, and leave them at a camp. They might stay out as long as three months. Then one of them would walk back in and Talley or one of the other young guys around town would drive out and bring in the rest and all their gear. Nobody seems to remember Bill's ever having a car.

The trips that often began in Connie Talley's Chevy, out to the Chuckwalla Mountains, were what most Palo Verde people knew of Bill's doings during those years when he "came and went." And soon everybody called him "Chuckawalla Bill" or just "Chuckawalla" or even "Chuck." Before long, few people remembered his surname.

Now a character named "Chuckwalla Bill" appears in three short stories in a book, the *Parson of Panamint*, by Peter B. Kyne, first published in 1914, and this character, who desert-rats it around Death Valley, could conceivably have provided an assist in Bill's rechristening. There are other versions of the name's origin, such as Grace's story of Bill feeding a priest chuckwalla for fish on a Friday. But there seems little doubt that the new name essentially originated in the line of low mountains that lie black along the horizon, west of Palo Verde.

Beyond those mountains, though, over in the Imperial Valley, Bill was still known as "Blackie" and rarely if ever as "Chuckwalla Bill." And he would have encouraged that. He always liked to keep the different sectors of his life almost watertight-separate.

During all his years in Palo Verde, Bill seems to have done nothing there, aside from the prospecting, that might have earned him money. His moneymaking sector remained the Imperial Valley. And he duly returned there at the end of the twenties when he decided that the time had come to make his bid for financial independence.

At least one man remembers Bill from that period.

When I met Tony Freeman he was eighty-four and drinking beer in a bar in Westmorland, a small village outside Brawley. He wore a thick flannel shirt and the same model of stained blue Chevy dealer's cap as Joe Bowers had worn. Yes, he said, he recognized the man in my photographs as a guy he had known as Blackie. Had met him first in the early twenties, right there in Westmorland, in Johnny and Edna's gambling joint.

Johnny and Edna's gambling joint was also the last place Joe Bowers had seen Bill.

"He always wore big hats like that one in the picture," said Tony Free-man. "I think he had one on that first time I met him, playing poker over at Johnny and Edna's." After that, they had met several times. Blackie played poker and blackjack, both. Pretty good poker player. And some-times he'd deal for Johnny. Edna used to talk about him a lot, even when he wasn't there. Could be she was kinda sweet on him. No, Edna died last year and Johnny the year before that. Johnny's real name was Gibhart or something like that, but he'd kinda changed it to Johnny Walker. Walker was really her name, though. Back then, it was all bootlegging, and Johnny and Edna used to move around: old houses, barns, everywhere. You had to. No, all those old buildings were gone now. . . . He'd always figured this guy Blackie was in on the bootlegging with Johnny and Edna. One time, Johnny had run out of whiskey and Blackie had driven off somewhere and come back with a jug. Could be it was from Niland: he was gone some time. Oh, an old car of some kind. Sure, it could well have been a Model T. Likely was. Could have been Johnny's car or his own. Either way.

"The last time I saw him? Around 1929, or maybe in the early thir-ties—once in Brawley and then again in Calipat. He remembered me— said I was a pretty lucky poker player, because he'd come in one night at Johnny and Edna's when I'd just won eleven hundred dollars. That time in Calipat, I remember, he said he knew where there was a good poker game. But I was busy. Come to think of it, seems like somebody called him Bill that time. Yes, I remember now—I kinda looked because I'd only heard him called Blackie. Can't remember who the guy was now, that called him Bill, but I knew him. . . ."

Another source—surer if less vivid—places Bill back in the Imperial Valley and pins him by both date and motivation: on June 19, 1929—six weeks before his fifty-fourth birthday—he applied in writing, from Calipa-tria, for an army pension.

Now the average human organism tends, as Lewis Thomas has said, to "wear out and become unhinged in the sixth decade." Put another way, most men tend to slow down around their mid-fifties. By 1929 Bill was slowing down and knew it—and saw an escape hatch.

He played the pension game to the hilt. He fudged his age forward to fifty-nine. He claimed to be suffering from "Rheumatism, Indigestion, Constipation, High Blood Pressure, Piles, No Teeth, Back of Scull Cracked, Poor Sight, Hearing, Catarrh, Heart, Kidneys, Dizzy Spells." A

Calipatria doctor added "bladder trouble" and "general debility" and sundry fractures and gunshot wounds, and summed up, "This brew of symptoms is due in my estimation mainly to a gradual failure of the heart muscle to respond to the demands of hard physical labor."

But Bill's pride almost caused his downfall. In his application he ignored his final service tour and desertion. But the pension board knew all about it; and they balked. For months, paper flowed. In one affidavit—notarized on October 21, 1929, three days before "Black Thursday" of the stock market crash—Bill supplied additional data but still eschewed all mention of his final army tour. This affidavit, the board replied, was "not satisfactory." Five months later, Bill moved quarter-way to meet them: he admitted his fourth enlistment and stated that after being hospitalized in Seattle he returned to duty at Fort Walla Walla, Washington, and "was with this troop short time there when I left." On April 30, 1930, the board awarded him a pension of forty dollars a month, backdated to June 1929.

In his pension applications Bill had naturally used the name under which he had always served: Anthony William Simmons. And now, with monthly checks coming to him under that name, he dropped "William A. Simoyne" forever.

That change marked another major threshold.

At last, Bill stood ready to embrace, totally, the new life he had tentatively begun at Black Horse Mine. World finance might be in chaos, but he personally had for the first time become a man of assured, independent means. Given his simple needs, he no longer had to work for mere money. He could begin to do, full time, the things he really wanted to do.

# 16   The Rock House

AFTER HIS INDEPENDENCE DAY, Bill wandered widely within his established territory.

He staked three mining claims—one in the Chuckwalla Mountains, near the territory's eastern edge, and two in the foothills of the San Bernardino Mountains, close to its northwestern limits. But his base became Banning, a small citrus-growing center a hundred miles up the highway from Calipatria. He wrote from Banning when, in November of 1930— that year of bank and business failures and mushrooming unemployment—he applied for a pension increase to fifty dollars. And his address was still Banning when, in March 1931, he asked for sixty dollars a month.

Although the world marketplace was now shuddering, Bill got both his raises.

But later in that year of 1931 he had cause to feel less pleased with government. He still kept returning to Palo Verde, where he lived in a cabin he had built for himself, across the lagoon from the village, back in the brush. He used to row across for his groceries and beer. The cabin stood on unused private land, and during 1931 the government sold the land for taxes and somebody bought it and Bill had to move out. So he may have been in an unsettled mood when, after barely eighteen months of unalloyed freedom, chance directed him toward a meeting without which you and I would never have heard of him, under any name. One day in December 1931, or possibly January 1932, he happened to drive out in his Model T Ford to Eilers' Place on the Salton Sea. And there he met Grace.

You may remember that I found an account of that meeting among Grace's papers. A few of its details differed from those she had told me back in her Santa Cruz hotel room. The earlier version had a week elapsing between the meeting and the prospecting trip, and it featured a mildly saucy scene in which Bill saw Grace swimming in the Sea and went for his swimsuit. The written version—perhaps because Grace exercised what she saw as dramatic license, or perhaps because she no longer felt a need to make the mating process sound slow and respectable—had them heading for the Eagle Mountains within twenty-four hours of meeting. And they went for no swim. But this written account—judiciously de-Hollywood-ized, and with due allowance made for hindsight—probably conveys the basic realities of a meeting that proved momentous for both of them.

Grace presents herself as a "victim of the times."

Not long before, she had been running an interior decorating store in Los Angeles.

> I closed the store and, clear of debt and with a few dollars in my purse, got in my car and rode away to the desert. Finally I made a turn in the sand and found myself at the Salton Sea, just gazing at it and enjoying the cool breeze off the water.

She ate at a nearby shack marked "Hamburgers, Hot Dogs" that was part of Eilers' Place, and fell into conversation with the owner.

> I could place him easily—broke now and away from it all. The Depression had cast him up on this beach of inland sea, as it had me.
>
> As we talked, a rattling old Ford car drove up and a man got out and came into the dining room. "Hi, Bill!" said my host, and I saw a man of about 65 years of age, five feet eight, with a military walk and a body that looked ten years younger than the gray hair and the Colonel moustache and chin whiskers. The piercing black eyes looked me over from head to toe. Then the man said, in a charming voice, "Pleased to meet you, Lady," as he removed his ten gallon hat and sat down close to us.
>
> The new customer was someone I could not place. I had never met his type. His sharp eyes and wit and friendliness on such a short time made me feel I had known him for much longer than the half hour he had his coffee and talked of his getting ready to leave for the hills the next day.

Eilers left them to serve new customers.

> Bill and I sat just looking at each other, leaving up to each other to talk first. Finally I said that I'd rather go walk on the

beach. Bill stood up and said he would like to walk with me if I would allow him to. I said sure, and we went out and walked on the beach. The sun was setting. And it was so pleasant I was forgetting all the unhappiness that brought me to this place. When suddenly Bill stopped and touched my arm. "Girl," he said. "How would you like to go into the Hills with me tomorrow?"

I stood looking at him. All I said was, "What for?" and I'll never know why I said that.

He answered very calm and with no emotion, "Because, Girl, I don't think you have any place else to go. And besides being educated and adventurous you could wind up with Gold in your pocket book."

We came to a bench and Bill said, "Sit down and let's talk."

So he talked and I listened.

"You are about 35 years old (I was 41) and you are broke and lonesome because you feel you are a failure. I can read you. So I am old enough to be your father, let's just say I am your 'Uncle Bill' and I assure you, you don't have to be bothered with details of my life and why I invite you to come with me. I am lonesome too but healthy and love the life I have chosen, which is a healthy one in the hills and desert. I am a mineralogist, and ex-soldier of the Spanish War in the Philippines, and I live a free and easy life now and I make money too. I also have a government pension and I am better off than the man up there in the shack—I'll never be broke and unhappy. And I can show you that you never need worry any more. Think this over tonight and I will be back early tomorrow for your answer."

With that we walked back to the shack where my car was parked. And we said "Goodnight" and Bill climbed into his Ford jalopy and was speeding up the road. I got into my car and slowly went the short distance back to the hotel where I got a room and went to bed. I slept soundly for the first time in quite a while.

The next morning I had breakfast in the dining room then walked out onto the big verandah of the hotel. There sat Bill. He didn't look surprised, just said, "Girl, I been waiting."

And I said, "When do we go to the hills?"

He said, "We will buy food and whatever, and can get started by late afternoon."

I said, "Bill, I trust you. But you must have patience as I know absolutely nothing about how to go about such a deal as you made me. As you said, I have no place else to go, so I am going with you. So let's go."

And by 4:30 that afternoon we were packed.

Grace's account does not describe Eilers' Place, but I have been as close to it as you can now get.

By the mid-thirties it was called Date Palm Beach and had become a world mecca for outboard motor racing. Later, it was the main site for the Hope-Crosby movie *Road to Morocco*. But soon the aqueduct that crossed the mouth of Long Canyon when Bill and Grace lived there—the aqueduct on which Grace's Stenderup husband worked—began to funnel vast quantities of Colorado River water into the Salton basin for agricultural irrigation, and all this water drained into the Sea. It began to rise. By the early fifties, the rising waters had covered Eilers' Place. When I went there, nothing remained above water except the thick periscope of one date palm, the upper skeletons of two bared tamarisk trees and the spar-crossed tops of a few ancient telegraph poles.

After a while I walked slowly back toward my car. Time and tide had—literally, this time—washed over a place Bill had known and had buried it, along with all echoes of the events that had happened there. It seemed sad that I would not be able to catch at least a glimpse of the way Eilers' once sat in Bill's memory.

That day, I drove directly to Peter Williams' oasis. I went mainly to discuss the rock house again, but our talk soon turned.

"Oh, sure I knew Eilers' Place," said Williams. "Knew it well. Yes, we talked about it with Bill, that day up at the rock house. Something relating to . . . swimming . . . We used to swim at . . . Horseflies! That's it! It began with horseflies. There was a horsefly chasing Mabel and me as we went up the road, and it seems to me that we mentioned this to Bill and he said, 'Yes, they're everywhere, even down at the Salton Sea.'

"And I remember I told him that we often went swimming there, and how at times it had been so hot and the horseflies so bad that it was like swimming in blood sometimes. And Bill chuckled, I remember."

"You mean he seemed to chuckle with . . . sort of about his memories of the place?"

"Yeah. Right. That was it, exactly. And he went on smiling, I remember, and nodded and said, 'Yes, I know Eilers' Place. I know Eilers' very well.' "

WHEN BILL AND GRACE came down from the Eagle Mountains after staking the first of the Trail's End group of claims, they naturally went to Banning, current terminus for Bill's pension checks.

Grace had said they put an ad for the claim in a local paper. Searching for it in the files, I kept catching flickers of how things had been there, that summer of 1932: "April 18: Yuma without a bank. The last survivor of that town's financial institutions, the Old Dominion Bank, closed its doors Friday [because of] inability to conduct a solvent business. . . . A federal tax of one cent per gallon of gasoline imposed because of over-production. . . . First Ford V8 in Banning." Eventually, in the Banning *Record* of April 7, 1932, I found what looked like an innocent news item but was probably, to judge by its position in the paper, indeed a subtle advertisement:

MINING CLAIM FILED

Anthony W. Simmons and Fred W. Palmer of Banning have filed in the office of County Recorder Jack A. Ross notice of location of the Solo Pal No. 1 Mine, three miles north of Mecca-Blythe highway, due north of the 129-mile post.

The name "Fred W. Palmer" intrigued me.

Half a dozen other men—including a Frank Coffee and a Charles E. Duncan, who had both cosigned Bill's claims in other places—appear as co-locators of the seven additional claims that eventually made up the Trail's End group. All are remembered locally—except Fred W. Palmer. I could not find a single old-timer, even in a nearby Palmer family, who had ever heard of the name.

Now Grace had clearly stated that she and Bill were alone in the Eagle Mountains when he found the galena outcrop that must have been Solo Pal No. 1: he came back to camp "all feathered up" and gave her the mine as a present, "for you and your kids." The claim's very name supports this script.

Yet the name Fred W. Palmer seemed vaguely familiar.

At last, I pinned it down.

When Bill got his discharge in Manila Bay in March 1901 he underwent a medical examination that was duly recorded on an appropriate form and signed by "Fred W. Palmer, A.A. Surg. USA."

It is possible that what we have here is mere coincidence. But I smell one of Bill's playful fantasies. I suspect that Grace wanted at that early stage of their relationship to run no risk of having her name linked in public with Bill's in a way that might reach her children. And I see Bill digging back into his past, producing this name with a flourish and pinning it on her, gleefully and proudly, as a nom de mine.

Anyway, name-playing or no, the ultimate result stands sure: on September 10, 1932, Frank J. Wiefels finally bought the Trail's End Mining Company from Grace Mason for "one 1928 Chevrolet Coupe Automobile and the sum of $300, payable in ten monthly installments of $30."

Grace gave the car to her son. She and Bill surely celebrated with a little whoopee. And then the happy pair, with Bill's pension now augmented by the more or less guaranteed if rather short-term income from Wiefels' installments—which were almost certainly paid—drove fifteen miles down the highway to Garnet.

Garnet was then in its pre-aqueduct, pre-Rolly Proebstel state: a cluster of wooden buildings, "a long ways from anywhere." The owner was "an old bootlegger and pool-hall operator who had never even finished the buildings or painted them or cut the ends off the boards that stuck out on the backs, so that some of them would be sticking out four feet or more: he was just that kind of a fellow, a boomer." The winds blew in Garnet then as they do now. But they had no smog to battle. And there were no bulldozers, so the real desert with its natural vegetation came clear up to the edge of the buildings, and there was therefore less windblown dust. But the winds had built a nearby sandhill, two miles long, just beyond Garnet Hill, on which you could still stroll and pick up garnets. No public power served Garnet, and water had to be trucked in. But it was the center of all things human in those parts. Desert Hot Springs, five miles northeast, up toward a line of parched, forbidding mountains, was little more than "a hole in the ground with some water coming out of it," though a chiropractor lived nearby, ready to minister to the few people who came to cure all.

For Bill, the keystone of Garnet was one of its wooden buildings. This post office became the new terminus for his pension checks. And he and Grace drove north into the mountains that looked so parched and forbidding to the ignorant, so beckoning to those who understood. And in Long Canyon they did what many desert dwellers used to and still do: they staked mining claims in a place that might never support a mine but made a first-rate homesite.

It was almost certainly in the fall of 1932 that Bill and Grace went to live in the old rock house that Bill renovated. But not until mid-February 1933 did they record two claims, Buck Horns and Papoose, that gave them loose title to squat. Then, in mid-April—probably because the out-side world now showed signs of crumbling—they protected their "prop-erty" with a third, adjoining claim.

Forty-five years later I backpacked up Long Canyon and lived for three days at the rock house.

I found everything much as I had left it, seven years earlier, and I camped, as I had in a sense been doing all those years, on Bill's doorstep. It was a big black flagstone, flush with the ground, directly outside his door-sill. It acted as table for my pots and cup, and it bore ancient scratch marks that had been made, I chose to decide, by nails in Bill's boots when he wiped his feet before stepping inside onto the rugs that covered the rock-house floor.

From this vantage point I commanded much the same view as Bill did that evening somebody snapped him standing beside Grace with their dog at his feet.

In those days, Peter Williams had said, a little stream "ran a ways down the wash." Fifty feet above, a waterfall cascaded down a rock wall. At its foot was "a little pool with a willow growing beside it."

Since my earlier visit, the drought had broken. The spring now flowed, and a pencil of water that trickled down the rock wall soon filled a little basin I scooped out at its foot. Spring flowers grew everywhere. Among them, lizards flicked and butterflies flickered. And I found the quiet little canyon—air-conditioned by faint echoes of the blasts that tarnished Gar-net, but superbly insulated from the human world—a delightful and satis-fying place to live. Like the cave, it would take time for your senses to ad-just to its coordinates, that was all. Already it was easy to picture Bill stumbling on it during a springtime prospecting trip, long before he met Grace, and deciding that one day, when the company was right, he would renovate the dilapidated rock house and move in. As I set up camp on Bill's black, scratched flagstone doorstep, I felt confident that I would soon find myself easing back into the world Bill had known. Here, alone, living much as he had lived, less than a half century down the roiling human road, all I had to do was sit and wait.

Perhaps I tried too hard. At such times, you often do. Anyway, I know I failed to push back the veil of years and embrace the reality of how it had been when Bill and Grace lived and laughed in that place and—in their own ways, for their brief span—loved.

There were only two moments when I even began to see beyond sur-face things and make connections.

In the cool and quiet of the first evening, several pairs of quail came strolling up the wash past the rock house, exchanging little love noises. I chose to regard them as descendants of those that had drunk at the spring in Bill's time. One male detoured to investigate me, up on the shelf. He advanced to within seven feet, expressed his uncertainty with a peevish "What? What? What?," then rejoined his mate. My second evening, the strolling pairs behaved even more trustingly. And on the third and last afternoon, just before I left, an early-arriving pair foraged from the wash clear up onto the shelf, billing and cooing contentedly to each other. They remained unfazed when my pots rattled at tea-making, and they ran enthusiastically for the salted nuts I threw them. Another few days, I decided, and they would have been eating out of my hand—as their ancestors, I suddenly felt sure, had once eaten from Bill's hand.

The other moment of near-insight stemmed from the rock house itself.

It was dusk on the second day. Time lolled in that shadowy interlude when bats gyrate and you feel the grip of mere daylight reality slackening. I stood in the doorway of the rock house, looking at the fireplace and gaping windows and the cement floor with grass pushing up through it. There was just enough light to make out the broad details—for the fire that had turned the rock house into a shell had virtually destroyed the roof. Only one charred beam still straddled the walls, front to rear. All at once, standing there in the doorway, I became aware of this beam, up and off to my right. I could see nails protruding from it, black against the pale sky. And suddenly I wondered if this had been the beam Bill was wrestling with when he told Grace that if only he had the instruments he had left cached in his trunk up in Nevada he would be able to make the crossbeams abut much better. Grace had come back with a smart-ass rejoinder. And standing there in the half-light, leaning against the solid doorjamb—"You can see how well Bill built the doorways," Grace had said—I found myself holding my breath and listening for long-dead voices, still echoing. I do not think I heard them. But at least I had listened.

As I left the rock house, late in the afternoon of the third day, I turned and looked back.

It seemed a pity that the place had not, for all its echoes, spoken to me the way I had hoped. The Bill who had lived there was the first Bill I had known, back in Grace's hotel room. So I had always tended, without really thinking about it, to picture him as a man of about fifty-seven—even though Grace had thought him older. I saw him as a man who still stood very upright but who . . . And all at once I realized that there at the rock house I had caught up with Bill. Because of that first imprint of a man almost sixty, I had always thought of him as much older than me: when I

stumbled on Trunkman at the cave I had been forty-six; and I had "met" Bill in Grace's hotel room just three days after my forty-ninth birthday. But now, here at the rock house, I was fifty-six. One more year, dammit, and I would catch up with the Bill I had always pictured.

In one sense, what had happened when I turned and looked back at the rock house for the last time was merely a playing with numbers. Yet the moment was a shock, a milestone.

I camped at dusk in lower Long Canyon. As I drifted down toward sleep, it occurred to me that a faint vehicle track that ran nearby, up on a shelf, undisturbed by many years' floods, could have been the one Bill and Grace used.

Next morning I began to drift out of sleep into the half-light of dawn. Almost at once, lying warm in my sleeping bag and looking up at the place the faint track passed, I found myself picturing Bill and Grace driving down toward Garnet.

Beside the track, spring flowers gleamed in morning sunlight. Grace was driving her Buick. Bill sat beside her and they were talking and laughing. The Buick sped by. Slowly, its dust cloud dissolved.

Time passed.

Another scene focused.

The grass beside the track had grown dry. Clouds now covered the sun. This time, they drove separately, in their own cars. Grace led. She still handled her Buick with confidence and flair; but now she looked pensive, as if wondering—the way she had often wondered, lately—just why she was living in this place with this particular man. She valued him still. But she knew the affair had been only an experiment, a stile. After all, she was a city girl through and through, and an ocean lover too, and it could not last. Besides, she was well past forty now and would soon be clear of this difficult period of her life. She swung petulantly around a curve. The dust cloud behind her Buick bulged, then began to dissolve.

A discreet distance behind the dust cloud, Bill followed. He sat very upright at the wheel of his Model T truck, concentrating on the driving—struggling at it, and aware he was struggling, and therefore feeling ashamed, because he did not like doing things incompetently. It had been a bad morning, anyway. Grace had been like that lately. And now, his contentment ruptured, he found himself looking back down the years and wondering just what he was doing, living in this remote canyon; found himself regretting, just for the moment, that he had not achieved the "better things" he knew he had in him; found himself raising the question—which was not like him at all—whether he should blame his failure to achieve those better things not on his scanty education but on his lack of money drive or on certain other deficiencies. Mostly, of course, he wanted nothing better in the world than the life he was leading. But this morning, following Grace down to Garnet, he was not so sure. He sped past my camp, frowning. He too swung fast around the curve, and slowly his billowing dust cloud also began to dissolve.

After breakfast I rolled up my sleeping bag and walked on out toward Desert Hot Springs and the present.


WHEN BILL AND GRACE moved into the rock house they no doubt planned, in an open-ended sort of way, to stay for a considerable spell. But the world outside Long Canyon was not standing still.

In Germany, on January 30, 1933, after years of financial chaos, Adolf Hitler became chancellor. In America, banks and businesses continued to fold. Unemployment snowballed, in less than three years, from 3 to 10½ million. In November 1932, Franklin Delano Roosevelt swamped Herbert Hoover. He took office March 4, 1933. March 6, he closed all banks for four days, called a special session of Congress, and launched his New Deal. Among the flood of new legislation was "An Act to maintain the credit of the United States Government." It became law March 20. Within two months its repercussions throbbed up Long Canyon.

May 4, a form letter went out from the Director of Pensions in Washington, D.C., to Anthony W. Simmons of Garnet, California. It quoted the Act, became clouded with bureaucratic circumlocution, scattered a layer of positive-sounding euphemisms, then slunk to the point: "On the evidence of record in your case it has been determined that you are entitled to, and there is being approved in your favor, effective July 1, 1933, an award of pension in the amount of $6 monthly, on account of Age."

In plain English, Bill's sole means of support had been slashed overnight from sixty dollars to six.

The shock to Bill must have been considerable; to Grace, stunning.

June 20, Bill mailed to Washington a notarized questionnaire concerning his means of support. His plaintive covering letter ended: "I do hope My Gov. sees fit to Continue My Pension for my few Remaining Years for I do not know what is to become of me if they cut me off. . . ."

Within a month, help came—but not from Bill's government. Thirty miles up the road from Garnet, a *deus ex machina* sat waiting in the wings.

# 17 Norton

AMONG BILL'S DESERT ADDRESSES that I had found in the National Archives was "c/o Mr. J. M. Roper, Cherry Valley, Beaumont." And in the same file had been a "To whom it may concern" letter about Bill, signed by Mr. Roper and dated September 1933.

Each time my researches took me through Beaumont I had tried to locate this man. Each time, I failed. But then the Beaumont librarian, who was compiling a local history, wrote giving me the address of Iretha, a daughter of his. Now Mrs. Chester Robinson, she lived in San Juan Capistrano, south of Los Angeles.

I immediately phoned Mrs. Robinson.

"Why, of course I remember Uncle Bill," she said. "He pitched his tent under the big apricot tree in our orchard. Two years he must have been with us, off and on. He didn't have nothing, but, oh, he was a wonderful old man. That's right, he was called Chuckawalla Bill, too."

Iretha had been only fifteen then, and did not remember many details. A younger brother and sister would probably remember even less. But an older brother, Norton, had known Bill "real well." He and Bill had even gone prospecting together. "And Norton is the one who can tell you best," said Iretha. "He didn't go to college, you know, but he took a home course. He lives in Sacramento now."

A few days later I met Norton at the International Church of the Four Square Gospel, where he and his wife did volunteer work. He was a short, cheerful man, plump and unpretentious, open-neck-and-sport-coated.

He had been twenty-one when he met Bill. "But we had a real good rapport," he said as we settled down in a small back room of the church. "I'd just as soon have Bill go with me anywhere as anybody."

It had been a two-way relationship. Norton, who used to enter public-speaking contests, would recite his pieces to Bill, who then gave his opinion of them. For his part, Bill was a natural storyteller.

"I loved to listen to him—and I'm a good listener," said Norton. Then he smiled. "Of course, I've never had much problem with talking either. I get a lot of kidding about 'the strong, silent type.' "

Like most compulsive talkers, Norton let his mind grasshopper around the universe. But for two days I let him roll—at the church, then at his home—and slowly, hop by hop, there emerged the story of how Bill had weathered the trough of the Great Depression.

It was July or August—"about cherry-picking time, I know that"—when Bill first went to live on the Ropers' five-acre ranch in Cherry Valley, three miles outside Beaumont, thirty miles up the road from Garnet.

"Uncle Cliff was the one who brought him," said Norton. "Uncle Cliff was always chasing rainbows—gold mines, oil shares, that kind of thing. He and my dad had met Bill earlier, down in Garnet. Then Uncle Cliff went back to talk to Bill about some fancy gold prospect and found his pension cut off and him and Grace running short on food. So he brought them both back to Beaumont—because my dad was a great humanitarian and looked after everybody. And Dad let Bill pick fruit and do a little irrigating and things like that—just to keep him going, you know, until he could get his pension restored."

For the first three or four weeks, Bill and Grace had lived in a little shack on Cliff Roper's property, a couple of hundred yards down the road from their ranch. Grace—known as Bill's niece, of course—had rarely appeared. "I think she had some kind of female disorder," said Norton. "Anyway, she was often in bed, and before long she took off for Los Angeles. That was when Bill moved onto our place and pitched his tent under the big apricot tree."

This apricot, which stood only fifty or sixty feet behind the Roper house, was a tremendous tree with a huge spread. Its lowest branches came out about eight feet above the ground and Bill's "tent"—no more than a canopy, really—stood in their shade, up against the trunk on its east side. And Bill liked to sit there outside his tent reading magazines and smoking his pipe. At night he would pull his old iron bed outside so that he could "sleep under the stars," but he was always up very early and would push it back inside before anyone else was about. Before long, said Norton, he was like one of the family.

"He was very even-tempered, Bill was. Never see him riled or mad. A real sense of humor too, and always had a nice smile. But he had a natural dignity. Never showed off. Always very gentlemanly. You'd never hear him using bad language to speak of, or anything like that, and he went to church with us and he'd sing like he'd been to church all his life. He was a diplomat too, right down to the last dot. Never put his foot in it. Had an ability to say the right thing. In church circles, we call it 'pouring a little oil on troubled waters.' . . . Oh yes, everybody appreciated Bill.

"My father, now, he was twenty years younger than Bill, but Bill had been a lot of places and done a lot of things and my father just loved to get him off in a corner." Norton held up two fingers, side by side. "Bill and my father, they were just like that.

"And my mother . . . well, Bill wouldn't let himself be a burden, you know—he was always doing a little something to help—and before long he offered to do the cooking. He was a good cook too. Real good. And if you paid him a compliment about his food, well, that was all the payment he could have. . . . Yes, he'd often do the cooking for my mother, and nobody had done that before, so she really appreciated him."

Bill had been fond of the kids, too—and they had idolized him. John was about thirteen and at the hero-worship stage. The girls were about ten and fifteen, and Bill would pick them up and sit them on his knee and talk to them. They were always asking, "Can we go out and talk to Uncle Bill?" But their mother would say, "No, you mustn't disturb him—he's just getting ready to go to bed." She understood that although Bill liked to talk he also valued his privacy. So he would sit there alone under the apricot tree, reading and smoking his old black pipe, "until the sun went out." There was an old family dog that became very attached to Bill and would sit out there with him and then sleep close beside his bed.

Bill had an old hat, Norton remembered—a big felt one, tan-colored—that he would put on first thing in the morning to protect him from the sun, because he was beginning to go a little bald. Norton used to accuse him of sleeping in that hat. But when he dressed up to go into town he put on a suit. It was a few years out of fashion but a good dark blue serge "that he had paid money for at some time." He would wear conventional little black shoes and a white shirt and string tie, or sometimes a little narrow velvet or silk one. Yes, he would sometimes put perfume on. And often he had a flower in his buttonhole. "Very distinguished, I can tell you. Looked like somebody. Oh, I can see him now, with his little goatee neatly trimmed and his mustache close-cropped and his hair brushed straight back. He looked a lot like you, really. But his hair was black, heavily shredded with gray—and receding, so that he had a high, intelligent-looking forehead. I remember I used to think he looked like a kind of Gabby

Hayes character—always on the go, always doing something—but always standing so upright, real military. And big around the chest, real big. Dr. Hartwell said he had an oversize heart inside there, so my dad was always worried he might have a heart attack. 'Better go take a rest, Bill,' he'd say after Bill had done something energetic."

"Ah, Dr. Hartwell!" I said. I reached into my briefcase and found a medical report I had copied at the National Archives.

Written by Dr. Robert Hartwell on September 27, 1933, it sounded like a pre-requiem: "arteriosclerosis . . . myocarditis, with enlarged heart, the apex being one inch beyond the left nipple line . . . complete absence of teeth . . . pulse somewhat irregular . . . precordial pain that he describes as 'like a needle stab' . . . stooping, he tends to fall; the same upon turning suddenly . . . a right hemilateral headache more or less constant. Diagnosis: Arteriosclerosis and myocarditis with angina; chronic colitis—this last service-connected with Cholera in the Philippines in 1899. . . . He is totally disabled for the earning of his livelihood by inability to do manual labor."

Norton read the report and nodded. "That's right, we were trying to get his pension back. I remember that visit well."

They had taken Bill up to see Dr. Hartwell because he had been their family doctor for years. One of the old-style doctors, he was. You'd call him and he'd come—so he toured all over that country in his old Buick. That day, Dr. Hartwell mentioned that he had been in the Philippines too and, like Bill, had been lucky enough to survive cholera. The doctor had a strange, deep voice that "vibrated like a key on an old woodwind organ," and after examining Bill he had laughed and said, "Nothing wrong with you, Bill—except that you ought to have been dead twenty years ago."

"That was him all over," said Norton. "Then he wrote this full report, to try to get Bill's pension back. Didn't charge him a dime, either. And it was probably him that advised Bill about writing to the congressman."

"Ah, yes," I said. "Congressman Sam L. Collins of Santa Ana."

"That's right."

From my briefcase I produced more documents. The first bore the same date as Dr. Hartwell's report:

> To Whom it may concern—
> This is to certify that I have personally known Anthony W. Simmons for some time, that he is in ill health in fact he is unable to secure employment or has any means of support other than his pension.

Being along in years he is unable to secure a job on account of his age in consequence he had to depend upon the kindness and generosity of his friends to enable him to live.

He has no other visiable means of support and no known living relatives that could possibly support him he is at present living in my home.

Very truly yours,<br>J. M. Roper.

When Norton had read the letter, he smiled. "Yes, I remember that." After the visit to Dr. Hartwell they had held a kind of family meeting, with Bill in on it, to hash out the words. John Roper, Sr., was no letter writer, and it was Norton, fresh out of school, who had actually written the letter and even signed his father's name.

I handed him the rest of the documents. The congressman had forwarded the Hartwell report and Roper letter to the Director of Pensions and asked that Bill's pension be increased to thirty dollars. It had, he said, been cut from sixty to fifteen.

"So by this time," I said, "Bill had at least gotten a small raise."

"Yes," said Norton. "That seems about right. The way I remember it, they'd actually canceled him out for a while there, and then as soon as he got some of it back we took off for the desert, prospecting—because by that time the fruit picking was through. Yes, we'd just finished picking the peaches, so that would be around mid-October. There were four of us went—Bill and me and two other young fellows. . . ."


LATER, I TRIED to sharpen my picture of how it had been for Bill during those first months with the Ropers, under the big apricot tree, before he and Norton and the other two young fellows went prospecting.

First, I went back to the old Roper ranch.

But house and apricot tree had both been canceled by the gravel access road to a big, impersonal chicken ranch that lurked, quarantined, behind a steel-mesh fence.

Next, I visited Iretha.

Modena, the youngest Roper child, had told me on the phone that she could remember nothing significant about Bill; but from Iretha and her brother John I hoped to come by something more than slightly shifted angles of memory.

In the Depression summer of 1933 Norton, at twenty-one, was an adult. But the mores of that time would ensure that Iretha, barely sixteen, and John, thirteen, looked out on a different world. They still stood on the magical side of the gulf protecting children from those sleazy and infectious "realities" that grip the lives of all but our freest human adults.

Iretha, now fifty-eight, turned out to be small, emotional.

"Oh, when we were growing up Uncle Bill was one of the outstanding people of our lives. I was just a snot-nosed kid running around, you know, and I didn't really care for too many people. . . ."

"Still that way," said her husband, Chet.

"But Uncle Bill, oh, he was just a very fine person. Always cheerful, too, and never grouchy, or I wouldn't have liked him. And I know my ma and pa really enjoyed having him. 'Cause Bill seemed to fit right in—he was economical, right along with us. Then he was an interesting person, very intelligent. Why, he could talk about anything. And he could just say things in the cutest way, like my father. Maybe that's why they clicked. Both of them had a knack of putting words together."

"You mean he was the kind of man you listened to because of the *way* he said things?"

"Yes, that's it! He'd make anything ordinary sound extraordinary. Somebody else would say the same thing and it would sound like nothing. He was very self-sufficient as well, and all man—not chicken in any way. We figured maybe he'd been kicked around a lot, but he shined through it all anyway. I remember he always said he just liked the wide-open spaces. That's why he used to pull his cot out under the stars. 'You can just look up and see the wonders of the world,' he'd say . . . And my dad, he just loved to get him off in a corner and talk."

"John Roper was one of the finest men I ever knew," said Chet. "He'd give you the last bite he had to eat. No, I never met Bill. I only come along five years later. But the family still talked about old Chuckawalla Bill."

"Since you phoned," said Iretha, "I've remembered all kinds of funny little things about him. Like the way he used to roll his own cigarettes. I remember I couldn't see how he could roll 'em like that, just with his hands, and John and I, we tried afterward but couldn't do it. . . . Then I remember how he always kept very clean. Daddy give him a bathtub to wash his clothes in, 'cause we only had an outside bath and toilet then. . . . Oh yes, and his notebook! He was always jotting down notes, there by his tent under the apricot tree. A little pad, he had. And most every evening he'd put it on his knees and write his little notes in it. Pa called it 'Bill's little black notebook.' And if you got up at five o'clock in the morning, there was Uncle Bill a-writing again, outside of his tent."

I asked about the tent.

"Oh, John's the one that could tell you about that. John was always a snooper. He loved to see what was inside places. And one day when Mom and Dad had gone to town he said, 'I'm going to look inside Uncle Bill's tent.' And I said, 'You'd better not, or you'll get a licking.' And he said, 'Well, are you going to be a tattletale?' And I said, 'No.' And I guess he went and looked. So you ask him about the tent."

I brought out my cave pictures.

"Why," said Iretha, "that looks just like the tripod Uncle Bill had! Only his was maybe shorter. . . . And come to think of it, I remember us kids played at digging caves around about then, and I think maybe it was because Uncle Bill had told us about living in a cave. I seem to kind of remember that—slightly. . . . I can't be sure, though."

But her memory of one event remained sharp.

"Oh yes, and then there was the day Uncle Bill bought us the shoes. Maybe that's why I liked him so much—because he bought me those shoes. Nobody else bought me shoes except my mom and dad, and that wasn't very often. My mom told Uncle Bill that I had an awful little foot and she doubted that I could get fit."

"She still wears a three and a half," said Chet.

Demurely, Iretha displayed a tiny, schoolgirl foot. "But Uncle Bill said he always thought girls should have one nice pair of 'Sunday-go-to-meeting shoes.' So we all went shopping together—my mom along with Modena and me. We went to Redlands, probably, or maybe it was San Berdoo, and Uncle Bill, he was just thrilled to death. 'You know, Rosie,' he said to Mom, 'they've got to fit the arch of her little foot or they won't be comfortable when she walks.' And he got right down there on the floor and was helping the fellow fit them. That was what tickled us all. It was a big thing. But the shoes, they were just as nice as could be. . . . Yes, Uncle Bill, he was so generous and kindhearted. Kind through and through. I remember we all felt bad when he took his tent down and moved on, out of our lives."

Before I left, Iretha sprang a surprise.

"Whenever I cook Spanish rice," she said, "I always think of Uncle Bill. Because of him it's always been a special dish in the Roper family. He was a very good cook, you know, and oh, he made the best chili beans. But his specialty was Spanish rice. He'd tell my mom, 'Now Rosie, don't you ever make Spanish rice without a Dutch oven,' and I remember once when we were eating hers he said, 'Rosie, I don't want to put down your Spanish rice, because it is beautiful.' Uncle Bill was always tactful, you know, never hurt your feelings. 'But the trick,' he said, 'is browning the rice dark brown. You think you're about to burn it, but keep stirring it—and you'd better watch it because it'll burn just like that. Make it real dark brown but not burnt, that's the trick.' "

Iretha beamed. "I cooked some last night—because I thought maybe you'd like some for lunch today."

So there in San Juan Capistrano I lunched on Spanish rice à la Bill Simmons—with corn bread and milk, "just the way Uncle Bill liked to eat it." And afterward Iretha gave me a little card with the full recipe for Spanish rice "from the kitchen of Chuckawalla Bill."

When I thanked her I said, "You know, eating Bill's favorite dish like that—just the way he must have cooked it, wherever he went—eating it like that with you seems in an odd sort of way to have brought me a notch closer to having known him."

For a moment I stood listening to what I had said, thinking about the way Bill had kept his life partitioned, so that few people knew anything about those compartments they did not share with him. Then, surprising myself a little, I said, "I hadn't thought of this before, but I think perhaps I know more about Bill's life, now, than anyone who knew him when he was alive."

"I think you know him better than he knowed himself," said Chet.


JOHN LIVED on the outskirts of Los Angeles. He was small, red-headed, very much a Roper.

At first he seemed reticent, almost cagey. "I really can't remember anything much about him," he said.

I kept prodding. Norton had said that when Bill lived under their apricot tree John was "in those impressive years—he'd just stand around and watch him."

"All I can remember is that I liked him. Really liked him."

"Can you remember why?"

Pause. An almost audible pounding away at a logjam of recall. "Because he seemed like a rugged old man. . . . He was just a good old man."

I waited.

"Yes, he was like the old pioneers—self-sufficient in every way, could turn his hand to anything. . . . And he really liked kids. . . ."

More waiting. I thought I could hear the logjam beginning to break up.

At last: "He was husky, I remember. Not tall—maybe five nine or ten—but husky."

"Actually he was five six and a half." I brought out Bill's desertion poster.

"Now that surprises me. Five feet six! That's what *I* am! Of course, I was only thirteen or fourteen then, and small. . . . You know, I can't honestly say that I'd have recognized him from that mug shot."

I brought out the snapshots. John said that one, showing Bill with a full beard, looked just like he remembered him. "And like you too—because of that beard. Why, when I saw you getting out of the car I wondered if you might be a distant relative. . . . But five feet six! Come to think of it, he always stood just as tall as he could. He'd tap me on the shoulders and say, 'Square up! Shoulders back!' and do it himself—and my God, he had a chest on him when he did that! Like a wrassler. He was well muscled all over, too, strong across his arms and shoulders. I'd think, 'I hope I have arms like that when I grow up.' . . . Oh, I do remember one thing—he had a hole in his thumb. His right thumb. He was out in the desert once, he told me, and he reached down for something and a scorpion struck him. He was real sick for a while, out there on his own, until a kind of hard core popped out with all the poison. After that it was O.K. But it left this little hole in the top of his thumb, just under the nail. Maybe a thirty-second or a sixteenth of an inch below the nail. It was old by then and all callused over and it didn't hurt him any more, but it was still big enough to push a wooden match into. I remember how he used to get dirt in it when he did things. And how he'd whittle a little stick to clean it. . . . Yes, I remember that real well now, because I used to think of him reaching down and that scorpion popping him. . . . He'd tell us kids all kinds of stories—but I can't remember any of them now. Funny. He'd talk to us out there under the apricot tree in the twilight, and when it got dark he'd go to bed. . . . At least, that's the way I remember it."

John leaned back, smiling. "Then when he got dressed up in his blue serge suit and cowboy hat he almost looked like a Baptist preacher—or a Colonel Sanders. Or you could think of him as a professional man, maybe a country doctor. He had a distinguished look, you know."

"But he wasn't, uh, stuck-up?"

"Oh no, no! Uncle Bill was just Uncle Bill. He'd probably been more and done more, and he didn't have to toot his horn. It's only those that haven't done anything that put on the dog. . . . Oh, there's another thing I remember. He had a little pension check, and every time it came he would go out and buy us kids a whole dollar's worth of candies. And in the Depression time you could get a lot of candy for a dollar, you know. A big paper sackful—like that." John's hands traced out a shape a foot tall and about eight inches across. "Yes, that big. Well, I imagine you could put it all in a three-pound coffee can—maybe. And Uncle Bill enjoyed watching us divide that candy, I remember—though sometimes it would cause a hell of a fight among the three of us. No, Norton was too old by then to divide candy with us. . . . Then there was that old shotgun. . . ."

By now the logjam was long gone. John flooded on.

"Yes, he did a fine job on that shotgun. He was real good with his hands, Uncle Bill was. There was one shovel handle he fixed for us that was a work of art. It lasted for years. And he mended all our axes and hammerheads and all that—handiwork just wasn't my father's line. . . . Anyway, I had this old twenty-gauge shotgun with the stock broken, and Uncle Bill, he took two of the hardwood faces off of the drawers of an old dresser and glued them together and then carved them out and made a new stock that fitted real good. A beautiful job it was. So I gave him the gun. And in return he gave me a twenty-two rifle. An old, old gun it was, with a long hexagonal barrel. . . ."

John lapsed into silence, smiling to himself.

I asked if he had ever gone into Bill's tent, the way he had told Iretha he would.

John laughed. "Oh, sure, I used to sneak in there. . . . Well, my dad had told me I couldn't go—it was an unwritten law, 'Don't bother Uncle Bill's tent'—so hell, I *had* to go. I wasn't really looking for nothing, you know, but . . ." His voice suddenly grew very warm. "But it just looked like I thought I'd like to be living right there. He had ways of putting a box in a certain place and things a certain way that looked real neat for a kid. . . . And then I'd go out and look at his tracks again."

"His tracks?"

"Yes. He wore high-topped shoes that come to just above his ankle. But like a workingman's shoe. Heavy leather. In those days everybody wore high-topped shoes like that. We called these"—he touched his ordinary city shoes—"we called these 'low-cuts.' And Uncle Bill had steel plates on the heels of his high-tops, like little mule shoes, and the leather wore out in the center so that they left marks on the ground like a mule track. Yessir, he sure left his tracks around. I can see 'em just as plain, right now."

I reached into my briefcase for the list of cave artifacts. There were four items I had taken to a shoe repairer. He had said that three were indeed horse or burro shoes, as I had thought; but the fourth was a metal strip for human footwear known as a horseshoe plate, once very popular for protecting heels. I showed John my tracing of this plate.

"Why yes, that sure looks like the kind Uncle Bill wore. Of course, I guess a lot of people wore 'em back then. But I can remember those tracks real clear. And when he went away, like he did sometimes, I'd go out into the orchard and look at 'em . . . because I missed him."

"Because you missed him?"

"Yes. It was a strange feeling I used to have . . . because I liked him so well. He was like . . . my hero. And there he was, gone. You know. And for days I'd feel real bad. When he would go away I'd cry like hell. I'd go off by myself, of course—heck, you wouldn't let nobody know—but I'd think about him being gone forever. You know how it is when you're a kid. Oh, I'd get over it, but when he would leave I'd go out and look at his tracks. It's like a guy goes off and leaves a young pup—it keeps looking around and sniffing his tracks. Like I say, I hero-worshipped him. Now my dad, he had a sense of humor and he'd see the funny side of Bill and his women, but I'd think of him with a sword in his hand or something. Hell, you know how it is when you're a kid."

And afterward, that was the picture of John Roper that hung sharpest in my memory: the thirteen-year-old boy standing in the orchard and looking down at Bill's "mule tracks" under the big apricot tree and then hiding where nobody could see him and crying his heart out because his hero had gone away.

THE TWO YOUNG FELLOWS who went prospecting with Bill and Norton in mid-October of 1933, after the peach picking was over, were Ralph Capps and Horace Roberts. Roberts had had to leave two weeks later, to help on the family ranch. Some years afterward, he was killed when a jacked-up baling machine fell on him. Ralph Capps was a high school friend of Norton's who had lived just down the road, and still lived near Beaumont. Ralph had stayed with them the whole prospecting trip, clear through to Christmas. It was his car they had used.

"A 1925 roadster, it was," said Norton. "A little coupe with no rumble seat. It was underslung, I remember, so that it had four inches less clearance than most Dodges, but it had big balloon tires and we used to drive cross-country when we had to, and sometimes we had the bottom of that old Dodge polished like it had been rubbed with sandpaper."

For almost three months they had camped in and around the Eagle Mountains. Bill was "heavy on the Eagles," Norton remembered.

Ostensibly, they were prospecting. Indeed, they prospected a great deal. But they did so in Bill's way. That meant spending considerable time moseying around old diggings and looking at Indian petroglyphs and doing anything else that took their fancies.

They worked out from base camps on foot, just carrying small day packs, never staying away from the car overnight. They set up only two or three base camps, so each of them was, like Trunkman's cave, a reasonably permanent residence.

They had slept in a tent—an old rectangular, ridgepoled World War I tent that they mostly had to hold down with big rocks and baling wire because the ground was too hard for driving in stakes. All three of them slept in the tent, always, because of the mosquitoes. Often, they built a smoke fire for mosquitoes outside the entrance.

Bill's bed was just inside the entrance, Norton remembered. "Ralph and I slept down the far end, on canvas army cots. But Bill didn't like cots. He had to have an old iron bed that we used to tie on the side of the Dodge when we moved. 'Got to have a good night's rest,' Bill would say. He didn't like sleeping on the ground in the desert—though whether it was on account of snakes, I don't know. Bill had old brown army blankets on his bed. You could buy them for practically nothing. And down beside the bed he kept his old trunk that he . . ."

"A trunk?"

"Well . . ." Norton screwed up his eyes with the effort of squinting back into the faded desert sunlight of 1933. "Well, maybe it was more like a footlocker—or an oversize suitcase. But it was strong and waterproof, and looked as if it had seen many miles of travel. When we moved we had to tie that on the side of the Dodge, too. Onto the spare tire. Bill just had stuff like papers and pictures and tools and clothing in it, as I recall, and we considered it spare baggage." Norton smiled. "Bill was always accumulating—and always a-losing. He brought along a lot of the cooking gear, I remember, like his Dutch oven. He cooked just about everything in either that oven or a heavy iron skillet. And he would set up a kind of schedule for foods. 'Today's our Spanish rice day,' he'd say. Or chili beans or prunes or whatever. On Sundays he'd cook biscuits in the Dutch oven, the whole bit, you know. Corned beef? Sure he liked it. Canned milk? Yes, that's all we had. In fact, Bill was an enthusiast for it and we'd buy it by the case.

"At our first camp, at Cottonwood Spring, where there were seven or eight other people camped, Bill might ask the others over for a meal and there'd be seven or eight of us sitting around. Bill just thought that was living. Yeah, he sure knew how to handle food. When we'd buy bread we'd get several loaves and we'd string it all up so that it would dehydrate and keep. Then Bill would store it in a metal box on account of the animals. . . ."

"Maybe the kind of big box that soda crackers come in?" I asked.

"That's right. Or tobacco. He'd see a big box like that in a store and he'd say, 'I'd like to have that,' and they'd just give it to him. Anyway, when we needed the bread we'd take it out of the box and it would be hard as brick, so we'd put it in this double steamer—the inside part like a colander, you know—and the steam would come up and soften the bread, and you'd have nice fresh bread. . . .

"Sure, we always brought stuff for a table. 'Got to have yourself a table,' Bill would say. Yes, always metal plates. Crockery would break too easy—and Bill just loved to eat off of metal plates, I remember. . . . Five-gallon cans? Lots of 'em—for storing and carrying water, mostly. Bill was pretty strict about conserving water. We'd use it twice if we possibly could—for foot-washing or something—and never pour a drop on the ground if we could help it."

"He didn't by any chance have a metate?" Nobody had ever confirmed Grace's story of the one Bill carried in his car, and I had begun to wonder whether she had invented it to support her Trunkman hypothesis.

"A metate?" said Norton. "One of those stone mortars and pestles the Indians used? Sure, he had a mortar and pestle when he and Grace came up to Cherry Valley. Brought them in the car. The first I had ever seen. The mortar was a big, heavy thing about eighteen inches across that he'd found out in the desert somewhere. He said he'd always had one around, and when we went prospecting he brought it along in the Dodge. We'd use it for grinding up soft rock samples.

"Bill kept a very clean camp, and his instructions about empty tin cans were specific: 'Take 'em out a little ways and bury 'em.' That way, he said, you did not attract animals. Besides, coyotes might get their noses in unburied cans and not be able to get them out."

No, Norton didn't remember Bill rolling cigarettes. He wouldn't have used the tobacco he smoked in his pipe, certainly. That stuff would knock you down at twenty paces. Bill was particular about it, though—used to order it in fifteen- or twenty-pound cans from back in South Carolina or somewhere. One of his few luxuries. He'd seen the tobacco advertised in some magazine or other.

Yes, he'd often read magazines. Western shoot-em-up stories and riding trail with herds, and that. Was *Argosy* going in those days? Also things like *True Romances* and *Popular Science*. He'd fold them two or three times and stick them in his hip pocket so that he could sit down anywhere and get back to reading. On that prospecting trip they had had mineralogy books from the library, too.

Yes, it seemed to Norton like Bill used to wear glasses for reading. His eyes weren't so good, and that was probably why he didn't drive—though he was too proud to admit it: didn't want anyone to think he wasn't hitting the pace. Come to think of it, he wore glasses most of the time, though not when they were hiking. He had three or four pairs—mostly little gold-rimmed jobs, just the store kind, not prescription ones. They'd never last long because Bill would keep pushing them into a pocket and they'd soon get all scratched up.

Anyway, about the tobacco—Bill had two or three different pipes and he was always loading them as he lay on his bed, and of course bits of to-bacco would fall down so that before long his blankets were thick with it. But although he was a very clean sort of guy, it never seemed to bother him. He'd just laugh and say it kept the bugs away.

When they went prospecting they almost always went on foot. "Talk about conserving gasoline," said Norton. "We could show 'em something today on that. But of course the Depression was part of the reason we were out there—in those days you had no work and no money but lots of free time. . . . Anyway, we'd hike out from camp pretty early in the morn-ing. If it was going to be a long day, we'd be half an hour down the trail before the sun came up, even though it wouldn't be too hot in daytime, that late in the year. And Bill could move along. Keep right up with us young ones, he would. It was amazing. We figured him pretty old, and Ralph and I were in athletics—we'd run and do calisthenics and that—but here was old Bill hiking along like he'd been a-hiking all his life. Which I guess he had. He walked very straight, very military, never bent over or a-humping or a-digging—just picking 'em up and laying 'em down, never acting like they were heavy. Still, Bill wasn't a pusher. It was no forced march. We'd stop for a halt every half mile or mile—every thirty minutes, say. Stop for fifteen, twenty minutes, you know, just for a rest. Bill would complain that he couldn't hike like he used to—and sometimes he'd need a day off. 'You boys go on out,' he'd say. 'I'll stay in camp today.' Oh, one little thing—he'd never go prospecting on Sunday."

I nodded. Bill had indeed been a diplomat. "Did he ever talk to you about his religion?"

"Well, he wasn't against religion. I mean, he believed in God—though I don't think he went to church, except the times he went with us because he knew we were religious people. But I always figured Bill tried to be as right as he knew how, in that he never swore a lot and never got mad. Outside of his little bit of drinking, that is, which was all hooping and hurrah and fun to him, you know. He just got jovial, not mean or anything. And by and large I think he was a contented man. Yes, you're right, the grass on the other side of the fence always looked greener to Bill. Keeping up with him was like keeping up with a grasshopper. But still . . ."

Norton paused.

I repeated the thought from Emerson that Bill had quoted to Peter Williams: "A man's happiness lies in his heart, not in the place he happens to be."

"Yes," said Norton quietly. "Bill believed and practiced that as much as anybody you've ever known. . . . That would be him, too, quoting from Emerson. He had good polish, Bill did. He might recite a little poetry now and then. But he was practical as well. He knew the desert real well. In broken country, off trails, he had a knack of finding the easy way through. He'd stop and look a little bit at the brush and the terrain, you know, and then he'd go on. And we'd follow—because we'd learned to trust him. Oh, he taught us a lot. He was subtle about it, though. Not 'now this is the way you do it,' but just doing it so that we could see how. Still, he laid down certain safety rules, such as for when we found some old diggings: never go down too far into a shaft because of the danger of dead air; and never go in somewhere that the roof could fall in on you.

"What did he wear? Seems to me he usually had on a white shirt and blue jeans."

"There was a piece of patched blue denim in the cave."

"Was there now? And jeans weren't common then, the way they are today. . . . He'd turn the sleeves of his shirt up a little ways, I remember—like yours are now, though maybe a turn more. Short sleeves weren't common then either, you know. But sometimes he'd go without a shirt—and his body was covered with black hair. He wouldn't go around being obscene, but it wouldn't worry him to take his clothes off in camp for washing or something . . . Oh, he wore long-handled underwear. 'What keeps out the cold keeps out the heat,' he'd say. But he only had this one pair, and he wore 'em night and day. He'd wash 'em in the heat of the day and let 'em dry, but he said he couldn't leave 'em off without catching cold. So he let 'em go until they started to fall apart, just rotting, and he had to keep 'em up by pinning 'em inside his pants. 'If I let 'em go slowly like this,' he said, 'I won't catch cold.' Yes, he had his little oddities, did Bill. Things had to be a certain way.

"There was his staff, for example. A solid ironwood stick it was, big at the top and pretty straight, and he wouldn't hardly leave camp without it. Clear at the start he told us, 'Now you've got to get yourselves sticks to walk with—you'll need 'em.' And we did. And we liked it. I still get me one whenever I go walking, and when I do I remember how Bill would say that he didn't feel balanced without it, and that you needed one, anyway, to move stones for prospecting or to thrash something out of the way and . . . oh, for all kinds of reasons like checking the depth of water."

I smiled. "I'm certainly with him there."

"Yes, I can see old Bill now, walking out across the desert there with the stick in his right hand and his little prospecting pick in his left and his ore bag hanging on his right side. My mother had made him a new bag just before we left. Cotton sack ticking, it was, with a wide strap that went over one shoulder. And along with the rock samples we collected during the day and the paper for making notes on the samples, Bill carried lunch and his tobacco in it. Hanging on his other side would be his field glasses. He carried them all the time and loved to study mountains and outcroppings and interesting formations and anything unusual, including mountain sheep and other animals. He had a magnifying glass, too, that folded into a little case that he wore on a string around his neck. That's right, just like the one you used just now to show me the details in that picture of the cave. The magnifying glass was really for checking rocks, of course, but Bill used it to look at plants and things too. Any kind of life interested him. Bugs, for example. 'Boy, this thing's sure got big eyes,' he'd say."

I smiled again. "Yes, I regard bug-watching as one of the great uses for a prospector's glass."

"Then he carried a canteen, naturally. It was the round, army kind, just like that one in your picture of the cave. Held about half a gallon. That would hang on his left side, along with the binoculars, and with all that stuff on him, walking straight and upright the way he always did, he used to look to me like a soldier walking fearlessly into some kind of anticipated adventure. Yes, I can see him now."

In its way, the prospecting had been very serious. They certainly put in some long days. Once, they started out at five in the morning, ran out of water in midafternoon and walked until well after dark. "According to all the dimensions of all the distances we could figure out," said Norton, "we hiked thirty-nine miles that day."

I held my peace. Thirty-nine miles is a prodigious day's foot travel, even when you don't run out of water—and you will not come close to half that total if you halt every half-hour for a fifteen- or twenty-minute rest. But then, Bill was by no means alone in talking nonsense about miles traveled. It is a common walker's syndrome.

By the end of that long day's walking, said Norton, Bill was very tired; and after dark he ran his leg into the point of a Spanish dagger, or bayonet—one of the cactuslike yuccas—and for the first and only time got mad at Norton. Even then he did little but snap, "That's right, laugh!" when Norton could not restrain himself at the way he was "hopping around and putting on an act." But that "thirty-nine-mile" effort exhausted him. He did not move out of camp for two or three days.

Even on more normal treks they covered a lot of ground. Bill was a great gatherer-in of samples, and they'd collect bits of "float"—rock fragments that had been washed down a canyon—and put each one in a little tobacco bag with a numbered note giving its location. These little bags would go in the sample bag, and when they got back to camp Bill would break the samples up with the hammer end of his prospecting pick and if there was anything interesting they would go out next day and try to follow the float up to its source. You traced similar fragments up the canyon until you could find no more and then backtracked and tried a side canyon until eventually you found the source.

Some of the stuff they'd find was "multi-ored," with blue copper stains and so on, and they'd do little tests with the chemicals Bill had for identifying minerals. Sometimes they even packed along a folding drywasher. Although they never really found anything that amounted to much they'd often come on something that got them excited and Bill would say, "Well, I dunno, maybe we'd better stake a claim here," and they'd build some stone cairns as marker monuments.

"Bill was a very enthusiastic person," said Norton.

He always carried claim forms with him because "you never know when you'll stumble on something rich." So they would make out claim forms for the new find and Bill would make sure the boys' names were on them as well as his own. But as far as Norton remembered they had never recorded anything.

In fact, in retrospect, Norton understood that what they were doing during those three carefree months in the Eagles was playing at prospecting while they learned to survive in the desert.

It had obviously been a good, satisfying, symbiotic arrangement. Ralph Capps had provided the car; Bill, with help from Norton, the groceries. Bill did the cooking; the boys, the heavy work. Above all, the boys learned a lot of desert lore. And Bill clearly had a ball showing them the ropes—

and also gloried in having a captive audience for his stories.

"What Bill wanted more than anything else was to feel free," said Norton. "When we were camped at Cottonwood Spring we'd often go visit Lee Lyons, an old prospector who had built himself a cabin over at Conejo Well, about ten miles away, and had lived there for about three years. He had three burros and would get a little gold, not much, from up behind his camp and sell it to some blowhard from Indio who liked to show it to people in bars and tell them how he'd got it from his secret mine back in the hills. Anyway, I remember Lee told us once how he had been working for the county, breaking rocks for roads, when one day he said to himself, 'Hell, I might as well be in prison!' And he went home and sold his motorcycle and bought his burros and had been prospecting ever since. And I remember Bill laughed and said he'd sure done the right thing. Yes, I remember that very clearly. And I remember that Bill really liked Lee's camp. Thought it was one of the most beautiful places in the desert. And it was a beautiful place he had there, right enough. Water piped down, and all that."

During those months in the Eagles there had been other things to do, of course, besides prospecting. Looking for Indian signs that indicated with a circle of rocks which way to go for the next water. Stumbling on some old bottles that the desert sunlight had turned purple—something that always gave Bill a real kick. Meeting people, too. Not that there were many people out on the desert in those days. But those you found tended to be characters. There was a geologist who was tracing "a dike that ran clear around the world"—and "an Egyptian linguist" who had deciphered the Indian hieroglyphics on Thumb Rock, near Cottonwood Spring. It told the story, he said, of how the Indians had waylaid a contingent of U.S. Cavalry traveling north from Yuma, Arizona, and had killed twenty-nine of them and buried them at the lowest place in the vicinity and buried their own dead at the highest point.

In those days, the desert was a quiet, uncrowded place.

"Palm Springs was just a sleepy little village," said Norton. "The wild burros would still wander in. Not much of nothing there, except for the hot springs, though the rich folks had begun to come for the quiet secludedness of it. You could see Shirley Temple and Jean Harlow on the streets."

The other little communities strung out along the Los Angeles–El Centro highway were even less event-ridden. Indio was a railroad siding where they added another locomotive to help buck trains over the hump to Riverside. But when the aqueduct started up, said Norton, construction

crews turned Indio into a rip-roaring, hell-firing place where "it was nothing to see people thrown out of bars onto the street."

You could see other things, too.

"In those days the freight trains would go through and there'd be hundreds, like hundreds, of fellows riding them, north and south both. Unbe-
lievable. Then there'd be families coming through by road from the dust
bowl, from Oklahoma. They'd have a flat tire and sit on the side of the
road for several days sometimes. So I'd get down and find what size tire
they had and I'd go down around the garage and I'd tell the guy these
people were out there and they can't go on, and I'd get a tire for fifty cents
or something and get them on their way."

Norton smiled. "I was very young then."

In those days, off the cement highway, it was almost all dirt roads—
which mostly meant sand roads. The ruts were sandy, anyway, and once
you got your wheels into them you often couldn't turn out. So the sidewalls of the balloon tires on Ralph Capps' Dodge got sandpapered bare. A
set of tires would often be finished in two or three thousand miles—the
treads still fine but the sidewalls down to fiber.

Back then, you had to go a long ways before you saw any vehicle tracks
across the desert, let alone cellophane or tinfoil or tin cans or garbage of
any kind. People did not deface rocks with their initials or other empty-
headed inscriptions, either. They had a respect for the country. Bill certainly did. He liked to leave things the way he found them. He'd get very
interested in some fragments of Indian pottery, say, but never take them.
And he went to considerable lengths to avoid encouraging other people
into unspoiled places. He never moved rocks or did anything to make a
place look more inhabited. And he had a kind of rule for the boys: "Don't
make a lot of roads, and don't make anything too good or there'll be more
people coming in."

He protected wildlife too, Norton said.

They would often meet rattlesnakes, and if one stuck its head out of a
hole Bill would just whack close by with his stick and say, "Get your head
back in there—you might bite somebody." Early one morning, when it
was still cold, Bill walked clear over a rattler and it was not until the boys,
following him, disturbed it that they saw it. "Oh, leave him alone," Bill
said. "He'll catch a mouse or something."

It was the same with all animals: Bill did not believe in just going out
and killing them for the hell of it. Killing for food was a different matter,
though. Bill was no hunter. He carried no gun. But he voiced no objection
when Ralph shot a bighorn sheep—even though that was already a serious

crime. In fact, he reveled in the free fresh meat and showed them how to make excellent jerky from it. And he always liked to have a couple of steel-jaw traps around in case they got troubled by larger animals. But he also told stories that showed he got very real pleasure from living in harmony with the desert animals.

In camp, if he wasn't just sitting and whittling, what Bill liked to do best, in fact, was lie on his old iron bed, puffing at his old black pipe, and spin stories off by the hour.

The stories were mostly about the distant past—often about army life. Not necessarily braggadocio affairs, though. Soldiers went into town, drank a little, had their girlfriends—with Bill always front and center. One night there had been a fight in a pool hall and some guy threw a pool ball and Bill ducked and the ball made a hole in the wall and just stuck there. "Boy, I got down on my hands and knees and crawled under the tables until I could get out of the place." Painting himself cagey, in other words, rather than intrepid—though he always "came out smelling like a rose." Norton rather thought he had even mentioned his desertion. Norton's Uncle Cliff had deserted from the Navy, so he saw nothing very wrong in that. "Oh, Bill probably just got drunk and went over the hill."

But a few of the stories were more heroic—and often, plain nonsense. "Bill was down around San Juan Hill with Teddy Roosevelt before he went over to the Philippines," said Norton. "And in the Philippines he was with Black Jack Pershing when they went over the wall and stormed the big fort that was the key to the surrender of Manila. That was one of Bill's favorite stories. They used ladders to scale the wall and had to jump down . fifteen feet the other side. Jumped down right in among the Filipinos, too close to shoot, so you had to take your gun and swing it around and mow them down. 'Man,' Bill would say, 'them guys was real tough until you got to putting the boots to a few of them—then they cleared out and got back and surrendered.' Pershing had gone over the wall with them, and Bill really appreciated that. Oh yes, he had some wild war stories, did Bill. You'd have thought he spent half his life in the Army—but it was difficult to see how he could have done that as well as all the other things he talked about. And after an evening of listening to him, Ralph and I would joke that Bill, who said he was sixty-seven, would have had to be a hundred and sixty-seven to have done all the things he talked about.

"Then he had these places he wanted us to go to—places we knew we'd never see. Just kind of dreaming. And always kinda shrouding his activities in mystery. In California alone, it seemed, Bill had been to just about every place in the desert, and a lot of others too. He'd been up in Nevada as well.

Yes, in Vegas, for sure—and that was years back, too. He used to call it 'The Sheep Corral' because in his day there'd been mostly sheep corrals along where the Strip is now. He'd talk about Beatty as well, but in that country Searchlight was the area he was most interested in. Then he'd been around Death Valley when he was cooking for the mule skinners hauling borax out of Trona—that's when he first got interested in minerals—and he'd known Death Valley Scotty and thought he was phony. 'He's getting his money from someplace else,' he'd say. And years later, of course, it came out that he did. Oh, Bill was no fool. Then before he came to California he was up in Seattle. He was cooking for some fellow in a restaurant and got kind of chummy with his daughter. . . ." Norton told me the story that ended with Bill outdistancing the shotgun-wielding father down a railroad track. Like Grace, though, he remembered Bill as saying he had traveled south from Seattle by rail.

But Seattle was by no means the only setting for the romances that Bill told the boys. Women featured in many of the stories he told as he lay on his bed in camp. The stories were set all over, and the plot often had him departing for fresh fields when the female was about to "nab him." Some of the stories were "pretty flowery," with Bill very much the ladies' man.

"But I always figured him to be a little shy around women," said Norton. "They were a little awesome to him. He wasn't just moving in and grabbing 'em. He'd be very polite, bowing and all that. Not servile, you know—just being a gentleman. But some of the stories he told us had him a super Don Juan. Once, when we were in Garnet picking up his pension check, he told me about a woman who cooked down there in the restaurant while he was living at the rock house with Grace. This woman was an all-right girl, it seemed, and he'd slip off from the rock house for a day's 'prospecting' and circle around and slip into Garnet to see her and monkey around some. One time, he stayed there all night and Grace got suspicious. And once, after dark, he met her coming down the canyon, looking for him, when he was walking back up, and he had to say he'd 'lost his way.' Yes, Bill always spoke affectionately of that lady."

"Would you recognize a photograph of her?"

"No, I never saw her."

"Was her name Rose?"

Norton hesitated. "I really can't remem . . . But wait . . . When he told me about his romantic sessions with her he'd sing 'The Rose of Tralee' and do the little buck-and-wing dance he'd learned in vaudeville."

"In vaudeville?"

"Yes, he'd done some trouping. Barnstorming, you know. Just filling in, he said. These little dance steps they called 'doing the clog.' Bill used to joke about it: 'They had to have someone to throw the fruit at.' But, whenever he'd get dressed up, or even when he was just standing around and feeling happy, he'd do this little jig, this shuffle and side kick, this buck and wing; and he was real nimble at it, so that you could tell he'd done that kind of thing. Then he'd built Grace up as an entertainer, and I seem to remember some story about him making some kind of tour or cruise with her in the Mediterranean. And some of his stories about getting involved with other women were when he was traveling with vaudeville.

"He'd done some horse riding in show business, too, though maybe not in the same outfit. He had a photo of himself on a white horse, in black clothes and a white Stetson. I asked, 'What did you do, Bill?' and he said he'd come charging into the rodeo grounds and do a few little rope tricks like Will Rogers. Oh yes, it was Bill in the picture all right."

I nodded. Show business was a new side of Bill. But I remembered now that *Young's Magazine* tended to run stories of stage life. And there had been a passage in the graphologist's reports on Bill's handwriting that read: "He would have made a terrific actor or movie star if he had more purpose. Even in his writing he puts on an act—when he is pleading it is shaky, though his signature puts on a bold front. But he does not have a strong enough will or purpose to have made an actor that could have held an audience for longer than a few minutes. He could probably spin a tale to friends and act a part as he was telling it. He would not really be a liar but would believe the story at the moment, so that it seemed to be truth."

Norton still remembered very clearly the ending of those free and sunlit weeks in the fall and winter of 1933, when Bill and Ralph Capps and he prospected in and around the Eagle Mountains. They had camped for almost a month on the eastern edge of the mountains, near a place called Buzzard Spring. It was a couple of days before Christmas, and they knew they had to be back in Cherry Valley in time for the family holiday. There in the low desert it was still warm. Reluctant to leave, they lay around naked on the rocks, sunbathing. When they at last tore themselves away, in midafternoon, it was still sunbathing weather. But in the Coachella Valley they met an icy, blustering wind. In Banning, rain began to fall. By the time they reached Cherry Valley, about nine o'clock, it was snowing.


AFTER FORTY YEARS, two men's memories of the same time and place and people can very easily mismatch.

Ralph Capps at sixty-two was a fit, solidly built, down-to-earth man:

clean-shaven, small glasses, crew-cut white hair; straightforward, honest and likable; but no poet.

I showed him Grace's rock-house and Garnet snapshots, taken a year before the 1933 prospecting trip. Ralph studied them carefully. "The way I remember Bill," he said at length, "he'd gained weight since these were taken. He'd got a belly, and his cheeks were out. I'd say he'd been living a little easy, because he was out of shape, no question about this. He'd puff real easy. I don't think that man could have done a day's work—I don't think he was well enough. And when he was tired one leg would give out on him. That's why he used that cane. So it was tough on him, hiking too far. No, the man wasn't sound."

"But Norton said he was an astonishing walker for his age."

Ralph smiled good-naturedly. "Well, you know, when you're talking about walking, Norton and Horace Roberts were good water drinkers. It was hot out there, even at that time of year, and you couldn't stop those two from drinking. Why, by nine o'clock theirs would be gone. And Bill wouldn't give them any. He'd told them, and that's it. Because Bill was desert-wise all right—he knew what to do and how to conserve water and that, and he had a good eye for country. But he really couldn't walk too well."

"But Norton said you did a thirty-nine-mile day, once."

"Hell, we never did no thirty-nine miles with Bill. For one thing, he walked pretty slow. And he had to stop to get his breath, especially if we were climbing at all. He'd learned to pace himself, no doubt about that. He was game—always willing to tackle something, but he was a little overambitious. He talked big, like he was going to conquer the world, but he ran out of gas easy. Just couldn't do it any more. I could see that he'd been a good man—he'd been tough, been rugged—but for my money he wasn't well. He'd go farther than he should have, and then he'd get tired and that leg would get to hurt him and he would start to limp. You say he was only fifty-eight then, but I'd have had him up around seventy—which is what he said he was. He lived till 1950? I'm surprised—I wouldn't have given him that long. Sure, he had a pretty good carriage still—but no stamina."

What Ralph Capps remembered best was Bill's way with names.

"No, we never recorded no claims—but I bet we staked at least fifteen or twenty. We'd go out prospecting every day, and we'd find something and I thought we'd hit a fortune because Bill would get all excited—oh, this was it, we had it made. And we'd stake it off and build the monuments and we had the papers and we had to get a nice name to put on it. And Bill would get so excited he'd just shake. This was it, it was just there, and he'd talk about how we were going to work it and the money and all that. I felt a few times that we were rich. And then I began to get puzzled. Because next morning he'd never talk about it. Ask him, and he'd brush it off, and we'd go looking for another one. Never went back to one of them. And after we did this for two weeks I got wise, I saw something was . . . not right.

"No, Bill was more of a monument builder. Building the monuments and getting the names right, those were the big things. When we staked a claim . . . let's see, the first thing was to step it off. There was a size or something. We'd mark the corners, then in the center we'd build the big monument. And we built those monuments all over. We were packing a lot of rock, I can tell you. And Bill was fussy about 'em. He'd get one started and then we had to finish it while he directed. And we sure had to fit 'em. If somebody had a rock he didn't like, you'd just put it back. By the time we were through I felt like I could've been a stonemason.

"And when we were through with building the monument, then we were at the main event—choosing the name. We'd think of names until . . . why, I can remember getting tired in the head trying to come up with one that pleased Bill. We'd have Rose Quartz and Iron Mountain and Gold Hill and all kinds of beautiful names, but they didn't quite do it—Bill would reject 'em all. And sometimes he'd get irritated at us. We weren't getting ideas fast enough. And then finally we'd hit it and he'd just go in the air. This was it. So we'd get this wrote on the claim paper and put it in a little tobacco can and put the can in the monument—not clear at the bottom but up *in* the rock in some way.

"But the name, that was the key part. And we had some dandies, I can tell you. I can't remember 'em now, but I'll bet some of 'em would startle you."

"Like Black Horse?"

"That sounds like one we might have even went through. We went through all kinds."

I began to read from my list of the claims Bill had recorded. "Solo Pal No. 1 . . . Trail's End . . . Lost Stag . . ."

"Lost Stag? Now *that* sounds like one of ours. It brings something to . . . I heard something about Lost Stag."

". . . Mockingbird . . . Blue Moon . . . Redwing . . . Black Beutt . . ."
Ralph chuckled. "Black Beaut! Now he'd have bought that."

". . . Silver Girl . . . Peach Blossom . . . Buck Horns . . . Papoose . . . Black Prince . . . Mary Francis . . ."

"Yes, I think we had some girl's names, too."

"Billy Wright . . . Gold Jint . . ."

"Well, there you are!"

"Silver Belle . . . Darling Sisters . . ."

"Yessir, they were all kind of pretty names, even though you often couldn't figure out what they meant. Sometimes I'd wonder. And sometimes we couldn't get a name that suited him right away and we'd go back to camp without putting the paper in the monument. Then Bill was pretty touchy and up-tight and we'd just sit around saying names until we found one that caught his fancy. He was fair about it, mind you—sometimes he got it, sometimes one of us got it. But when we'd got it, he'd know. I mean, there was no question, no in between. It wasn't nothing till it suited him, and then he knew it right off—and he hit the sky. He'd get so excited and thrilled that he'd shake. I used to worry about him—thought maybe he was going to have a heart attack. . . . And if we'd left the monument without the name in it, why next day when we had the right name, he hustled us back there. He'd talk about how we could lose 'em and how somebody could jump claims and that. Yessir, we went back fast, we moved—we almost ran."

"In theory, in other words, you'd take the risk of losing the claim just because you hadn't been able to hit on a suitable name right away?"

"That's right. That's the kind of thing he'd do." Ralph Capps looked at me over the top of his glasses. "I'd have to say Bill was little bit unstable, you know, even a bit childish in some ways—like with the names—so that you'd feel sorry for him. To me, it was kinda sad. . . . And he could be pouty. When he was happy, nobody was happier—he was just happy as a bird. Then all of a sudden he'd go into one of his moods and get snappy, real snappy. If one of us would ask him a question he'd snap back. Just like a kid. And then five minutes later he'd be smoking the pipe and everything was fine again. I always thought his moods were because he wasn't well . . ."

I nodded.

"Then when he got some booze he'd go till it was finished. He didn't get violent or anything—he was happy for a while but then he'd get high and kinda morose, and in the end it would fold him, just knock him out. Of course, he didn't get it too often. He knew the Ropers didn't like it— Rosie Roper wouldn't allow drink in the house—but when Bill got loose, he drank. I'd say that could have been his weakness, a real weakness. He'd have went for that, because I'd say he couldn't resist it. He seemed a strong man in other ways, but not with booze. I think he'd have went right down the river if it had been there."

I hesitated. "I get the feeling you aren't really sure whether you liked him."

"Oh no, no, no. I liked him very much. You couldn't help but like him—except when he'd get to drinking. You couldn't like him then. But oh yes, I really enjoyed him. He was quite a guy for us young fellows going out with him. He was very knowledgeable, so we learned a lot, and I got the impression he was just tickled to death to be out there with us. But though he was the chief, he wasn't bossy—and he wasn't fussy either. No, he was nice to be around, he was nice to talk to. And he was no dummy. No sir. The guy had a lot of natural intelligence, and a lot of knowledge about things. Yes, you're right, he didn't seem interested in money. My impression was that if you gave him a fortune he might buy a freight train—but he'd probably throw it away, scatter it around. He was an impulsive man—and proud. . . . Oh no, I liked him, don't make any mistake about that. I enjoyed him very much. Why, I never heard anybody could tell stories like him."

"What sort of stories?"

"Well, I've been thinking about that. It's a funny thing, but I can't remember most of them. What he liked best of all, though, was to lay there on his bed with the pipe and talk about finding gold. He'd use the pipe as a kind of prop, you know. Sometimes he'd stop cold in the middle of a story till he'd got the pipe fixed. He'd maybe tamp it out and then fill it and then get it lit again—while we'd sit there open-mouthed. Oh, he was good at it. He was an artist, I tell you. . . . Some of his best stories were about the Lost Dutchman Mine, and he had it built in that it could be right where we were at. And we looked for it for a week, maybe two weeks. Covered a lot of ground. And I expected to find something. We were just out of high school, you know, and Bill had a way to pep us up. And we never acted like we doubted any of his stories, you know, because he wouldn't have liked this."

"But in spite of his stories, people seemed to find him an honest man."

"Oh yes, Bill was honest. I'd have trusted him, sure. But in his stories maybe he just let his imagination go. He was what I'd call an honest liar. . . . I figured he'd like to have been some of the things he told. In a lot of his stories he loved to come up with something where he told them to go to hell. He'd worked for somebody and they'd told him to do something and he told them to shove it. I mean, he liked that. No, I don't remember anything about vaudeville, but it wouldn't surprise me one bit. I'd say he'd have been the type that could do something like this. He could have performed, yes. Because he had that ham in him. And the bigger the audience, the better. If he saw that his story was going down good and everybody liked it, he could make it a little better. Yes, I'd say he could have been very good as an actor. Very, very good. In fact, I would have pictured him at his best at something like this—as an actor or something before the public. Oh, I can see him now, laying there on his bed like a king with three, four pillows propped up behind him. . . . Then I got the impression that he fancied himself as a ladies' man, kind of a lady-killer. But I'd say Bill could stumble his way into woman trouble, easy."

"He wouldn't be alone in that. But would you say he was a happy man on the whole? Contented?"

"Yes, I would. . . . Although there was something sad that would come out. . . . He was lonesome, this man was lonesome, he'd been lonesome. I would say he didn't like being alone but I'd say probably his makeup made him be alone. He liked people and he could adapt—and he gave the impression he could fit any place, in any company. But I think maybe he could have spats pretty easy, like he did with Lee Lyons, the prospector with the burros that we met out at Conejo Well. Lyons was a serious man, not humorous like Bill, and he didn't buy some of Bill's stories, and after a few days they just didn't get on. . . . Then there was another thing. Bill was very bitter about his pension. He figured he hadn't been treated right."

"Oh, but that was only temporary." And I explained about the reduction from sixty to six dollars.

"Well, maybe that was all. But something way back had left something empty."

"A woman?"

"Yes, that could very well be."

I explained that Grace had departed just before they went camping.

"Well then, I guess it could have been just that. Or it could have been something deeper. I don't really know. But although he was mostly happy, he had sad spells. There was something kinda sad about him. He was a dreamer, and sometimes you'd feel sorry for him because he seemed in a way to be alone."

I smiled. "At least some of that was by choice, you know. And I find that most people tend to feel sorry for a man who chooses to spend a lot of time alone. But being alone doesn't necessarily mean loneliness. It can be solitude."

"Maybe," said Ralph Capps. "Maybe . . ."

For a moment we sat silent.

"Tell me, when you say you found something sad about Bill, do you mean that he was a pitiful character?"

"Oh no, not at all. But the way he talked, you'd get the feeling like he'd been hurt or something, some way. Or something hadn't been fulfilled in his life or he'd had something happen to him. Oh no, no, no—not pitiful. Not at all. I just felt like there was something . . . he had been something or done something and it hadn't worked out, and here he was, and he would have rather been in different surroundings. Oh no, Bill had dignity. He was very proud. But now he was in his twilight, and he knew it too, deep down. He was still independent, though, very independent. He didn't want to be obligated. And he liked to tell people to go to hell. Oh yes, he was a free man."

MOST OF THE COUNTRY that Bill and the boys prospected in 1933 now lies within Joshua Tree National Monument. But not all of it.

Conejo Well, where Lee Lyons built his cabin after he quit breaking stones for the county, stands deep in the Monument. The little canyon that cradled the camp remains fairly inaccessible to humans—and therefore uncrudded.

The camp itself has almost gone. You can still see a few pieces of weathered lumber, though, and some rusty water pipe and the scattered remains of an old stove. The well is part sanded in now and barely ten feet deep, but in spring it harbors a little water and hummingbirds bathe there and then perch for sun-dry treatment in the branches of the gnarled and ancient mesquite tree that overhangs the well. Around the tree, grass grows thick. Down toward the mouth of the little canyon stand blocked outcrops of warm brown granite, tumbled yet compact, squared off and stalwart yet also rounded off and strokable. Beyond stretches wide plain, then distant hills. Above hangs wide sky and silence.

No wonder Bill thought the place "one of the most beautiful in the desert." It is a place fit for a king. In such a realm, a free man lords it over the world like a genuine monarch. He lacks serfs, of course, to do his bidding—or to be insubordinate or temperamental, to whine or revolt or, almost worse, to sap his fiber, slowly, with their daily sycophancy. Instead, a man sits there alone, his own master and servant, lord of all he surveys, content, in harmony with his domain of grass and mesquite tree and hummingbirds and square, smoothed-off granite and wide plain and wider sky and silence and evening shadows lengthening across distant, changing hills.

Bill had understood all that, clearly. "If I never saw a speck of gold," he had said to Norton one evening as they sat outside their tent at Cottonwood Spring, "I'd still rather be here than anywhere else." No wonder he coveted Lee Lyons' camp at Conejo Well.

Cottonwood Spring also lies within the Monument but it is close to a Visitor Center, near the Monument's only highway. A blacktop feeder road from the Visitor Center ends at a blacktop parking lot, a hundred yards from the spring. And a manicured trail, complete with signs, leads down into the little palm-fringed oasis. So the place has been diluted, vacationalized, part varnished. It remains desert, though; remains beautiful.

The last place that Bill and the boys camped—at the eastern edge of the Eagle Mountains, near Buzzard Spring—lies outside the National Monument, unprotected from humans.

In 1933, the plain on which they made this final camp was still almost unspoiled desert. So were the mountains that rimmed it. But the industrial world had begun to encroach. A few miles east of their camp, construction work had started on the Colorado River Aqueduct—the same aqueduct that crossed the mouth of Long Canyon, sixty miles away. And three or four miles north of camp stood a prominent outlying peak of the Eagle Mountains that was pockmarked with what Norton remembered as looking like "gopher holes," but which Bill said were pits dug by men paid by the big company that owned the mining rights, just to keep the assessment work up to date so that they would not lose the rights. Bill would often stand outside the tent, said Norton, and look across at the mountain through his binoculars.

I wonder, now, if he was reading the signs.

Today, at the foot of what was once that prominent outlying peak of the mountains stands a town; a company mining town, population 3,750. It is called Eagle Mountain. It has paved streets and rows of rabbit-hutch buildings. From it, during working hours, there floods across the once quiet desert, for twenty or thirty miles or even more, downwind, the whine and grind of huge machines at labor.

These machines have expunged the outlying peak of the Eagle Mountains that Bill would often study through binoculars. They have ingested it, then spewed it out. All that remains is an immense gray slag heap—neat and orderly, terraced into the straight lines beloved of engineers. Lifeless. And the machine tentacles continue to embrace and cancel. Zigzag roads slash up and out across warm brown granite toward other peaks that still stand unviolated, still creased with lines of subtle meaning.

I wonder if Bill, looking at the original peak in 1933, read the gopher-hole signs. I wonder, that is, if he saw, as he stood outside the tent peering through his binoculars, that Braddock's Industrial Defeat would soon come to the Eagle Mountains. I suspect that by now, in his own way, he did. For many years after that winter of 1933, when he would stand looking across the plain at the "gopher holes," Bill went on prospecting. But he recorded only one more mining claim.

AFTER THE LONG prospecting trip, Bill went back to living in his tent under the apricot tree in the Roper's orchard. And during the first three months of 1934 Norton took him on several short desert trips in his 1924 Maxwell.

"The Maxwell had no top," said Norton, "but old Bill would sit there smoking his pipe, calm as you please, even when the wind blew his hat off. We'd go puttering out to Twentynine Palms and Mecca and Indio and places like that, sometimes camping out but mostly stopping over with friends of Bill's that we had dropped in to see. Bill would tell his friends, 'I've got my little place up Long Canyon, you know,' and make it sound like he was very established. No, I can't remember any of the friends' names. They were mostly older people he'd known from times past. Oh, there was a Frank somebody we were always going to see at Dos Palms, down by the Salton Sea, but we never made it. Bill said that this Frank—I think that was his name—had a cabin there, in among some palm trees."

Bill and Norton called in several times at the rock house. The place was fully furnished but livable rather than comfortable. There were no soft chairs or anything like that. Once they stayed overnight while Bill collected a few things. No, you didn't lock places in those days: just shut the doors to keep the animals out.

"One time we were up there, Bill offered to turn the rock-house claim over to me. I thanked him but said there was nothing I could do with it. I guess Bill felt a bit melancholy because he'd shared it with Grace and couldn't face living there alone. He was funny like that. I don't think his feelings for the place were really all that strong, but I remember he appreciated the way it was sheltered from the wind that often blew in Garnet and Palm Springs. He'd often say, 'Bet it isn't blowing like this up Long Canyon.' He loved the animals up there, though. Felt he was their protector. He said he had at least three coveys of quail there, and people would come up and try to shoot them and he'd go out after them. Those quail were just like his chickens." Then one year, two bighorns had stayed all winter, just a stone's throw from the rock house. " 'One of 'em would lay down in full view,' Bill said, 'and the other would stand there looking at me.' And he got a real kick out of that."

Toward the end of that spring of 1934, or in early summer, things began to look up, economically.

"We weren't quite so poor then," said Norton. "We'd had some luck with onion seeds—sold them through the Chamber of Commerce to Brownsville, Texas, and got four hundred and seventy-five dollars. Made us feel pretty rich, I can tell you. We went out and bought a new Philco radio. And about that time Bill got his pension restored."

"His records show it went to forty-five dollars in June," I said. "Back-dated to March."

"That sounds about right. I remember he got quite a lump sum. And being Bill, and grateful to us for looking after him, the first thing he thought about was doing something for my sisters. 'Let's go down to the store and buy the girls some shoes to go to church in,' he said. Bill was always so free with his money that you had to hold him down not to buy too much. My father said, 'Now Bill, don't let all your money get away from you.' And Bill said, 'But I want to do that, you know.' And he did."

"Yes, Iretha told me about it. . . . Bill seems to have been really big on shoes."

"Yes, it seems to me he said he'd done a little cobbling."

"Come to think of it, some small green shoes that I found in the cave had had the holes in their uppers very neatly stitched."

"Sounds right. I know Bill would take old automobile tires and cut them into pieces and just nail them to shoes for soles.

"After he got his pension back he bought himself a big new hat, I remember, and dressed himself up and went off to L.A. I went with him once. He'd go into a hotel lobby there, all dressed up like that, looking like an old boy just come in from his mines, you know, and he'd sell a number of his prospects that way. 'Going to L.A. to shyster some of my claims,' he'd say. 'Got to get some money around this stinking place.' And he might salt his mine, just a little bit. You know, he'd take a little sample he knew was rich and plant it, and the guy would take it and it would assay out like a house afire—and Bill would have his money, a hundred or three hundred dollars or even more, that would get him grubstaked for the next round. He had these places, you see, and he'd sell them, and then people would give them up—wouldn't do the assessment work, so that the claim lapsed—and Bill would go and restake them and start over."

"But I've always thought of him as an honest man!"

"Oh, Bill was as honest and straightforward as they come. You could trust him with anything. At home, he had the run of the place. But he figured this was a way to sell his claims and he knew the guy would find gold there all right and if he didn't choose to do his assessment work, well, that was his affair.

"After he got his pension back we didn't feel so responsible for Bill, and he wasn't one to impose, so he went back to Garnet. But when we went down that way we'd always call in to see if Bill was around. And for several years he'd drop by our place from time to time. He always seemed able to get rides because if he had a little money and met some guy with a car on the next bar stool . . . well, you know as well as I do how it is with these fellows who hang around these places—they're always kinda restless and wanting to get out and do something else. And that suited Bill—swashbuckling about. So he was always with somebody when he dropped by our place, and always in a hurry, always off somewhere to pull a big deal or something. 'That old boy's sure a goer,' my dad would say. Bill would just maybe stay for a meal, but he was still like one of the kinfolk. We had real uncles just like him who would drop by from time to time. Yes, we all felt very close to old Bill. . . . But then he moved down to Palo Verde. Permanently, I guess. I'm not sure when it was but . . ."

"He changed his mailing address to Palo Verde in December 1936."

"That would be about right, too. The last time we saw him, he was with somebody who was going to take him down there. He said he was going because he was getting a little rheumatism and it was warmer there in winter, with none of the wind you got up in Garnet. We told him that on the way to Palo Verde he could go back up to our last camp in the Eagle Mountains, near Buzzard Spring, and pick up the tent and all the other stuff there—but whether he did or not I don't know."

"I think he did. . . . When did you last hear from Bill?"

"I guess we kind of lost touch with him after he moved to Palo Verde. But we'd keep asking down at Garnet. And then after a while we heard that he had died. I don't know just what year that would be, though."

"He died January 11, 1950."

"As late as that? My dad died in 1949, and it seems to me that we thought Bill had died some years before that. . . . Anyhow, I know we all had the warmest memories of him—and still do. . . . What's that? Oh no, certainly not a disappointed man. Not at all. Bill didn't regret anything. He was free, he didn't feel that anybody owed him anything, and he was happy if he could give anybody anything or do anything for them."

"The more I learn about him," I said, "the more I wish I had met him."

Norton nodded. "Yes. Not knowing him was your loss."

# 18 Last Wanderings

SOMETIME DURING THE SPRING or summer of 1934, Bill and Grace got together again and moved back into the rock house. At a guess, Bill persuaded Grace to do so on one of his visits to Los Angeles to sell "mines," after his pension was partially restored.

The living arrangement no doubt remained open-ended; but in November Grace slammed it shut. By then she was waitressing and singing at de Courselles' bar in Garnet, and there she met and peremptorily married Nils Stenderup.

According to Grace, Bill was at first "just broken up." His pride, if nothing else, must have ached. But it seems likely that, as Grace maintained, he soon recovered. They certainly remained good friends. Bill often went to see Nils and Grace at their ranch near Garnet.

Nils died about 1962, but two of his nephews still live in Los Angeles. Both used to visit their uncle at the ranch. Both remembered Grace—and Bill.

One of the nephews was still at school then. "Me being a teen-ager, Grace always leaned over backward to help me. She was a good-hearted soul, and I liked her. If she had two dollars and you needed one, you got it. If you really needed them, you got both. She was getting kinda chubby, I remember, but was a lot of fun and had had a wild kinda life. For my money, a real charming girl.

"Bill often seemed to be around the place, and as far as I could see, he and Nils got along fine. But I don't remember that I ever talked to Bill. He had a goatee, and . . . Oh yes, and he had a dog that I liked. Half coyote, it was. He'd had a bitch that was bred by a coyote, and he'd raised this pup. Real close to him, that dog was. He was the only one could play with her. She had some kind of a squirrely name—began with an 'R.' Renee, or something like that. . . ."

"Reina," I said.

"Yeah, that's right. Reina. . . . Now Chuckawalla Bill, he was kinda renowned, I remember. Lived out in the desert someplace. Had this mine, back up some valley. I never knew he had any money, though. All he wanted to do was live."

The other nephew had been in his early twenties. "Yeah, they were colorful characters, all three of them. Frankly, I didn't care too much for Grace. She could drink, and I guess I saw her at her worst. They were an odd couple, her and Nils. He was always immaculate, and Grace was pretty scruffy—though she could dress up if she wanted to. But to hear her swear—now that was a beautiful thing. All carefully constructed it was, I remember. . . . She seemed to spend a lot of time looking for minerals with Bill, up on Garnet Hill. She was supposed to own part of the hill, though I don't think she really did, and the story was that she'd shoot at strangers looking for garnets up there. But the sheriffs could never pin anything on her. . . . Yes, I heard something about Bill bringing minerals for the fireplace. An unusual fireplace it was, sort of Mexican. And I remember Bill sitting in front of it once and talking about all the things he could see in the shapes and colors of it—animals, water, skies . . . He sure had imagination. Yeah, you're right. Poetic. That would really describe him."

Nils left the ranch to go to Hawaii, made money, and got together with Grace again for six months in a big new waterfront house at Seal Beach. But then the money ran out and they broke up for good.

Meanwhile, Grace was continuing her "fight for the ranch." County records show it as a leeching legal battle that did not smell of roses.

By this time Bill's wanderlust had resurfaced.

His pension file clearly signals a new restlessness—though now it was a strictly local lust. In October 1935, just after his pension went back up to sixty dollars a month, his address changed from "PO Box 24, Garnet" to "Box 93, Coachella"; then, in February 1936, to General Delivery, Niland; and then, five months later, back to Garnet.

At the root of these vacillations I read both Grace trouble—now further soured by the smell of non-roses—and some twinging intimations of mortality: the move away from Garnet came less than a year after Grace's marriage and just two months after Bill's sixtieth birthday. And your sixtieth birthday, they tell me, jolts.

I do not mean that Bill threw in the towel. Far from it. But a decade is a decade is another decade. And the obituaries say—and said it louder then than now—that the sixties are prime dying time. By Ralph Capps's account, Bill knew he was slowing down, and I see him during those unsettled months moving reluctantly but inexorably toward the decision he was to make at the end of 1936.

Meantime, though, he gathered little moss.

During that unsettled year, for example, he put in one or two spells of prospecting with a Mexican friend.

I WENT TO SEE Juan DeLaGarza on spec.

Several people had suggested I talk to him. No one knew of any connection with Bill, but Juan DeLaGarza had been around that part of the desert all his life, they said, and his life had now lasted ninety-odd years. He was still in full command of his faculties, though. And everyone spoke highly of him. In Blythe—a place that accords no extravagant respect to Mexicans—a woman who had once worked for Steve Ragsdale, founder and baron of nearby Desert Center, referred to him as "Ragsdale" but spoke of "Mr. DeLaGarza."

So on one of my desert visits I turned off the Blythe–Indio freeway near Desert Center at Chuckwalla Road—hoping that was a good omen—drove eight miles down a dirt road to Corn Springs and swung west toward Aztec Well.

I drove among strong, granitelike outcrops. Paloverde trees greened the washes. Ocotillos reached for heaven. Cholla and other cacti clustered in bizarre natural gardens. It was a pleasing country that would change with every light.

Juan DeLaGarza's cabin stood in a little canyon so soft and shallow as to be, more accurately, a gentle valley. The cabin itself was a thing of no great beauty. It had a corrugated-iron roof, and its walls were a patchwork: gray asbestos sheeting; wood, both weathered and New Deal; tar paper; inserts of shiny aluminum sheeting. On the slope behind the cabin stood an aluminum water tank, conical-capped and unlovely; and above that, a gray wind pump.

Yet the place had a looked-after air. By "looked after," though, I mean "left untouched": the canyon had none of the scuffed and littered, poor-white feeling of so many human-occupied desert places. It was clean, uncrudded.

Juan DeLaGarza turned out to be a tall, slim man who moved slowly and carefully but with none of the labored stiffness of old age. He wore a nondescript gray shirt and slacks, impeccably clean, and a nondescript gray hat, honorably soiled. His white mustache was neatly clipped. Brown eyebrows roofed pale blue eyes. His long face, its pale skin faintly blotched, was almost expressionless.

But as soon as I mentioned Bill's name, the face smiled. It still smiled, though, from a slightly different world.

"Chuckawalla Bill Simons? Yeah, sure. I used to go prospecting with him. He was a Spanish-American War pensioner. The last I heard, he was in Palo Verde." The Spanish-accented voice was still strong. And quietly sure of itself.

With a courtly gesture, Juan DeLaGarza motioned me indoors.

Inside, it was cool, shadowy. Juan DeLaGarza apologized for the bareness of his home, motioned me into a chair and sat down on another.

The cabin was sparsely furnished but had everything a man needed: two small tables, two easy chairs and one upright, a heavy iron stove, an alarm clock and an oil lamp, even a copy of the *National Geographic.*

I brought out Grace's snapshots of Bill. Juan DeLaGarza put on a pair of steel-rimmed glasses and tilted the prints toward one of two small yellow-curtained windows. He peered at the photos, readjusted his position, peered some more. Then he smiled—and this time the smile broke the drawn and wrinkled mask of age and revealed the living man.

"That's him all right enough. Used to wear a little goatee. . . ."

Juan DeLaGarza went back to peering at the photos. I took a magnifying glass from my briefcase and handed it to him. He smiled his beautiful smile, re-peered—and went on peering.

Time passed.

I asked several questions. There was no response. The silences filling the cabin grew longer, heavier. I felt my muscles begin to tighten. Then the obvious struck me and I bellowed a repeat of my last question.

"What's that? Oh yes, we went prospecting together, in the thirties. Bill used to live in Niland then. He was a good fellow. . . ." Juan went back to his peering. But now he kept emerging. "Yes, that's him all right enough. But he never did wear a hat like that. . . . Yes, Bill was quite a character. We were good friends, him and I. He was a man I could trust—a true friend. I wish that he was alive. . . ."

Juan leaned back, took off his hat and scratched the top of his head. He had a healthy crop of gray-white hair. "By God, we teamed pretty good, him and I. I remember once, down at a place on the old Bradshaw road from Palo Verde to Mecca, way over the mountains . . . a beautiful place . . . You used to be able to see the walls of the old stage station . . . Grassy, and a lot of brush. . . . And Bill wanted to homestead there—him and I.

Bill would say, 'We'll call it the Simons and Garza Ranch. . . .' " Once again, Juan pronounced "Simons" with the "i" as in "pie."

I nodded. Bill had certainly been slowing down in those post-Garnet years. Rolling stones do not ranch.

"Yes, we were good friends. Traveled together in Indio, Mecca, Niland. . . . Always I come back to Imperial Valley. Brawley is my home town." Juan looked past me, back down the decades. "I knew Calipatria," he said softly, "when they put up the first building there."

He and Bill would go prospecting back in the mountains in Juan's Model T Ford, sometimes for two or three weeks at a time before returning to Niland and going their separate ways. "I always on the go, you know," said Juan. "I never stay very long in one place. And Bill, he was the same. Very much by himself. We were here in Corn Springs a couple of times, and I told him, 'Bill, you'd better come with me, and stay with me.' 'Well,' he says . . .

"But I always knew where to find him. Used to be a place in Niland, an old empty house—oh, just a shack, but a big one. Sheepherders used to camp in there, just in the season. And when I wasn't doing nothing I'd go there. That's where Bill stayed, and I would stay with him."

They had never actually staked any claims together, but they made a number of trips. They lost contact for a while, then got together again.

"Oh no, Bill wasn't what I'd call a seasoned prospector or anything like that. He just liked the idea, liked to go out in the desert. Yes, for Bill it felt like home, being out in the desert. He was like a rabbit: he'd make a bed anywhere, behind a rock or in the brush. Anywhere. When he was on his own he'd walk, but we never walked. Always went in my old Model T. No, I never knew Bill drive a car. But I remember he bought a couple of tires for me once in Niland. In those days we used to pay three dollars and a half."

Beyond Juan's head, a quail sauntered past, barely three feet from the yellow-curtained window.

"How did you find out about Bill in the first place?"

I explained how I had stumbled on the cave while walking through the desert. And how I had called in at Palo Verde during my long summer's walk.

Juan looked up sharply. "You walked from Mexico to Oregon!" For a moment he sat silent. Then: "Well, my name is John DeLaGarza. What *is* your name?"

I told him, again.

Juan held out his hand. And after we had shaken hands there was no more of the lingering restraint that had lain between us.

"Bill was a walker, too. He'd been all through the mountains, over in the Little Chuckawallas—but not over this side in the Big Chuckawallas, where I went. Oh yeah, he had a pack, sure." One of the slow, revealing smiles transformed Juan's face. "A papoose saddle. . . . No, no frame to it. Just a big brown canvas bag with straps to put over his shoulders. He'd pack water, grub and everything. And an overcoat for the night, for a blanket. He was a very active man, you know. In his day he must have been very quick in action. . . . He was quite a man for the girls, too. One time, he came up here from Garnet with a Russian woman they called Long-Legged Anne. He was in some sort of deal with her. . . . But he was a good man, was Bill, and we teamed good. I wish he was still alive. . . ." Juan waved aside a fly that had buzzed into our silence, then asked cheerfully, matter-of-factly, "When *did* Bill die? . . . Nineteen fifty, eh? . . . Do you know when he was born?"

"Eighteen seventy-five."

"Well! So he was older than me, eh? I was born eighteen seventy-eight. Then he was only around seventy-five or eighty when he died. . . . I've got ninety-seven on my back now. . . ." For a moment, Juan seemed to be surveying that near-century. Then his face broadened into one of its sunburst smiles. "The first time I saw Bill was somewhere around nineteen two or three, in Colorado."

"Colorado?"

"We didn't get acquainted but I knew *him*. It was out of Denver, when they was building the Moffet road, and he used to make the stones on a horse, and all of that, you know. . . ."

"Making the stones for the road?"

Juan did not hear me. "We was working for the railroad, the Moffet railroad, Denver to Salt Lake. I was quite a teamster then, driving long-team wagons and scrapers and all of that. And when they unhitched the horses for lunch this fellow would get on a horse and buck, you know, and make a lot of stunts and all of that. . . ."

"Ah, stunts. You mean just for fun?"

"Yeah, it was remarkable. Everybody watching him making the stunts—bareback and different positions and all of that. And we was waiting there for the bell to ring, to go to the dining room, and he was telling us he learned all of them tricks in the calvary. . . . He was a remarkable fellow and very handsome. . . . As I say, I couldn't say that I got acquainted with him, or spoke to him, but I remembered him. And I *think* it was Bill. I don't say for sure it was him. But from what I learned afterward, I say, 'That is the man that was doing them stunts on horseback in there.'"

"What made you think it was Bill?"

"Because of his features—and all of that."

"Did you ask Bill about it?"

"No."

I hesitated, plunged: "Why not?"

Juan shrugged and gave an odd, lighthearted "Eh, deh, deh" that could have meant "Oh, I don't know" or "Well, I really couldn't ask, you know" or something entirely different—but which certainly meant "That's all the answer you're going to get, friend."

I took a Xerox copy of Bill's desertion poster from my briefcase.

"Well I'll be damned! He never told me that! Nineteen eight. . . . that's ten years after the war, huh?"

"But he *was* in the war, earlier. . . . Does his picture look like the stunt rider?"

Juan studied it with the magnifying glass. "Something like him."

I found a clearer copy. Juan studied it carefully. At length he said, "Eh, that's him! At least, I think so. . . . When I knew him in the thirties he did tell me that he had been in the calvary—and a sergeant in the Philippines. I remember once he told me about cutting his foot on a bamboo. . . ." It was a long and interesting story about Filipinos at a water hole, and Juan had reached a point at which Bill "got to be a cook for some of the officers" when he abruptly broke off.

"No! What a fool!" he muttered. Then, out loud: "I am sorry. I am wrong. That was a different Bill. Bill Dixon, not Bill Simons. I am very sorry. Oh, my memory! It is going!" His voice expressed the kind of resignation a man of forty feels when he finds he can no longer remember names as he once could.

And sitting there in the little cabin, I marveled. It is not every day that you find a witness—a witness of any age—so honest that he will ruin a good story when he discovers in midstream that memory has slipped a cog; especially if his listener has no way of checking facts.

"Yes, that was Bill Dixon, not Bill Simons," said Juan. "But Bill told some war stories, too. He never told me about his family, though. He never would tell much about his past history, and I never was inquisitive. I never ask to find out about anybody else's business. If he want to tell me, volunteer, fine. . . . But Bill—sometimes I thought he was dodging something."

"Dodging?"

"Yeah, I thought he was dodging something because he'd talk this way and that. Never finish up a thing. Mind you, we were two good friends. But jumping from one thing to another, it didn't come out, sometimes. . . . A great man—but it seems to me, the way I size him up, that in some way or other he was hiding something. He had a guilty conscience in some goddam way or other.

"He was very honest, though. A man that I could trust. He told me once about a pocket of gold ore, high grade, that he dug. And I said, 'Bill, don't give me that line of bull. You don't look like a miner to me.' 'By God,' he says, 'I'll show you where I got it.' So we went out from Niland, away across the sand and the old beach line—no road—in my old Model T, and he showed me the place and, by God, it was just the way he had described it, with running water and all, and he showed me the place he had dug the ore.

"He used to tell some bullshit stories, though. He was telling one time about rattlesnakes that were so bad they came from Mexico by the *millions*. And there was a regiment of calvary or something there . . . cavalry? . . . and it scared the hell out of 'em. Oh, and bullshit like that, you know. But he was right enough about the place he dug that gold ore.

"Yes, you're right there—he wasn't a man who was very interested in money or possessions. The only damned thing was, he used to get his pension check, and then he'd gamble. I remember once in Indio . . . We was to have come out here to Corn Springs but I lost Bill in Indio. So I put out and camped outside of town. In them days it was all open spaces. And the next morning I went over and told one of the cops that I'd lost my partner—because it don't look good for me, you know, after we got there together. And this young cop, a hell of a fine fellow, he says, 'I'll look around.' So it wasn't very long—I was getting some groceries—when he came over and says, 'Your man is down in the cellar over there, gambling. Been gambling all night.' So I left him there. And after that I lost track of him. . . ."

Juan was to see Bill only once more—a dozen years later.


DURING THOSE unsettled months in 1935 and 1936 when Bill temporarily moved his base south from Garnet, he was often in Niland. "In those days," one longtime resident told me, "the place was full of old guys like that. They'd go back up in the mountains and come back with aspirin bottles of gold and try to sell it in the bar."

But Bill also traveled widely around his territory, visiting friends. He would call in on the Ropers, at Cherry Valley. He was always in a hurry, and John Roper would say, "That old boy's sure a goer." And down around the Salton Sea there were other old friends, such as Fig Tree John, a small, dark-skinned Indian who called himself "Chief Johnny Razon, Chief over all this territory, Chief over all the Cahuillas," and who used to ride around his "territory" on a burro, wearing a U.S. Army general's coat and a black silk stovepipe hat, complaining that "white men pay no tribute" and extracting it whenever he could. There was Frank Coffee too—clearly the man Bill had talked of visiting when he was driving about with Norton Roper in the spring of 1934. His name appears along with Bill's on several mining claims, and he lived alone at a little oasis called Dos Palmas, near Mecca. (He always called it "Dos Palms," just as Norton had done and therefore, presumably, Bill had, too.) Coffee—a small, leathery-skinned man with gray whiskers and sloping shoulders, who owned a burro, of which he was very fond, called Blackie—had much in common with Bill. He, too, was the son of a coal miner and also ran away from his "back East" home at sixteen. He had prospected "almost every mountain" in those parts, including the Chuckwallas, and appreciated the desert's beauty as keenly as Bill did. If Bill indeed visited Coffee during those unsettled months when he moved around the Salton Sea—and I find it difficult to believe he did not—then he can hardly have avoided making comparisons between himself and this man with a wandering background so like his own who had now hunkered firmly down. And when he moved back to Garnet in July 1936 he may have intended to make the rock house his own hunkering-down place, his own Dos Palmas. It makes sense. The grass on the other side of the fence, down around the Salton Sea, had once again failed to taste all that damned wonderful. And in Garnet he still had friends. Grace, for example, was still out on her ranch. For a long time there had also been the people at the post office and bar, whom he trusted to take care of his pension check and to protect his privacy. ("When you asked about Bill," Norton had said, "they wouldn't tell you unless they knew you.") Sadly, they were no longer there. But two old friends from the Imperial Valley had now turned up.

I found out about both these sets of friends by chance, while searching through Riverside County records.

The postmaster's name had been de Courselles. His wife ran the bar in which Grace had worked. "In the evening," Grace had said, "I'd sing for them, and Martha played the piano. Poor Martha! She and her husband both committed suicide." And among the county records I stumbled on an entry dated January 1935 reporting that Martha de Courselles Smith, married only two days to Mr. Smith, had killed herself with the gun her previous husband had used to commit suicide a year earlier. Buried in the evidence was a mention of the distraught new husband's telling of the tragedy to "Johnny Walker and his wife." And I confirmed from Rolly Proebstel that about that time "Johnny and Edna Walker" operated the beer joint in Garnet that had previously been run by the de Courselles. So Johnny Walker, also known as Gibhart, and his wife or partner, Edna, who might have been "kinda sweet" on Bill—the gambling-joint pair for whom Bill had dealt and maybe bootlegged in Westmorland during the twenties—were now in business in Garnet. And that may have encouraged Bill to go back to live in the rock house.

But Garnet had changed, physically, since the day he and Grace first went there together, after selling the Trail's End claims to the German undertaker in Banning. Most if not all the changes stemmed from the aqueduct. Garnet, though still not exactly close to anywhere, had become the center for local construction crews, and the young Rolly Proebstel, detecting entrepreneurial opportunities, had torn down all but one of the old "boomer's" wooden buildings and built the huddle of practical, unlovely, cement sub-mausoleums known as Rolly's Place.

In a different way, things would also change up at the rock house.

I have talked to two men who met Bill during his final stay there.

Jim Blankeley is an engineer. At that time he was working on the aqueduct, and he went up Long Canyon to shoot quail. "The company did a lot of blasting," he told me, "so we'd get one of those big dynamite boxes and when we'd filled it with quail we'd stop."

One fall, he and a friend went hunting high up Long Canyon and stumbled on the rock house. Bill was standing at the door, and as soon as he saw them he went inside, then came back out strapping on a belt with a holstered six-shooter. And at once he began shouting at them to get the hell out. "It's funny, the way those people want to live isolated like that," said Blankeley. "And he was a typical shriveled-up old prospector—so naturally he resented us and wanted us off. They're all like that. Don't want you across their land, no sir."

Bill stood at the door with his six-shooter and cursed and swore at them about shooting his quail. "A regular outburst, it was. He was sure competent with words. But my friend went on up and talked to him. Things looked pretty hostile and I walked down the canyon a little ways. The quail were flying down the hillsides toward the water, and I could see where the monuments were that marked this old guy's claim, so I began shooting the quail. My friend, he stayed up at the cabin talking to the old guy for maybe fifteen or twenty minutes, and when he came down he said, 'We'd better be careful of him. He's pretty mad.' So we went back down the canyon.''

A year later, in the fall again, they had gone back up. The rock house was empty. Everything had been taken out, and it looked as if Bill had been gone all summer. The quail would fly down from the hillsides in flocks of forty or fifty and drink from the little creek, no more than a dozen feet from the rock-house door. And a year later Blankeley had filed his own claim on the site, "just so's we could hold on to the water and go up there and shoot the quail."

Eventually, I found the record of the claim he had filed. It was dated 1938. So Bill's encounter with the two hunters almost certainly took place in 1936, during his final months in the rock house.

During those months he also had one very different visitor.

Charlie Gaskell had been to the rock house a couple of years earlier. He and his partner were interested in the minerals in that country and somebody had told them to go up Long Canyon and talk to Chuckawalla Bill. "Bill was very friendly," Gaskell told me. "When my partner and I decided to walk on up to the head of the canyon, Bill said, 'Leave your lunches behind and I'll put the whole thing together and we'll have a good dinner.' We did, too. We must have talked, there in the rock house, for at least three hours. Bill sounded like a good prospector. He showed us a bottle of acid he kept for testing minerals that would cut most everything except gold. And he certainly knew about minerals and formations—about footwalls and hanging walls and that. Knew the lingo, anyway. Yes, he was an interesting man. And pretty sharp. That's why I remember him. I mean, that's a long time ago.''

Gaskell went back to the rock house the second time, in 1936, because he had heard that Bill knew the location of a mine he was interested in, up in Nevada, out of Las Vegas. But although Bill had known the man who owned the mine, he did not know exactly where it was. On that second visit, Bill was sick. There was no car up there, and Gaskell brought him out to Rolly's Place. That was the last time he saw him.

Having to be brought out by a chance visitor could have been the last straw for Bill. It is not difficult to picture his frame of mind. The load had been building up. Grace, though still on the ranch, was up to her ears in unsavory legal hassles. The authorities had written claiming that his rock house lay within the boundaries of the new Joshua Tree National Monument, and that he would have to leave. Across these hard facts lay shadows: not so much the distant though disturbing news from Europe—

where March saw Hitler's Germany reoccupy the Rhineland and July brought civil war in Spain—but his own sixty-first birthday looming in August and the unshruggable fact that he was physically no longer the man he had been. He had no car up at the rock house: his eyesight was fading, he could no longer drive. And it was a long, long walk down to Garnet, even when he was fit. So now this indignity of having to be brought out by Charlie Gaskell felt rather like a sign—a final straw.

Anyway, he moved out.

On December 3, 1936, he changed his address again, and I feel sure he knew that would be the last change—knew that his wanderings were over. Perhaps he even recognized a certain resonance, rich in family echoes: his wanderings would end, as they had begun, in a valley beside one of America's major rivers.

# 19  Palo Verde

MEMORY CAN BE a capricious cuss.

I turned away from the window of the unfamiliar little post office, built into a corner of the grocery store I did not remember either, and walked out onto the street that I could recall only in a skeletal sort of way. I got in my car and drove slowly south, searching the double line of small, widely spaced buildings for one I could recognize.

I passed two gas stations, three modest motels, then the B & B Bar and Trading Post—"Open 6 a.m., Beer." The place was just another small desert community, lying quiet in the low afternoon sunshine. Undistinguished. Indistinguishable from a hundred others.

I drove on down the main and almost only street, still searching, still failing.

The Sleepy Burro Cafe. A bait and tackle shop. The Wheel Bar— "Beer and Bait, Pool." A few homes and old cabins, all modern-desert rabbit-hutched, without concession to architecture. Stretching away on either side, farmland, flat as Holland; but the flatness mostly hidden from you because big, billowing tamarisk trees lined and softened the arrowlike street. The trees grew tallest around midtown, at what must have been the old nucleus. Without them, it would all have been pretty grim.

I drove on.

The air felt pleasantly warm: cooler than when I passed through a week after the start of my summer-long walk from Mexico to Oregon. It had been March then, and the sun hung higher.

Beyond the last building, the road now ran black and paved.

Seventeen years earlier, as I walked the last few miles into Palo Verde—where I stopped over for the inside of a couple of days—the foot-wide Wetback Trail had given way to a jeep track and then, at the very end, to a narrow dirt road. I had been almost sure of that, even before I asked, back at the post office—the post office at which I had picked up my first mail since leaving the Mexican border. But that was about all I had gotten right. And the failure had been disconcerting, the way it always is. I had been right to harbor misgivings about coming back. It is nearly always sad.

They had all agreed, back at the post office, that the paved road had made a big difference. In 1958, when I passed through, there had been just the old wagon road winding south. So Palo Verde had been more or less the end of the line. But nowadays, with the fast paved road leading to Yuma and Brawley and El Centro, all kinds of traffic passed through, and many more visitors came, mostly for the fishing. Booming, the place was. Why, there had to be twice as many buildings as there were in 1958. No, none of the people there in the post office or grocery store could remember how it had been in 1949, let alone 1936.

I drove on south. A loose, scattered string of cabins, trailer parks and other "improvements" lined the river. There had been none of that when I last saw it, seventeen years before. And it was now almost twenty-five years since Bill had last seen this place; almost forty years since he came back for good.

That raised, as always, the question of human memory; and my only real probe so far in Palo Verde had not looked very promising.

Tentatively identifying one of the modest, cabinous motels as the place I had stayed, and hearing that the woman who owned it in 1958 still did so, I investigated. "That's right," said the owner, without hesitation. "You stayed in number ten." I went and looked. Cabin number ten failed to activate a single memory molecule. Then, a little later, I found on the map I had used in 1958 a note of the motel I had stayed in. It stood on the other side of the street. And when I went there I found that I remembered quite clearly the small, enclosed square around which its cabins clustered.

But the hard fact remained that, with a few exceptions, the only marks Bill had left on the world lay in the minds of people now mostly dead or heading that way. So scattered human memories—some fuzzy and porous as netting, others meticulously monitored precision instruments like Juan DeLaGarza's—were almost my only tools for opening windows into Bill's life. In a sense, of course, that is almost all that history has, beyond documents and tapes and photographs and other mechanical capturers. When it comes to warm flesh-and-blood history, the differences tend to

lie in whether you measure in minutes or hours or decades the gap between a perceived event and its consignment to paper or other recording
instrument.

It was already obvious, too, that here in Palo Verde my difficulties in
understanding would not end with the retrieval of information from other
people's minds.

I drove on southward. The improvements petered out. The road swung
close to the Colorado and I stopped the car and began to walk down toward the river.

I found myself walking along a flat-topped spur, a miniature mesa.

The spur was clean and open. Its level crust of small stones had been
sandblasted improbably smooth into what is known as "desert pavement."
Yet shrubs and cacti filigreed it. And the tiny "paving stones," burnished
and baked to a rich, chocolate-brown patina, were intricately seamed with
small cohering gullies and other, softer meanings.

I walked on down toward the river. It was odd, the way you always forgot the cleanness of real desert—of unspoiled desert, where man had not
crudded things up.

Beyond the spur lay a narrow strip of bottomland. I picked my way
through mesquite and salt cedar. I had forgotten that part of it, too.

It had all been new, then, at the start of the Walk, and I had noticed
everything: the desert's apparent sameness and simplicity; its constant surprises and cohering complexities; above all, its cleanness.

A belt of arrowweed lined the water's edge. I pushed through it.

I had even forgotten the arrowweed. Yet for that first month I had
clung close to my lifeline, the river—camping close beside it, eating most
meals on its sandy, weed-fringed banks—and the green, straight-stalked
arrowweed had been as constant a part of my life as walls and curtains are
in "normal" living. Arrowweed, I remembered now, had been good stuff
to live in: clean; non-snagging; easy to move through. When you sat in tall
stands, it was even shade-giving. Yes, it had been good stuff to live in. And
I had forgotten it.

I sat down on a sandy bank at the edge of the arrowweed. The river slid
softly by. Upstream, half hidden in a tule bank, waterfowl clucked and
fussed and sent small, secret circles widening across the pewter surface of
the river.

Out over the river it was all light and space. And far beyond the low
green line of the distant bank hung the Arizona mountains.

That first month of the Walk, whichever way you looked, there had been distant mountains. And there was always something exciting about them, especially when you knew them, had been back in them, and understood.

It had been a good time, that first month up the Colorado: one of the best stretches of a very, very good summer. It had been clean, sweaty, simple and satisfying.

And I had almost forgotten the feel of it.

I sat on the sandy bank on the edge of the arrowweed and looked out across light and space at the line of distant mountains. And as I sat there I saw why Bill had chosen Palo Verde.

He had chosen it because the things that had attracted me that summer of 1958 had, not too many years earlier, attracted him. He had chosen a place that was then almost untouched by man. Unplundered. Uncrudded. He had chosen a place where desert and river still ruled—where it was the little, complex, natural things that mattered, that held hidden meanings: stones burnished to a patina; intricate meshings of small gullies and mesquite trees and arrowweed; birds that sent circles widening across calm water that was all space and light.

When Bill chose Palo Verde, these were the things he had chosen—this man who "loved all God's works," this "first of the flower children."

Upstream, a wind rustled the tules. They whispered together. And all at once I remembered a riverbank scene, seventeen years buried.

A dozen miles south of Palo Verde, the Wetback Trail had swung out to the tip of a spur and skirted the burnt-out site of a house—the first sign of human habitation I had seen for several days. Uncut stones, barely a foot high, traced the outline of a single small room. Outside stood a massive iron cooking stove, cracked and rusty. The house overlooked a tule-ringed lake and commanded a view of the river, upstream and down, for many miles. The view was blue and green and pink and brown.

When I saw the stone outline, I hesitated. Then I walked forward, slipped off my pack and sat down beside the stove.

Below me, a light wind sandpapered the lake. Tules whispered. The world held nothing but openness and color, stillness and subtle movement, silence and gentle murmur.

And as I rested beside the stove I found myself dreaming of an old man living out his last years in that simple rock house—alone, untroubled, content. It would be difficult, I had decided, to find a better place for a man at peace with himself, and I imagined this old frontiersman ferrying his new, unassembled stove downriver and carrying it, piece by piece, up to the house he had built, stone by stone. I imagined him sitting each evening in the shade of its walls and smiling to himself as he looked up and down the river that was "his."

I had found these stones and stove, remember, more than a decade before I stumbled on Trunkman's cave—thirteen years before I first heard the name Bill Simmons. And I am not really suggesting that Bill built that other desert rock house—even though it is not impossible he did so during his early years of coming and going around Palo Verde. Obviously, he did not "live out his last years" there, the way I had imagined my "frontiersman" doing. Yet that peaceful riverside scene had just flicked up into my mind's eye, unbidden. . . . It was odd, really, that I had never recalled that other rock house and made a connection in any normal, cold, straightforward, logical way. It had been very much Bill's kind of place. Yes, memories could be capricious cusses—my own and other people's. I must not forget that.

Somewhere out behind me, beyond the arrowweed, a car pounded down the paved road.

Upstream, at the tules, the waterfowl were quiet, or gone. Circles no longer widened across the river.

I stood up and pushed my way back through the arrowweed.


WHEN BILL FINALLY pulled up his stakes in Garnet in December 1936 and came back to Palo Verde to live out his days, he persisted for a while with the active habits of his wandering years. He still went prospecting occasionally, and he recorded one final claim, out in the Chuckwalla Mountains, with Henry Whittle, who ran the beer joint.

But mostly, now that he had made his decision, Bill puttered.

Palo Verde then amounted to five buildings and a dozen trees, but Bill had no lack of co-putterers. A hard-core group of old-timers still holed up in and around the village. A woman who used to cook Christmas dinners for these loners was always amazed at the way "about fourteen of them would come in out of the bushes." The names of some of the old-timers who were particular friends of Bill's still echo around human memories: George Fitz, for example, who homesteaded; Rattlesnake Jim, whose real name no one could remember; and Emil Dekens, who drove the freight but wintered in Palo Verde and whose brother wrote the book of the valley's history, *Riverman, Boatman,* with its admiring passages about Floyd Brown. (Brown had been killed in an automobile accident near Searchlight a year earlier.)

But Bill had young friends, too. Bob Stallard—whom I had found

Aerial shot, Palo Verde, *ca.* 1938. Bill's tamarisks and Ma Gahan's cottages stand at center; the Whittles' bar, just across the road.

drinking deeply of life in Indio—was by this time married and living south of Palo Verde.

"Bill used to baby-sit with the kids while the wife and I went dancing," Bob had told me. "Looked after 'em good. Wouldn't let a goddam fly set on 'em. And the kids liked him. . . . He used to cook for us sometimes too. A good cook he was . . . Oh, that reminds me, I found a photograph of him. Not sure where it was taken, but it was around about that time."

The photograph showed a man in hat, shirt and slacks standing at a table. His shirt sleeves were rolled back from the wrists and he seemed to be preparing a meal. He wore a full-set beard, and the face did not look much like those in Grace's photographs. Yet there was something familiar about it.

I studied it carefully. And suddenly I recognized the resemblance.

"Well, I'll be damned!" I said.

Bob was grinning at me over the top of his beer can. "Yeah," he said. "The moment I saw you I said to myself, 'Why, he could be old Chuck's brother!' "

Bob paused for further thirst-quenching.

"He'd tell me stories, Bill would, by the hour. I've forgotten most of 'em, but I remember one about the Spanish-American War. He used to cuss old Teddy Roosevelt. Plain didn't like him. He was Teddy's orderly, you know, and he said the niggers took San Juan Hill. He said old Teddy

Roosevelt was lying down there under a tree and he was carrying him beer from a tub full of ice while the niggers took San Juan Hill."

Bob re-refreshed himself.

"Once, Bill built a patio for us. Flagstones. Carried the damn things himself. Old Bill, he just went and went, wouldn't stay still. We'd go prospecting sometimes, and it was the same then. He'd go like a bat out of hell over the top of them hills, just to see what was on the other side. Walk the ass off of me, any day. Yeah, that was Bill. Ambitious. Always had to be doing something. But not for money. Hell no. Money up his ass. But he had to be doing something. I remember one day I came back from work and he'd built us a shithouse. He'd taken an old damn saw—you couldn't cut butter with the sonofabitch—and some old boards and stuff, and he'd built this thing—an outside crapper, you know—complete. Cut holes and everything. All in one day. He must have been sixty-five or seventy then, but he was always alert and on the ball. A wonderful old guy—you should have met him."

It is easy to picture Bob Stallard and Bill, in spite of the age difference, having good times together. Beneath the booze Bob had poetry, even when I met him. And once Bill settled down in Palo Verde he helped his puttering on its way by drinking. He drank methodically. And while it may or may not be coincidence that he moved to Palo Verde permanently within a year of its first beer joint being built, that beer joint and others that followed became the fulcra of his daily round. The beer joints' owners therefore played major roles in his life. And it is from them—supported by

a cast of citizenry—that I have patched together my picture of how it was for Bill in his final thirteen years.

The original beer joint—now called the B & B Bar and Trading Post—was built by the Whittles.

Henry Whittle is long dead. His widow remembers Bill only as "one of the nicest old guys I ever seen. . . . I'd cut his hair for him sometimes. . . . He wore it kinda long, like in this picture I've found for you. It was taken

beside the lagoon, around about 1938." But the Whittles' eldest daughter, Lucile, though only a teen-ager then, was perhaps the person who understood Bill best during the late thirties, when the crescendo rumbles of approaching World War II must, in Palo Verde, have sounded very faint and far away.

When I met Lucile she lived near San Francisco, was about to move to Idaho, and showed every sign of having freed herself from her beginnings.

"Back then," she told me, "I used to sit on a stool in the bar and lean against the refrigerator. That was my life. And many's the hot beer I've served Bill. Like a lot of those old-timers, he didn't like his beer cold. Of course, I was underage, and if anyone was around who wasn't a close friend, I wouldn't do any serving."

In those days, said Lucile, you never saw an outsider during the week. You knew the locals well, though—like Old Mrs. McGee, who put vinegar on everything and painted everything green, including her shoes. Back then, Palo Verde still used to flood every year and was a beautiful place with cottonwood trees everywhere, and green grass. The forty right around town wasn't farmed, and hadn't been for years, so it was full of mesquite trees, high as a house, and right there in Palo Verde you lived in the desert. Not like now. Lucile often went back, and she knew what "progress" had done.

The original beer joint looked pretty much the way it did today, except that now they had inside toilets and a new top on the counter, and a few years back the wind blew the front off the building and they'd never put it back on. Out front, in Lucile's day, there had been a homemade sign, strictly rough, that said WHITTLES—a red sign with white letters. And there were gas pumps that you operated by hand. Inside, they had a grocery store as well as the bar.

"Bill had his special place at the bar. It was the best damned seat in the place, down in one corner, against the wall, and Bill was very particular about it. Locals always gave it up to him, and if anyone who didn't know about his 'ownership' sat there, he'd wait until they went out to the outhouse and then take it. I can see him now, sitting there in the corner, with his pipe in his left hand, going in and out of his mouth."

It never seemed to bother Bill toward the end of the month when his money got cut off and he couldn't buy any more beer. Lucile's stepfather, Henry, looked after all the old fellows and had a real feeling for them, and when he knew they'd run up enough for the month he'd cut them off, so that they'd have enough left for groceries. That was what kept Bill in good shape, kept the weight on him: half the month he could eat and live a normal life.

"Of all the old-timers down there," said Lucile, "there was a feeling about Bill that . . . oh, he had an air about him. He wasn't one to get drunk too often, and he never got out of hand, even when he did get drunk. Always so dignified, that's what impressed me. Not just another sloppy drunk. Even as a kid I looked at the inside of people and was always fitting things together. I mean, I sized up people. And Bill's stories fit. They made sense. They connected. Not like with most of the guys there. He believed in his stories, I could tell that. He was a dreamer, sure, and maybe some of the stories were a bit fantastic, but there'd be a basis behind it. . . . I remember he used to lift up his shirt and show his wound, where he'd been stabbed—run through with a sword—during some war. . . ."

"Well, actually, he fell on a stake while searching a Filipino hut."

"Could be. But while he was telling it, he believed it. And he had a wonderful way with words. He could hold people—because his education came from life. And he was a person who was very determined in life. He was a loner, but he liked people, even though he never wanted *close* connections with people. Me, I was only fifteen or sixteen, but I've always had a feeling for old people. And you could see him reaching out. I really think he had a close feeling for me. I was the only young girl there. I mean, that was it. I was the belle of the town. And I was always doing little things for him. He was kind of a . . . grandfather figure to me . . . in a mysterious way.

"I remember once . . . When his check came, you know, he'd buy a few groceries and take them home, and then he could get gloriously drunk. And one such time, he'd been sitting in the bar, probably drinking all day, and my folks closed the bar and went down the road to visit. And I went to bed and . . . well, on the south side of the building there used to be a big sump hole, for drainage when the floods came, before they put Hoover Dam in . . . and from out by that sump hole I kept hearing this 'Mother! Mother! Help me, Mother!' So I got up and I took a flashlight—because you know there wasn't any electricity down there then, or anything—and there was old Bill clear to the bottom of this hole, all wrapped up in a roll of chicken wire. He'd slid right down into it, head first. Well, I tried to pull him up by his pants but I could get no leverage and I'd just begin pulling his pants off. So I'd say, 'Back up, Bill! Back up, Bill!' But he was awful drunk and he'd just keep saying, 'Mother! Mother!' And I'd say, 'Come on, Bill! Just keep on backing up!' And we'd get him almost up and then he'd slide back down to the bottom. And I'll bet you I was out there half an hour getting him out of that hole. . . . So after that I got in the habit of waiting. When he would start home from the bar I would walk out, and if it was a moonlight night I could see him all the way down to his house, and if it wasn't moonlight then I would go and I would watch for him to light a lamp. And then when he lit the lamp I knew he was home."

"He knew you were watching him?"

Lucile hesitated. "He knew that I watched out after him. I mean, he had a very close feeling. And I had a very close feeling for him."

"Did he call anyone in Palo Verde 'Mother'?"

"Oh no, he was calling back to his mother. I mean, he was very, very drunk. He probably didn't remember anything about it afterward, and I wouldn't have embarrassed him by bringing it up. . . . Yes, Bill told me about planting those tamarisk trees. If he had done anything, he had pride in it. Yes, the trees are still there, right across the street from the bar."

Bill had planted the trees for shade, he had said, when he camped there years before. But then Ma Gahan bought that lot and built her cabins there. For a while, Bill had been on good terms with her; before long, though, they weren't speaking. "But that's not surprising. Ma Gahan wasn't on speaking terms with a lot of people, especially men. She was fat and dirty too, and Bill couldn't abide obese and dirty people, smelly people.

In that hot climate, you know, with no running water . . . Then Ma Gahan was always getting things out of everybody, finagling everybody, and that wasn't Bill's cup of tea. And he couldn't stand stupidity. He put himself above most people, and he would let them know in a certain way. Yes, if Chuckawalla Bill didn't like you, he didn't like you."

"I'm with him there."

"But that was Ma Gahan's life—finagling. She was my first mother-in-law, you know, the old bitch. I married her son, John. But they're both dead now. . . ."

When Lucile knew Bill, he still used to get out into the hills a bit. "He'd disappear, and when he came back you'd ask him where he'd been and he'd answer, but somehow you never really got to know. He always liked to be mysterious, Bill did—even though if he liked you he'd talk as free as free."

I brought out my snapshots of Bill.

Lucile had been there, she said, the night someone took the shot Bob Stallard had given me. It was up in a cabin owned by Bob's brother, just north of Palo Verde. Lucile rather thought that was the night she smoked Bill's pipe. Bob or his brother had smoked a cigar half down and she took it and stuffed it into Bill's pipe and lit it. "The pipe was kind of raunchy, I remember. But I proved it to them, that I could smoke. Bill worried about me, I remember. But I always had to prove myself. . . . Yes, sometimes he'd wear a beard like that, like yours. And then he would shave it off and leave the goatee, according to his moods."

Lucile also recalled her mother's taking the picture out by the lagoon. "Now that's the way I remember Bill. Always *that* hat on his head. And that was his hair—always a bit long like that, the way yours is now. . . . You know, so much of you is like Bill. . . . And I'm talking to you as if you understand. . . . Yes, we've figured out the same man, you and I. And I can tell you now that when you got out of the car I said, 'My God, he looks just like Chuckawalla Bill.' . . . Maybe it was fate brought you to that cave."

When Lucile came to the desertion poster picture she said, "Yes, you can see those eyes! When he got mad, they *snapped*. But he was mostly a very peaceful man. I think he only went off to his wars for the adventure of it. But if somebody pushed him, look out!"

"Oh, I'm with him there, too."

"Come to think of it, the only time I remember him getting real ornery was when my grandfather was behind the bar and they were all throwing bottles at him. Chuckawalla Bill was in on that. I think that was the time he pulled his pipe on my grandfather and held it like a gun and said, 'I'll blow your damned head off.' I can remember it now, remember it so plain. . . . But mostly, you know, Bill wasn't at all ornery. Oh no, he was very cheerful. I remember when he was loaded and happy he'd do a funny little shuffle of a dance, like a Spanish fandango."

"You mean a buck and wing, like in old vaudeville?"

"That's right." Lucile laughed at the memory of it. "Mostly, Bill preferred young people, like me, and he had a special fondness for little girls about three or four. He had a picture of a little girl he carried around in his wallet, an *old* picture it was, that he would take out and show to me when children came into it. I think he said she was a niece of his. And when he went up to Blythe he most always brought back some little thing for my sister Pat, who was about two or three. One time, I remember, he bought her a pair of beautiful little cowboy boots. Tiny, they were. And Pat, she wouldn't take them off. All around the house she went—clog, clog, clog. She even slept in them for several nights, too. I remember my mother telling me how excited Bill had been over getting them and making sure they fit and all. . . . Oh no, nothing like that. I never wore shoes when I was down there in Palo Verde, and Bill . . . Oh no, never anything out of the way."

(Later, though, I mulled over this latest clue in a line that had begun in the cave.

In the cave, there had been the pair of very small and tattered green shoes, about which I had jokingly jotted down "foot fetishist?"; then there had been the five dollars Bill had mailed Aunt Marie "to buy the new baby a pair of shoes"; and then the shoes he had not only bought for the Roper daughters but had insisted on helping fit, there in the store.

Seen from the outside it might seem a very minor matter, even a mildly comic one. But Bill had seen it from the inside. And it was the kind of thing that could have helped color his life—the kind that can color all our lives. So eventually—not without misgivings, because it felt rather like prying—I discussed the matter with a psychiatrist friend who is also a poet. We agreed in advance that, whatever the verdict, we were not necessarily talking about anything pathological, only about an erotic topographical preference. There are, for example, leg fanciers and callipygiophiles of both sexes. And a mild fetishist, said my friend, might not even be aware of his tendency.

I unfolded the clues. My friend listened attentively. He commented that Bill had bought shoes only for the Roper girls, not John. He explained the Freudian model for foot fetishism and pinpointed possible sources in Bill's childhood. Then he summed up. The data all fit. They were consistent with foot fetishism. Nothing took him sharply away from it. Clinically speaking, though, the evidence was far too skimpy. As a doctor, he could not feel convinced. But poetically speaking, in his heart, he was with me all the way. He liked it. In fact, it was beautiful.

And that, frankly, was good enough for me.)

Lucile told me one other story.

When Byron wrote in *Don Juan* that

> *What men call gallantry, and gods adultery,*
> *Is much more common where the climate's sultry,*

he might almost have had Palo Verde in mind.

I do not mean that the village was a throbbing whorehouse; but it does seem to have been a place horizontally active well beyond the demands of reproduction.

I had glimpsed this side of local social life long before I talked to Lucile—at first from old-timers' hints and sidelong smiles, then from specific stories. Many of the stories revolved around Harriet Robinson—who had been on more than nodding terms with Bill.

Harriet no longer lived in Palo Verde, but everyone—men and women alike—remembered her with affection and respect. She was a very kind person, they all said, who would do anything to help anyone. She was very beautiful, and mostly very quiet. She rarely got drunk—though when she did she would "whoop it up like a coyote." She never talked about conquests of men, even to her closest friends, and from time to time she would marry the man she was living with. But that rarely proved enough. Harriet simply loved making love. She had seen the light: biology was beautiful, sex next to godliness—and she became a lay missionary.

Her ministry remained strictly nonprofessional. It just had to be, one woman assured me: some of the men who went down to Harriet's house plain didn't have the money.

I visited Harriet. She had a very poor memory: she could recall Bill only as "one of the people around the place." But later, several old Palo Verdeans told me that she had stored furniture in the house Bill rented and used to cook food and take it to him.

And then Lucile told me her story.

Even as a teen-ager, she had known about the steady stream of men that visited Harriet's house, and she still remembered it because during her high school days she had put her knowledge to good use.

"I went down to Harriet's one day for some reason," she said. "There was a place you could pull a car around, where it was hardly seen, and that day I saw a car standing there. I looked at it and I said, 'You're kidding!' So I walked around to the steering wheel and looked at the registration. . . .

"Well, I didn't say nothing—until the next time I was called on the carpet before my high school principal. I was ornery in those days and I was always being called in. But that next time I just says, 'Harriet Robinson.' And the principal, he blushes. Yessir, he actually blushed. And he says, very quick, 'You're dismissed.' And after that all I had to do was say 'Harriet Robinson' and we got along fine. . . . Oh, sure I know Chuck-awalla Bill was one of them. I've seen him go down there. Besides, they were buddies. Yes, I guess you could be right—she could have forgotten. You see it was, well, every Tom, Dick and Harry."

Now I am not suggesting that Bill during his autumn years was a Don Juan running rampant. But he clearly retained a friendly gleam in his snappy brown eyes. Palo Verde stands beside a big river and may therefore be a shade more humid than most desert places; perhaps its climate is a shade more sultry.

For most of the seven years the Whittles owned the beer joint, Bill lived in the house, just down the road, to which Lucile would "watch him home." He rented it from George Covington.

"I wouldn't have dared rent to most of those old prospectors," Covington told me. "But Bill was different. We'd been living there ourselves and left most of the furniture, and Bill looked after things as if they were his own. I never worried a minute about the place. On the rare occasions I went down there, everything was in tip-top shape. He kept house, he really did.

"Bill was a very honest man, too, totally to be trusted. And meticulous about paying the rent. Always paid cash, on the nose. He'd bring it himself, on the dot, and never ask for a receipt. Now I remember . . . Well, old Bill liked his liquor, you know. But he could pick himself up. He was never sloppy. We lived in Blythe then, and one day my wife and I were sitting there visiting after we'd had our lunch, and I looked out the window and there comes Bill. He was so loop-legged he was just taking the whole street almost, from one side to the other. So I met him at the door and stuck my hand out and shook and said, 'Come on in, Bill.' And when he was inside I remarked that he looked much better than the last time I'd seen him. 'You must have quit drinking,' I said. And old Bill, he drew himself up and shook himself and said, 'I'll have you know I haven't had a drink in six months.' "

Covington laughed. "That was our Bill. Never lost his dignity, no matter what he'd drunk. Everybody liked Bill."

But Covington was wrong.

Carol Shaw, for example, remembered only warts.

"He was just an old drunk," she said. "Just another barfly—and an old goat. He was about eighty-nine and he got his name from eating chuckawallas. I was in the bar once, waiting for somebody, and I moved past him, close, and he says, 'Quit rubbing yourself up against me—what do you think I am?' It shocked me and I said, 'Why, you old . . .!' That's all he was, a dirty old man. That's where his head was all the time, in the gutter."

Then there was Bill Rains, who dredged up a memory of Bill's having told him about walking alone in the desert in a high wind with all his clothes off. But hell, he figured Bill must have dreamed that. After all, it was difficult to believe a grown man would do such a thing. "Still, you never know with a guy like that. I never did attach to the man. He had a way about him. . . . His attitude. . . . He was different than most any people I knew. He had . . . he had plenty of ego. . . . He was going to come up and live with me once, at my place four miles north of Palo Verde, but he cooked some stew and I put chili in it and he walked straight off out the door, back to Palo Verde. Hell, I didn't give a damn. He was just an old man to me."

There were Johnson Bunker and his wife, too. One summer, they parked their trailer next door to Bill, and to reach his outhouse Bill had to pass close by.

"Chuckawalla wasn't much to stop and talk with anybody," Johnson Bunker said—and that observation told me a lot. "Still, he'd stop on the way to his outhouse if I insisted on stopping. . . . Old Chuck, he was just a bar hound. A barfly. A typical desert rat. When he wasn't sitting in his den a-reading magazines he was up at the bar. Or sleeping. He was clean enough but he didn't go visit nobody and nobody come visiting him, so you never saw old Chuck unless he was either going to the outhouse or he was going to the beer joint. His drinking never bothered no one, mind you. We never saw him real drunk. But we don't even like beer.

"When he wasn't up at the bar he was down in his den, just a-reading. All the time he was able to, he'd read. He wasn't interested in none of the things going on around town. Like the time we called a meeting about having a survey done so that we'd know where the property lines ran, and people kinda divided into two factions. Well, you see, we'd bought a seventy-five-foot lot for ten dollars, just to get the fill out of it, and . . ."

"But most people seemed to like Bill."

"Oh sure, everybody liked him well enough. But you couldn't really say you liked him or you didn't like him because you didn't have too much contact with him unless you went up to the bar and listened to him tell his stories. And, like I say, we don't even like beer. Besides, we had better things to do. Yessir, at different times, we owned nine places down there in Palo Verde. But we didn't get in on the good grab. Now the Robertsons, they bought thirty-two lots for a dollar and fifty-four cents apiece. And Mom Gahan, she paid ten dollars a lot for her place. . . ."

"So you never really got any feeling for Bill, as a man?"

"Well, no more than you would for anybody. We didn't really have anything in common—only he lived there and we lived here, so we'd say good morning. . . . And he liked his drinks—and we don't even like beer. Like I say, we didn't really have anything in common."

But it seems clear that by this time old Chuckawalla Bill was, in spite of his occasional oddness, a sort of minor Palo Verde landmark, or at least fixture, whom most people found they "couldn't help liking."

The Whittles sold the beer joint in 1942—just before it became a gold mine because General George Patton's troops, who trained for North Africa in the surrounding desert, had savage thirsts to quench. During this interlude, Bill struck it rich, too. His years debarred him from active participation in this, the last war of his lifetime, but he still brought his military experience to bear: in return for his stories of past wars, the soldiers supplied him with more beer than even he could always drink.

The Whittles sold to the Harvells.

Joe Harvell is now dead. His wife rarely served in the bar and did not know Bill well, but she told me of one quiet, recurring scene from those years when Bill was moving serenely toward his seventieth birthday. "He used to come 'most every day, I remember, and sit on a great long bench out in front in the porch, under the window. Palo Verde wasn't above three or four buildings then, but a lot of the old fellows would come over around eleven o'clock and sit on that bench and wait for the mail to come."

In the spring of 1945, with Patton's soldiers long gone and the war almost over, the Harvells sold the beer joint to Al Workman. He would be its last owner in Bill's lifetime.

By the time I returned to Palo Verde, Al Workman was eighty-two and long retired, but he still lived in a trailer parked beside the beer joint—now known as the B & B Bar and Trading Post. Before I went to talk to him I walked in among the old cabins, opposite his trailer, that had once be-longed to Ma Gahan.

They stood in a grove of six or seven tamarisks. They were mature, confident trees with thick, heavily ribbed trunks. Their dense, feathery foliage softened the cabins' ugliness.

I walked in deeper. There, the foliage hung low, cutting off the street, framing a view of the placid, sunlit lagoon. Even before the trees were planted—when there were almost no buildings in sight, only desert trees and brush—it would have been a beautiful, secluded place to camp. And it would have made sense to plant seedlings, with an eye to shade and the future.

I walked back out onto the street and craned my neck. The billowing green treetops stood tallest of all the trees in town. And they stood at the very center of things—at the nucleus of a town whose name meant "green tree." A man could hardly leave a better memorial, I decided, than that tranquil little grove, whether people remembered that he had planted it or not.

I walked across the street to the trailer parked beside the B & B Bar. Al Workman was very cordial. "Sure," he said. "Old Chuckawalla was one of my regular customers. He was a happy enough guy then. Walked around with that old pipe in his mouth, ready to talk to you anytime. And he was a pretty smart old hombre. Been all over the world, pretty near. . . . I don't know how he come to land here. . . ."

In 1945, said Al Workman, the beer joint was still the only building on the west side of the street. Back then, though, before they dredged the river and ruined it, Palo Verde had the best goddam fishing you ever seen in your life. You could go right out there behind Mom Gahan's cabins and catch all the catfish you wanted out of the lagoon. No, Bill wasn't much of a fisherman. He just passed the time away. Didn't do a damn thing, really, except maybe jump in the lake for a swim now and then. He loved his little dog, though.

"The dog was getting old, too. Must have been sixteen or seventeen when Bill died. He didn't bother nobody but he stayed at Bill's heels all the time. If Bill would be in a place, that dog would be laying right outside the door, waiting for him. A shepherd, he was. No, not a German shepherd— a long-haired red shepherd, about half as big as a setter. Always at Bill's heels, he was. Real affectionate. A real one-man dog."

Back in those days they used to have Saturday-night dances down in the old schoolhouse, near where the Sleepy Burro Cafe stood now, and Bill used to go to those. Somebody always had a bottle. No, Bill wasn't interested in women then, only just to talk to. He'd lost all that. But mostly you'd see Bill in the beer joint. He'd tell a whole lot of stories there. Talk all the time. He'd prospected all over the desert and could tell you all about it, but most of his stories were about other places, twenty, twenty-five years back—mucking around through mining districts, prospecting, and about his time in the service.

He'd often play euchre in the bar, but the big deal back then was the slot machine. "I paid them two hundred and fifty dollars a month but that there machine stood two years and it took me four hundred dollars a month. And Bill spent just about all his money in it. Hell, his pension check was only ninety dollars, but I'd give him a five-dollar roll of dimes pretty near every day, and I'd always loan him a little because, after all, I got his money anyhow. And when I wouldn't give him no more until his next pension check, he'd get so mad at me. He'd say, 'Goddamnit, Al, just give me another roll of dimes.' So I'd carry him along awhile longer. But then I'd say, 'Goddamnit, Bill, if you're going to eat you'd better cut out that playing that slot machine, 'cause otherwise you ain't going to have nothing to eat.'

"Yeah, sure I liked him. You couldn't help but like the guy. Oh, we'd have our arguments. Old Bill could be pretty hard to get along with some-times. Yeah, he could be an ornery old bastard. If he was about half drunk he'd cause a man to kinda get mad at him. Hell of a temper. Why, I re-member one night, he was going to kill me."

"Kill you?"

"Yeah. At that time he was living with Dick Parsons and his wife. It was the first year I was here, and Bill didn't like me then, didn't like me at all."

That night, someone had told Al there was trouble out in front of the bar: Dick Parsons had hit another man over the head with a pistol. Al went outside.

"There was this guy with blood all over him. He was going to get mar-ried that night, and he did, afterward, with his bloody shirt on, too. Dick Parsons' car was down a ways, just a few yards, and Parsons and Bill were sitting on the running board of the car. And when Bill saw me he come a-running toward me. He was mad, and he said, 'You dirty son of a bitch, I'm going to kill you.' And I said, 'Bill, what the hell have I done to you?' And he said, 'That don't make a goddam bit of difference. I just don't like you, and I'm going to kill you.'

"Now I knew that Parsons had a gun with him, and Bill had been sitting there beside him on the running board of the car before he come a-running toward me. It was kinda dark between us, and you couldn't see real good, but I looked and by God I thought he had the gun in his hand. So I said, 'Bill, I ain't got no gun or anything, and I ain't got nothing against you. . . . So that'll just be your goddam meanness.' But Bill kept a-coming toward me. Then when he got up close enough I saw that what he had in his hand was his damned old straight-stemmed pipe that he smoked all the time—he had the bowl in his hand and the stem pointing out toward me. So I said, 'Oh, Bill, you couldn't kill nobody with your pipe.' And he said, 'Well, by God I can knock the shit out of you.' And he hauled off and made a hell of a swing at me with his left, a real wound-up swing, and I just vermeered back and he missed me and swung himself clear off his feet. Well, we'd just put some blacktop down, out in front, and it was pretty rough, and Bill he just skinned the insides of his hands just good. Burned them like it was with a rope.

"And I said, 'Oh, come on, Bill, get up, and forget it. I wouldn't hit an old man, and you ain't got no reason to hit me, either. So go on with the Parsons and go home.' And sure enough, they all got in the car, Dick Parsons and his wife and Bill along with them, and went home. . . . Yeah,

he sure took a hell of a swing at me with that left. And hell, he was old—
he must have been up there in the last of his seventies then. And he wasn't
very tall. But he was solidly built. . . . Yeah, he swung good.

"Later, I heard that somebody kidded Bill and said, 'You sure fixed Al
Workman, didn't you?' 'Yeah,' says Bill. 'I fixed him good. By God, I
been wanting to do that a long time. I don't like that son of a bitch.' "

Al Workman laughed, almost without rancor. "I guess I'm the only
man that old Bill really didn't like. I don't know why. Shit, I couldn't have
treated my father any better. He could have laid down and died any night,
but I still carried him along, there in the bar, month to month, until his
next pension check come. . . . But he just took a . . . I think what he got
mad about that night was a married woman he knew that done a lot of
skinning around on the side. Now I don't say that he had nothing to do
with her. He was too old by then. But I guess he figured I was skinning
around too—'cause I was fifty-one years old and not married, and that's
not too old. . . . Anyway, Bill never would come out and accuse me of it,
but I always figured that's the reason he got mad at me that night. And
after that he didn't come into the beer joint for a long time.

"He was living with Dick and Anne Parsons then. They had a kind of a
bar up at the first corner, three miles north of town. When they sold out,
Bill moved back down and rented an old cabin, half a mile up the lagoon.
But soon he moved across the road and lived in a tent, just outside of town,
down on the flat below a levee. Just him and his dog. There was a tree
there then, I think, and that gave him some shade. But it was brush all
around. Just river bottom. Why a guy would want to live there beats me. I
guess it was because it was so close. Up till then, Bill had been pretty
lively, but suddenly he just didn't have the pep any more and I guess the
walk was too much for him. So he set up his tent down there in the river
bottom. It was just an ordinary city block from town, and he could still
make it into the post office and the bar. That must have been why he
moved. I can't figure out no other reason.

"Later, after he died, they burned the tent and the stuff he'd left there.
Hell no, there wouldn't be any sign of the burning left. Not now, after
twenty, twenty-five years. The place has been cleared over several times
since then.

"But before that—before he began to go down, fast, that last year—he
made it up with me. I mean, he got over the spat and come back in. So in
the end it was like it had always been. He'd come in and sit there and drink
beer all day. And we'd carry him along again, month to month. No, just
beer. We didn't have no liquor license. But I don't remember that Bill got

drunk much until he got in with those Parsons—Dick and his wife
Anne—and began drinking hard liquor. Like that night he swung at me. I
know they'd been drinking then or he wouldn't have done what he did."


I EVENTUALLY tracked down the Parsons in a trailer beside the Salton Sea,
midway between Niland and the place that had once been Eilers'. Dick
was now seventy-seven, Anne a little younger. They had met Bill in 1945,
the very first day they went to Palo Verde.

"I happened to sit down beside Uncle Bill, there in Al Workman's beer
joint," said Anne. "And we just started up talking, like I knew him forever."

"He was that kind of guy," said Dick. "You would just look at him and
he wouldn't say a dozen words to you and you'd say, 'Hell, I like that old
boy. He's all right.' "

Two weeks later, when they moved up to the beer joint they had
bought, three miles north of Palo Verde, Bill went along. He lived in a little cabin that had been a shack for storing beer. They fixed it up for him
and he paid ten dollars a month for room and board. From the cabin to
their back door was no more than twenty feet.

Bill would spend most of the daylight hours sitting outside the cabin in
an old rocking chair with his pipe hanging from a corner of his mouth,
reading. If you interrupted him while he was reading, he'd get mad, so you
just let him sit there with his old pipe in his mouth and his old dog at his
feet. Some guy had shot at the dog with a shotgun and crippled both his
front feet, so that walking seemed to hurt him. He was an old, old dog that
sounded like he had asthma or something because he wheezed like he was
going to die anytime. But Bill really loved that old dog. Called him "Old
Fellow." "Come on, Old Fellow," he'd say. "Come over here and sit in
the shade." And wherever Bill went the dog would go, and sit down right
there beside him.

As the Parsons saw it, Bill liked to get drunk whenever he got half a
chance. In fact, that was the only way to stop him reading. You didn't
need to say anything: just show him a bottle and he'd put the book down
and be ready to talk.

By that time, Bill didn't often care to go anywhere. Not even into Palo
Verde with Dick—and Dick went in just about every day, because they
had no electricity then and had to buy all their ice. But Bill would often ask
Dick to bring back a bottle of whiskey, and he'd take it and stuff it under
the pillow, over in his cabin. He'd never share that bottle of whiskey. He

wasn't mean about it, but he just thought of it as his own bottle.

Bill ate all his meals with the Parsons. Most evenings, he would go over and sit around in the bar. Weekends, when the place was full, he had to be there, and if there was a poker game going he liked to join in.

"Old Bill, he sure liked to win at poker," said Anne. "In the end it seemed like he figured he ought to win every pot, and when he didn't win he'd get to tearing up the cards—until I told him to quit or I'd have to bar him from playing."

One night when Dick was away somewhere, Anne had one customer in the bar, a young married fellow. "Old Bill, he got drunk and come over stripped stark naked, with a meat cleaver in his hand. Well, I got him back to his cabin all right, but pretty soon he was over again, still naked but carrying a shotgun. I got pretty angry and took the gun away from him and waltzed him back to his cabin and throwed him down on his bed and told him to lay there and not dare get up. . . . And next morning he come in like a little whipped dog, because acting like that was all against him. He was such a gentleman, you know. He loved us and we loved him. He was just like an uncle. The kids loved him, too. The girls were just babies then—about three and five—and Bill would walk them around the yard and sit them on his knee and even offer them his pipe, until I stopped him. One time, he wanted to give me some money to go buy the girls a pair of shoes each. They didn't need any shoes, but that's what he wanted. I told him he ought to keep his money because he needed it all. Aside from the rent, he spent most of it on beer.

"He was always full of stories," said Dick. "Funny thing, though, I can't seem to remember 'em now. But I do remember one thing he told me. He rode out in the pickup with me one day to an old mill there used to be, beside an irrigation ditch on the edge of Palo Verde, just west of town, right on the county line. The land beyond there, over on Joe Clark's ranch, was all flooded and I could sneak up this little road along the drainage ditch where the brush grew down beside the bank, and when the ducks come in I could knock 'em off. This day, like I say, Bill rode out there with me. And we was down there in the corner, in among the arrowweed and the mesquite trees, when Bill suddenly stops and says, 'You know, Dick, the first time I come to Palo Verde, I camped in a tent, right here.' He looks around and takes a couple of paces and then stops again and smiles. 'Yessir, right here was my first home in Palo Verde.' "

"He was always the gentleman," said Anne. "Kept that little goatee of his real neat. Stand in front of a mirror, he would, and trim it down to maybe four or five inches. He'd wash and scrub it, too. He still had a good head of hair, though it was gray then—kind of iron gray, with dark streaks. And he always stood pertly and straight, so that he looked younger than his years. And if he was going someplace, even across the road to Charlie Herrington's new beer parlor—that was after we'd sold our place and moved back into Palo Verde and Bill lived in a shack up along the lagoon—why, he'd put on a fresh set of clothes. And then he'd get his cane and start down the road. Gosh darn, to see him go, you'd have thought he was a millionaire."

I went back to the place Bill had lived with the Parsons, north of Palo Verde. Progress had begun to catch up with that quiet corner.

On the site of the old bar stood a modern house. Its owner vaguely remembered that when he bought the place there was a kind of old chicken shack out back, and he showed me where it had stood. From an arbor of gnarled and ancient tamarisks you looked out across plowed fields to distant mountains. In Bill's time, the land beyond the arbor had still been unplowed, was still natural, and the moment I saw the place I understood why he had been happy to live there.

"When I came," said the new owner, "it was a hell of a mess back here. Inches deep in tamarisk needles, so that your feet sank into it like it was a carpet. There was none of this landscaping then." He swung an arm. Its sweep encompassed a level and lifeless patch of gravel, a concrete barbecueing block and three or four red reflector lights nailed to tamarisk boles. "You can't believe what a difference the landscaping made."

"Oh, I think I can," I said.

Finally, I went to see Charlie Herrington.

"You'll like Charlie," the Parsons had assured me. "Bill liked him better than anyone else down there in Palo Verde."

Charlie had moved to Palo Verde in 1946 and two years later had built the village's second beer joint, a hundred yards down the road from Al Workman's. Now retired, he lived in a trailer camp, a dozen miles downriver.

From the start it was obvious that although he had known Bill for only four years, he had been genuinely fond of him.

"Oh, he was one nice man, old Chuckawalla Bill. He'd come over to my beer joint every day and stay about an hour and drink maybe three beers and then go home. Oh, he could drink beer, that man, but he didn't get drunk too often and if he did it was just a-singing. Mind you, he'd get in a fight, too. Wouldn't take nothing from nobody. Give old Dick Parsons a black eye once—and he was on into his seventies then, and maybe more. But he was gentle, too, Bill was. He didn't like you to kill nothing.

Not like these people who come in now there's a paved road and drive around the desert in their Hondas and four-wheel drives killing everything that walks or crawls or flies. Call themselves varmint hunters! Huh! They don't leave the animals no place to go. But old Bill, he wasn't like that at all.

"I can see him walking down the street now with that little goatee of his, wearing nothing but a pair of shorts and a pair of shoes—tennis shoes or just a pair of slippers. No shirt. Never wore a shirt in summer. He always walked real straight, too, with his chest sticking out like this." Charlie demonstrated. "The hair on his chest had all turned white, but hell, that man, he'd walk better than I could. Yeah, I can see him now. . . . Hell, I think I've got a photo somewhere of him and Lonny Lannerman a-standing outside of my beer joint."

"You have?"

"Sure," said Charlie.

He brought an album stacked with loose snapshots and began sifting. "Jesus Christ, he's dead . . . and he's dead . . . and she's dead, too. . . . That guy was ninety-four when he fell in a ditch and drowned himself. . . . Christ, they're all dead. . . . That guy hung himself with a piece of wire. . . . Yeah, here's that photo. There's old Bill in the middle with the stick, a-sucking at his old pipe. Must have been wintertime for him to be wearing all those clothes. That's Lonny Lannerman on the left. He's been dead these ten years. Cancer. And, hell, that's me on the right. Must have took it right after I built my place. Forty-nine, probably."

The faces in the snapshot were all shadow, mere daubs of black. But the middle figure, leaning on a stick, was somehow consistent with what I would have expected in the last year of Bill's life: shoulders still thrown back; yet a stance more relaxed and unposed than the other two had managed.

"Hell, that takes me back," said Charlie. He smiled, back down the years. "Old Bill, he'd sometimes come along when I went down the river, plugging for bass. He didn't fish, but he'd go a-swimming naked in the river and then fool around with my old dog, Jacob. That dog, he was crazy about old Chuckawalla Bill. One time, Bill had fallen down and cut his hand and it wouldn't heal. And that dog, every morning he'd go out there and lick Bill's hand. And he kept licking it until, by God, it healed up and you couldn't even never tell. Yes, you're right, old Bill had a dog too. I'd forgotten that. Old mixed-up dog with hair hanging down over his eyes. Always there a-sitting beside Bill when you went up to see him."

Sometime in early 1949, Bill had moved out of the cabin he rented, up along the lagoon, and pitched his tent just outside the village.

"I used to go up there to his camp a lot and bullshit about the places he'd been and the women he'd lived with. We'd talk about Pennsylvania, too, because I was born about sixty miles south of Pittsburgh, where he came from. And sometimes four or five of us guys would go up—Lonny Lannerman and George Cox and Little Red and Pete—and we'd take a couple of six-packs of beer and just chew the fat and maybe play three-handed cutthroat pinochle, fifteen cents a game. Old Bill, he'd get so mad he'd jump up and down. But half an hour later he'd forgotten it all. . . .

"A nice little camp, Bill had, out there in the arrowweed. Nothing fancy, you know. Just a piece of canvas over it for shade—though there was a big cottonwood for shade, too. Hell, you don't need no roof in this country. But when it rained, old Bill, he could lie on his bed there—a couple of two-by-fours and some blankets—just lie right there and watch it rain. Come to think of it, maybe he had a little tent, too. But he didn't sleep in it very often, so far as I remember. He had a bucket with a rope on it and when he wanted water he'd just throw it in the irrigation ditch and then let the water stand for a while for the mud to settle. He always had a pot o' coffee set back there on his stove, and all he had to do was throw another stick of wood on it and it was boiling. A nice little stove it was. But I remember he had some rusty old stovepipe on it that was full of holes and the smoke bothered him, and one day I went into town and bought him three lengths of stovepipe and we drove a length of half-inch pipe in the ground and wired the new pipe to it and then he had a real good stove.

And old Bill, he liked to cook. You'd walk along the ditch bank and hear him down there a-singing. A-singing and a-cooking.

"He was a good cook, too. And he liked to eat. But hell, he didn't never get fat. Usually he had a pot of something stewing there on the stove, like chili and beans. Yessir, he really liked chili. In summer, sometimes, when it got to be a hundred and ten or a hundred and twelve, his beans would be sitting there in the sun a-boiling and a-bubbling all by themselves."

I asked where the camp had been.

"Just west of town, in old river bottom," said Charlie. "Right on the county line, beside an irrigation ditch. There used to be an old mill there, and a lake where it was all flooded, over on Joe Clark's ranch."

"Wait a minute. That sounds like the place Dick Parsons told me about. Bill said it was the first place he camped in Palo Verde."

"That's right," said Charlie. "He told me about that. Said it was the same place he'd pitched his tent the first time he came here. Old Bill, he didn't give a shit if he died. But he didn't want to owe nobody nothing. 'I don't want to die until I get my check and pay everybody,' he used to say. And he wanted to die in Palo Verde. 'I love this desert and this country,' he told me once. 'And I want to die right here.' "

Charlie grinned. "Me, too. I don't never want to live nowhere but right here till I die. . . . Yessir, old Bill said that that camp of his was where he wanted to end up. He would have done, too, if they hadn't carted him off to Sawtelle. But he went down real fast, that last year. Just getting old, I guess. Toward the end, he got pretty cranky."

"Yes," I said. "I was talking to Mrs. Mills, who was postmistress then. She only knew him for about a year, and all she could remember was a cranky old man who was kind of frail and would boom his cane on the floor of the post office if he didn't get prompt service, no matter how many people were there before him—as if he figured he'd been around long enough to be privileged."

Charlie smiled.

"Mrs. Mills was still the postmistress," I said, "when I passed through in 1958, on a walk up California, and picked up my first mail here."

But Charlie was still smiling back into his own past. "Yeah, old Bill got cranky all right, there at the end. But don't let that fool you. He was just a nice old guy. One real nice man."


NEXT MORNING I drove up toward Bill's first and last Palo Verde camp.

There was one other person I knew who had visited him there.

A dozen years after Juan DeLaGarza left Bill down in the Indio cellar where he had been gambling all night, he happened to pass through Palo Verde on his way to some mining claims. He had heard that Bill had moved to Palo Verde and he pulled into the bar there for a beer.

Twenty-five years later, he still remembered it all vividly.

"I asked the lady there, 'D'you happen to know a man here they call Chuckawalla Bill?' She looked at me—and then she jerked her head down toward a dark corner of the bar. And by God, I looked, and down there in the dark where I couldn't see him was old Bill! And he took me to his camp. It was a few hundred yards west of town, over by a canal. They had a lake in there then. And he had his camp away out there in the brush, like a rabbit, right in the arrowweed. Just river bottom, it was. 'Jesus Christ, Bill!' I said. 'For Christ's sake, you might get bit by a rattler here. You ought to have a bunk or something, anyway.' But he was there right on the ground, and that country was full of rattlers. He had just a little bit of a tent, a little brown tent. . . . Poor old Bill! He said he wanted to come and stay with me, but he couldn't get away from there. So he gave me his Spanish-American War button and a shotgun. He said, 'You keep these, John. Someday we'll be together again, and I ain't got no place safe here to keep these things. I can't trust nobody here for that. And someday we'll be together again. . . .'" A beautiful button it was—real gold with the colors and the coat of arms and all of that. And I had this button along with my pin, just the same. You know, I used to belong to the Spanish-American Alliance, and I had this pin—past president of the Alliance. I had them together. And goddamnit, somebody stole the button while I was in the hospital. I had the shotgun around here for quite a while. Twelve gauge, it was. . . . Anyway, Bill told me, 'You keep these, John. We'll be together again.' So I'm figuring that someday he will be showing up here."

"No. I think the place you saw him there, it must have been just before he died."

Juan had nodded. "Maybe you're right." He paused. "Yes, I'm sure you're right."

I pulled off the highway just beyond Palo Verde, at the county line, and walked along a track toward the levee of an irrigation ditch. You could see that the land had once been "just river bottom" but had, as Al Workman said, been "cleared over several times." And now a big square of it, an acre or more, was freshly bulldozed.

I walked down the track to where Bill's camp must have been, over in one corner, close to a ten-foot levee. The only whole and living thing the bulldozer had left was a belt of arrowweed growing along the slopes of the levee.

I stood looking at the arrowweed.

An alien sound broke into my thoughts. Over on the far side of the bulldozed square, a pickup had turned in off the highway. It stopped. Two men got out and began to inspect a mound in the middle of the cleared land. The mound was the only part of the square with any unevenness left, any spirit. I walked over and said I hoped it was all right to be on the land: I was just looking for something that had been there, way back.

No sweat, the older of the two men assured me. They were just clearing the land for a horse corral. Sure, it had been used for a lot of things in the past twenty years. For a while there had been a portable concrete mixer, right over where I had been. Yes, he had done the first clearing—and just about every clearing since.

A tent? Now it was funny I should ask that. Around about November 1949 he had been doing some work for the Clark ranch, just over there to the west, along the irrigation ditch, and there had been this old guy living in a tent, down among the brush, right in that corner. The old guy had taken sick and they had hauled him off to the hospital. No, he had never met the old guy, but while he was doing that job he had passed by every day along the road on top of the levee. The tent? It was an old brown army type. Rectangular, not conical. Sloping sides, then maybe two- or three-foot walls, straight down. Oh yes, and an open flap on the front, that you could roll back. There had been a separate awning for shade too—canvas, or maybe an old blanket. Trees? Mostly, it had been salt cedar and mesquite . . . but, wait a minute, there'd been a good-sized cottonwood, right there by the irrigation ditch.

After they hauled the old guy away, the camp had stood there quite a while. But it got kind of run-down, and in the end, after they'd heard the old guy had died, they fired it. Yeah, that was right. Chuckawalla Bill they'd called him. He'd forgotten that.

Sure, he could show me pretty near exactly where the camp had been.

We walked back across the bare, barred soil to the corner below the levee.

While the contractor stood trying to fix his bearings from time past, I examined the freshly bulldozed soil. The place the concrete mixer had stood was clear enough: a jagged concrete block and several fragments; gravel mixed in with churned-up soil. Nothing more.

I began to move away.

It was then that I noticed, just off to the levee side of the churned-up gravel, an irregular patch. It was roughly rectangular. And it was black, as if burned.

I went down on one knee.

A fine ash permeated the soil. There was no sign of charred artifacts, but something had definitely been burned there, long ago. Something about eight feet by twenty.

I called the contractor over.

He inspected the blackened rectangle. Could be, he said. Could well be. The tent must have stood just about there. And that was no recent burn. The soil we were looking at still retained its structure; just the top few inches had been skinned off, and the rest had never been disturbed—never chewed up like the stuff with the gravel in it, a dozen feet away. He stood up, smiling. It looked as if I lived right. If the concrete mixer had been parked a few feet further over, the blackened soil would have been all chewed up, too. And until yesterday, when he skinned this section, it would have been covered with sand and arrowweed and I would never have seen the blackness. So I was pretty lucky. Yeah, I must live right, or something.

Still shaking his head, still smiling, he walked back across the bulldozed lot with his assistant. They got into the pickup and drove off.

I went up onto the levee. The "irrigation ditch" was a sizable canal, twenty-five feet across, perhaps thirty. It cut down from the north, made a right-angled bend just beyond Bill's campsite, then ran due west, true as an arrow. Ran due west, toward the mountains. Toward low, flat-topped foot-hills, less than a mile away. Toward distant black peaks that floated above the foothills. Toward the Chuckwalla Mountains.

I went partway down the far slope of the levee and sat in the curving outer side of the bend, looking west along the canal. The light was still morning-fresh. The water lay blue, placid, mirrorlike. Its bounding levees, tapering toward the mountains, fitted it like a frame. Their slopes were the pale yellow-brown of dried-out grass. On either side lay plowed fields, darker brown. The rest of the world was green and pink—and distant black.

It was very quiet, there on the inner slope of the levee, cut off from highway and village and scarred flatland. Very peaceful. The road along the top of the levee was just a dirt track and it did no real damage.

The contractor had said that in 1949 there was indeed a lake off to the left, where it was now plowed land, and the lake would have made the place even more peaceful. You would fairly often sit down, there on the levee, when you walked up from camp to draw water or just for a routine check on the universe. You would sit there and look down the strip of blue, mirrorlike water that was so neatly framed by the long, tapering, yellow-brown levees. And you would keep looking beyond the water, beyond the flat-topped foothills, at distant black peaks. For you knew those peaks, those mountains. Knew them well. Young Connie Talley used to drive you out there in his stripped-down 1927 Chevrolet, and you and a couple of friends would set up camp there for maybe three months at a time; then one of you would walk back in and Talley or one of the other young fellows in town would drive out and pick up the others with all the gear. Down the years you had spent many long, hot days back in those mountains—those mountains whose name you bore. You were too old and frail now to go back among them any more, but you were content. For you knew, in your mind's eye, what was there. Knew all about the clean, open stretches of desert pavement with tiny paving stones sand-blasted flat, baked chocolate brown and burnished to a patina. You knew about the delicate filigree of shrubs and cacti. Knew about the intricate patterns of small, cohering gullies. And knew about other, softer meanings. You knew about them all, and knew they were all out there still. Safe. So you were content. And grateful. By and large, anyway.

Most people did not understand, of course. They would not know why you had camped there in the river bottom. They would not know that it was a good place to live, there in the arrowweed, among the mesquite and salt cedar, with the big cottonwood beside the levee for shade. But to you it was home now. A good home. A very good home indeed. Good enough to be your last home, just as it had been your first home here in Palo Verde.

Far down the canal, a waterfowl sent circles widening across the mirrorlike surface. The sunlight, flattening toward noon, had lost its morning freshness.

I stood up and climbed back over the levee and went down through the arrowweed onto the bare, bruised flatland that would soon be a horse corral. I skirted the black rectangle. And as I began walking the ordinary, easy city block back to the highway it occurred to me that it had not been sad, going back a quarter of a century, to the place that had to all intents been the end of the trail for Chuckawalla Bill. Not sad at all.

It had seemed sad at the time, though.

"At the end, there," Al Workman had said, "Bill was in pretty bad shape. Wet his pants and that. And he went down pretty thin before he died. Didn't cook anything to amount to anything, and I think that's what killed him—didn't have any clean food. Right at that time there wasn't really nobody to take care of him. I was new in the country, of course, and didn't know him—or only just knew him as one of my customers. And he was pretty cranky by then.

"Those last few days, I think he just laid there. Maybe he got up on his feet, but he didn't leave the tent. And I doubt if he ate anything very much. He just laid on the goddam ground, in the tent. Almost died here."

The last day, Charlie Herrington had been away. But Al Workman remembered.

"I went up there when Harry West hauled him away to Sawtelle Hospital. Harry West was our deputy sheriff then. Old Bill, he was in bad shape. They pretty well had to carry him into the pickup. And that camp! Oh, it was . . . I don't know how in the world he ever lived there like he did. That tent, it wasn't as high as the ceiling in this trailer of mine. And he cooked outside. It was a mess, I tell you."

I came to the highway, stopped beside my car and turned and looked back across the freshly bulldozed soil toward the corner by the levee.

During those last days in his last camp under the big cottonwood tree, out there among the arrowweed and mesquite, Bill had known that his life was drawing to a close. In a sense, of course, he had known it for a long time. That was why he had moved back. That was why he had given the shotgun and his Spanish-American War medallion to his old friend John DeLaGarza when he turned up as if by accident. But toward the end Bill must have known that the light was failing fast.

It was not difficult to see how things had gone.

For a while he continued to cook meals. But the shadows kept drawing in. Eventually he stopped bothering about food. Old Fellow sat beside his bed, eyes mournful, and occasionally licked his hand.

For a long time, Bill just lay there.

Out of the shadows emerged memories that were no longer mere memories. He lay in his enormous, tiny bed and heard another load come clanking down No. 2 Incline, then swoosh out with a sound that began as a roar but softened to a whisper as the coal covered the floor of the wagon. He crouched among Braddock greenery, in a magical, pulsating universe of firefly dances, and dreamed of Indians and the young George Washington, on that very ground. He sat in the little frame house in Twin Lakes, Colorado, listening to the prospecting stories of his Uncle Anton—who had been important in some way, though it was difficult, now, to remember just how. It was midnight, and he peered out of the speeding train at the wide, beckoning expanse of Nevada desert; that place they had just passed through was called Winnemucca, the captain told him. He opened the door and saw Marge, hair black and tangled on the pillow, and the policeman lying beside her. He stood looking at the stones with which he had just blocked in, neatly enough, the entrance to the little natural chamber at the left end of the cave—the chamber in which he had cached his trunk and everything else; stood there and knew that when he went back up and out into the world again he would be starting, like a new man, the rest of his life. He sat outside his little old shack, stroking his little old black cat and letting his eyes run with pleasure past the two small, round hills that protruded from the plain like islands; looked past them, out across the plain, to the lines of distant hills that humped across the horizon like huge caterpillars. He came to a small, quiet place beside a river, where nothing much happened in a human herd sense, and fell in love with it and camped nearby among arrowweed and mesquite and a big lone cottonwood tree that gave shade from the desert sun. . . . He stirred and tried to look up at the cottonwood tree. But he could not see it. Old Fellow licked his hand again. He knew that the dog's eyes would be even more mournful now, but somehow he could not see them either.

And then out of the shadows, differently, came people. They were vaguely familiar but not very real—like people in a dream. They lifted him up and carried him and put him in the cab of a pickup. They would not let Old Fellow into the cab. And then one of them drove him a long, long way.

# 20 Sawtelle

BILL DIED SLOWLY.

So there at the very end, when he was off his last legs and just plain running down in the way most of us will likely approach the gate that is the sure terminus for all things born—when he was no longer alive in any warm and human sense—he generated the densest written chronicle of his threescore years and fifteen.

Anthony William Simmons was admitted to the General Medical and Surgical Hospital, Veterans Administration Center, Los Angeles 25, California, on November 2, 1949. On admission, he had forty-two dollars in his possession. He gave his age as eighty-one, his religion as Catholic, his marital status as divorced. He said among other things that he had no children and no known living relatives, was retired and had lived in California for fifty-five years. He designated Patricia and Harold Swafford, friends, of Palo Verde, California, to receive all his property in case of death. According to Charlie Herrington, the Swaffords at that time ran what is now the Sleepy Burro Cafe; but they had long ago left Palo Verde and no one had heard of them since.

Bill was brought to the hospital by "a friend," Harry West, Jr., Deputy Sheriff, also of Palo Verde, "because he was unable to care for himself."

The initial diagnosis was "gastritis and emphysema of lungs. . . . Hypertension. . . . Heart disease with failure."

During the first weeks he must have rallied a little.

"After they hauled him off to the hospital," Charlie Herrington told me, "I knew he'd want to come back. And sure enough, he wrote to my wife, Dorothy, and said he was feeling much better and wanted to come back. He didn't want to die in that damned hospital. But I hadn't got a car good enough to drive to L.A. and none of the other guys would go get him. I felt real bad about that. Always have done. 'Cause old Bill, he wanted to die right here in Palo Verde. . . . He wrote Dorothy about some effects he wanted, too, and we went up to his camp and got a folder with a bunch of damned old letters and junk in it. Didn't amount to nothing. . . ."

Other things were happening, too, around Bill's last camp. "After they took Bill away," Al Workman told me, "that old dog of his just left the tent and never come back. Went half a mile north up the ditch and laid down there. And a few days later, Lonny Lannerman went up along the ditch and found the old dog a-laying there. He wasn't dead, just laying right out there. And Lonny shot him. . . . No, that dog never come back to the tent, not after they took Bill away."

The improvement in Bill's condition did not last.

Three weeks after his admission he suffered a "small cerebral vascular thrombosis. . . . He became confused, disoriented, deaf, delusional. . . . Hypomanic behavior not controllable in his ward."

By December 3, when he was transferred to the Neuropsychiatric Hospital, he was "inaccessible for interview due to his extreme senility and loss of memory. . . . Patient is in bed with rails to prevent him from getting out. He is very hyperactive, talks constantly, irrelevantly and incoherently, and there is a marked paranoid trend to his mutterings. He is always talking about money matters as if he had great wealth and someone was taking his money from him. When further questioned he states that he had about $200 somewhere but does not know where. . . . The simplest questions are not answered by this patient. No information of value is available from this 82-year-old man. . . . Hallucinations are not noted, but delusions of paranoid nature are manifest. He has no insight or judgment and he is definitely incompetent." Diagnosis: "Severe arterio-sclerosis with resultant damage to cerebral cortex, the myocardium, the lungs and the peripheral vascular tree . . . enlarged heart . . . EKG revealed old postmyocardial infarct . . . cerebral sclerosis . . . senile psychosis."

There was a lot more, too: poor old Bill was simply breaking up.

The patient "became progressively weaker." January 11, he sank into a coma. He died at 12:40 p.m., in Ward 258-B.

He was buried six days later, at nine o'clock in the morning. At the Catholic burial service, a VA chaplain officiated. The VA provided pallbearers and music. A check for ninety dollars, dated December 31, 1949, being the "balance of funds on deposit at this station," was returned to the Veterans Administration Treasury Department, Washington, D.C. No records appear to exist pursuant to the forty-two dollars in cash that the patient reportedly brought to the hospital.

Out in the real world, in the January 26 edition of the Palo Verde Valley *Times*, published in Blythe, there appeared near the foot of a list of social trivia headed "Palo Verde Items, by Mrs. Mattie Lee Gahan":

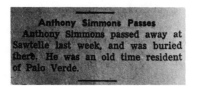

Bill had, of course, been off speaking terms with Ma Gahan for years, and the perfunctory coldness of the notice, which few people would have connected with the well-known local character Chuckawalla Bill, was no doubt bitchily deliberate. The pen can be knifier than the sword.

"Right after he died," Charlie Herrington told me, "some of the guys went up and burned his camp. There wasn't nothing there, really. Just old pots and pans and things, and they buried 'em in a big hole that Bill used to throw things in. . . . Then for a long time, Dorothy and me had a little leather thing with papers in it—army discharge papers and the like. But in the end I burned all that damned stuff. You know how it is—the years go by and what the hell would we want with them? . . ."

Governments, of course, operate differently. Back in the bureaucratic world, papers continued to flutter like autumn leaves, covering the patient over. At last, on July 25, 1950, in Washington, D.C., someone wrote "Closed—no heirs" on a legal-size sheet, then stamped it "Ready for File." And for nearly a quarter of a century the file lay untouched.

WHEN WILLIAM ANTHONY SIMON, lying and dying under the name Anthony William Simmons, made his final lonely exit from our stage on January 11, 1950, in Ward 258-B of the Neuropsychiatric Hospital, Veterans Administration Center, Los Angeles, California, Harry S Truman was President of a nation that bestrode the postwar world like a colossus and loved it, Konrad Adenauer had just been elected the first chancellor of a Federal Republic of Germany that was already beginning to rise again from the shame and shambles of a thousand-year Reich that had crumbled after twelve, and King George VI reigned over Great Britain and Northern Ireland and an Empire on which the sun was rapidly setting; the human population of the United States was 150 million and still booming, that of the planet 2.3 billion and booming even harder toward bust; the Scopes trial was twenty-five-year-old history, yet the law that had provoked it still stood on Tennessee's books and, almost everywhere, evolution was still called "a theory"; in Russia, the first state established according to the principles of Karl Marx had recently celebrated its thirty-second birthday and Joseph Stalin his seventieth, while in Asia the red flag had just been hoisted over the most populous country on earth—and, back home, Alger Hiss was on trial; within three weeks, President Truman would instruct the Atomic Energy Commission to proceed with its work on the hydrogen bomb; the word "ecology," though born before Bill, had barely entered general scientific usage, let alone popular consciousness— or jargon; in private homes all across Europe and the United States, little boxes portraying black-and-white blizzards were breaking out like a rash (though it is unlikely Bill ever saw one); Henry Ford had died two years earlier but Albert Einstein was seventy and still counting, while Congressman John Fitzgerald Kennedy was thirty-two, Lieutenant Jimmy Carter twenty-five, Lee Harvey Oswald ten and Paul McCartney seven. Meanwhile, all over the world, the weather remained essentially unpredictable.

On that Wednesday evening of January 11, 1950—the last of Bill's 27,191 days on earth—the sun set in Los Angeles, technically speaking, at 5:14 p.m. All day, though, it had sulked behind clouds. The clouds had decanted almost an inch of rain, and the rain had temporarily cleared away the haze of pollutants that had for seventy-five years been spreading outward from Braddock's Industrial Defeat and was now beginning to smog up the most westerly of God's own skies.

# 21 Goodbye, Bill

I WENT BACK one last time to Bill's desert.

On the way, I visited his grave.

The Veterans Administration cemetery in Los Angeles, close by the hospital complex that used to be called Sawtelle, is a vast, carefully tended lawn, cradled by trees. Today's traffic, blasting along the bordering arteries of Wilshire Boulevard and the San Diego Freeway, leaves the place strangely serene. Even the helicopters, chopping overhead, rarely seem to penetrate that timeproofed world.

I found Bill's grave near the cemetery's southern corner.

His monument is a plain gray stone, flush with the mown grass. Around it stretch precise military rows of similar markers. But Bill's marker is

simpler than most. The others give place and date of birth, rank and unit and wars fought; also a cross or, in a few cases, Star of David. I was not sure Bill would have approved of the place they had buried him, but I knew he would have liked his stone's distinguishing simplicity, its hint of mystery.

I stood for a long time on the manicured grass, looking down at the small gray stone, failing to feel what I had expected to feel, what I thought I ought to feel. Such numbness often comes, I suspect, when people attempt premeditated emotion—when, for example, they visit an old friend's grave.

Anthony W. Simmons—January 11, 1950. Almost thirty years had rolled by since that unflagged day they buried Bill's husk—and almost ten years since I happened to come around a corner in a remote canyon and see a beautiful, humpbacked trunk. A lot of sand had sifted since that November Nevada afternoon. And I had come a long, long way from what I thought I was doing when I went back a year later to live in the cave.

You could argue, of course, that I had still not solved the Trunkman mystery. I had certainly assembled no concrete, linear proof. But it seemed to me that I had long ago built, item by jigsaw item, a case that would convince most juries. I believed it myself, anyway—all Mondays and most Tuesdays; and not only because of the undeniable convergence between the Trunkman I had pictured and the Bill Simmons I had come to know. The really vital evidence still lay in the lack of a single serious negative: in ten years I had turned up nothing about Bill Simmons at odds with what I knew of Trunkman. And that was pivotal. You had to stop and think about it before you appreciated its weight.

Looking back, I could see that the Trunkman part of the search had turned out at least as well as I could have hoped. (One of the few sad ingredients had recently surfaced: through carelessness, the Park Service had allowed the trunk to be stolen—and thereby vindicated a friend who at the very start had warned that, if involved, they would infallibly foul things up.)

But as my project evolved, so the Trunkman component had faded. Other magnets had begun to pull me along.

Even now, though, I found it difficult to say just what had kept me blinkered down the years; had held me obsessed. One friend persisted in seeing the quest for Bill Simmons as part of my Americanization. It had certainly given me glimpses of what "history" meant in certain corners of my adopted country during the century before it adopted me. That I had been unaware of such motivation did not, of course, rule it out. But I remained skeptical. It seemed to me that the most intriguing element of the whole quest had been . . .

A helicopter chopped over the cemetery, low. I rejoined the world of sunlight on mown grass. And after a while I went looking for the place Bill had died.

But Ward 258-B no longer existed. The wing in which it once stood was now devoted to research and administration. The chief administrator seemed to remember that 258-B had been small, with three or four beds, and I had to settle for that. Perhaps it was just as well.

I drove east from Los Angeles into the desert to visit Bill's quiet places.

As I drove, I found myself looking back over the whole evolving, ten-year Trunkman/Bill Simmons project. From the start, the business had danced with coincidences. Or you could say, as I often had, that during it my serendipity quotient seemed abnormally high. For many links that had kept the chain of events moving seemed happenstantially tenuous. That first day, when I walked down into the rock basin, I had chosen the "right" route. If I had returned to the cave a year later than I did, after the storm that spread four inches of gravel over the wash, I would have found few telltale artifacts outside the cave. A chance conversation with a friend who was Sunday editor of the San Francisco *Chronicle* led to the re-printing in that paper of my $100-reward Trunkman article. And so it had gone on: Grace; Helen Harriss; the door marked "Nau."

Today, in the West, we clothe and color such events with the kinds of words I have used: coincidence; happenstance; serendipity. A few people, harking back to earlier times, may still speak of "omens." Many settle for "getting the breaks when you need them." Then there are Tom Robbins' "second clockworks": an alternate monitor of the universe that measures progress not by the linear, ticking pulse of time but by erratic, apparently arbitrary events, by "breathless, giddy signals." And one Eastern sage has offered: "Nature supports a right action." But a comfortably Western and scientific notion is the "hologram effect": a small hologram, the mind, moves into three-dimensional harmony with the large hologram, the universe, and thoughts and events mesh. True, my Trunkman search had been riven by frustrating interludes during which it looked as if my grasping hand would never light on anything at all. But you could say that at those times I was simply out of sync with the universe, with Bill, with my goal or Grail, and that the seminal things began to happen when my mind moved into harmony with these elements.

One aspect of the hologram effect showed up in the congruences be-tween me and this obscure man into whose ghost I had bumped by apparent chance in a remote canyon at a cusp in his life—in symmetries that could not all be explained by the selective process that had drawn us both to the cave. We both began life as Christians but saw the light. We were both wanderers who worked at other jobs until able to devote ourselves to what we really wanted and were determined to do. We both had early military training that gave us, among other things, an eye for terrain. We were both hairy men. By the age of thirty, we both seem to have had a bellyful of leading others. I suspect that neither of us attained until rather late in life—around about our thirties—a really good, surging, bed-breaking appreciation of sex. We both came to the desert late, because of women, and both discovered there that life re-began at forty-one. We were both meticulous beyond the call of necessity, yea unto the borders of fussiness. We both valued solitude and silence and square, smoothed-off granite boulders. Bill called his last dog "Old Fellow"—and when I talk to dogs or even passing foxes or coyotes I tend to address them as "Fellow." We even shared certain date coincidences that I have refrained from mentioning because I do not believe in such things—or rather think I don't.

In some ways, of course, we stood worlds apart, Bill and I. I am no gambler; not for money, anyway. And Bill, far from coming equipped with blinkers, was always ready to lift his hand from a plow. Physically, we were never even on the same continent together: Bill left Britain three years before I was born there; I first came to America three years after he died. But our convergence was nevertheless real. Others detected it. The graphologists who decoded Bill's and Grace's handwriting pounced on my scrawled covering note and commented: "You and Bill are very alike in many ways, though not all. Both of you are, like Grace, suspicious: people need to prove themselves to you before you will accept them." Four or five people who knew Bill and saw my Trunkman self-portraits in the cave assumed, without thinking, that they were of Bill. One of them, when I explained, said, "Yes, I can see now that it's you. It's funny, though— that's just the way he used to sit." One friend of Bill's said to his wife as I walked up to his house after phoning ahead, "Hell, he looks more like old Chuckawalla than Bill did hisself. Must be his son." Then there were the psychiatrist and his wife, friends of mine, who came to dinner and discussed the whole Trunkman business. Just before they left, the husband said, "You know, there's an odd thing been going on. Sitting here this evening and talking about Bill Simmons, it has been exactly as if we were talking about Colin Fletcher." His wife nodded. "Exactly," she said.

There was also the matter of Bill's friends. Looking back, I could see that, with very few exceptions, the people Bill liked, I liked. The people he disliked, I disliked, too; but the friends were what mattered. You can tell a lot about a man from his friends—and the more of his friends I had met, the more I had liked Bill. Juan DeLaGarza, for example, had banished one of my small but nagging worries. Because Bill always seemed to see the grass on the far side of any fence as greener, I had sometimes wondered whether, meeting him, you would have felt a sense of shiftlessness. But Juan had been the same sort of man: "I always on the go. Never stay very long in one place." And the last word you would have used about Juan was "shiftlessness." He was a rock.

Time being what it is, almost all of Bill's friends I had met had been elderly. His acquaintances, too. In fact, that had been one of the great Trunkman bonuses: talking to so many wonderful old people. For the vibrantly young-old, no matter how many years they have on their backs, remain open, aware, growing, wise—and therefore giving. One yardstick of wisdom is the way a person has come to terms with the tiresome facts of mortality, and this, of course, is a matter in which age counts. At eighteen you are, roughly speaking, immortal. In your sixth decade, as far as I can see, the best response is to think you are going to live forever but to know you might die before lunch. At ninety-seven, lunch no doubt looked pretty imminent. For Bill, at seventy-five, it had clearly done so, and he had come to grips with the knowledge. "He didn't give a shit if he died," Charlie Herrington had said. Come to think of it, that had been another Trunkman bonus: the search had been an exercise in *memento mori*—had sharpened my understanding of the transitory nature of human lives. . . .

In my rounds of Bill's quiet places I looked for his claims. But they were no more the true object of my journey than they had been of Bill's prospecting.

I visited for the first time three places that I have already described in their proper niches: Black Horse Mine, Crystal Creek and the Eagle Mountains. I failed to find a single physical sign of Bill's claims or camps. But I saw a lot. Places were as important to Bill as they are to me. And at many of them, as you now know, I often just sat and daydreamed about the place and about this man I knew well because I had, in a sense, lived with him for ten years.

It seemed odd now, but only once in those ten years had I really dreamed about him. In the dream he remained half-focused, as dream-people often do. He seemed much as I had expected, though: amiable but ordinary. Mostly about sixty, he oscillated to forty and even younger. I had met him—in some vague, unpinnable, dreamlike way—through a big board lying on the ground that referred to the Black Horse Mine. The mine had prospered (though the dream occurred before I "learned" that this is what had happened), and I remember that Bill was surprised I knew of his friendship with Floyd Brown. We had a couple of drinks at a bar. But we had discussed very little when it occurred to me that I could nail down the Trunkman mystery simply by asking if he had in fact lived in the cave. For some reason—I think it had to do with needing a moment's respite to frame the question's wording—I did not immediately ask him but said only that I had a very, very important question to ask. And at this precise point I woke up.

When I had finished visiting Bill's quiet places I finally drove down to the Chuckwalla Mountains.

I had often driven along the freeway that skirts them a few miles to the north, several worlds removed. But I had been saving until the end these mountains into which Bill often disappeared for weeks on end, these mountains that gave him his final name, these low mountains he could see in the distance, black beyond blue, whenever he climbed up onto the levee above his first and last camp in Palo Verde. But now the time had come for me to do what I had long intended to do: walk though Bill's mountains as Bill had done—and emerge at the end at his last camp in Palo Verde.

Instead, I caught the flu.

The bug was sweeping through the human population of the desert and it swept me onto my back in a Blythe motel. I emerged feeling fragile as thistledown and drove slowly south into the Little Chuckwallas.

In a sense, I was prepared. Tommy Jones, a poet friend of a friend of Bill's, had written:

> *God must have been tired when he made the Chuckawalla*
> *Mountains.*
> *He must have let the earth fall through His fingers into*
> *crumpled heaps.*
> *Then He gave the winds dominion over the wrinkled,*
> *twisted chain of hills.*
> *The winds sulked and pouted and beat the hills fiercely,*
> *to show their contempt of such a forlorn domain. . . .*

But in spite of this warning I found that once again—as at cave and rock house—I was at first repelled.

It was midafternoon. The sun beat down on mile after mile of somber, sullen rock. Mourning doves mourned: "My *Good*ness, how sad!" By now, though, I knew that I had only to wait. I found a faint track that led back to the foot of one of the mountains' side ridges, and I camped beside a dark, conical hill.

And slowly—aided by the aftermath of the flu, which braked my modern haste and forced me to change gear, down to the pace at which Bill operated—I began to learn the language of that country.

The light shifted. Cholla gardens glinted in evening sunshine. Out across a plain that often seemed less a plain than a curiously sloping sea, mountains rode into the night like dark, low-lying battleships. At dawn they reappeared as the jagged spines of aquatic dinosaurs caught cruising past, half submerged, through a time warp that night had hidden. Soon, a new day was flooding across the plain and the distant dinosaurs re-battle-shipped, then became twenty-mile-long caterpillars that humped two thousand feet tall.

By noon of the second day my eyes could embrace the sky. In such country, earth forms only part of the parade. Plain and mountains can become mere footnotes to the huge and lofting heavens.

By midafternoon I could hear the wind—the wind that came from God knows where and headed likewise. Before long I could begin to decipher its messages; then, the messages hidden in the silence that lay beyond the wind.

I sat on into the twilight of that second day, still weak, resting in my camp beside the dark, conical hill and looking out over the curiously sloping plain. Once you had accepted such country, it was beautiful and true. It forced humility on you. Like cave and rock house, like Black Horse Mine, it was no land for a man afraid of the world. To live in such places, especially alone, you had to have come to terms with yourself.

By late afternoon of the third day I felt strong enough to walk up a ridge behind my camp.

I moved slowly. But after half an hour I needed to rest on a black volcanic outcrop. I sat on its west side, in the warmth of the sinking sun.

My car, far below, was a mere speck beside the dark, conical hill. The hill stood just beyond the tip of a long ridge. It protruded from the plain the way an island protruding from the sea often shows you that a rocky promontory persists, down there below the waves—the way salient facts from a man's history, standing uneroded by the years, can reveal the submerged and ongoing realities of his life. I felt that Bill, too, must have recognized this echo of the two hills at the north end of the McCoys, beside his old Black Horse Mine.

Now that I had stopped, my legs felt like floss. I wondered how many days I would have to rest before I felt strong enough to begin my walk through these mountains and on over to Palo Verde. I even began to consider the unwelcome possibility that I might have to come back some other time to make that final journey.

It was very quiet, up there on the ridge. The sun slipped toward the horizon. A raven cruised past, quothing. I looked out beyond it toward distant, caterpillar mountains.

From up on the crest of the Little Chuckwallas, not far above, you would see such mountains circling the horizon. Bill must often have stood there. And when he did so he would have been standing at the center of the desert domain that he had established. For the mountains he would see circling the horizon would be the Chocolates—where he had staked the Green Bay Mine with Joe Bowers and Fred Hansen, and had traveled with Grace and later with Juan—and the Eagles and the McCoys and finally, to the southwest, the Palo Verdes—where I had been told he once lived beside a spring. So he would be surveying, from there on the crest of the mountains that had given him his name, the heart of the country that had been the stage for most of the second half of his life—that part of his life he had constructed, the part he had begun to build after his sojourn in the cave, when he had decided what he wanted out of life, and what he did not want.

Far below me, shadows were reaching out across the plain. The sun was slipping toward the horizon and its light had lost all thrust. The desert was ready to call it a day.

And suddenly I was sitting bolt upright.

I would not be coming back to make my final Trunkman journey, on foot across the Chuckwallas to Palo Verde. I would never make that journey. I no longer needed to.

There on that dark and rocky ridge of Bill's mountains I had succeeded in burying him; had buried him in a way they had not done, for me, beneath the manicured green grass of the cemetery. And this time I had buried him decently, in a fitting place.

So now at last it was over.

There on that rocky ridge my blinkers had fallen away. And now that it had happened, there was no way I could set the clock back. It was like an affair: once the magical bonds that hold you together have snapped, there is nothing that either of you can do about it, no matter how hard you try.

I do not mean that the bonds binding me to Bill had broken. For ten years he had been a shadow on and in my life. And he would be there, as a shadow, for the rest of my days. I would often see him, this independent shadow that I had in a sense created. Mostly, I would picture him walking through the desert pretending to look for gold, content. Occasionally I would smile and nod to myself and say, "Bill would have liked this place," or "This is a guy that Bill would have gotten along with." But now, for the first time since I embarked on my search, I was willing to stop, was ready to call it a day. Come to think of it, I wanted to stop. For the obsession that had bound me to the search with a persuasive logic apparently invisible from outside had, without warning, evaporated. So it was time to go; time to say goodbye.

And once I had adjusted to the shock I saw that leaving Bill's last mountains unexplored was a fitting way to end it. He had known that man needs mystery.

There remained, of course, many other bays of mystery. Did he ever marry? Or was that one of his long-term fantasies? Where did he get the name "Ashee"? Had the name "Simmons" stamped on mousetrap and yellow measuring tape really been pure coincidence? There was his "diary," too—the little black notebook the Roper children said he used to write in, out under the apricot tree: what had happened to that? Was it among the papers in "the little leather thing" that Charlie Herrington eventually burned? Then there were simpler, everyday mysteries that would not have lingered had I met Bill: Was he a moviegoer? In such places as movie houses, where did he habitually sit? What music moved him?

Bill's understanding of the need for mystery was part of his sense of privacy, and down the years I had become acutely aware of that sense. It was not a very difficult thing to do: I share the sense, fanatically. And when I finally decided that I must write a book about him I began to worry about its being a posthumous invasion of his privacy. To my relief, no less than three people who had known him said, spontaneously, that Bill would be "tickled pink" and "proud" had he known about the book. One even added that he would not have minded if I did not hide his faults. So I had stopped worrying.

I became aware that the light around me was changing. Westward, the sun was slipping down behind the Eagle Mountains. It was suddenly cool, there on the ridge. I stood up and began to walk back down toward the darkening conical hill.

The lingering mysteries should not worry me. It was always like that. You can never enter fully into someone else's mind, so that you understand, consistently, all the fluctuating, enveloping miasmas that color their daily lives—that color all our lives. Even old face-to-face friends can surprise you. But now that my long search was over and I had the jigsaw pieces assembled into as sharp a picture as they would probably ever make, I seemed to know more about Bill than I had dared hope to discover. And now that I had finally buried him, decently and softly—with a recognition of his frailties, but with affection—I found myself looking back on his life as a whole.

What I saw was essentially the kind of life I had pictured, though vaguely, when I lived in the cave, ten years earlier.

I saw the normal mix of human paradoxes.

I saw an ordinary man who was far from ordinary. I saw a contented malcontent. I saw a highly imperfect organism, as impelled and constrained by the tides of its time as we all are. I saw a man who was born at the birth of his country's Industrial Revolution and died a quarter of a century before the onset of the Industrial Devolution, but who, long before he died, had escaped the merely-human-world myopia that infects industrial-world thinking, and who therefore recognized the canker in the golden apple. I saw, that is, a dreamer, not built for the place he was born, who revolted against the steel and ugliness of that place and learned that the butterflies are free. I detected, I mean, another print of time on energy with an ear for harmonies that reach out beyond our beguiling artifact, the human world—an ear for rhythms that, though not necessarily better than the artifact's, certainly run deeper. I saw a maverick diplomat, a chameleon with a mind of his own. I saw a bright man who had never reached his potential, and knew it. I saw an uneducated man with an alcoholic Achilles heel who for most of his life kept changing and growing. I saw a man of impeccable honesty in all daily dealings but wholly and unholy free-lance in his fantasies. I saw an individual with a solid sense of his own worth who followed his own small and uncertain star and to his own self was very true—and yet could be riven through with resurging regrets; a man who in one sense lived a life of almost quavering discontinuity but who mostly had the wit—whether prospecting or building stone monuments or anything else—to keep his eye on the process, not the goal; a man who chuckled and was not afraid to die. I saw, in other words, the standard human amalgam of crud and magnificence.

I saw a man who could be a bit of an ass, even quite childish, yet of whom most people said, "You couldn't help liking him." A man who to some people looked like a loser but who remained a poet and by and large chose poetic friends who were all, in their own ways, free. A man with a wide spectrum of such friends—not all of them heavy drinkers, not even all free of the money grub. Above all, in the end, for all his faults and foibles, a very decent, human man. A man with the spark.

I came down onto a broad wash and began walking toward the tip of the ridge with my dark, conical hill at its foot. The light was failing now.

More than anything else, Bill had been a man who chose freedom. Faced with our recurring choice between the joys of sharing and of solitude, he had come down on the unencumbered side. Like all of us, he sometimes wavered. But by and large he knew what he wanted and what he did not want. And he paid the penalties and reaped his rewards.

In its way, the second half of his life had been a work of art, a triumph. He had decided, then held fast. He had taken what the world threw onto his plate, had chosen and rejected, and then molded. Toward the end, just before they took him away to die—took him away from the place in which he wanted to die—he might with advantage have put a bullet through his head. But otherwise he had, according to his own lights, handled things pretty damned well.

I came to the foot of the ridge. The light had almost gone. I began to walk the last few yards to my camp on the far side of the dark, conical hill.

That little gray stone, flush with the manicured cemetery grass, was not Bill's real monument. Neither was the rock house in Long Canyon; nor even the tamarisk trees he had planted beside Palo Verde lagoon. In time, these would crumble away. The real monuments he had left to mark his passage were those we all leave: the ripples he had sent reverberating forever down the widening, weakening circles of cause and effect. From what I had seen, peering back through such windows on his life as human memory had opened, Bill's ripples had been almost entirely benign. No one had even come close to calling him a shit. Grace had said, forty years down the road, "I could never raise a monument high enough for Bill Simmons." And there had been no lack of others. Eusibio Savalha, remembering old Blackie with his backpack and annual vagabond homily. John Roper, for whom Bill had left tracks worth leaving. And on down to Charlie Herrington with his final epitaph: "Hell, he was a nice old guy. One real nice man."

All in all, it seemed to me, you could do a lot worse. Most of us do.

A nighthawk came sideslipping around the hill. It saw me and banked. For a moment it seemed to hang there, very close, and it was as if I could see through the white windows in its underwings and out into the still-pale western sky. Then the bird had slanted away, as silently as it had come, into the advancing shadows of the night.

Early next morning I began the long drive home.

# Acknowledgments

HUNDREDS OF PEOPLE helped build this book. Many contributed memories or photographs or documents. Others assisted with written research or suggested leads or supplied background.

I list such contributors, gratefully, below. A few deserving individuals will, inevitably, have escaped my net of notes and memory, and to them I apologize. My regrets, too, to those whose names I only heard spoken and may therefore have misspelled.

The list embraces those major contributors who appear in the text—five or six of them under aliases, either at their own request or because I had unpleasant but necessary things to say and did not want to inflict pain. It includes several people who, although involved only in the course of their work, went beyond routine response; but it does not include many whose aid was peripheral—or the one man, apparently a pathological liar, who deliberately misled me.

Any list like this imposes a degree of injustice: it cannot distinguish between players with walk-on parts and those who, like Dennis Casebier— "the man in Los Angeles who often went to the National Archives"— contributed swaths of time and enthusiasm and encouragement. But it is the best I can do. And I thank all concerned. They brought my building blocks.

C.F.

CALIFORNIA

Ansel Adams; D. B. W. Alexander; Billie Allen; Marna Anderson; Ruth M. Anderson; G. Stanleigh Arnold; Robert Ashmore.

ACKNOWLEDGMENTS

Janie Barnard; Marjorie Bennett; Mrs. Betts; Benny Betz; Clair Bigham; Charles Bigley; Colette Cassidy Blair; James H. Blankeley; Bud Bogust; Dorr Bothwell; Floyd Bowen; Joe and May Bowers; Gwen Bronson; Ray and Irene Brown; Thelma Bryant; George Bucklin; Vern Burandt; Catherine B. Burke.

Ralph Capps; Cliff Carney; Mickey Carson; Dennis G. Casebier; Louis G. Castner; Paul Cassidy; Joseph L. Chiriaco; Stan and Kathy Christian; Gene Christman; Geneva Harlan Chronister; Nick Clapp; Rolly Clark; Nevada C. Colley; Gail Colton; Glen Colton; George Covington; William B. Cox; W. Crivelli.

Jim Davenport; Mildred Davenport; Sahras Dekens; Juan DeLaGarza; Charles Demetrius; Fred Denewiler; Chico De Rouen; Agnes Dimwiddie; Barbara Ferron Doyle; Noel Drady; William J. Dykes.

C. J. "Chuck" Eddinger; Benjamin B. Ehrich; Lawrence Elders; Colbert H. Eyraud.

Keith Farrar; Sam and Alice Faubian; Patricia M. Flanagan; Harry Free.

Charles Gaskell; Janet Gaynor; Judge Gillespie; Paul Gillette; Cliffton H. Gray; Robert Griffith.

Mrs. C. Eilers Hall; Gilberta Harmon; Arden Harlan; Mr. and Mrs. Arden Dean Harlan, Jr.; Lee Harlan; Norman Harlan; Mrs. Harvell; Robert Harvell; Jan Hauptli; Modena Roper Hawley; Bill Hayes; Bob Heizer; Sidney Henking; Charles Herrington; Lon Hettinger; Foster Hewitt; John Hilton; Cy Hopkins; Betty Hudspeth; Cliff Hudspeth; Douglas Huff; Herb Hughes.

Adolf and Marie Idol; Iron Jaw.

Roberta Jenkins; Donald P. Jewell; Frank Jones; Tommy Jones; Bunker Johnson; Joseph Johnson; Stancil and Kristen Johnson.

John A. Kay; Norma Kays; Mr. and Mrs. John Kee; Ruth Kelly; George Kenline; Dolores Kleinkey.

Tom Laughran; Axel Lauridsen; Gray Laury; Chester Longwell.

R. H. MacDonald; Charles Maddis; Jack Marlowe; Otis "Dock" Marston; Jack Masson; J. Maynard; Grace Mazeris; Garnet McBride; Bea McCambridge; Gerry McCarthy; D. McComas; Mary McDonald; Andrew J. B. McFarland; John McGee; Carol McGuire; Rickie Meehling; Louis Merrill; Ellen M. Mills; Mr. and Mrs. Archie Mixon; Jean Molleskog; Leslie Moore; Chester and Patricia Moorten; David B. Morrison; Betty Mullins.

Clyde Nichols; Russell Nichols; Forrest Noffsinger; Ole Norland. Peter Odens.

Jack Page; Dick and Anne Parsons; Joe M. Paulk; Tom Pierce; Phil E. Pister; George C. Pipkin; Lee Portis; Rollin and Edith Proebstel. Lloyd Quick.

Stan and David Ragsdale; Bill Rains; Jim Reay; George R. Repaire; Charlie Rhodes; Jimmy Richardson; George Ringwald; Iner W. Ritchie; Ulva Harlan Robertson; John Roper; Norton Roper; Harriet Robinson; Iretha (Margaret) Roper and Chet Robinson; Ward Russell.

Elizabeth Sale; Eusibio Savalha; Ben Shank; Carol Shaw; Dixie Shaw; L. E. Short; Lucile Harvell and William I. Short; Nina Shumway; Bill Sidel; Betty Smith; "Dutch" Smith; Roger Smith; Norbert E. Snider; Arthur Bill Sonneborn; Bill Sorenson; Welda Harlan Stahli; Sherman R. Stallard; Robert C. Stebbins; Carl and Peter L. Stenderup; Moyle Stewart; Charlotte Stocks; Mary Wiefels Stockton; Geraldine Sutterfield; Norma Sutton; Cecil Swan.

Connie Talley; Lillian M. Talmage; Grace Tarbutton; David and June Taylor; Frank Terrill; Mary Trainor; Lutz Trautmann; Hazel and Bob Tucker.

Bob Vanderver; Frank Van Hoorebecke; Aron B. Vaughn.

Ethel (Whittle) Wagner; Alton Walker; Byron Walker; Tommy Walters; Clarence Washburn; Marion Weddle; Harvey Wells; George Wende; Ellie Wenzlaff; Jim Westerfield; Halstead G. White; Edward Whitehead; Mike Widman; Howard Wiefels; Jane Wiefels; Peter Williams; Fred Wing; Dora Wolf; June Woodward; Al Workman; Grace Workman.

Bill Young.

### PENNSYLVANIA AND ENVIRONS

Al Abrams; Frank Benkovich; John Bischel; Lorraine "Dolly" Nau Clark; Lynn Ferraro; Father Cornelius Finneran; Olyn Simon Fowler; Walter Gregg; Theresa and John L. Gross; Mrs. Harper; Helen and Gene Harriss; Father Charles Heupler; Gene Hughey; Father William J. Hutnik.

Sister Adele Kasper; Ron Lucas; M. Joseph Martinelli; Mrs. Mooney; Charles Nau; Robert and Mary Ann Nau; Virginia Oakes; Sister Barbara Obringer; Mrs. Pristera; Edna Simon Roley; Arthur J. Rooney; Sister Rose Marie; Father Rutledge.

Father Savage; Marie and John Schuster; Edna M. Simon; Joseph Simon; Joseph P. Simon; L. W. "Boots" Simon; many other, unrelated Simons; David Solomon; Arlene Schuster Somple; Virginia Simon Tabron; Tom Walsh; Mary and Jack and Gene Yost.

ACKNOWLEDGMENTS

OTHER PLACES

*Arizona:* Louis Bishop; R. G. Eberhart; Patty Ferro.
*Colorado:* Ray B. Hall; Lula Kirsch; Harry and Teddy Lane; Sue Nicholson; Neil V. Reynolds; Myrtle Ryan.
*Connecticut:* Tom E. Hall; Paul Holmberg.
*District of Columbia:* Bernard A. Bernier; Beulah M. Cope; Elane C. Everly; James D. Walker.
*Florida:* William Gelder; William and Jay Weintz.
*Massachusetts:* George F. Mason.
*Nevada:* Elbert B. Edwards; Murl Emery; R. C. "Red" Ellis; Vern Freher; Sherwin "Scoop" Garside; Robert B. Griffith; Robert Grom; Stella Hawkins; Mike Leavitt; Frank Long; James C. Maxon; "Red" McElvane; Stanley W. Paher; Ed Schroeder; Gene Schultz; Robert Sparks; Janis S. Thurman; John H. Wittwer; Otto Westlake; Dorothy Winter.
*New Jersey;* V. E. Kelly.
*New York:* Anita Loos.
*North Carolina:* William T. Hodge.
*Washington:* James R. Cumming; Phoebe Harris; Russell Heather.
*Wisconsin:* Fred Hansen.
*Wyoming:* W. Don Nelson.
*England:* D. A. Johnson.
*Germany:* Father Franz Czarnecki.

B O O K S from which material or quotations were taken:

Kenneth Alsop, *Hard Travellin': The Hobo and His History.* New York, 1968.
Nevada C. Colley, *From Maine to Mecca.* Indio, Calif., 1967.
Camiel Dekens, *Riverman, Boatman.* Riverside, Calif., 1962.
George H. Lamb (ed.), *The Unwritten History of Braddock's Field.* Braddock, Pa., 1917.
Samuel Eliot Morison, *The Oxford History of the American People.* New York, 1965.
Stanley W. Paher, *Las Vegas: As It Began—As It Grew.* Las Vegas, 1971.
Margaret M. Wheat, *Survival Arts of the Primitive Paiutes.* Reno, Nev., 1967.

Colin Fletcher was born in Wales and educated in England. He went to East Africa in 1947, farmed for four years in Kenya, and later surveyed and built a road over a virgin mountain in Southern Rhodesia (now Zimbabwe). In the 1950's he crossed the Atlantic and prospected—among other pursuits—in northern and western Canada. In 1956 he moved south to California, where he wrote *The Thousand-mile Summer, The Man Who Walked Through Time, The Complete Walker* (and its revision, *The New Complete Walker*), and *The Winds of Mara.*

A NOTE ON THE TYPE

This book was set, via computer-driven cathode ray tube, in Caslon, a modern adaptation of a type designed by the first William Caslon (1692–1766). The Caslon face has had two centuries of ever-increasing popularity in the United States—it is of interest to note that the first copies of the Declaration of Independence and the first paper currency distributed to the citizens of the new-born nation were printed in this type face.

The book was composed by American–Stratford Graphic Services, Inc., Brattleboro, Vermont. It was printed and bound by The Murray Printing Company, Westford, Massachusetts.

Design by Dorothy Schmiderer